THE RISE AND FALL OF RATIONAL CONTROL

The Rise and Fall of Rational Control

The History of Modern Political Philosophy

Harvey C. Mansfield

The Belknap Press of Harvard University Press

Cambridge, Massachusetts · London, England

2026

Printed in the United States of America
Second printing

EU GPSR Authorised Representative
LOGOS EUROPE, 9 rue Nicolas Poussin, 17000, LA ROCHELLE, France
E-mail: Contact@logoseurope.eu

LIBRARY OF CONGRESS CATALOGING-IN-PUBLICATION DATA

Names: Mansfield, Harvey C., Jr., 1932– author
Title: The rise and fall of rational control : the history of modern political philosophy / Harvey C. Mansfield.
Description: Cambridge, Massachusetts : The Belknap Press of Harvard University Press, 2026. | Includes bibliographical references and index.
Identifiers: LCCN 2025032456 (print) | LCCN 2025032457 (ebook) | ISBN 9780674298859 cloth | ISBN 9780674303829 epub | ISBN 9780674303836 pdf
Subjects: LCSH: Political science—Philosophy | Political science—History
Classification: LCC JA83 .M264 2026 (print) | LCC JA83 (ebook)
LC record available at https://lccn.loc.gov/2025032456
LC ebook record available at https://lccn.loc.gov/2025032457

This book is based on lectures from the Harvard University course History of Modern Political Philosophy (Government 1061), delivered in alternate years from 1968 to 2022. It is dedicated to those who could not or did not take the course.

Contents

Preface

We begin from this book's subtitle, *The History of Modern Political Philosophy*, and ask, what is modern? And what is its history? These two questions come first. One surely does need to know what political philosophy is, yet we come upon it as something already existing, with a tradition, invented long before modern times by Socrates (470–399 BC). "Modern" implies a change, something new, a *new idea*. It's not that we look first at a starting date for what is modern, a crucial event such as 1492 or 1789, then find the idea. One must start from the idea that identifies and explains the event. "Modern" refers to an idea that came at a certain date with a distinct author, Niccolò Machiavelli, the first of our modern thinkers. To introduce him we begin not from his two main works but with *Mandragola*, a play written in about 1518. This comedy will reveal its great author having fun with a very serious idea.

Machiavelli lived from 1469 to 1527, a long time ago. Can the modern idea be this old? Yes, that is the thesis of the book. With Machiavelli was born a single idea with many aspects, versions, currents and countercurrents—the idea of rational control. Reason is to be used not merely to *understand* our problems but to *control* them. Rational control is most obvious in the modern science familiar to us, where knowledge brings power. Take the discovery of DNA as the program of life: when you know what a being's DNA is, you can control it, at least in principle. The modern sciences of medicine, physics, chemistry, economics, psychology, etc., all have the aim of improving our lives by using human reason in a new form of science that links it with technology. Francis Bacon (1561–1626), after Machiavelli, stated it with beautiful clarity: "Enlarging the bounds of human empire to the effecting of all things possible," and doing this "for the relief of man's estate" (*The New Atlantis*, 1626).

Rational control would also come in the form of political science—a new political science to bring that idea to politics. There, this new politics would manage and reduce conflict, dependence, and slavery; it would make humans strong by making them free. With his political science, Machiavelli invented the notion of rational control that we now see better in the modern sciences outside politics mentioned above. Yet rational control came first in the new political science, ahead of all other modern sciences. Politics is about governing or ruling human beings, which is a form of control existing since Socrates. But Machiavelli believed that old science needed to be corrected, and he set out on an enterprise—*his* enterprise, he said—to bring "new modes and orders," a new political science. Although political science today does not seem to be the most advanced of the sciences, because, to put it mildly, the ancient problems and questions of politics do not seem to be safely under human control, modernity began with a new politics. Machiavelli's politics preceded the creation of more exact, more successful sciences doing more good for humankind—above all others, medicine. When Bacon spoke of "effecting all things possible," he was following Machiavelli, who first explained what *effecting* is and why it is fundamental.

Several versions of the modern idea of rational control arose, and several critics of it responded. Of these versions, this book studies Niccolò Machiavelli, Thomas Hobbes, and John Locke; of the critics, it takes up Jean-Jacques Rousseau and Friedrich Nietzsche, who attacked the idea and yet returned to it. After Machiavelli, his modern idea continues in Hobbes, Locke, and the others to be studied (let's not forget Karl Marx), but not unchanged; it is *developed*. The later philosophers react to the earlier ones, both accepting and revising. All modern philosophers are indebted to Machiavelli, but not all, indeed few, would be considered "Machiavellian." A Machiavellian is one who rejects justice for necessity and resorts to dirty tricks with a clear conscience because they are *necessary*. Machiavelli made a principle of necessity, but his successors looked for a modern justice to replace the classical justice he rejected. This modification gives each of Machiavelli's successors a doctrine of moral and political principles of the sort he avoided. He preferred to use striking examples, as in his play *Mandragola*.

In this book, Machiavelli receives the special treatment due to the founder of the modern idea, and the seven philosophers who follow are examined in their relation to him, as well as others preceding him. Besides honoring Machiavelli, this book reflects a choice of depth and argument over shorter, superficial treatment of many additional philosophers. Modern political philosophy could be thought to field a larger team—for example, Francis Bacon (already mentioned), Baruch Spinoza, David Hume, Montesquieu, Edmund Burke, and John Stuart Mill, and other worthy names. But our eight are enough to present the case for and against rational control. With too many players, we might lose sight of the theme.

Thus, in developing the idea of rational control, modern political philosophy has a particular *history* of its own within itself. It grows through the seventeenth century in a manner to be shown in Hobbes and Locke, and then meets a crisis when Rousseau confronts them and criticizes the modern idea fundamentally. Rousseau makes two opposite moves. He continues the earlier notion of the social contract, which rationally controls human freedom. But he also introduces historical change to the very idea of reason; instead of being the permanent principle of a rational animal, reason itself grows. After Rousseau one sees history come to the fore, first as a problem in the work of Immanuel Kant, then fully developed in G. W. F. Hegel and Karl Marx. The second crisis of modernity arrives with the work of Nietzsche, who shows that history is as little reliable as rational principle. Historians will object, and with some reason, that this book makes modernity too orderly, as if it were following a plan and were never interrupted by events or accidents. We show an internal history of modern thought, however, more orderly than historians commonly suppose, that moves on its own in a sequence of thinkers, reflective of those past and instructive or inspiring to those ahead.

The modern idea, with its development and its two crises, has a philosophic history from Machiavelli to Nietzsche: the rise and the fall of rational control. It moves from the belief that reason supports and enlivens humans, freeing them from slavery, constituting their very being—René Descartes said "I think, therefore I am"—yet ending with the belief that reason deadens humans, stifling and enslaving them—the view of Nietzsche. Nietzsche is the thinker behind the trend of "postmodern" sentiment today doubtful of modern science and concerned for its consequences in environment, climate, and weaponry. "Human empire" does not seem as beneficial to us as it did to Bacon. Yet the solutions to the troubles of science are more science, as, for example, with climate change. Will science save us from science? The promise of rational control, once accepted, dies hard. The word "postmodern" displays an attitude critical of what is modern yet is unable to get beyond it or find a name for it. *Postmodern* is unable to escape *modern*.

Do we really want to escape the modern idea? That is the problem for us moderns today. Can we progress beyond present unease with what is modern, or will that simply continue modernity with all its difficulties of defining an identity that never stops changing? Or should we try to return to what came before, what is premodern, the medieval philosophers and, before them, the ancients? In this case we might seem to endanger our freedom and our comforts. Not everything that happens in our time of modernity is modern. Accidents occur, and permanent features of human life—such as politics itself—may escape rational control and cause it to fail. To meet our doubts about modern life, we need to understand it. That is the purpose of this book.

CHAPTER ONE

NICCOLÒ MACHIAVELLI

(1469–1527)

NICCOLÒ MACHIAVELLI BELONGS to the Renaissance; some believe he defines it. But Renaissance means "rebirth." Of what? Of the ancients. Machiavelli wrote of the Romans yet offered "new modes and orders" for a republic and the ways of the new prince for a principality. No one else in his time called for novelty that has value merely for being new. No one else called Christianity "the present religion" as he did, implying it was temporary. The corruption of the Church was a common topic but no one else attacked its doctrine, its concern for the honor of the next world. Machiavelli was a philosopher who made himself the prophet of a new sect, one that would advance to a new conception of this world as *the* world. A native of the city of Florence where Botticelli, Raphael, and Michelangelo were at work, Machiavelli set beauty and nobility aside and put his mind to considering the necessity of evil. The term *Machiavellian* goes to deeds and thoughts we hold to be evil, and we take our word *realism* from his belief that evil is more real than is good.

For an approach to Machiavelli's play *Mandragola,* one more step beyond the analysis in my preface is needed. Rational control gives humans greater power that also gives them greater liberty than ever before. It has two aspects: liberation and reform, or deconstruction and reconstruction. Why say "liberation" rather than simply "liberty"? Liberty appears as liberation because to establish liberty one must be liberated from *irrational* control. Modern thought does not come out of chaos, as if created from total disorder. Before rational order there was a certain order, irrational order, the order of custom. Custom is what children learn from their parents, who get it from their parents, and so forth back to the origins of custom in one's ancestors. Then where did they get the idea of custom? From a superhuman source, from God or the gods. The foundation of irrational order is a deity of some kind. Rational order requires liberation from God, understood as the origin of irrational order.

Yet liberation from the divine in favor of the human cannot be total because order of some kind is necessary. Hence liberation points to reform, not abolition, of the old order of custom. Perhaps there is a place for a reformed God in the reformed order made by humans. But the religious question is very important in understanding modernity. It is the first and fundamental question facing modern thought; it must assert human rights as against divine right. All premodern regimes are based somehow on divine right; even Socrates, who founded the application of reason to human affairs, was obliged to refer to the Delphic Oracle as the source of his philosophy. But modern reason, as we have seen, goes beyond understanding in the way of Socrates to control, and control must replace divine right with human rights. This replacement is what we know as *progress*. The two aspects of rational control, then, can be called liberation and progress. Liberty requires liberation, which is for the sake of progress—and progress means expanding the scope of liberty. Liberation and progress interact to their common benefit.

So, is there no problem? Yes, one: There is no liberty to be irrational—or less liberty. For example, today it is held to be a central quality of progress that women are at last equal to men, or at least much more equal than they used to be under the irrational order of patriarchy. No doubt this is for the good, but this means that for men there is, in a sense, less liberty.

MAJOR WORKS OF MACHIAVELLI

Mandragola (1524): The dramatic comedy relating a trick played to seduce a pious woman and cuckold a foolish doctor.

The Art of War (1521): A dialogue led by a mercenary captain, Fabrizio Colonna, on war as a distinct art.

Discourses on Livy (1531): A commentary interpreting Livy's *History of Rome* to consider republics, principalities, and all "worldly things," published posthumously.

The Prince (1532): A treatise on the new prince offering advice to Lorenzo de' Medici and all other readers, published posthumously.

Florentine Histories (1532): Histories or inquiries about Florence, related to Machiavelli's "universal treatise" and his overall "undertaking."

The old sexual stereotypes have been abandoned but new, nonsexist ones have been set in their place. These are new customs taught by one's parents and schools with new, less direct techniques of control, but control is still in force. In the *Mandragola* we shall see liberation, reform, and the problem of continuing control. Does liberation have a limit, so that it reforms but does not abolish human government? It might seem, and some opponents of rational control would insist, that liberation once begun is hard to stop. This difficulty appears in all of modern political philosophy, for the internal history we shall study suggests that it wants to stop but does not know where or when. Each of the proposed reforms by the eight philosophers we consider finds a critic in the next chapter calling for more liberation and a new reform. This book concludes with Nietzsche, where modern progress seems to have reached the dead end of the postmodern, as our thinkers in the twentieth and twenty-first centuries generally yield to Nietzsche's diagnosis yet cannot accept his solution. We believe in liberation and cannot agree on where it must be declared to be defined, and brought to a stop, as reform. That is why this book, having begun with Machiavelli, closes with Nietzsche, thus beginning and ending earlier than readers might expect.

Using Evil for Good

Now for a preview to Machiavelli's famous play *Mandragola*. It is not usually the first work of his that one would read, but it gives access to the use of evil he is known for. We postpone the study of his two major works, *The Prince* and the *Discourses on Livy,* but they will not be slighted. In the play, then, two desires are shown. First, Callimaco, the erotic young man, wants to seduce Lucrezia, the beautiful and pious married woman. Second, Lucrezia and her older husband, Messer Nicia, want to have a child, a son, which they can't have because Messer Nicia is impotent. The first desire is for adultery, an evil in Machiavelli's day and still in our time when we speak of "cheating" on someone. The second is a good desire that is thwarted. In the play, both desires are satisfied; Callimaco gets to seduce Lucrezia and the result is to produce a son for the family. The old form of morality (the Bible) does not permit saving a family by resorting to adultery; having children is good, but adultery is wrong. One is not permitted to do evil for a good result. This means that old-fashioned "family values" might lead to the extinction of a family, having no heir or given the misfortune of impotence. A very pious couple would not be allowed to "be fruitful and multiply," as the Bible commands (Genesis 1:28).

Machiavelli's play says that this old morality is irrational; a better solution would be to relax the moral prohibition against adultery in order to save the family. By this means one could in principle make the family perpetual by reducing or eliminating dependence on the chance of one's fertility. One could increase human power over chance and human freedom together. Those who follow the old way of morality and piety do good but receive evil; those who follow the new way do evil—but is it so evil?—and receive good. With rational control over the chancy character of human life, one lowers the moral standard and achieves a better result. The notion of using evil for good is typical of modernity. Modern economics is based on self-interest, perhaps not evil but certainly lower than generosity and justice; modern psychology teaches you to reduce stress and be timid and docile rather than be courageous; modern political science shows you how to achieve stability rather than justice. *Mandragola* shows an instance of what is today called "birth control": You take an event that happens spontaneously and you control it. Today, birth control means to avoid having children; in the play, the characters use control for the sake of having children. But the principle of birth control is the same whether the child is unwanted or wanted.

One might object that the *Mandragola* is about sex, about rational control to continue a family, but since this is a book on political philosophy, where is politics? Politics is behind the irrational control of custom; the power of Church and state enforce custom's decrees. In Machiavelli's time, a woman had a right, with limitations, to say "no," for as today women need protection against the aggressiveness of men. In *Mandragola* it is assumed by all that Lucrezia has to be persuaded to have sex; adultery is against the law of both Church and state. Sex and love need to be controlled because there is something essentially lawless about them. One person is attracted and falls in love without the consent of the person one loves, and one falls out of love also without that consent. Moreover, reason plays a limited role in love. One can fall in love with someone who is not a reasonable or suitable choice and fail to love someone who would be reasonable. Love is fervent; it takes over your mind, and it makes you want to claim the mind of your beloved. You want your beloved to return your love; if he or she doesn't, you get angry as if the person you love is obliged to love you back. This can lead to stalking and violent jealousy, as well as heartbreak. Love, to the extent that it claims and acts without consent of the one loved, is in its nature invasive and tyrannical. With the possibility of tyranny we begin to see how sex is related to politics.

The name of the heroine, Lucrezia, makes this relation explicit. It recalls the Lucretia in a famous incident in the history of the Roman republic at its very founding, which Machiavelli discusses in his *Discourses on Livy* (D 3.2, 5, 26). Lucretia was raped by the son of the king, Sextus Tarquinius, and committed suicide afterward out of shame. This rapist crime was used by Junius Brutus to overthrow the Tarquin kings and to found the Roman republic. A king is a tyrant who permits his son to commit a rape, and the republic began from a vigorous reaction against a rape. Machiavelli, however, does not accept this story. He denies the importance of this incident; it was a mere pretext and some other accident would have been found if this one had not existed. He even suggests that the king could have retained his kingship if he had sacrificed his son to the popular anger at the crime.

In the *Mandragola* Machiavelli shows a case of successful persuasion. To get the woman he wanted, Callimaco did not rape her or think of doing so, but instead he uses a fraudulent argument that overcomes Lucrezia's resistance to adultery, and to her husband, Messer Nicia, he offers the belief in a magic potion, Mandragola or Mandrake, that makes sterile women conceive. He makes the rape of the Roman Lucretia into the seduction of the Florentine Lucrezia, and thus turns tragedy—for Shakespeare and others treated this incident as a tragedy—into a comedy. To flip tragedy into comedy, he makes rape of an outraged Lucretia into seduction of a persuadable Lucrezia a question of fraud. Is fraud distinct from rape or is it a kind of concealed rape? Machiavelli, we shall see, is an instructor of fraud. No one can become great without using fraud. Why? Because when one sets out to be a prince, one is weaker than the existing prince; the only way to advance is for the weaker to gain the advantage by somehow fooling the stronger. Lucrezia is in a stronger position than Callimaco; she has the law, including both Church and state, on her side. So Callimaco must use fraud, which he does.

Conspiracy Against the Law

Callimaco mounts a plot to gain the woman he wants. Callimaco's plot is the same as the plot of the play: a conspiracy consisting in one surprise after another. The first is that Callimaco is not in charge, as he gives it over to his hireling, Ligurio, who is a fixer or, to speak plainly, a pimp. Ligurio points out to Callimaco that his first idea, of getting Lucrezia to the public baths where she can see him and become attracted, will not work. She may be attracted to him or may not be, and some other, handsomer man might enjoy the benefit of his scheme. It's too chancy, because attraction or love is not easily controlled. If you love someone or someone loves you for your looks, your wealth, or even your virtue, someone else may still come along who appears to have more than what you have. To keep the object of your love, you must bring her or him to a place where there is little or no competition. You must domesticate your love, put it in the family where it is more safely yours and doesn't depend on a *reason* for love. Ligurio makes Callimaco jealous of Lucrezia before he has her, and it is here that Machiavelli's comedy begins to go beyond the fun of sex in private to the gravity of respectable and stable love in the family.

At this point, now in Act 2, we see Callimaco in contact with Messer Nicia, the husband of Lucrezia, whom he is going to cuckold. According to the domesticated plot, Callimaco will have his success with Lucrezia not outside but inside her family. To manage this feat, Messer Nicia will have to be persuaded to accept being cuckolded by Callimaco; the pious Lucrezia will have to be persuaded that the God she worships will permit the indiscretion. The plot has to be in Messer Nicia's interest and it has to respect Lucrezia's belief. Neither party is coerced and both are persuaded, but in each case with a fraudulent argument. Machiavelli is not going to force himself on us—how can he? But is his fraud so different from force? In the *Discourses* he speaks of force as "open force"; what, then, is hidden force if not fraud (D 2.13)?

To persuade Messer Nicia, he has to learn of a magic potion called *mandragola*, and we thus encounter the name of the play. Ligurio tells him that this potion makes sterile women conceive with the first man who beds her, as if the infertility was Lucrezia's, as Messer Nicia believes, and not himself. But there's a rub: this first man dies after his performance. So it cannot be Messer Nicia who beds Lucrezia but rather an unfortunate stud, who of course must be deceived. To accomplish this goal, Callimaco appears in two different disguises: as a doctor who tells Messer Nicia of the mandrake, and as the not-so-unfortunate stud. But on hearing this scheme from the disguised doctor, Messer Nicia exclaims, "What, make my wife a whore and me a cuckold?" (Act 2, Scene 6). He is brought around by the news that this scheme is often used by the king of France to keep his hereditary monarchy intact when the queen is infertile. Messer Nicia is induced to compare his family situation as one who wants a son so as to maintain his family, with a king's and a country's need for an heir—a political need. Machiavelli's play, apparently about the family, is politics in disguise.

With Messer Nicia on board, the more difficult task of gaining the consent of Lucrezia awaits. She is a pious woman unlikely to submit to adultery, or as Messer Nicia put it, to become a whore, but it is through her very piety that she will be persuaded, in very indirect fashion. To appeal directly to her piety would contend with her distrust of the Church, because she had had a bad experience with a priest. But she does trust her mother, who will get her to go to a priest, a certain Brother Timothy. We see him in a scene listening to the confession of "a woman," an apparent digression from the plot, asking her whether she is willing to accept God's commands as conveyed by him (Act 3, Scene 3). It is a picture of indirect government of a kind Machiavelli appreciates and will use in his own cause: the priest, the real ruler of the anonymous woman, presents himself as an intermediary between God and man, or God and woman. The truth, or to use a phrase from Machiavelli's *The Prince*, the "effectual truth," or actual outcome, of traditional divine right is the human rule of unarmed priests who claim to know what God says and then pass it on to their pious clients. It is government that rules but pretends not to rule itself, but merely to execute the will of higher authority. Much of Machiavelli's political science is contained in this brief scene.

Next, it is necessary to enlist Brother Timothy in the plot. Ligurio approaches him, pretending to need an abortion for a young woman, Nicia's nonexistent daughter, who was betrayed by the nuns in a convent and now needs absolution for her abortion. The purpose of this dodge is to hook Brother Timothy into a crime usual with him, absolving an abortion, when the real objective is to get his connivance in the contrary: adultery for the sake of having an heir. Ligurio goes offstage for a brief pause and returns with the happy news that the daughter has had a miscarriage; nature has done God's work, and Brother Timothy is not needed. But then he is informed that he is needed for the true plan, a crime (or sin) unusual for him that he would not have consented to if it had been proposed to him first. Committed to a lesser, more typical crime, he finds himself responsible for a greater one and obliged to conspire against the law, both human and divine. Machiavelli's maxim, we shall see, is to rely on your own arms, and in no way rely on others to help you. That maxim would imply trusting no one. But that's impossible; to survive, you need the help of others, and hence their trust. How is this possible if no one is worthy of trust? In the *Mandragola* every ordinary human trust is betrayed: husband and wife, mother and daughter, host and guest, master and servant, ruler and ruled, confessor and confessed. The only trust that holds is that of coconspirators in a plot to seduce Lucrezia. As we shall see, Machiavelli believes, as he conveys in *Mandragola,* that government is essentially conspiracy, rather than open, transparent rule for the sake of public principles.

The following scene, the central one in the play, shows Lucrezia being persuaded by her mother, Sostrata, to go to Brother Timothy and thus join the plot. She does not give in readily. Instead, she declares dramatically that she couldn't believe that she would be permitted to commit this crime if Callimaco were the last man on earth and it was necessary to regenerate the human race—let alone produce a son for Messer Nicia. Lucrezia is a good woman with a conscience; her goodness consists in a sticking point, something one will not do regardless of the consequences. Machiavelli exposes his view of the nature of morality. The moral person must act as if all morality depended on refusing to commit an act that might be prudent in an extreme case. Morality is a whole; one cannot divide it into discrete actions that may or may not be prudent. Once you bring prudence to mind, you can always find a reason not to be moral in a particular case. The moral law must defend itself as an indivisible whole so that all morality is at stake in every moral question. Morality cannot afford not to make an issue of itself in every case or it will fall victim to alleged human necessities exaggerated to suit and excuse oneself.

Yet when Lucrezia says she would not commit this crime if it were with the last man on earth, Brother Timothy has her in his grasp. He shows her from the Bible that it would be allowable, as when Lot's daughters were permitted to have incest to repopulate the world (Genesis 19:30–32). Well, then: if incest, then adultery; if to repopulate the world, then to have a baby herself. This is the Bible read, as Machiavelli says, *sensatamente* (judiciously) (D 3.30), which means according to human necessities, not God's commands. It's as if God was not omnipotent but himself obeyed the rule of necessity that Machiavelli legislates for human beings.

When Lucrezia hears this, her goodness is engaged. Goodness consists in things one does, but also in certain things one doesn't do, even to save the human race; such goodness creates a terrific pressure that needs to be relieved. The purpose of religion is to relieve it, to provide a release—from goodness or conscience. This is the natural purpose of religion, of a natural religion, which is what Christianity could be if it were interpreted *sensatamente*. Lucrezia's belief in Christianity relieves her from her goodness. God says it is all right to abandon morality in an extreme case, which means in effect to abandon morality when one feels it to be unnecessary or inconvenient—in Lucrezia's case, to satisfy her desires for sexual pleasure and generation. She is forced to trust the man (Brother Timothy) who shows her how to obey human necessities. He shows her also how to disguise those necessities, first as God's will, then as her own will in obedience to God's. At the end of the play, when Lucrezia realizes how she has been played upon, she says to Callimaco, "You are my father" (Act 5, Scene 4). She understands her adultery with him as incest, like that of the daughters of Lot with their father. Her reasoning goes like this: I wouldn't have done this myself, but I did it; therefore heaven willed it; therefore I will it. She wills necessity in the guise of religion. She says she is "born again."

Conspiracy in Favor of the Law

Machiavelli does not simply reject the divine right typical of irrational control, but he uses it himself for the purpose of "bringing common benefit to everyone" (D 1 pr.). It is not enough to escape morality and religion, let alone to go so far as to reject them. The conspiracy against the law must become a conspiracy in its favor. Morality, he shows, consists of two opposite things: a denial of necessity, such as by Lucrezia's pious chastity; and an acceptance of necessity through Lucrezia's religion. Lucrezia is seduced not despite her morality, but precisely because she is moral. Her seduction reveals both the strength and the weakness of morality, both its ability to hold off human necessities (or desires) and its final surrender to them. Lucrezia, we see, would not have surrendered if she hadn't been so moral; she would have shrugged her shoulders at this silly idea and said, "Don't bother me." But because she is moral, she is forced to make an issue of morality, and in the test, morality is found weaker than necessity. Yet without morality, necessity would not have been tested. The result is to show that humans need their moral conventions.

The conspiratorial plot in *Mandragola* is opposed to public morality in a number of ways, but it requires a relation of trust among the conspirators. The relation has to be a private one because the conspiracy is directed against the ruling morality. But the relation cannot remain private lest it leave the ruling morality untouched. If, like Machiavelli, one wants to overthrow and revolutionize the ruling Christian morality, one must offer some ruling convention in its place. The private conspiracy must become a new public respectability. And this is what happens in the play. We have seen in the abandoned scheme of the public baths the instability of beauty as a principle of trust. Beauty needs to be brought home from the baths and domesticated in the family, where the status of wife (or husband) does not rest on her good looks. Still, this hardly prepares Machiavelli's audience for the surprise ending of *Mandragola*. Callimaco not only succeeds in seducing Lucrezia, but he is invited by the prize booby Messer Nicia to remain living in his house indefinitely. Callimaco will be "the staff of my old age," Messer Nicia says proudly. This is not the only unseemly joke in *Mandragola*.

Everyone profits from the conclusion of the plot. Messer Nicia gets a son, with which he hopes to make the case for the political advancement of his family; Callimaco delights in his romp with Lucrezia, repeatedly and with impunity; Lucrezia has a son and enjoys her fling with Callimaco, yet she maintains her disguise of respectability; and Ligurio and Brother Timothy are well paid. In the last scene Nicia invites Callimaco to live in his house. Lucrezia says, as if seeing him for the first time, "I am delighted to meet this man and want him to be my godfather." In private she calls him "father," in public "godfather." The happy ending of *Mandragola* requires that respectability be maintained, but therefore also the deceit that makes it possible. Messer Nicia must be deceived, or he must pretend to be deceived. One wonders who is the master conspirator of this plot: who conceived it? Might the stupidest character in the play actually have been the most prudent, pretending to be stupid? Machiavelli says in one of his major writings, the *Discourses*, that it is very wise sometimes to play crazy (*pazzo*, D 3.2).

Unlike most comedies, which end with a general enlightenment and deceptions exposed, this play ends with a deceit that must be continued. It may not last forever, but it can be renewed when Messer Nicia dies or Callimaco runs dry. Machiavelli shows that his attack upon the dominant values, the sexual morality of the Church, has for its purpose not to abandon those conventions but to strengthen public trust by renewing them periodically. It is as if the family, instead of being subject to chance when the principals die, could be made to last in perpetuity, secure from misfortune and accident. Tyranny—that is, the tyrannical desire of Callimaco to have Lucrezia at any cost—requires respectability. But vice versa, respectability requires tyranny; without the plot, Messer Nicia's family line would have expired. On a political level, the marriage of tyranny and respectability is shown in founding. *Mandragola* is a comic founding or refounding of a family. Following the analogy of family and politics from the example of the king of France, the play reveals how a Machiavellian prince might conduct himself. He could observe Messer Nicia to learn how to maintain a state or imitate Callimaco to become a new prince in a new state.

Kind and Ruthless

It is time to turn to Machiavelli's two major works, *The Prince* and the *Discourses on Livy*. In each of these, Machiavelli states at the beginning that it contains everything he knows. In a letter of December 10, 1513 (a famous letter we shall consider), Machiavelli says that he has "composed a little work" on princes, and the *Discourses* seem to have been written from 1513 to 1517. There is very little evidence and very much scholarly analysis, but the upshot seems to be that they were written at about the same time. We cannot say that one of them supplants the other in importance. Both, being very subversive of Church and state, were not published until after Machiavelli's death in 1527—the *Discourses* in 1531, and *The Prince* in 1532. After his death, Machiavelli was of course safe from reprisal but at the same time incapable of presiding over their publication. How he managed to get them published, and with the approval of the Pope, is a story of great interest but quite unknown.

Both major works pose the problem of how they are related and which has more authority. *The Prince*, with its twenty-six chapters, is "very brief" and dedicated to an actual living prince, Lorenzo de' Medici; the *Discourses* has 142 chapters, the same number as the books of Livy's *History of Rome*, is much longer, and is dedicated to two young friends of Machiavelli's who are not princes but perhaps deserve to be. Their subject matter is not as different as one might think from their titles, as *The Prince* is mainly about princes but also discusses republics, while *The Discourses* is the same in reverse. Perhaps the difference in dedication is a clue: *The Prince* is for a busy executive with not much time to read; the *Discourses* are for those who have the time and are able to study an ancient work of history. One could say Ins (actual princes) versus Outs (potential princes). This difference, however, is not as great as one might first think: both Ins and Outs have to be at work and also on the prowl for new acquisitions. The Ins have to think about how the Outs might displace them; the Outs have to think about how the Ins might be displaced.

Machiavelli makes much of "acquire" and "acquisition." Normally used both before and after him to refer to economic goods and activity, he uses them militarily and politically in the sense of "conquer," as in this passage early in the *Discourses*: "The fear of losing generates in him [who wishes to maintain] the same wishes that are in those who desire to acquire, for it does not appear to men that they possess securely what a man has unless he acquires something new" (D 1.5.4). These striking words say that conserving or securing one's position leads to acquiring more than one has; nobody is or can reasonably be satisfied with what he has. This statement is made to justify the acquisitive imperialism of the Roman republic. Early in *The Prince*, Machiavelli says, "And truly, it is a very natural and ordinary thing to desire to acquire," adding that acquisition is blamed only when attempted by someone who can't achieve it (P 3). Here appears the moral aspect of endless acquisition latent in its political aspect and blatant expression later in the book when Machiavelli advises that if a prince wants to maintain himself, he must "learn to be able not to be good" (P 15). Machiavelli's enterprise of rational control begins not from scientific technology designed directly to give humans more power, as with the modern science of Francis Bacon, but from a new liberating attitude toward politics and morality that prepares and justifies Bacon's science. Yet a certain knowledge is required: the prince must *learn* how to be not good, and republics instructed as to how to acquire.

What is this knowledge and why is it needed? It would seem that there have always been evil men capable of dirty tricks, and that to follow them leads sometimes to success but just as often to defeat, in which evil gets its just deserts. But Machiavelli claims to "depart from the orders of others," their principles and institutions (P 15). In the preface to book 1 of the *Discourses,* he says he brings "new modes and orders," an "enterprise" as dangerous as "seeking new waters and lands"—comparing himself to Columbus, who sought a new world. He recounts some of the dangers arising from "putting oneself at the head of introducing new orders" in *The Prince* (P 6). This is what today would be loosely called "realism" or *Realpolitik,* a familiar viewpoint that Machiavelli presents as perilous, exciting, and new. He stresses its novelty. He is not the first political philosopher to present something new, but he is the first to announce it, make a point of its being new, and in general to praise "innovators" and new princes. He does not learn how to operate from evil men; he teaches them and everyone else what they do not know.

What is it? His advice is summed up in a famous passage already partly quoted: he departs from the orders of others to teach men—not just princes but "whoever understands"—the "effectual truth of the thing" and not just what is imagined: "Many have imagined principalities and republics . . . never seen nor known to exist in truth." One who tries to live on what should be done "learns his ruin rather than his preservation." One who makes a "profession of good . . . comes to ruin among so many who are not good." "Necessity" compels us to learn how not to be good, and to use this knowledge or not "according to necessity." This very brief passage of condensed brilliance states the modern project of rational control at its inception. Our discussion of Machiavelli can be taken as explaining what it says.

We note again that Machiavelli begins from the difficulty of living a moral life. To do so "among so many who are not good" risks *coming to ruin,* not a small loss. These many who are not good nonetheless need the advice to learn how not to be good; again, we see that mere practiced evil apart from knowledge is not enough. The not good many apparently live under the "profession of good," which fails to make them good but leaves them exposed to ruin. They try to live by what should be done rather than by what is done. They praise others and are praised themselves, however, not for being good but for having succeeded, whether good or not. They should take their guide from how men are praised and blamed in fact, in the "effectual truth," rather than from unthinking praise of what is good and blame for what is bad. Philosophers up to now have made imaginary republics like Plato's *Republic* or imaginary principalities like St. Augustine's *City of God*. Such marvelous creations are based on the illusions of ordinary morality and feed those illusions by trying to give them imaginary substance "never seen nor known to exist."

Taking a closer look, one can see that the world is divided between those who live by what should be and those who do not; one might call them "the kind" and "the ruthless." The kind believe that because they do good, others will do good to them. They are wrong; there are many who are not good. Yet there are many who wish or imagine that others are good. If they understood better, they would see that good people submit to evil when it is useful or successful. Their kindness is unaware of its own inconsistent propensity to admire successful evil. The ruthless engage in acquisition, believing correctly that since it is done (others do it), it is necessary. One might wish to combine ruthless and kind, using one or the other when appropriate. But this is a wish for persons with both qualities, who are rare. Hence one must choose to be one or the other, which means you must choose to be ruthless unless you are weak, and therefore have to be kind. Your choice is determined by the necessity arising from the incompatibility of the two qualities. No one ruthless understands kindness except as weakness, and those who are kind never rise in politics. There are anomalies, to be sure, politicians who might be a good neighbor, or a good baby doctor, like Machiavelli's boss in the Florentine republic, Piero Soderini (see D 1.52.2), but these are not princes over men.

The issue between ruthless and kind becomes clearer with a quick look at the philosophers writing imaginary republics, like Plato and Aristotle. They would agree that the best is rare but claim that the best, rather than how not to be good, is necessary to know in order to guide practical politics. They suppose that politics is a matter of choosing, even when choosing the lesser evil. Choosing better from worse, even worse from worst, implies a standard of good and bad by which to choose, or in political terms, the best regime. If politics is choice, one must focus on the best. But there is a complication in going from the standard of good to the best regime that seems to provide an opening to Machiavelli. In book 1 of Plato's *Republic,* Socrates reminds Polemarchus that politics is not merely a matter of helping one's friends but helping them and harming enemies (*Republic* 332b). The distinction fundamental to politics between friends and enemies is obviously in good part arbitrary, an accident of birth. Everyone is born with friends—fellow Americans—and enemies, or "adversaries," as President John F. Kennedy liked to say with statesmanlike coolness. No thinker has succeeded in overcoming this arbitrary difference, and Plato and Aristotle did not even try. Their best regimes are small, based on trust rather than inclusiveness, and outfitted with a military strong enough to fight wars with neighbors and other enemies.

Despite this arbitrariness of political friends and enemies, which makes kindness in foreign policy impossible, the ancient students of the imaginary best regime thought it possible for the best regime to be decent in behavior. Both Plato and Aristotle give rules of war that ought to be obeyed, since without them the best regime would lose its pride and its sense of what it stands for (*Republic* 470c–471b, 422d; *Politics* 1333b–1334a). Ruthlessness to outsiders extends to insiders and gradually spreads into mistreating former friends, for all regimes throw together friendly groups that, owing to their differences, could be corrupted into enemies under pressure. The ancients thought there was always a choice, even in the direst circumstances, and they did not draw Machiavelli's conclusion that one must choose necessity. But one should not make an early decision between the two abstract principles of necessity and choice. To clarify them, Machiavelli turns attention to the beginnings of regimes and offers the example of Rome.

Necessity is most visible at the beginning of human institutions when men are most exposed to danger, and this is especially true of the most comprehensive human institution: the political regime. As if conceding the point to Machiavelli, Aristotle shows at the beginning of his *Politics* that early humans were uncivilized and lived like barbarians, capturing one another to serve as slaves, robbing and pillaging, and perhaps even cannibalizing one another like the Cyclops. But in contrast to Machiavelli, Aristotle covers over these unseemly facts lest they cast doubt on later civilization. He says that whereas men first came together out of necessity for the sake of life, they stayed together for the good life. Once secure, humans can live together for higher, nobler activities.

Machiavelli disagrees. Men come together for the sake of life but they cannot remain together for the good life. The necessity of protection is best shown at the beginnings of civilized life, but it is not confined to the beginnings. Humans can never afford to relax from concern with necessities to enjoy the good life. In the *Discourses* Machiavelli makes us aware of this truth gradually as he discusses the founding of Rome. He asks, Why are states founded? Because they do not exist and are needed. Neediness is the state of humans at their beginning, for they get nothing but what they make for themselves. The earliest men were not born in a state, and all those who come after them, born into states, presuppose the first beginning. That earliest beginning arose from nothing, from no previously existing state or culture. Rome had such a beginning, so that Rome is typical, archetypical, of human beginnings: a comprehensive beginning in which everything is made anew, a *founding*. The one who makes everything anew necessarily receives the highest glory any human being can attain. Such glory is deserved and cannot be blamed. But what is necessary to this highest human glory as founder? You must be yourself the sole cause of the founding. Still, suppose someone else founds alongside you—your brother, for instance?

Romulus, founder of Rome, killed his brother Remus, thus ensuring undisturbed possession of the throne and its glory for himself. Machiavelli says this: "This should be taken as a general rule. . . . He who is violent to spoil, not he who is violent to mend, should be reproved" (D 1.9.2). Here Machiavelli says that Romulus "acted for the common good, not for his own succession but for the common fatherland" in "contriving to have his authority alone." Note that the common good is equated with the common fatherland, a patriotic definition replacing an abstract one. Nine chapters later, he says Romulus acted "so as to be alone," not mentioning the common good (D 1.18.5). This is a typical Machiavellian contradiction, not evidence of a loose mind but meant to teach the reader something—namely, that the different intentions of acting for the common or private good are immaterial and merely verbal. If the murder or "homicide" of your brother can produce a result as glorious as the greatness of Rome, then go ahead. A man who won't hang back at his brother's murder will not save his full attention for the common good; he might cheat on his taxes. This crime may make you think of another great fratricide, if you have a wandering mind—the crime presented as the first crime, one could say *the* crime (as opposed to the original sin) in the Bible (Genesis 4:8). No other assumption is safe if applied to a philosopher who blasphemes as cleverly and often as Machiavelli. One begins to suspect that his teaching is not fully compatible with the Bible, not even under the most relaxed interpretation of it. One could also note that Machiavelli does not justify Romulus's fratricide but *excuses* it as if he were in the office of forgiving offenses.

Generalizing from the example of Romulus, one could say that Machiavelli wants to show that nothing great is made unless it is founded on some great crime. Why is crime necessary to greatness, to founding? Building means building anew, and except for the earliest beginning, building means the destruction of an old building. Every new state destroys an old state, an old status quo. There are no vacant spaces left in the world, nor have there been for a long time. Therefore, if you want to found something new, you must destroy something old. If this is true for Rome, which did not begin with a revolution or conquest of an existing state, then it is all the more true of other states. Romulus's fratricide was a crime of necessity. America, the splendid land of opportunity, is founded on a ruthless policy toward the Indians that its settlers encountered. But there is no call to feel guilty, according to Machiavelli's argument; every other great deed demands blood and misery at least at the beginning. No doubt the Indians were savage and brutal to the people they displaced, as can be inferred from their endless warfare with one another. Or they would have been, if forced to. "Native" and "Indigenous" are misnomers based on forgotten crimes.

This advice, be it noted, applies at the level of a private individual, as well as to the public. Every individual, like every state, is either humble or exalted. If exalted, one can look back far enough to a time when one was humble, in the spirit of Franklin D. Roosevelt's famous words when addressing the Daughters of the American Revolution, a conservative group proud of its lineage: "Fellow Immigrants!" All men and all states have beginnings, which means humble beginnings. All humans are bastards if you look back far enough. All who reflect on their beginnings can see that their present place, if they have one, was not given to them without effort. One cannot assume the place one has. At the same time, reflection on one's beginnings shows the correct assumption—that every place is occupied. If you, or your ancestors, were once humble in fortune, then at that time other men and other states were in command. Everyone was once a new man, every state once a new state; all who have "made it" have done so by displacing others. Either they pushed others aside or the way was cleared by some natural disaster like an earthquake or a flood. Since every act of construction presupposes an act of destruction, to act anew is to renovate the old. The Good Book may say men were originally placed in the Garden of Eden where it was unnecessary to sin, and the good-hearted may believe this. But this is just a comfortable illusion because the origin of present comforts is not comfortable to examine. Our friendly surroundings were once held by enemies who had to be displaced.

Man is exposed at the beginning—born naked, and therefore needing to acquire. He cannot acquire enough without living with his fellows; the state is necessary for his acquisitions. Fortunately, the state itself can be an object of acquisition, and fortunately too, there are people who desire the glory of acquiring command over others. On this basis, there can be a coincidence of interest among the weak and the strong. The selfish acquisition of glory redounds to the power of human acquisition generally, as will be described when we come to Machiavelli's politics. But for the present, if you see that acquisition is necessary, and that it is done necessarily by taking away from others (since every rank or status is at some time acquired rather than inherited), wasn't your position acquired from others, and therefore won't others do this to you? Doesn't this thought have to enter the complacent head of every prominent family and every citizen of a powerful state? Then, how else can one preserve the status quo than by acquiring more, before that scheming fellow displaces you?

In *Discourses* 1.5, Machiavelli takes up the question, Which men are more harmful—those who desire to gain, or those who fear to lose? Contrary to what one might suppose, he says it is the latter. Fear of loss produces the same, if not more threatening, wish to acquire as the desire to gain, because those with more power need to keep increasing it and are able to make great changes. In this view, maintaining is just as active as acquiring. There is no such thing as inheriting rank or status; if you wish to keep it you must expand it—that is, change it. If you don't rise, you will fall. Old power is always feeble power, complacent, and ripe for overthrowing. Newness is everything. All power is new at its beginning, and all old power must renew itself to maintain itself. *The Prince* begins with a classification of states in chapter 1. The argument builds up from hereditary principalities (entirely old), to mixed principalities (partly old, partly new), to acquired states used to living under a prince (easier to acquire), to acquired states used for freedom that must be reordered by the conquest, to a peak of newness in chapter 6: a new prince in a new principality acquired by his own arms and virtue. Then the argument subsides and gradually rises to a new peak in chapter 19. The lesson is that states should be understood by how they can be acquired, not by their ends or by their behavior. Machiavelli's stress on the necessity of novelty is shown in his own claim to novelty, as said above. This is not mere boasting on his part but an attempt to raise the status of novelty in political science and in politics. As shown with Aristotle, what Machiavelli says about human nastiness at the beginnings of states especially is not new; what is new is his open talk of it. He lifts the veil that covers the unrespectable beginnings of every respectable institution; other philosophers had only peeked behind it.

The Manufacture of Gratitude

Machiavelli's necessity is the necessity to acquire. We humans have nothing at the beginning and can never assume that we can keep what we hold. We survive to the extent that we acquire and keep acquiring. We must be ready to renew and reorder everything old, and we must do it with our own arms. To depend on the arms of others, on help from any quarter, means making yourself into an object of acquisition, a fat sheep or cow to be milked. On a deeper level, this means that man is indebted to no one and nothing—neither to God nor to nature. Aristotle, too, had seen that men are ruthless at the beginnings of civilization, but they have in them a natural desire to live together for the good life: "Man is by nature a political animal." Humans are indebted to the gift of their political nature for their highest creations. Thomas Aquinas said that a natural inclination to society has been implanted in us by God; we are indebted to God. For both of them, acquisition is not the fundamental fact for men; for them, the things we are given are far more valuable than the things we make or create. We make only because of the gifts we have received. So, for them the fundamental demand of human beings, despite their seeming nakedness, is gratitude.

Machiavelli denies this in an analysis of the nature of gratitude (D 1.24, 1.28–32). What is gratitude? It is good will in return for benefits one has received. If the benefits are distributed justly, then gratitude would be good will in return for justice, for a just regard for one's deserts. Now, suppose a state adheres to a policy of justice. Can it expect gratitude from its citizens? The answer is no. In the first place, the state makes enemies of all those who benefit from injustice, who may be powerful. Second, those who receive just benefits would come to expect them as a matter of right. They would fail to be grateful. Indeed, no one is grateful for deserved benefits. If a student writes an A paper, he is not grateful for the A; he deserved it. Moreover, no one is grateful to another for not harming him, because everyone believes he is entitled to security for himself, his property, and his wife and children (D 1.17; Machiavelli's sexism). When ushering dinner guests out the door, it would be regarded as an offensive sarcasm to thank them for not raping your wife or stealing your silver (not Machiavelli's example). Conclusion: since nobody is thankful for receiving his due, justice cannot be the basis of the good will of citizens or the state. Justice cannot be the basis of trust or obligation. Consequently, when Machiavelli lists the virtues and vices of the prince in chapter 15 of *The Prince*, he omits justice. He never mentions, let alone discusses, the notion of natural justice (or natural right) or natural law, which were so important in the prior history of political philosophy and which remained the common currency of political philosophy in Machiavelli's day.

How, then, does a person or a prince or a free state gain friends if not by treating them with justice? Machiavelli shows that one must add severity to justice. He tells a story of Junius Brutus, founder of the Roman republic, who after that founding was troubled by the conduct of his sons, who expected special favors from their prominent father. In an access of statesmanship, Brutus had them killed. Machiavelli fixes on this act and makes it a motto: "To kill the sons of Brutus" becomes the byword of necessary cruelties. Notice, by the way, that the formula changes when made general. From Brutus's point of view it should be "kill your own sons"; Machiavelli makes it "kill someone's sons." One must not only reward justice but severely punish injustice to dispel any trace of favoritism. People walk ever so much more softly after a timely public execution.

Machiavelli goes beyond severe justice. He censures the Romans in one case because they did not punish Horatius, who had rendered great service in the war against the Albans (D 1.22). After a combat of champions between three Romans and three Albans, Horatius emerged as the only one alive; on his return, Horatius met his sister, who wept at the death of one of the Albans to whom she had been betrothed. Horatius promptly killed her for this unpatriotic sentiment, and the Romans, out of gratitude for his timely or lucky service, failed to punish him. This was bad, Machiavelli says, because even a citizen who is duly rewarded may become arrogant and dangerous to the republic. Not only is he not grateful, but he may think he deserves more than the reward he received. So, while it is useful to reward merit when that merit helps you, it is necessary not to reward it fully, thus to keep everyone, not only the unjust, under fear of punishment. When a person believes that he may suffer punishment, no matter how great his merit or how useful his services, then he will be grateful when he does not suffer punishment. A justly rewarded person is not grateful, but a citizen who fears punishment, even *unjust* punishment, will be grateful for justice when he receives it. His fear makes him value his rewards and obliges him to the giver of rewards.

In terms of grading papers, the prince makes no friends by giving an A paper an A, and a B paper a B, etc. He could make friends by giving B papers A's, as with grade inflation, but this is expensive and arouses envy and contempt. It's much better to give the A paper a B occasionally; then the A student will be grateful for an A when he gets it. Since no one is perfect—even the greatest hero may murder his sister—the reminder that every lapse from perfection will be punished regardless of good deeds serves to maintain fear and hence gratitude. Fear is fundamental, because man is naked and given nothing. Gratitude is derivative; it goes to whoever relieves men from their aching fears. Gratitude is not owed to God; it is humanly created and manipulated. It is perhaps created, however, on a certain model. Compare what Machiavelli says about the true policy of republics in regard to rewards and punishments with what Christianity says about God, and note that the remission of sins is far more important in Christian theology and practice than reward for good deeds. In the parable of the prodigal son, the most notable example, the prodigal son who repented for his disobedience is preferred to the obedient son who never strayed (Luke 15:32). Perhaps according to Machiavelli, fear is the basis of gratitude to the Christian God: in which case, Christianity would admit what Machiavelli asserts by implication—that God has given men nothing to be thankful for.

Caesar's Strange Career in Machiavelli's *Discourses*

Machiavelli is sometimes praised as the author of a new scientific political science that in its realism forswears the making of value judgments and sticks to facts. This is true insofar as his realism leads him to denounce a morality based on what people should do instead of what they actually do. It is also true that what they actually do is related to "facts," a word that did not yet exist in its present sense, but that Machiavelli gave the impetus for in his phrase "effectual (or factual) truth." But he certainly uses value judgments on behalf of his realism. It is from the initial facts of the human situation, which is a predicament, that he draws his analysis of the morality of gratitude. That morality is expressed in a politics of manipulation, as we have seen, so that the connection between his morality and his politics can now be developed. Some commentators—Benedetto Croce, Federico Chabod, Sheldon Wolin—praise Machiavelli for a discovery of the "autonomy of politics," free of morality and metaphysics. It would be better to say that he invented a political science that owes nothing to higher sources above or beyond human necessities. But to do this it was necessary for him to deny the opposing Christian view that man is the creature of God and the Aristotelian view that man aims at the highest good. For this, Machiavelli had to be a philosopher and offer a metaphysics or anti-metaphysics of necessities.

Machiavelli's denial has to be presented gradually from the assertions of wishful imaginary morality to the harsh conclusions of human necessity, and he does this by revealing step-by-step an argument that is appropriately based on examples (a word used frequently) seen from diverse aspects, rather than logic that marches by syllogisms directly to its end. One prominent example is to be observed in his treatment of Julius Caesar, in which Machiavelli begins by reproaching Caesar for the moral fault of corruption and ends with a quite contrary judgment. The steps of the argument are eye-opening turns of direction within what seems at first to be simple morality.

Discourses 1.10 has for its title: "As much as the founders of a republic and of a kingdom are praiseworthy, so much those of a tyranny are worthy of reproach." In the chapter Machiavelli merely contrasts the fame of good princes with the infamy of bad princes, and he concludes near the end: "And truly if a prince seeks the glory of the world he ought to desire to possess a corrupt city—not to spoil it entirely as did Caesar but to reorder it as did Romulus." In this we have a clear contrast between the founder of Rome (demoted to re-orderer?) and the execrable despoiler of Rome. What happens to this contrast? If we follow the career of Caesar in the rest of the *Discourses*, it is completely wiped out. Machiavelli's rhetoric serves the needs of his plan of reform. He is bringing "new modes and orders" to Italy, or to the world, but he is aware of the dangers of introducing them. He is not above using fraud to conceal the extent of his novelty, as he himself tells us in the chapter on fraud (D 2.13). We have seen him apparently forget the common good when speaking of the intention of Romulus (D 1.9 and 1.18). To introduce his novelties, his shocking novelties, he must shock his readers—but not so much that they turn away in disgust. So he gives a consolation, a sop to the conscience of moral folk, which is elsewhere taken back. Romulus's fratricide must be excused, but at least he meant well; on second thought, however, he didn't mean well or it didn't matter what he intended. What mattered was the effect.

If you read carefully, you notice these changes and learn much more about Machiavelli than first appears. If you don't read carefully, you are led insensibly and by degrees from your old prejudices against corruption to new ones excusing it. In this case you are led to a new understanding of social corruption, which is the one prevailing today, as we shall see. Machiavelli doesn't conceal his novelty; on the contrary. But he conceals the extent of it. He exaggerates, as with the example of Romulus, but his purpose is to lead you further, not merely to bid you to applaud. He gives you a glimpse of different aspects of the teaching he wants to impart, and you must put them together yourself. The most general example of partly hiding and partly revealing his new modes and orders is in his use of Livy and of Rome in the *Discourses*. He disguises his new political science in a commentary on an old history of a defunct, or apparently defunct, state, Rome.

After making his debut in *Discourses* 1.10, Caesar appears next in 1.17. This chapter is about the difficulty that a corrupt people has in keeping free, and there it is said that Caesar, as head of the Marian party, "could so blind the multitude that it did not recognize the yoke it was putting on its own head." In this ambiguous sentence it seems that responsibility for the ruin of the Roman republic is not merely Caesar's alone but shared with the Roman multitude that was fooling itself. That multitude was a "blind animal" according to 1.16, where Brutus is praised for killing his own sons in order to please the multitude. In 1.18, as we have seen, Romulus committed his crime, when he killed his brother, of wanting "to be alone." With so much crime needed to found or renew a republic—perhaps the simple allocation of praise to founders and blame to despoilers like Caesar is not accurate.

Machiavelli is not through. The next reference to Caesar turns the argument around to show the true defect of the distinction between a corrupt and an uncorrupt people (D 1.29). Now the Roman republic is blamed for not rewarding Caesar, who merely "took by force for himself what ingratitude denied him." The cause of this ingratitude was the corruption of Rome, which explains and excuses Caesar's despoiling of Rome, as well as the ingratitude of the Romans to Caesar. Then we learn in 1.33 that the remedies that the Roman general and statesman Pompey used too late against Caesar hastened the ruin of the republic, but the creation of the office of dictator (of which Caesar took advantage) did not aid Caesar to establish his tyranny. Indeed, Caesar could have established his tyranny only in a corrupt city, where he could be very rich and be supported by his own partisans. Machiavelli says in 1.37 that the contention over the agrarian law much earlier ruined the republic, so that Caesar and Pompey only headed already existing parties. Caesar did not start the fight; he merely won a fight that was begun nearly a century before by the Gracchi but that could have been sparked because Rome was then so corrupt.

Then why was Rome so corrupt? It had become large in consequence of the growth of the empire, caused by the virtue and strength of the Roman people under the republic. That virtue turned against itself through its very success: the people became dependent on the booty of their imperial gains, turned lazy, and ended tumultuous and disloyal to the republic. It was not the *fault* of the Roman people that they became corrupt any more than it was Caesar's fault that he came along when the people were corrupt. Far from using "corrupt" as a term of moral blame, Machiavelli seems to use it as a moral excuse. His last word on Caesar in *Discourses* 3.24 shows how little he is to be blamed: "Caesar could seize his fatherland" because of the prolongation of military commands in the republic, a policy found necessary by the Senate for the public good but fatal to the republic when the extension of Rome's conquests took its armies too far away for frequent and easy recall. Thus Rome's army lost its loyalty to the republic and became Caesar's. The beginning accusation that Caesar wholly despoiled Rome becomes the assertion that he seized his fatherland. Caesar did what any man of virtue and ambition would have done in those circumstances. In the heyday of the republic he would have been a republican hero like Scipio. Machiavelli's last word does not blame him at all; in *The Prince* (16) he praises him as an excellent man worthy of imitation by a prudent prince.

Comparing all these passages carefully, one can read them without a sense of contradiction but with growing comprehension and a widening smile. Prudence consists in acting "according to the degrees of corruption" (D 1.18.1) or "with the times" (D 3.9.1), characteristic Machiavellian phrases. The virtue of a republic is not virtue plain but according to the times. Here is "situation ethics," in today's language. Machiavelli was not a philosopher of history, and his concerns were wider and deeper than those of most historians, but he introduced into political science something of what is today referred to as "a sense of history." That expression is used by historians to praise or more often to denounce non-historians, as it means the ability to look behind an action to the background or mood that determined it. The usual consequence of the phrase is to provide a moral excuse for characters and actions that might otherwise be damned and dismissed with blame.

Machiavellli's Dubious Republicanism and Patriotism

If Machiavelli's devotion to morality is questionable, could one perhaps take heart from his republicanism and his patriotism as substitutes? It could be and has been said that his willingness to praise and advise republics in his *Discourses* cancels, or at least counteracts, his immoral advice to princes in *The Prince*—as if a man who shows tyrants how to succeed could redeem himself by showing republics how to repel tyrants. But are republics morally preferable to princes, according to Machiavelli? According to some commentators, Machiavelli says that only republics observe the common good. But we must look more carefully at what he says: "Without doubt this common good is not observed if not in republics" (D 2.2.2). But what is "this common good"? It is the good of the many who "can go ahead with it against the disposition of the few crushed by it." No wonder the double negative, "not observed if not," leaves open the possibility that there is no common good that includes all. In crushing the few, republics do not avoid oppression. Even the best republics will have a necessary element of injustice in their rule, as we saw when considering the necessary ingratitude to those with merit.

Romulus killed his brother to found Rome as a kingdom; Junius Brutus killed his sons to found Rome as a republic. The moral superiority of republics does not exactly shine in this comparison. In one place Machiavelli asks whose alliance is more to be trusted: a republic's or a prince's? The answer is the republic; it is slower to act, hence slower to break faith (D 1.59). The Roman republic made its way to the top through successful fraud and in doing so destroyed the liberty of all the surrounding republics (D 2.2, 13). The most successful republic, the Roman, became an empire from its success. For Machiavelli, the common good, we may say, is the suppression of the few by the majority and aggression against foreigners, followed by their oppression. The common good as collective selfishness does not seem to be preferable to the private good of individual selfishness.

Nor is Machiavelli's patriotism so generous as it might appear from the ending of *The Prince* in a quotation from Petrarch proclaiming "the ancient valor in Italian hearts" (P 26). A close examination of chapter 26 will show that Machiavelli did not really expect Lorenzo de' Medici to unify Italy. It would be tantamount to a miracle if he did. And Machiavelli in his mood of enthusiasm does not discuss the *means* by which he might succeed. Those are discussed earlier, and among them he tells how the French kings unified France by killing its barons (P 3, 4, 7, 8, 11). In chapter 3 Machiavelli explains the errors that the French king made in invading Italy and does not criticize the invasion itself. In the *Discourses* he tells the right way to invade a country, and only after reading the unnamed example does one realize that the country being described is none other than Italy (D 1.23.2). Machiavelli was an Italian patriot, to be sure. As one instance of his ardor, he suggested sending the pope to Switzerland so as to corrupt the Swiss and purify Italy (D 1.12). But Italy unified by a single prince or republic would do away with the Florentine republic that was also his *patria* (fatherland). Which of the two came first for him? He said in a letter that "I love my *patria* more than my own soul," but what is his true *patria*? Perhaps it is humankind, since he says he works for the "common good of each" (D 1 pr.), rather than for Italy or Florence alone.

Knowing the fragility of all human institutions, including the Church (D 2.5), Machiavelli was concerned first and above all with the cause of his own principles, "Machiavellianism," which would bring benefit to the freedom and virtue of everyone within the limits of necessity. It is *necessary* for humans to acquire; that is his realism. It is *possible* for them to anticipate their necessities, to choose necessity; that is his idealism. Men are dominated by their necessities, but they can regain their freedom by forestalling those necessities. Choice becomes dominant over necessity by choosing necessity. The ancient skeptics were resigned to human necessities; Machiavelli anticipates them so as to overcome them. The ancient realism of Epicurus and Democritus was nonpolitical, and the ancient idealism of Socrates and his followers was political but imaginary, based on the best regime. Machiavelli fuses the two, combining the materialism of the skeptics with the politics of the Socratics, and thus avoiding, he hopes, the objections to each. Idealistic politics becomes realistic, and skeptical realism becomes political.

Machiavelli goes beyond the necessity of selfishness that excuses it from blame. He encourages it and tries to enlighten it. The essence of his morality, therefore, is the opposite of selfishness—impartiality. If you endorse selfishness in everyone, then you must be impartial as to who wins. If you generalize selfishness, you create impartiality. This paradox in Machiavelli is the germ of the social contract in Hobbes and Locke and the general will in Rousseau. Machiavelli presents no solution so formal and exact as these, but he attempts something similar, a common basis in selfishness that seems to divide men from one another. He redefines Aristotle's moral virtue in his own conception of *virtù* to mean prudent selfishness. But Machiavelli thinks it is prudent to teach everyone to be selfish, and in this queer way his doctrine is impartial. He does have a special quality for the weak who are incapable of acquisitive selfishness, which is goodness (*bontà*) and will come up later.

For Aristotle, moral virtue is a mean but it is not impartial. He holds the virtues to be a mean between vices, such as courage between rashness and cowardice. His purpose is to display the virtues as worthy of choice for their own sake and to make men partial to virtue. Aristotle is certainly not impartial between the virtuous and the vicious. For Machiavelli, virtue is a mean, as we have seen, between virtue and vice. Justice requires a mixture of injustice, as in the example of professors' grading. As noted before, in chapter 15 of *The Prince* Machiavelli lists eleven pairs of virtues and vices and does not mention justice, for justice is entirely equated with necessity. The virtuous person is impartial between kind and ruthless, and one chooses each "according to the times."

Parties: The Benefits of Disharmony

After the first chapter in the *Discourses,* on the beginnings of cities, Machiavelli supplies a study of the regime in the seven chapters that follow (D 1.2–1.8). This study constitutes the first defense of party government in the history of political philosophy, amounting to an argument that reason in the form of modern rational control is better served with disharmony, rather than harmony. This argument advocates the benefits of what would today be called "pluralism," stating the paradox that it is better and *more rational* for citizens to disagree than to agree. Not only is discord valuable for philosophical argument but also for the political environment of ordinary citizens. Today we take our opposing parties for granted, but this is the first argument to conclude that their existence is a sign of health (on the whole) rather than sickness. In this feature of Machiavelli's thought, as well as generally, we can learn about our practices and beliefs at their origin, when the alternative of classical political science was still alive and dominant—for Plato and Aristotle sought the reason that would unite our differences in the political claims we advance, a search Machiavelli did not abandon but transformed. His political argument can be seen to emerge from the moral outlook we have seen. How can impartial benefit come from Machiavelli's paradoxical advocacy of selfishness? In political terms, how can the common good—an impartial good—be derived from the most ruthless partiality to one's own good?

In the first chapter of the *Discourses,* as seen above, Machiavelli began by speaking of the beginning of Rome as the ordering of its lawgivers and declared that it was responsible for the virtue and greatness of Rome. What was that greatness? It was the ultimate greatness of the Roman Empire, he says, despite the fact that Rome went through two great reorderings after it was begun by Romulus. These were the founding of the Roman republic by Junius Brutus, who not only killed his own sons but, just as much to the point, exiled the last Tarquin king; the second was of course the destruction of the Roman republic by Caesar and the construction of the empire by Augustus. Then in chapter 2, Machiavelli offers a brief discussion of the six classical forms of government in the rule of one, few, or many in its good and bad forms; this discussion is based on Polybius and derives from Plato and Aristotle before him. He shows the ruinous consequences to which each form is subject—the three good ones because they are short-lived, and the three bad ones because they are bad. These regimes succeed one another in a cycle like that spoken of in the classical writers, but with the difference that those writers spoke of a natural cycle, and Machiavelli says that governments arose by chance. Man is *not* by nature a political animal, contrary to Aristotle's words. Could the three good regimes of one, few, and many be combined into a mixed regime, as the classical writers suggested?

Machiavelli considers this traditional solution and works a striking contrast between Sparta and Rome. Sparta was the classical city celebrated for its mixed regime and enjoyed eight hundred years of stability, he says. Rome was the regime that expanded as it grew from kingdom to republic to empire without stability and without harmony, suffering from faction and discord between the nobles and the people. Those writers, Machiavelli says, who favored the Spartan example have always condemned the agitations in the Roman republic. One of them is Titus Livy, Machiavelli's grand authority in the *Discourses,* but Machiavelli does not make a point of his disagreement at this stage, early in his book. He makes an argument in favor of Rome and against the harmony of reason proposed (if not accepted) by classical political science and seems to leave it as a standoff between two attractive possibilities: Sparta or Rome.

Which is better: Sparta, the representative of classical political science; or Rome as understood by Machiavelli—that is, Machiavelli's Rome, representing his transformation of that political science and rejection of its bias toward self-sufficient harmony? On the one hand is Sparta with its way of self-sufficient moderation and satisfaction with its borders; on the other, imperial Rome dissatisfied with moderation and willing to endure the troubles of party dissent as the price of unlimited expansion. Polybius, the Greek historian of Rome, had stated the same alternative between desiring greater things like the Romans and following a stay-at-home policy of moderation, like Sparta (D 1.4–1.5). But having seen what

Machiavelli thinks about the necessity of acquisition, we are not surprised to see that he rules out this alternative. It appears that Sparta had an empire after all, lost it and "showed its weak foundation upon one slightest accident" (D 1.6.4). So, could a mixed republic like Sparta or Venice (a "modern" example he adds) find itself in a situation where it could not be conquered but was yet too small to trigger fear in its neighbors? No, that is not possible to sustain. Sparta had been in a lucky equilibrium, too lucky to imitate, and in the end was forced to expand, which brought its ruin.

"But since all things of men are in motion and cannot stay steady, they must either rise or fall: and to many things that reason does not bring you, necessity brings you" (D 1.6.5). Machiavelli concludes with his characteristic shocking statement that the "more honorable part" for a republic is to order itself so that "if indeed necessity brings it to expand, it can conserve what it has seized." He had come to this conclusion about foreign policy in discussing domestic policy. He had said that every republic has two parties that dispute each other: nobles and people. One can either suppress the dispute with strong laws and rigid education like in Sparta, in which case there must be a small, homogeneous citizen body, and let us not forget, a class of slaves for dishonorable tasks. Or one can have a free country with hostility and pitched battles between nobles and people, as in Rome, in which case the only way to bring and keep them together is to take both parties for an occasional outing in an imperialistic war. The choice is between harmonious peace and agitated imperialism; one cannot separate domestic policy from foreign policy, as Plato and Aristotle wanted to do. All government is oppression. If you are lucky like Sparta and neither conquer nor are conquered, then you oppress your own people; otherwise, you oppress foreigners, unless you are oppressed. One possible alternative might be a league of free republics with strength in unity so that each republic can be small. Machiavelli considers this, but he says that the success of such a league would require special circumstances, and that those cities that remain free do so because they have a "wholesome" habit of killing all their gentlemen (D 1.55; 2.19).

Domestic and foreign policy are interconnected, meaning that in fact the imperialistic necessities of foreign policy determine the domestic regime or constitution. Sparta and the classical mixed regime, one could say all classical political science, depend on the illusion of "the middle way" of moderate self-sufficiency. The domestic order of a classical polis (city) aimed at a just balance of classes that resolves claims to justice from each class in a public order. This order elevated the public over separate private claims. Machiavelli argues that this could be done only by excluding foreign policy, especially the necessity of conquest, from consideration. The regimes shown by Plato and Aristotle were certainly not pacifist and included a provision for the military. They both expected that wars were inevitable, but they did not accept the necessity of conquest and the policy of imperialism. Thus, classical political science depended on the primacy of domestic policy over foreign policy and of public justice over private interests. In Rome, as Machiavelli portrays it (not as Livy has it), one sees the reverse: the primacy of foreign policy over domestic policy led to the primacy of private interests over the public good.

One can argue the connection between domestic and foreign policy either way: from party government to imperialism, in order to keep the state united by war; or from imperialism to party government, as Rome's conquests brought new citizens and made a people less homogeneous and more tumultuous. Then it was necessary to allow them to vent their ambition and hatred against the nobles. What is the effect of allowing foreign policy to have primacy over domestic policy? Fundamentally, it is to challenge the distinction between friends and enemies, based on the presumption that your fellow countrymen are on your side. Rather, all humans must be considered possible enemies. This new presumption doesn't prevent temporary or even long-standing alliance with other humans, but it does question the self-sufficiency of the classical polis. There is no alliance, no grouping, that you can count on and trust. According to Machiavelli's morality, selfishness is dominant; everyone should try to be *uno solo*, by himself, like Romulus. According to his politics, foreign policy is dominant. At first that dominance would make one think of patriotism and self-sacrifice for one's country. But the real truth of foreign policy, the "effectual truth," is imperialism. Imperialism is the common good on which people can unite after their selfishness is expressed in party government.

For Machiavelli, it seems that the common good can be an effect, but not a cause. You cannot get people to act *for* the common good, but you can get their selfishness to *result* in the common good as an effect. This we saw in the *Mandragola*. The next task is to see how this happens in politics through the interplay of princes and peoples, the two orders that can be found in every regime. Meanwhile, we are left with the necessary connection between the pluralism that free people favor today and the imperialism they abhor. Having forsaken the self-sufficiency of the classical polis in order to answer our necessities and improve our freedom, is there any way we can stop short of empire? Is empire the only alternative to the polis?

Machiavelli's Indirect Government

Machiavelli is not merely content to attack classical political science by giving primacy to necessity over choice and arguing for a necessary connection between party government and imperialism. He also has a replacement for classical political science that provides the founding principle of a new political science both for his own use and its lasting influence in all succeeding modern political science. "A new mode of ruling" that governs people "more quietly under a dominion they do not see," as he describes it (D 2.21.2). Here it will be called "indirect government" to describe the leading feature that makes it invisible. Indirect government seeks to avoid the impression of those who are ruled that they are being imposed upon by their rulers and bossed around. It wants to make government, apparently a harsh necessity, more acceptable and received more quietly, because it is not seen as imposed. And why will it not be seen that way? Because it comes from oneself. Machiavelli remarks on a fact of human psychology: "For wounds and every other ill that a man does to himself spontaneously and by choice hurt much less than those that are done to you by someone else" (D 1.34.4). Noting how this impersonal statement turns personal, we can surmise that the reason self-harm hurts less is that it comes without a sense of being slighted by "someone else." Applied to politics, this means that government does well when it can convince those governed that government not only benefits them but also *comes from them*. That is the feat of indirect government, and it is the crucial first step toward modern self-government as practiced and understood today.

We see indirect government in contrast to direct government in the regime as presented in classical political science, most notably in the third book of Aristotle's *Politics*. The regime (*politeia*) is the rule of the whole of society by a part of it, which gives a characteristic stamp and style to that society as well as its type. There are different types, based on the number of rulers—one, few, or many. Monarchy, oligarchy, and democracy define the rule of the whole by these parts, so that, for example, the result of democratic rule is a democratic society, a certain way of life. No society stays together without rule; it must be ruled by some part of itself. This rule shows itself in the most open and public ways, each a kind of display of who is in charge. The ruling part is the most powerful part, always the most publicly visible. There are private parts kept hidden in every society, but the reason that they are hidden is that they are less powerful than the power that doesn't have to hide. The ruler of any society is always its most respectable power, and vice versa, the most respected is the most powerful. The Communist Party in the former Soviet Union, the mullahs in the Islamic Republic of Iran, and the American electorate are three very diverse examples of rule by the most powerful and respected part. Thus, the most impressive fact of politics everywhere is who rules. "Take me to your ruler," the demand of an alien from Mars, is the same as the prime object of earthly political science. This is direct government as shown in classical political science.

Machiavelli undertook to replace the classical regime of open, public rule with manipulation (modes) and ordering—"new modes and orders"—existing in every regime regardless of its public character. The most powerful part is hidden rather than public—it manages rather than rules; what is public is misleading and deceptive. Machiavelli's success in establishing his indirect government can be seen in the words used today for what in classical political science was called rule (*archein*). Start with the very word "management" (*maneggiare* in Machiavelli), current today in "schools of management." What does it mean but getting things done without demanding obedience, which is ruling without seeming to? In politics today, accomplishing something usually means *managing* to do it. The terms used today to designate the ruler try to conceal his predominance: *executive*, as if the ruler merely executes or carries out someone else's rule; *president*, as if the ruler merely presides; *chairman*, as if the ruler sits in a special chair; *leader*, as if the ruler were merely followed; *prime minister*, as if Winston Churchill had been merely the first minister, or assistant, or servant. *Civil servant* is a nauseating sarcasm that sums up the hypocrisy of the modern ruler. Machiavelli interprets Livy and makes a point Livy does not make about the Roman Senate's opposition to a tyrant: The

Senate, acting "with art . . . was unwilling to show its authority" (D 1.40.3–4). This is the hidden character of indirect government.

Hypocrisy, however, is not Machiavelli's style. Rather, the reverse: his shocking analysis exposes the hypocrisy of every attempt to aim at some imagined good. In killing his brother, Romulus did not aim at the common good but instead to become "one alone." But to become one alone, the goal of Machiavelli's prince, one must conceal one's aim and use fraud. Most people do not believe that being one alone is a proper goal; they do not have enough nerve to grasp this necessity. Those who do have this degree of prudence must hide it and manage their way around common morality. Machiavelli thus both exposes and justifies hypocrisy. After his death, his advice of practicing dirty tricks came to be known as *Machiavellianism*, a term of disgust. But disgust expressed with Machiavellianism is often an instance of the fraud that characterizes Machiavellianism, signifying the necessity of hypocrisy. It is no small part of the influence of Machiavelli today that we try to deny his influence—or is it his rule?—over us. No modern government is ashamed to rule, but every modern government is ashamed to admit it. Our rulers do not rule; they *represent* us. The notion of representation will be found in Thomas Hobbes, the next modern philosopher to be treated, who never mentions Machiavelli.

Indirect government arises from Machiavelli's analysis of human nature into two orders or "humors," a simplification of Aristotle's direct government. According to the latter, any of three parts of society can rule; according to Machiavelli, there is one ruling part in every society.

Machiavelli says, "For in every city these two diverse humors are found, which arise from this: that the people desire neither to be commanded nor oppressed by the great, and the great desire to command and oppress the people" (P 9; cf. D 1.4–1.5). Not speaking of "ruling," Machiavelli abandons the notion of Aristotle's direct government that rule is for the common good (however defined). For him, rule is commanding and oppressing—mastery. Who are princes? They are young, ruthless, ambitious, and desirous of mastery. The best prince is he who makes everything anew, and Machiavelli prefers potential or illegitimate princes, full of steam and lacking in scruples, to hereditary nobles, who as such are likely to be complacent and conservative. It was to the great advantage of the Roman republic that it allowed people of virtue to rise to high office when young, "without respect to age or blood," before their "vigor of spirit" grew old

(D 1.60). Illegitimate princes do not follow established ways, and while they secure greater glory than hereditary nobles because they make anew, their rise actually makes their countries safer, for nothing is less secure than trying to stand still, since human things are ever in motion.

A people will never wish to be conquered. Perhaps they would wish to conquer others if they could, but they are too weak. The people proper must be distinguished from people of popular origin who arise from the people with the ambition to become great. Such individuals are potential princes from but not of the people. Without a prince (our term "leader" is too tame) the people are passive; they can show constancy, but they do not become active or agitated unless they are supplied with a head (D 1.44.1). Machiavelli says that he differs from all other historians in appreciating the quality of constancy, and even wisdom, in the people (D 1.58.1). Whereas princes are superior in establishing new modes and orders, the people are superior in keeping things already ordered. The people are slow and ponderous; they are the maintainers, the conservative element. If this is so, then the party division between the nobles and the people that Machiavelli describes is actually between nobles and popular individuals who want to be nobles. All dissension is confined to the order of princes, actual and potential. The multitude is mere body or material without a head to form it, the head being always a prince. To ascribe constancy to the people is to absolve them of responsibility for their moods and deeds when excited. These are the work of their heads (their *capi*), not themselves. In Machiavelli's terms, the people have goodness (*bontà*), and the princes have virtue (*virtù*).

Thus are the two diverse orders natural to humanity and found in every regime: peoples and princes, weak and strong, kind and ruthless. These are opposed qualities that cannot be mixed, yet both are needed. They cannot be combined for the sake of a common good that all citizens more or less consciously make their own. The people are religious (as will be seen) and dedicated to the established common good, but the people do not and cannot rule. The ruling class is not and cannot be dedicated to the common good because it is composed of selfish and ambitious individuals eager for glory. The princes have prudence and virtue, the political qualities. In sum, the class or order dedicated to the common good does not know how to achieve it, since as we know "goodness is not enough," and the class that knows how to achieve it is not dedicated to it.

Yet there is a common good, a public good shown in the "idealism" that goes with Machiavelli's "realism." The regime does not aim at the common good but rather has two orders that contribute diversely to it. Under classical direct government it was thought that one could not have a common public good unless the rulers were public-spirited. If you thought that was rare or impossible, as did the ancient skeptics, then you dismissed politics as a worthy subject and refused political philosophy. Machiavelli for the first time conceived a common good that is merely a result of private goods, a regime that does not aim at its end. Aristotle had conceived of such a possibility, but he did not recommend it. For him this would be a regime without a final cause, to use his term. Final cause, we know, was expelled from modern science, which denies that nature has purposes. But it was expelled from political science by Machiavelli before modern science came into existence and its apostle Francis Bacon wrote its eulogy. In Machiavelli's politics, the Aristotelian questions of who rules and for what end—for the answers are the same everywhere—become the modern question of *how* they rule. Government does have a form, as Machiavelli uses Aristotle's term, but it signifies a temporary, shifting alliance of private interests. No form can change the nature of the two orders; no formative education can produce a country dedicated to the common good. No Machiavellian form can last unless it changes and stops being itself.

In Machiavelli's terms, "republic" is distinguished from "principality," but not because it has a different ruling part with a different intent. The ruling part of a regime is the same everywhere and always: the prince or princes, never the people. Machiavelli speaks of "the princes in a republic" to make it clear (P 6, 9; D 1.18, 1.20, 1.58, 2.9) that the people, as we have seen, need a "head." Moreover, all states have the same intent, which is to acquire; states must also maintain, but the only reliable way to maintain is to acquire more (D 1.5.3). "Rome" can be understood as one state despite the fact that it began as a kingship, changed to a republic, and ended as an empire. Names and forms are flexible, open to change, and subject to the underlying necessities of princes and peoples. Two classical forms are affected by Machiavelli's analysis by orders and humors. One who wishes to make an absolute power, "which is called tyranny by the authors," should "renew everything" (D 1.25 end; P 6, 7)—which is to say, give no respect to the republican form. The term "tyranny," vital to classical political science, is purely nominal for Machiavelli and is not used in *The Prince.* A second consequence is that the people do not rule and democracy as rule of the people is impossible. Democracy in its classical sense would, for Machiavelli, be rule of the weak and rule of the good, neither of which can be sustained. The people have a conservative quality that serves to sustain a state, or would do so if states could be sustained by conservative sentiments. But they cannot. Constant renewal of forms—in Machiavelli's words, "new modes and orders"—is a necessity.

Extraordinary Means

Necessity has a double aspect that Machiavelli must contend with. It means what is urgent and compelling in the present, when it can be understood immediately—a danger that today is often called "existential." But it also refers to dangers that might arise in the future, in which case it will not be immediately understood and must be anticipated with prudence. Necessity as compelling, when there seems to be no choice, must be distinguished from choosing "according to necessity" when necessity is not apparent (P 15). In promoting necessity as a principle, Machiavelli must look ahead to consider everyone's necessity and thus predict the behavior that will come about. This outlook produces a certain impartiality that prevents him from preferring one person's or one group's necessity over another's. Everyone does what seems necessary to oneself. Yet some make mistakes—typical ones, such as the greatest human mistake made by the weak of believing that God or human justice will care for them. We have seen this false presumption at work in Machiavelli's analysis of corruption, which ends in the necessity of acting according to the times.

At times a principality is appropriate; at others, a republic is better. But a republic is in general more favorable to indirect government. In a principality, the prince has more difficulty in disguising his government as necessity rather than for his own advantage; in a republic, the existence of rival princes allows the government—in Rome, the Senate—an opportunity to use one prince against the others in a system that disguises the rule of the nobles as a whole in the actions of one of them. This general advantage of a republic does not prevent the prince in a principality, like Cesare Borgia, from using a henchman, Remirro de Orco, to do his dirty work and then dispose of him afterward to the approval of the populace ("satisfied and stupefied"; P 7). Machiavelli points out that Cesare Borgia played front man himself to his father, Pope Alexander VI. Yet the ordering of the Roman republic provided an arena in which a number of princes, as consuls or tribunes, could attain individual glory in rivalry with others of their nature. Machiavelli provides a contrast between two republics, ancient Rome and modern Florence, on this point.

At the beginning of the *Discourses,* Machiavelli presents Rome as the model for the beginnings of states, particularly in the necessity that excused Romulus for the murder of his brother. He also discusses the successful ordering of party government that enabled Rome to be free and strong. Among its orders was a law and a practice of accusation allowing citizens the power to bring charges before the people against those who "sin" against free government (a kind of impeachment; D 1.7–1.8). This was used both to deter overambitious princes and to purge the anger and resentment of the people against them. In the tumults that resulted from the disunion of people and nobles, Machiavelli introduces the word "extraordinary" to describe the modes resorted to by both sides (D 1.4.1). That word occurs frequently in *The Prince* and the *Discourses* in contrast to the ordinary. The ordering of founders creates ordinary modes by which government operates, but ordinary modes are made by extraordinary modes that impress people by causing shock. Ordinary modes have the disadvantage that over time they result in complacency and a sense of entitlement, followed by too much ease and disobedience. Ordinary modes cannot sustain themselves; they need to be enlivened, so that people are suddenly made aware of the presence and power of the prince over them. Government must consist of an alternation between the ordinary and the extraordinary. Ordinary does the work of maintaining but becomes enfeebled by its routine, which needs to be revived by the sudden intervention of an extraordinary deed or event. Such a thing might be an extraordinary execution—such as "to kill the sons of Brutus"—after which people walk around less presumptuously and more fearfully and reverently.

Recalled to the fear of its beginnings, a republic might succeed so far as to become perpetual. With a remedy for every circumstance of emergency or corruption, a perpetual republic might be possible. Machiavelli both affirms and denies this idea (D 3.17, 22.3). On one hand, it seems unlikely that a single republic can so perfectly conquer fortune in one country that "despite the motion of human things" it could solve every problem that might arise; on the other, perhaps Machiavelli has in mind that if a republic following his advice should fail, it could be replaced by another republic that followed it better or with better luck. Machiavelli will perhaps always be needed and his advice must always be available, but his advice cannot succeed so well as to make its functioning automatic and his republic a machine. Fortune will continue despite the war of humanity led by Machiavelli the prince against it, and so freedom will continue, as well as the need for virtue in the use of freedom. One successful republic will not take over humanity as a whole and make its necessity into the fate of all for all time. Weak as Machiavelli is, complaining of his "malignant fortune," he has to consider, if not worry, that he might succeed too well and tyrannize over all humanity (P Let. Ded).

It is well to speculate on the goal Machiavelli sets for us and for himself, but one must not overlook the extraordinary means he advises to get us there. To do so we may return to the discussion of accusation and calumny near the beginning of the *Discourses* (1.7–1.8). Accusation refers to a law permitting the people to bring charges against those citizens who "sin" against free government; calumny consists in private charges that do not require evidence made public or allow a public defense by the accused. Rome had such a law, or such an institution, as Machiavelli shows in two cases of accusation against Coriolanus and Manlius, and Florence, the modern regime, had no such law and suffered from the sort of party discord that brings ruin to republics. Party discord made Rome free and strong but it was fatal to Florence. What made the difference?

Machiavelli makes a distinction between ordinary means (*modi*) of dealing with an ambitious single citizen by means of a law and public proceedings; and extraordinary means that have to be resorted to when ordinary means do not exist. This seems to be the difference between legal and illegal means: Rome had a law and Florence did not; so the Florentines punished that citizen with riots directed against him. But there were also riots in Rome, and Florence did have a law establishing accusations. The purpose Machiavelli cites for accusation is not just punishment of unjust behavior; it is to "vent the animus" of the multitude "ordinarily" against a single citizen. If it doesn't happen ordinarily, it needs to happen extraordinarily. Executing the law isn't the point; rather, it is executing the man. A republic needs such executions at least once every ten years in order to survive the corruption arising from complacent routine, by which it slides into disobedience and ruin (D 3.1.3). Whether that individual found guilty is indeed guilty doesn't matter; rather, such people must be "eliminated" so that the established order of government can be cleansed. Government, we have seen, must necessarily be oppressive according to Machiavelli, but the appearance of oppression can be disguised by the sacrifice of one of its members as a scapegoat to save the rest.

The necessity to focus punishment on a single person in order to save the class of nobles or princes is matched by the equal necessity to allow single persons—that is, princes—to gain the glory of victories in war. Thus, accusation is not just a requirement of legality, as first appears, but a general necessity of government. The focus on individual responsibility, whether for good or evil, emerges as another feature of indirect government. A single prince can make one of his henchmen take the rap for the outrages of his behavior, as we have seen Cesare Borgia do to Remirro de Orco, gaining both the advantage of Remirro's misdeeds and the favor of punishing them (P 7). A republic can do the same, as when the Roman Senate managed the unruly animus of the plebs against itself by offering parades for victors, set off against punishments for unsuccessful rivals. Glory is most appreciable when contrasted with ignominy and execution. For Machiavelli, virtue (*virtù*) must be visible to be effectual, and visible virtue is clearest in contrast.

The Roman regime was a succession of princes, holding individual responsibility, rather than a collective rule of law with a constitution, like one in our time, of fixed institutions having defined powers and an aura of lawfulness. To be sure, this is Machiavelli's Rome shown in his interpretation of a Roman historian; it is not intended as an accurate historical account in our sense. Now accusation culminates in an execution, and we must take notice of the importance Machiavelli accords to execution and executive power. Since government is necessarily oppressive, punishment is more essential than reward, just as fear is more motivating than love (P 17). The most impressive punishment is capital punishment, when a miscreant is executed. The execution of government culminates in the execution of rival princes from among the princely class, whether guilty of breaking the law or not. The two meanings of execute, "carry out" and "punish capitally," are connected; the second is necessary to the first.

The idea of an executive function or power is yet another aspect of indirect government, whereby the government claims or pretends not to be acting on its own but submitting to the will of someone or something else—the law, the will of the people, or the will of God.

The institution of accusation culminates in the punishment of an execution. But the same may be said of government as a whole, for all government is essentially punitive and must culminate in a periodic execution (every ten years) to keep its power active. Gratitude from citizens for benefits received is unavailing. To execute its policies, government must occasionally execute its enemies, as we have seen. But if we take another step, another grand feature of Machiavelli's political science is revealed. If government must stress punishments over rewards, its necessary strictures must be managed privately out of sight. Indirect government cannot operate in the light of day with the transparency and accountability of our constitutional government. Machiavelli's regime has two opposed humors: princes who want to master others, and peoples who do not want to be mastered. Neither humor can appreciate the insistence of the other, and, consequently, princes must use fraud to conceal their mastery from peoples who hate it. Accusation leads to the conclusion that all government must be understood as a conspiracy. All its executions must be planned in secret so as to have its chilling effect as a shocking surprise to the public. Machiavelli indicates the centrality of conspiracy in his political science by making the longest chapter in *The Prince* (19) and in the *Discourses* (3.6) consider conspiracies. In the latter he gives the first analysis in the history of political philosophy on how to accomplish a conspiracy by its stages—before, during, and after. Previous philosophers had occasionally discussed the justice of conspiracy against a tyrant, but without supplying directions on how to do it. In his *Politics,* Aristotle discusses revolutions, but also not with a manual. Machiavelli excuses himself from arguing the justice of conspiracy and, ignoring the rights and wrongs, devotes himself to explaining the execution. He reveals his impartiality by showing how, despite the dangers, a conspiracy against the government might succeed and, correspondingly, how a government might conspire to prevent the very conspiracies he advises. As in his play *Mandragola*, Machiavelli's political science works behind the scenes.

Machiavelli's Conspiracy Against "Our Religion"

The same chapter of the *Discourses* that promises renewal of a republic through well-timed executions also contains the last of Machiavelli's three open attacks on Christianity (*Discourses* 3.1.4; see also 1.12.2 and 2.2.2). These criticisms are worded in such fashion that one could think charitably that Machiavelli was opposing only the corruption of the "Roman Church" and the misinterpretation of its doctrine "according to idleness and not virtue," but they contain a searing indictment of "our religion" as having made the world "effeminate" and an account of an attempted revival of it that did no more than revive its corruption. For even after the renovations of Saint Francis and Saint Dominic, its prelates "do the worst they can because they do not fear the punishment they do not see and do not believe." Christian priests are actually atheists in this description. Are they perhaps capable of being enlisted in a movement against "our religion"? In these striking and memorable passages, Machiavelli takes a stance against Christianity that no other philosopher or theologian in his time dared to take. Not only was he not imitated but his name became too dangerous to pronounce unless to revile and reject it. A century later Francis Bacon implied praise in his statement that "one of the doctors of Italy" had shown the harm done by Christian priests. Machiavelli had to say this so that Bacon could repeat it a century later. This was the second step of calling attention to Machiavelli's first step of rejecting the rule of Christian priests. Machiavelli's boldness had to be seconded and advanced by Bacon's appreciative boldness. But all philosophers read Machiavelli and some of them followed him. His plan to free the world from the "Christian republic" and to set it on the way to the "new modes and orders" announcing the new world of modernity was well begun.

Where could Machiavelli find the structure of his political science? He looks in two different places, both pertaining to religion. Religion contains the general secret of indirect government, which is to disguise the human will and the work of chance as the will of God. First, he relates two beautiful episodes contrasting the prudent pagan Roman treatment of priests with modern Christian practice (D 1.14). The Romans had priests known as "chicken-men" (*pullarii*), who had care of the chickens used for auspices. When auspices were needed for the success of a battle—indicating the favor of the gods—the chicken-men would cast grain to the chickens. If they ate, auspices were good; if not, the army would be advised to abstain from battle. Obviously, the chances for favorable auspices were good. But, in the first example, the consul came upon a good opportunity for an important battle, but the chickens did not eat. The "prince" of the chicken-men reported the sad fact to the consul, who lied to the soldiers that the chickens had eaten. When some of the chicken-men told soldiers that the chickens had not eaten, the consul repeated his assurance to the soldiers and added that any chicken-men who said otherwise were lying and would be punished. Then, in order that "the effect would correspond to the prognostication," he commanded that the chicken-men be placed in the front line of battle. It happened "by chance" that the prince of the chicken-men was killed by a Roman javelin in his back. Whereupon the consul declared that the army had been purged of its guilt by the death of this liar.

In a second example, however, the consul was not so careful to maintain "the orders of their religion." This consul, hearing that the chickens had refused to eat said, "Let's see if they wish to drink," and had them thrown into the ocean. While the first consul won his battle, this one lost. The first was honored and the second condemned, not so much for the result of the battle but because the first went prudently against the auspices and the second rashly. Machiavelli does not mention the possibility of pious obedience to the auspices. But this is what Christian priests—or the "princes" of Christianity, so called to accord with the "prince" of the chicken-men—enjoy. Their exemption from public, political accounting allowed them to claim private revelations from God, hold private confessions, and instruct private consciences. They demand loyalty to the Church in this world and teach loyalty to the next world, where the pious will find their reward. The Church disarms the pious but uses the arms and the wealth of strong men to gain worldly strength it cannot achieve on its own. For all its enormous power, then, it can do no more than weaken the strong. It is strong enough to keep Italy divided but not strong enough to unite it.

Machiavelli does say that our religion, "having shown the truth and the true way," makes us esteem less the honor of the world" (D 2.2.2). Does this mean that after all his criticism he remains a Christian, if perhaps a somewhat unorthodox one? This forgiving view is held by many, who underestimate the power of the Church in Machiavelli's time and consequently underestimate the rhetorical concessions that prudent authors found necessary. Machiavelli was very bold in his criticism of Christianity—not just the Church but its doctrine—because he could point to statements such as this one. And consider it carefully: Machiavelli does not say Christianity is true; it could "show the truth and the true way" and yet be false if Machiavelli could appropriate it and use it for his anti-Christian purpose. He is impressed by the success of Christianity, a doctrine from an "unarmed prophet" that somehow "acquired" or conquered the world. Initially, he seems to present the "moderns" of his time as weak and in need of reinvigoration by the ancients, who are strong. Yet somehow the strong ancients were defeated by the weak moderns when ancient Rome submitted to Christian Rome. How did this happen?

Machiavelli is not above using the Bible to suit himself. He retells the story of David and Goliath in a manner to suggest that he takes the mantle of David. In chapter 13 of *The Prince,* Machiavelli cites David's refusal to accept Saul's offer of his arms, saying that David would rather meet the enemy with his own arms, his sling and knife. His knife? The Bible says that David used his sling to kill Goliath and afterward picked up Goliath's knife and used it to cut off his head (1 Samuel 17.3, 37–40). In the Bible, David gives credit to "the Lord, who will deliver me out of the hands of the Philistine"—the very contrary of "one's own arms," Machiavelli's phrase, which he uses as a motto for his enterprise. If there is one thing taught in the Bible, and that without any possibility of confusion or misinterpretation, it is that man is not self-sufficient. Man cannot rely on himself alone; he cannot rely on his own arms. He needs the help of the Lord. For Machiavelli, the political truth that one must rely on one's own arms is traceable to the cosmic truth that man is alone.

We may now summarize the clarion call of Machiavelli to his time and the later time of his successors. To rely on "one's own arms" rather than God implies that human necessities come first, even when they conflict with divine commands. "Necessity" signifies the ways humans must adopt to save themselves from "coming to ruin" (P 15). These are "extraordinary modes" shocking to the princes and peoples who live enthralled to the Church and its unbelieving priests. Humans can and need to be awakened to their necessity by a revelation counter to the one in the Bible, with its same promise to bring freedom—but now by means of human prudence rather than submission to the will of God. Thus, the origin of the modern project of rational control must necessarily appear as an irrational shock *ad uno tratto* (with one stroke), a bold annunciation of the new "effectual truth." Moreover, Machiavelli's counter-revelation inverts and adopts the indirect government characteristic of the Church, as one can see from another look at the example of David and Goliath. David, the new prince confronting the champion Goliath and killing him with nothing but a sling, picks up his fallen enemy's knife to cut off his head, thus using the enemy's arms as his own. Machiavelli, a writer who is even bolder than he seems, affords us a modestly concealed portrait of himself as David.

CHAPTER TWO

THOMAS HOBBES

(1588–1679)

SUPPOSING, as we have, that modernity is the idea of rational control, one can see that control can be exercised over human beings and over nonhuman nature. The former control is by politics and political science; the latter, by natural science. Now, is political science the same science, using the same scientific method, as natural science? This would be because human nature belongs to, and is no different from, all nature. Or is human nature a special part of nature requiring a separate sort of science? That is the first question to be posed about Thomas Hobbes since, following the study of Machiavelli, it is the most obvious difference between the two.

Hobbes guided himself safely through a long life of perils both political and religious. Some were brought upon him through civil war between the monarchy and Parliament, between Protestants and Catholics, and among the disputatious Protestant sects. Others he brought upon himself in reaction to his materialist doctrines and in response to the scathing wit that makes him a delight to read. In contrast to Machiavelli, whom he never mentions, Hobbes brought a new morality of justice and rights and replaced Machiavelli's politics of significant examples with an abstract political science that is, for its simplicity and universality, still studied by all political scientists today.

In agreement with Machiavelli, Hobbes's original notion of the state of nature made a theoretical system of Machiavelli's *uno solo,* and his science came out of Machiavelli's effectual truth. Hobbes introduced the term *fact* to political science, now as common a word as there is. While Machiavelli openly attacked Christianity, Hobbes did the same for the philosophy of Aristotle, which he mocked as "Aristotelity." If it were not for Machiavelli, Hobbes would be the founder of modern political science. In fact, Hobbes declared that political science began with one of his own books, denying Aristotle (who began political science), ignoring Machiavelli (Hobbes's predecessor), and surpassing Baruch Spinoza (his contemporary rival). In this claim of innovation, one could say, Hobbes crowned himself the latest of Machiavelli's new princes. Machiavelli does speak of "effectual truth" in a manner to suggest the cause and effect of modern science, but he does not develop that suggestion and lived before Galileo (1564–1642) brought the new science into view. Hobbes was a contemporary of Galileo and of René Descartes (1596–1650), who developed the modern "method" that still characterizes science, and Hobbes was also the private secretary of Francis Bacon, who with noble inaugural speeches made himself the founder of modern science.

Hobbes went beyond Bacon, his teacher, who spoke of the "advancement of learning," the title of his most famous book. Bacon based science on experiment to free it from the "idols" of Aristotelian philosophy and common opinion, but he did not show how to apply experiment to politics. For Hobbes, however, the new science was for him not merely an advancement, implying the extension of existing learning; it was the only science deserving the name. In the dedication to his book *De Corpore* (Of the body, 1655), Hobbes said that though natural philosophy was young, "civil philosophy" concerning politics was no older than his own work *De Cive* (Of the citizen, 1642). So much for Plato, Aristotle, and Thomas Aquinas—and for Machiavelli, as well, whose guiding spirit was much more to Hobbes than a lingering presence though quite unacknowledged

MAJOR WORKS OF HOBBES

The Elements of Law, Natural and Politic (1640): Hobbes's first effort to reform political science with the deductive method of geometry.

De Cive (1642): Along with *De Corpore* (1655) and *De Homine* (1658), the last planned but first published work in the three-part *Elements of Philosophy*, putting forward the social contract, the state of nature, the rights of a sovereign, and a manufactured Christian theology.

Leviathan (1651): Developing *De Cive*, this rhetorical masterwork contains Hobbes's theory of representation (the first) and an expanded purported Christian theology.

Behemoth (1681): A history of the English Civil War documenting abuses caused by neglecting Hobbes's new theory.

by him. Why was civil philosophy brand new? It was the first political philosophy that used the method of modern science to guide the answers to political questions and thus to consider human nature as no different from nonhuman nature. Hobbes considers it obvious and true that human beings are the only beings capable of science, as one sees in the first five chapters of his book *Leviathan* (1651)—his greatest work and the one we shall analyze. These chapters are directed not to *what* we see by looking at politics but to *how* we see when we look at anything, human or not. The subject matter of politics does not require special treatment to understand it; one does not have to begin from the political opinions that humans have and offer to explain themselves, nor is it necessary to consider the claims they make in their opinions. Galileo did not take a survey of popular opinion to discover whether the earth moved or not, and Hobbes does not take his civil philosophy from political opinions. Modern science works through experiments rather than opinions, though it is necessary at first to explain why opinions are untrustworthy, as Hobbes did. He takes pleasure in contradicting what previous philosophers have inferred from what people say. Modern science wants to prevent disputes rather than try to resolve them through disputation and argument.

Yet Hobbes cannot quite set opinion aside, for he does not succeed in reducing civil philosophy to the exactness of natural philosophy. He still regards human nature as distinct from the rest of nature, and he still appeals to nature in the older sense that regards it as a guide to mankind. Hobbes's notion of rational control puts man in charge of nature, hence above it—but he also needs nature to explain and justify human empire over nature. So today a tension remains between science and human nature, between scientists and humanists: is politics part of science, or science part of politics? Today's political science is deeply indebted to Hobbes as its founder; he is the first to apply the scientific method to politics, as we shall see. His political science is now, perhaps too optimistically, regarded as obsolete, but is its principle, which he boastfully asserted as his, still valid? Political scientists are divided now between those who accept Hobbes's political science and those who reject or resist treating human actions like natural or physical objects in motion; the latter believe that humans can intend what they do, so that their purposes, opinions, and ideas must be consulted.

The current debate over climate change illustrates the question of the status of science raised by Hobbes. Climate change is caused by the growth and application of modern science in unrestricted technology. Science wants to be on its own, independent of political control, which it regards as ignorant and invasive. Science should lead, with scientists at the helm, the rest of us following. But science seems not to have correctly considered the consequences of its unrestricted growth for the climate of the earth, the home of human beings. These inhabitants, partial to their home, need to defend themselves by defending the nature that is much more kind to them than is the rest of the cold, fiery, airless universe. The earth gives benefits to humans that they depend on. In this view humans should follow humanism, rather than science; they should put politics in control, rather than science; and their politics should be exercised to some extent against science, rather than meekly obey it. In philosophy this thought is behind what is called postmodernism, a movement that goes beyond science without ignoring it or leaving it—merely "post" or after, instead of against. Later, we shall find it in Nietzsche, but we must now return to Hobbes to see how he treats this issue of today.

Nature and Naturalism in Hobbes

To understand Hobbes, one must distinguish two notions that I shall call "nature" and "naturalism." "Nature" appears above all in Hobbes's concept of the "state of nature," or in *Leviathan*, "the condition of mere nature." Here, *nature* is a term of distinction between what is natural and what is unnatural. As term of distinction, nature can serve as a guide, perhaps not a guide to good but at least a guide by which to escape what is bad. "Naturalism," on the other hand, is the belief that all things are equally natural; nothing is more natural than anything else. All things are caused, and events are nonetheless caused, nonetheless natural or unnatural, for being frequent or infrequent. Homosexuality, for example, may be less frequent than heterosexuality, but this does not make it unnatural. If naturalism is true, and nature is no guide, nothing is usual or habitual or normal. Political science is a simple part of science understood as physics or as the method of physics. Such would be the "standard model" today of the universe. But if nature is a term of distinction, some things natural, others not, if the state of nature that Hobbes introduced is a guide for human action, then political science has a special character because human beings have a special character. When this special character of nature is found in the "state of nature," then that nature serves as a guide and as a separate basis for political science that would justify its independence from the naturalism of the natural sciences.

Hobbes wavers between these two positions: He is closer to nature in his two early works *Elements of Law* and *De Cive*, and closer to naturalism in *Leviathan*. His contemporary and friendly rival in Holland, Baruch Spinoza (1632–1677), sailed closer to naturalism and was declared by Hobbes to be "bolder" than he was. The naturalism of modern science had sources that will help to understand it, in Machiavelli and especially in Bacon and Descartes. Machiavelli spoke of the "motion of human things" and of "worldly things" of which they are part, but he insists on the special character of mastery in politics. He lowers the standard of politics from what is special to humans to the imitation of certain lower animals like the fox and the lion. But these are qualities of common sense, not physics, and they are invoked to explain human acquiring and maintaining, which remain necessarily on a higher, human level. What Machiavelli denies to politics is a higher level than politics; he is the master of politics, as politics that does not transcend politics with a view to the city of philosophy or of God.

It is Bacon who first developed the scientific method of naturalism. He did not formulate a political science but composed a scientific utopia, *New Atlantis* (1626, published after his death), the end of whose foundation he declared to be "the knowledge of causes, and the secret motions of things; and the enlarging of the bounds of human empire, to the effecting of all things possible." "Enlarging the bounds of human empire," a phrase we have encountered before, sounds much like the necessity of acquiring in Machiavelli's realism but expanded beyond politics. The question arises, Is this realism a conclusion of science or the motivation of science? Is it naturalism or nature? When Machiavelli's realism is restated in the terms of modern science, does this mean it was *derived* from modern science, so that political science is derived from natural science and that Machiavelli's philosophy of anticipating was not necessary to the formation of the modern world but redone later and better by Bacon? Or was Machiavelli's realism the motive and the cause of the realism of modern science, so that political science has a special status as the master of modern science? Aristotle had said that political science is the master science because it is the gatekeeper science that decides which science and how much science can be pursued. Perhaps this reason applies also to the modern political science—especially in Hobbes—that opposed Aristotle.

Bacon's statement of the end of modern science did not issue in a new political science. His political philosophy had two parts: the utopian *New Atlantis*'s promise of fantastic innovations, such as submarines, as the fruits of science under a regime vaguely ruled by scientists; and a provisional policy of Elizabethan imperialism for the present. Whereas Machiavelli, with his new modes and orders, was innovative in politics but not in physics, Bacon—with his *New Organon* replacing Aristotle's *Organon*—was innovative in physics but not in politics. A new science of ethics and politics was the work of Descartes contemporaneous with Hobbes. Descartes was the founder of the scientific "method," by that name, with his *Discourse on Method* (1637), and he applied his method to human affairs in a marvelous work *Passions of the Soul* (1649), a work of ethics worth considering as a friendly rival to Hobbes's political science. It is friendly because it emphasizes human passions, like Hobbes, but does so without producing a whole new political science.

The title of the first part of Descartes's *Passions of the Soul* is "Of the Passions in General and Incidentally of the Whole Nature of Man." Descartes thought that the passions were much more important than had been held by the ancients, whom he criticizes. This was their most defective science, he says. While Descartes's (and Hobbes's) ethics were oriented toward human passions, Aristotle's ethics depended on human actions as voluntary, not determined by passions.[1] Descartes does not deny the power of free will in humans—he affirms it—but it becomes a problem for him, and for modern philosophy in general, because of its emphasis on the utility of passions. Aristotle seems to take voluntary action for granted in his *Ethics*, and merely discusses practical difficulties in deciding whether an action is voluntary. For example, when on a ship in a storm one throws one's baggage over the side in order to save the ship, is the action voluntary? But for Descartes and Hobbes, the very idea of voluntary action becomes questionable and they spend effort to address a theoretical perplexity as if there were a practical need to resolve it.

The new science of ethics has two advantages: realism and universality. The realism is in the link between soul and body; passions of the soul dispose the soul to will movements already begun by the body, preserving and perfecting it. Descartes presents a physiology of the passions now entirely rejected, to explain what happens in the body when one gets angry, for one instance. Today's neurology, though more accurate, is a version of the same idea. Now, virtue, says Descartes, must rule over the passions—but how does it do this? By not suppressing but *managing* them (recall that Machiavellian word). There is no passion without its useful side. Reason is needed, of course, to correct the shortsighted or blind character of the passions, but it can do this with the aid of the passions. Descartes's ethics do not preach to human reason; they show practical instruments for getting people to obey reason, which is the main problem. This is his ethics' realism. In Aristotle's ethics the passions, generally speaking, are the enemy of rational perfection; here in the founding of modernity, they become instruments of reason. With Descartes we are on the way to the more radical dictum of David Hume that "reason is the slave of the passions."

As for the second advantage of the new ethical science, universality, we find in Descartes and Hobbes a movement from less universality to more. For Descartes, the key to all the virtues is generosity, which is not the usual sense of freely making gifts but a general resoluteness, an awareness of one's identity in the strength of one's will. Generous minds are strong and noble, making up an aristocracy of the strong-willed. Such people are not so much magnanimous, as in Aristotle's supreme individual virtue, as naturally strong like Machiavelli's princes. They are *benevolent,* neither disdainful like Aristotle's magnanimous man nor cruel like Machiavelli's princes. They will receive admiring glory from the multitude for their goodwill to humanity as a whole rather than the shocked "satisfied and stupefied" reaction of the multitude to Machiavellian ferocity. The conclusion of Descartes's scientific ethics in generosity was nonpolitical benevolence that offered no basis for a new political science such as was to come from Hobbes. Its formal adherence to free will sustained an inequality of those aware of the strength of their will. For Hobbes, the key virtue was justice, the political virtue studied by Plato and Aristotle, now in a new guise but still political. His rejection of free will, in accordance with naturalism, made justice possible for all on a fundamentally democratic basis of fear. His naturalism culminates in political or civil philosophy that treats all alike.

What does the scientific method shared by Hobbes and Descartes show? Science is a whole with a method that applies everywhere, without reference to the subject matter that might call for a special method or treatment. Human beings and their politics do not call for a method different from any other items that might be found in nature. There are no differences between things or beings but only *names* for things that men are free to impose on nature; nature has nothing to say or suggest to us. The so-called beings that Aristotle spoke of are actually matter in motion that can and must be understood in the same way, with the same laws of nature, as a rolling ball. The ruthless desire for power after power in men would represent inertial motion. Indeed, the very concept of power, we shall see, represents an import from physics. Inertial power may seem to have an end as in Aristotle's physics, which is self-preservation. Yet perhaps this is not motion toward an end but motion away from the beginning, a flight from danger rather than man's natural end. The constant use of power today is mostly in Hobbes's sense of the word: by virtue of their motion to nowhere, humans have power for anything. By this new understanding of power, the project for rational control we have been following in modern political philosophy is not limited by nature but develops only by its own scientific method. That method recognizes no set limits and encourages experiments of new possibilities for human power. Hobbes's *Leviathan*, he says in the introduction, makes "an Artificial Man . . . of greater stature and strength than the Naturall" (L Introduction, p. 9).

Hobbes's Prescientific Peeking

Hobbes did not hold exclusively to the view of naturalism with its scientific method, for he also thought that nature could be a guide for humans and their actions as opposed to a merely scientific description of the laws determining their behavior. This guide is the "state of nature," Hobbes's original contribution to political philosophy, a new foundation for it. This new "concept" is newly conceived rather than dictated empirically by the nature of things, but it does make use of half-concealed observations of human nature that may be considered "peeking," rather than openly looking, at nature. What do I mean by "peeking"?

The purpose of scientific naturalism is to derive politics from physics, and to do so methodically. This means that it is against the rules of method to observe men as they are now, before their behavior has been derived from physics. To observe men in this way is to assume that they have something in their nature that needs to be to be observed before they can be understood. These special characteristics might seem to require a method distinct from the laws of physics. Scientists can look at men to verify the conclusion of their derivation from physics, but they must not *peek* at them first in order to guide their derivation. If they do, they import common sense into their scientific system, whose supposed merit is to rise above common sense. In today's parlance "stereotypes" is the word used to describe reliance on unscientific common sense—that is, on what science labels fixed prejudice, superstition, and tradition. At the end of his introduction to *Leviathan,* Hobbes says to his readers "Read Thy Self" to demonstrate his doctrine. This is ambiguous: does it mean to check the doctrine by examining yourself or to examine yourself in order to demonstrate the doctrine? The latter is untrue to naturalism because it implies that the science depends on a preceding, prescientific peek.

The best example of Hobbes's guilty peeking is the reference to curiosity, nestled among other passions in chapter 6 of *Leviathan* and defined as "this singular Passion from other Animals."[2] Hobbes calls it a "lust of the mind," making man delight in generating knowledge. He considers reason specific to man as well, but by connecting reason to passion, almost reduces it to something that men share with other animals. Yet humans have reason and animals do not. The exercise of reason is science, which is to conceive possibilities, while prudence, common to humans and animals, is to reckon probabilities. This special character of man to conceive possibilities produces two special problems for him that other animals do not have. The first is for Hobbes himself, the scientist. Hobbes's science says that humans are things in motion, but also admits that only humans are capable of science. How does one explain the capacity for science out of science? Science says that men are nothing special yet asserts that science itself is something special. How does Hobbes fit himself into his system? He says that the reader must read mankind in himself, but where is Hobbes explained? He seems to know himself beforehand by peeking, then explains the rest of mankind from this knowledge.

The second problem is that only men have politics. They are not simply gregarious like bees, nor solitary and familial like peacocks. They have politics instead of the overwhelming passions of animal instinct, and their politicking seems related to the capacity for conceiving possibilities. Humans are insecure like other animals, but their insecurity is made worse by the imagination enabling them not only to see but also to imagine dangers. They can imagine the "state of nature" to which Hobbes's political science introduces them. Yet in describing human nature, is not Hobbes joining in the "frequency of insignificant speech" that he inveighs against (L 1, p. 14)? Perhaps so, but only if naturalism is true in asserting that everything about humans is equally natural. The state of nature is when everything necessary to define "man" is revealed, as opposed to normal political life when the defining function, capacity, and character of human beings is covered over with accidental features such as religious dogmas. For Hobbes, man's definition can be found only if it is stripped of all normal, civilized qualities. Aristotle had said that "man" (human being) is by nature a political animal, a definition based on the behavior and opinions of normal people in a civilized state. Hobbes's state of nature, by contrast, is where men have no political community, where they live dangerously and anxiously, where their lives are always at stake.

Whereas Aristotle said that man is political by nature, Hobbes states that he is nonpolitical by nature. Both cannot be right. Before Hobbes, some had supposed that society might be artificial, the result of a contract (for example, Glaucon in Plato's *Republic*), but none had combined the social contract with the view that man is by nature antisocial. Surely the ability to accept a social contract implies a measure of social feeling for one's fellow human beings—but not for Hobbes. Hobbes seems to follow Machiavelli in denying that by nature humans have either the goodness or virtue needed to live together in justice. And yet Hobbes declares that they do. Hobbes follows Machiavelli's opinion that men are selfish but dissents from the conclusion that they have no justice. "The fool has said in his heart there is no such thing as justice," says Hobbes, echoing Psalm 14 (in which the fool speaks of God, not justice). He gives the reason explaining why the fool, for his own "conservation and contentment," might keep or not keep a "covenant" (contract) only when it was to his benefit, and adds, in an obvious reference to Machiavelli, "from such reasoning as this, successful wickedness hath obtained the name of virtue." And he supplies an answer to the unnamed Machiavelli: that this course of betraying one's promise and committing injustice presupposes an error by the person being fooled, "which errors one cannot reasonably reckon upon as the means of his security" (L 15, pp. 101–102). Hobbes thought he had found a means of securing the same end as Machiavelli, "conservation and contentment," more reliably and safely, and without resorting to deceit. Here is Machiavelli transformed into a new kind of natural right or justice that preserves his goal—Machiavelli without Machiavellianism.

What, then, is the state of nature that Hobbes has refashioned and implanted so successfully in the modern mind?

Four Aspects of the State of Nature

The term "state of nature" is used in Hobbes's earlier works, *Elements of Law* and *De Cive*. In *Leviathan* it is called "the natural condition of mankind" or the "condition which man by mere nature is actually placed in" (L 13), but we shall use the simpler phrase by which it is known later in Locke and Rousseau and at present. Four aspects will describe the "state of nature": first, it is anti-Christian; second, it is concerned with the origins of society rather than its ends; third, it forms the basis of a new natural right of self-preservation; and fourth, it underscores the artificial character of civilization.

Perhaps surprisingly, Hobbes borrows the phrase "state of nature" from Christian theology. There it describes the innocence of men before the Fall and sometimes extends after the Fall to those living in ignorance of the true God. Living in innocence, men are ignorant of the original sin for which they need to be redeemed by the grace of God. For Hobbes, the state of nature is anything but innocence, yet totally dismissive of the grace of God. Men in that state cannot sin, because it is a state of war in which every man has an equal right to live and hence the right to choose whatever means he judges most fitting to keep himself alive. Human necessity is the necessity to sin. In the Bible things are reported otherwise. Men are said to have had everything they need and more in the Garden of Eden. To enjoy this state, they had to obey only one small prohibition, which they did not. This act, the original sin, was unprompted by God and in no way necessitated by the penury or savagery of man's original condition. Human responsibility for the original sin is made quite clear. Christians of most every kind differ from Machiavelli and Hobbes by averring that the evil of man is his responsibility, not necessitated by nature or by God. But if, on the contrary, men are *forced* to do evil, they cannot be blamed for it. The artificial Leviathan they make appears not as punishment for evil, as with St. Augustine and Martin Luther, but as the way out of the necessity to do evil.

The Hobbesian doctrine that men are free to appropriate anything they need in the state of nature is directly contrary to Christianity (L 13, pp. 87–88). Placed in the state of nature, Hobbesian man is not obliged to behave as if he were a creature of God. Indeed he has the right not to behave so. Fighting for his own preservation, which does not seem to be assured to him by Divine Providence, Hobbesian man has occasion neither for Christian humility nor Christian zeal, and the promise of afterlife, so far as he believes it, can only distract him from the main task, or the main chance. By Christian revelation, it was argued that the origin of humans was perfect and their present plight their own fault. By classical political philosophy in Plato and Aristotle, those origins were considered very imperfect, so that it was necessary to look toward natural human ends in the good life to find guidance. Hobbes agrees with the latter that the origins of man in the state of nature are very imperfect, yet he concentrates on the origins rather than the end and denies the existence of the good life (or *summum bonum*). Why the origins? Because he believes that the end of man can be seen only in the beginnings, as the *escape* from the beginnings. The state of nature is a negative guide. Where does it take us?

Looking at human origins, we see equality. Chapter 12 of *Leviathan* on religion ends with a shot at "unpleasing Priests," and chapter 13 on the "Natural Condition of Mankind" begins with the assertion of a universal truth in answer to that unpleasing inequality, that nature has made humans equal—or more precisely, "so equal" that one man cannot claim for himself any benefit that another cannot pretend as well. Thus, the fact of equality is less important than the claims or pretensions that may be offered by one person against another. In the state of nature, no one is so superior to another in body or mind that the difference cannot be made up by the ability of the weakest to kill anyone stronger, either by himself or by "secret machination" with others. This has to be a disturbing thought to those stronger in body and mind. But it is supported by the vanity of weaker people who might be supposed deferent, rather than hostile, to the stronger. Men will admit that others are more witty, or more eloquent, or more learned than themselves but not wiser, at least as regards their own affairs: "For there is not ordinarily a greater sign of the equal distribution of any thing than that every man is contented with his share" (L 13).[3]

The decisive consideration for Hobbes is not that we are equal to one another but that we think we are. We can look around at the apparent inequalities of human nature and circumstances, and scientists can carry out careful investigations, but all common and scientific observation on this point can be dismissed, for supposed equality is more effectual than actual equality. To endorse the fundamental principle of human equality, Hobbes appeals to the very democratic vanity that might seem to deny it. It's not that humans are equal in fact, but that they are equal in their vain pretensions to inequality: a paradox, a reason taken from unreason, to found the new political science.

Now from equality, actual or supposed, proceeds an equality of hope in attaining our own ends. But in a condition where our end must be self-preservation, we are very likely to bump into each other, from which arises "diffidence," as Hobbes calls it, and thereafter war. The state of nature is a state of war, where the life of man, in his memorable phrase, is "solitary, poor, nasty, brutish and short." From the natural equality of humans, Hobbes deduces that the end of man is self-preservation. The end of man is decided by the condition of his beginning. That condition is so overwhelming that a human being must never forget it. Civilization is a veneer of deceptive thinness. In trying to be good we are too confident of the condition of goodness, which is being alive. Even in the midst of civilization, it is hard for men to keep at peace, to forsake every end but the peace necessary to keep them alive. Who knows what the good life is, anyway? Hobbes says that man has no *summum bonum*, no highest good—or does this mean none on which we can agree?

The end of man is nothing positive to aim at, but rather something to be escaped from. It is to escape from his beginning, always with his eye over his shoulder, fearful and wary. Life is like the escape of a prisoner of war in enemy country: He doesn't know where he is going, but he knows where he is coming from. Thomas Aquinas had it that self-preservation was part of the natural law guiding a human being, but it was not exclusive; it was below two other inclinations to the common good and to God. What Hobbes has done is to adopt the lowest right of Aquinas and to make it absolute against the inclination to be sociable to other men and then impudently to substitute the preservation of one's own body for the highest inclination to the love of God. For Hobbes, as for Machiavelli (and Descartes), self-preservation means the preservation of one's own body. This is not how self-preservation was always understood by modern thinkers. Later, Kant and perhaps also Locke understood the self to be something more than preserved; they saw the self as something like a soul. Yet, for Kant, the universal law to guide one's behavior is still a generalized selfishness (of the rational mind). Hobbes's notion of self-preservation left a lasting imprint in the history of modern political philosophy.

The state of nature further implied a new kind of natural right. Humans by nature aim at their self-preservation; they have no natural inclination to be good to others, but rather the reverse. Men are not *by nature* good, as they necessarily have a right to everything as the means to their preservation deriving from the right to preserve themselves. Yet they can be good despite this necessity by following natural law. How can this happen? Men can become good by relying on their reason, which is promoted by fear for their self-preservation. Since they are equal by nature, each has a right to life, and the mere exercise of this right leads to war in which men are not blamable but certainly not good. Men become good, and leave the state of nature, by following natural law, which consists of rules of reason. Nature teaches men to preserve themselves, but reason shows them how; reason teaches men to seek peace by consenting to a common power over them, the sovereign.

Aristotle had a doctrine of natural right, a doctrine that certain things are just by nature; but these dictates were not sufficiently specific to amount to a natural law. Aquinas had a natural law, which had to be made specific by human law and divine law. Hobbes has both natural right and natural law, but natural right comes first. Natural right is not so much what is right for you, as a human, to do as a right to do what you judge necessary for self-preservation—in a broad sense, in comfort. Natural law tells you what ought to please you—namely, peace. The rules of reason show you how to escape nature or the state of nature. Reason is opposed to nature, whereas in the classical tradition of Aristotle and Aquinas, reason shows you what is good in your nature. According to Hobbes we know that reason shows that every man has the right to do what is necessary to preserve himself, and that this right includes the killing of another person who is dangerous or in the way. Who is the judge of that necessity? You are. If someone else is the judge, you in effect cede your right to life to him, which you cannot do reasonably without a common power to enforce laws on everybody—so you judge. But aren't you likely to be trigger-happy in these circumstances? Hobbes says yes; you are likely to anticipate your opponent and right to do so.

Again in chapter 13 there is a paragraph that begins: "And from this diffidence there is no way for any man to secure himself, so reasonable, as Anticipation. . . . And this is no more than his own conservation requireth, and is generally allowed" and that ends: "And by consequence, each augmentation of dominion over men, being necessary to a man's conservation, it ought to be allowed him." Anticipation *is* generally allowed and *ought* to be allowed: the factual judgment becomes a value judgment. But recall that anticipation was the key to Machiavelli's political doctrine (see esp. D 1.52). Anticipation is a vicious cycle; is there any way to break it? Yes, for Hobbes, by natural law—that is, by rules of reason that teach and impel unjust men not to anticipate by stratagem and deceit but to seek peace. Natural law in Hobbes is not a mere leftover from the classical tradition, hence an inconsistency; it enables Hobbes to advance beyond Machiavelli's risky princes without sinking back into Aristotle and the Kingdom of Darkness he invites. If by rules of reason we all agree upon a common power, then we need not continue to anticipate the animosity of others. Others will see that peace is to their interest just as it is to ours, and we can avoid the turbulence of Machiavelli's succession of "virtuous" princes. Hobbes brings peace and domesticity to Machiavelli's principality.

Finally, the state of nature signifies that civilization is artificial. Recall that in the introduction Hobbes says, "For by Art is created that great LEVIATHAN, called a COMMONWEALTH . . . which is but an Artificial Man though of greater Stature and Strength than the Naturall." But does "man" create out of whole cloth? No, he has the model from nature, which in the *Leviathan* is man himself. Man copies himself, and the Leviathan consequently has all, or almost all the power of a man in the state of nature. Civilization is artificial but imitates human nature. If the human in the state of nature is the model for political action, then nature is Hobbes's standard. It is not, to repeat, that nature tells us what is good, but it tells us what is evil, which is a great help. Moreover, the natural passion of fear impels people away from evil. Altogether, this is a notion of nature distinct from naturalism. Is it an adequate notion? Does not knowing what is evil imply knowing what is good, a well-preserved human body?

Our original question was, Which comes first: nature or naturalism? Does human nature set the problem, whose solution is political realism aided by scientific method? Or is naturalism the solution, so that political science is drawn from physics, or science generally? The answer seems to be the former. At least in the case of Hobbes, naturalism is used for the sake of his natural understanding of humans, revealing humans in the state of nature. His science *served* his political realism, rather than being the *end* that includes realism. Modern science had an end established by Machiavelli and (to repeat) stated by Bacon, "the enlarging of the bounds of human empire, to the effecting of all things possible." When people chose this modern science as a means to this end, the end seemed to disappear. The reason for science became itself, apparently, a conclusion of science. Science derives or demonstrates the realism that inspired it. The Machiavellian necessity to anticipate becomes the scientific explanation of inertial motion. This result has helped to make Machiavellianism respectable, but it has hindered our self-understanding; the issue of whether humans fundamentally have a necessity to acquire is obscured. Modern science progresses by covering over its own tracks.

Hobbes's Modern Political Science

At this point we can consider further the meaning of "modern." In Machiavelli's work, "modern" refers to what is Christian as opposed to the "ancients," the pre-Christian Greeks and Romans. But Machiavelli had proclaimed that he was bringing "new modes and orders" to contrast with those of the ancients and, as it proved, of the Christians as well. In his thought there is self-advertised novelty as contrasted with the ancients—the reliance on necessity as opposed to Aristotelian moral virtue. He presented the ancients admiringly at first, as stronger and more invigorating than the moderns enfeebled by Christianity, and then turns on the imaginary republics and principalities of the ancients, showing that, seemingly virtuous in this world, they made way for the weak yet cruel reliance of Christians on the imaginary next world. As we have seen, he appropriated their techniques of indirect government for his own use against them. Hobbes, however, pays little attention to the ancients. He does not bother to refute or even address them. He mocks the "Aristotelity" of the "Schools," the Scholastic philosophers who still based their thinking on Aristotle. He delivers himself to the advances of modern science and leaves the ancients behind, ignored as they deserve. Machiavelli gives the reasoning behind modernity but does not display it in modern science. Hobbes skips the reasoning and instead supplies the new science in its early stages.

What is it that modern science supplies? A few of its features may be discerned so that we can see just how important Machiavelli and Hobbes are. There is, first, the fact that modern science is comprehensive over all nature, and therefore does not change according to the subject matter studied. There is just one scientific method. Hobbes tries to assimilate the science of humans to the science of moving things; Machiavelli speaks of political regimes as "mixed bodies" (D 3.1) Since the subject matter does not determine the method (as in Aristotle when considering the human virtues), one does not have to look at the subject matter when beginning its study.[4] Hobbes's *Leviathan* is a work of political science, but it begins from "Of Sense" as the first chapter and "Of Man" as the first part; it does not begin from men in politics but arrives at its subject only in part 2, "Of Commonwealth," after the true picture of politics has been generated from a covenant. No study of actual politics in its own or at any other time is attempted in this fundamental work, which is said to establish political science newly and completely. In this regard Machiavelli differs from Hobbes; Machiavelli begins with politics and manages to stay with politics, politicizing everything. While in Hobbes everything is power, in Machiavelli it is acquisition, the forerunner of power (L10; P 1). With no subject matter in nature, nothing is to be seen reliably, no things or beings, but only names given by human beings for their own convenience and by their own domination. Part 1 of *Leviathan* consists of chapters on human faculties—sense, imagination, passions, reason—rather than the activities and objects of their exercise. Before one sees, Hobbes tells you how to see: the faculty of sensing and imagining must be fixed so that one sees properly. He does not want you to have to rely on your natural, prescientific sight. Machiavelli has no scientific method, but he wants you to see as the acquisitive prince sees (P Let. Ded.)

Since there is no subject matter, no boundaries exist that would have been determined by the subject matter. For Aristotle, political science is about the polis, the only comprehensive human association—not about the household, which is subpolitical not merely in degree but in kind.[5] Hobbes explicitly denies this; commonwealth is the same as family because both have the same end of seeking power to preserve peace. Political science is essentially the economics of the household, as all associations are concerned with the necessity to acquire power. Machiavelli had preceded Hobbes with the same politico-economic usage of "acquisition." Nor are there any natural wholes. All wholes we think we see are composites of matter in motion, and all are divided into complex and simple. The complex is a composite of simple; method reduces complex to simple elements and then reconstructs what it has taken apart to make an artificial whole. This is the resolutive-composite method, a feature of naturalism obvious in the structure of *Leviathan*, in which a visible individual composed of human nature and opinion is resolved into a state of nature containing simplified individuals in naked equality and then reconstructed into an artificial commonwealth also called an "artificial man." For Aristotle, the polis is also a composite, but it has a part more important than any other part: the citizen. The citizen is the part that emerges only with the whole and thus presupposes the whole that the citizen rules. As ruler, the citizen cannot be understood apart from the polis; by contrast, Hobbes's individual must be sought only in the pre-political state of nature. For Aristotle one joins society for the sake of survival but stays there for the sake of the good life. For Hobbes, individuals remain what they were before joining the artificial whole of society and never escape the fear for survival and the pressing need for peace.

Another feature of Hobbes's political science is that it has no distinction between theory and practice. If there is no articulation in nature, no essential distinctions, no natural wholes, then there are no unchangeable distinctions. Things are in motion, and so to the extent they have any regularity, like the seasons of the year, a thing is the law of its motion. Understanding things becomes understanding how they change—hence, how to change them. The perfect theoretical understanding is the same as the perfect practical understanding. For Aristotle, theory is about unchangeable things; practice, about changing changeable things. He had one comprehensive science about human things, political science; and one for nonhuman things, physics. And because having two comprehensive sciences created a problem, he invented metaphysics. One could look at things from two perspectives, he proposed: one, the human perspective of practice; the other, the nonhuman perspective of theory. Humans, it appears, are capable of a nonhuman as well as a human perspective—which creates the metaphysical problem.

For Hobbes, however, the difference between theory and practice seems to disappear: knowing is making. Practice is built into theory, and theory ends in practice. When you know what a commonwealth is, you will be able to make it. It is similar with Machiavelli's prince: when he knows what the state is, he will be able to found or acquire it. In science today, a distinction is stated between pure and applied science, but the older distinction between theory and practice means that practice is not "applied" theory. The possibility of application is built into the scientific method, so that the result of knowledge is the ability to act on the basis of knowledge. When Plato's philosopher-king knows what the best city is, he doesn't therefore have the ability to bring it about but only the ability to admire it in imagination. It is different with Hobbes's sovereign—and with Machiavelli's prince, for Hobbes is a fellow member of Machiavelli's grand conspiracy, to which he contributes the application of scientific method. Machiavelli had spoken of "effectual truth," which is the sort of truth that produces an effect and applies itself (P 15).

Still another feature of scientific method is a new attitude toward chance. Whereas Plato's philosopher-king has to await a favorable chance, a coincidence between knowledge and power, Hobbes's sovereign is ready for instant application, just like Machiavelli's prince, who was encouraged to take his chances with Lady Fortune, who favors the young and (in Machiavelli's sense) virtuous (P 25). The later invention of calculus made it possible for modern science to discount the possibility of one's death with "life insurance" without the necessity of practicing incautious Machiavellian virtue and very much in the spirit of Hobbes's steady, fearful self-preservation. The drama of science exemplified in the boyish impudence of Hobbes is apparent more in its conception than its application. A last point from this view of modern science is that it takes no great experience in politics, in its subject matter, to excel in political science. Aristotle said that the young are not fit for political science, and Hobbes himself had a long life during turbulent times in which he had much opportunity to observe the most baffling and unsettling changes of regime in his country and on the Continent. But he was not content with the sort of ad hoc, compromising solutions to practical difficulties that would challenge and satisfy the classical statesman. Hobbes wanted a theoretical solution that would fix the problem of religious warfare so that it could not arise again. His statesmanlike comment on the English civil war, apparent in other writings such as *Behemoth,* is quiet in *Leviathan,* where all is theory and theory is applicable. Science leaps ahead through great scientists and then settles into a collective enterprise of incremental discoveries in countless specialized articles adding to the number of things "we know." But it fails to go back to its fundamental principles, especially in regard to politics. It takes the state of nature for granted and assumes that politics is an artificial remedy for it.

Modern Science Applied

So much for scientific method—Hobbes's and ours. It can be summarized as thinking about how to study before looking at what is to be studied. It is not quite like singing in the shower, for that is an amateur act, but it is rather like practicing seduction on an empty couch. Hobbes did not apply this method consistently, as we have seen. He was more interested in the human than he was in science. His picture of the human was more likely the premise than the conclusion of his science, but both views can be found in *Leviathan.* Part 1 of that work is titled "Of Man," and which man is it—man as Hobbes saw him in his predicament, or man as he presents him methodically through science? Clearly it is both, but which view is primary? To answer, one must take seriously Hobbes's claim to be the first political scientist by making political science a part of physics.

Chapter 9 of part 1 contains a remarkable chart showing a table of the sciences. Science (or philosophy) is knowledge of consequences (compare Machiavelli's "effects"), and this whole is divided into two branches: natural philosophy and civil philosophy. Civil philosophy, the second and shorter branch, is political philosophy, the science of "politique bodies." Natural and civil philosophy would correspond to Aristotle's distinction between theory (physics) and practice (politics), except that for Hobbes, both are equally theory. But if one follows out the longer branch of physics from "bodies permanent" to "bodies terrestrial" to animals to men to speech, one discovers that it ends with the "science of just and unjust." The two branches have the same end, and one must ask whether political science is in contrast to physics (the short second branch) or a consequence of physics (the long first branch). This is in Hobbes's own summary chart the same ambiguity we have been considering between nature or naturalism.

We must now see how Hobbes applies the science he has discovered to the problem of man in the state of nature, where he lives in intolerable misery. There men are shown equal in the ability to kill, in the first instance, followed by equality of pretension or vanity. From this it follows that there is no natural rule by one man over another, but that there is natural right in equality, the right of self-preservation. This is the right to secure everything one thinks necessary to one's own preservation and therewith the right to be the sole judge of what is necessary. This right is not limited by any thought of self-rule or self-restraint, but rather by natural law distinct from natural right. Natural law introduces the duty to seek peace, but it comes second to the natural right to judge and act as one thinks necessary. All duty is subsequent to right. The classical doctrine of natural right, by contrast, proceeds from the judgment that men are not equal but unequal in several respects, the most important being inequality in wisdom. The wise have a natural right to rule over the unwise and a duty to rule them in accordance with wisdom; the unwise have a natural duty to obey the wise.

For Aristotle in particular, wisdom in practical matters is prudence, and he says in his *Politics* that prudence is the virtue of rulers; and "sound opinion," the virtue of the ruled (*Politics* 1277b). Machiavelli agrees with Aristotle that most people are not prudent, but he takes the view that necessity is paramount and that men cannot afford to be just or right. It is prudent calculation, not right, that counsels an individual to be selfish, and most people in their goodness are incapable of obeying necessity. Hobbes enters with two changes: As opposed to Aristotle, he moralizes selfishness in the right to self-preservation; and as opposed to Machiavelli, he democratizes the prudence of claiming that right. Hobbes says that all men are roughly equal in prudence. In chapter 8 of *Leviathan,* he sets a formula: "A plain husbandman is more prudent in affairs of his own house than a Privy Counsellor in the affairs of another man" (L 8, p. 53). Thus, governing a family or governing a kingdom is the same kind of prudence, since politics does not make a whole greater than its parts (cf. L 17, p. 118). And the possible greater wisdom of the privy counsellor or of anyone that might make him more prudent in another's affairs, even if more prudent in his own, is denied. What Hobbes has done is to equalize prudence by adding self-interest to it: "I may be less wise than you, but I am more interested in myself than you are."[6]

Equal prudence means that the bellicose equality of men in the state of nature is not calmed by the presence of an unequal few more prudent than most others. Then what to do in this impasse of equality without authority to make peace? Aristotle laid it down that "man is by nature a political animal." But Hobbes has abandoned the assurance that human beings, however intractable and given to rebellion, are naturally social beings who like living with one another. If men are naturally free of obligation, as Hobbes has it, then authority as such becomes a problem, not merely which kind of authority, democratic or oligarchical. For Hobbes, and for all of his unconscious followers today, *any* authority is questionable. There is no natural rule, and men will use their prudence against one another; the more they deliberate, the more they seek ways to get the better of one another, and the more they consult their experience, the less can they find a way out of the state of nature.

The way out of the state of nature is to use science. Science is based on conceiving possibilities, not on reckoning probabilities, as is prudence. With science, men can conceive of a new condition that is completely unlike any in their experience up to now—that is, if they accept Hobbes's political science, which describes an imaginary republic and principality that Machiavelli, for all his aversion to them, might approve of. A leap against all experience will make the authorization of the sovereign. Hobbes is criticized for leaving men in the state of nature in a vicious cycle from which they cannot emerge: they cannot get out of it without a common power, but a common power cannot exist there. But humans have the capacity for science that makes such a leap possible. They can conceive of the possibility of a common power before it exists, and in so conceiving, make it come into existence. This solution is not available to other animals, who have no means of transcending experience, but humans can obey a natural law to seek peace through political science regardless of all previous experience. They do not have to wait for a common power to arrive in the form of a conqueror; they can authorize it before it exists. Hobbes shows a new problem, the state of nature, and he has a new political science to resolve it. No wonder that he made a point of boasting that political science began with him.

This science is not a mere abstract possibility that might or might not occur because Hobbes supplies an analysis of the passions that lead to its acceptance once it has been formulated. The equality of human abilities in the state of nature leads to an equality of hope or vanity in all men; all believe they are equally worthy of life, and all seek every means possible to preserve it. Each person tries to accumulate as much power as he can, producing a "restless desire for power after power that ceaseth only in death" (L 17, p. 70). Since men are curious, having this "singular passion," they are capable of science, and they abuse this capability, until instructed better by Hobbes, to imagine dangers, especially those that arise from "invisible spirits" (on this, more later). Since they can imagine infinite dangers, they require infinite security and seek the conceit of absolute assurance. They fear risks of death, especially violent death. The other side of absolute assurance is the absolute dread of death. Their vanity in seeking power after power is rooted in the fear of death or "violent death" (in the Latin translation of L 11), and that fear makes them willing to entertain the possibility of a common power. Some might do so in a desire for a better life, but most do so for fear of losing their lives. "The passion to be reckoned on," Hobbes says, "is fear" (L 14, p. 99). Humans have a super-animal curiosity that leads them to super-animal vanity that can be cured only by super-animal fear. Humans have a problem other animals do not have; they live by nature in a state of war. They need a solution not available to other animals, which is science and the support for science in passions that are specifically human or that have a specifically human intensity. Thus do human beings stand out in the science that does its best to level them to physical objects.

Hobbes's science is based on the power of ordinary selfishness, which is common sense, but it transforms selfishness into self-preservation. What is the difference? Selfishness is looking out for yourself regardless of morals and manners. It is common in humans and everyone has had experience with it and can readily appreciate that it makes for success in politics. Machiavelli builds on this fact with appeal to experience and the use of startling illustrations ("examples," he calls them). Self-preservation is the preservation of the body from death; Hobbes takes this right to life to the extreme (in the state of nature) of justifying the right to kill when necessary to preserve one's life. Of this extreme, the life-or-death situation, most people have little or no experience, whereas selfishness is a daily temptation. But Hobbes presents self-preservation as a factor presupposed in every action, from which one can make a theoretical abstraction that renders it powerful in daily life, even if rare by itself. Selfishness is a vice that Hobbes transforms into a virtue, or rather the support of virtue. The result is that selfishness and society are not opposed: the more selfish you are—that is, the better you reckon the benefits to yourself and forget about others—the more secure society is. Society in the past and in Hobbes's time has suffered from too much togetherness, from the belief that people are sociable. This belief forces them to prescribe too much, especially to make good Christians out of unregenerate citizens. The hope in this belief is forlorn, and the practice of it is cruel. By prescribing common life with demanding conditions, one creates partisans and brings on civil war, like the civil war in England and the Thirty Years' War on the Continent. So Hobbes looks for the security of society precisely where one would least expect to find it. It has taken humanity a long time, but the moment of clarity has at last come: the discovery of rules that "neither poor men have had the leisure, nor men that have had the leisure, have hitherto had the curiosity, or the method, to find out" (L 20, p. 145). Hobbes is using a method never before tried for a problem never before solved or even stated. By considering humans as a natural multitude of disparate individuals, and only as such, can their latent oneness be brought out and made politically effectual. This is to be done by *method*—that is, science—and the fact that all previous experience of selfishness runs to the contrary is no argument against its success. Here is the combination of realism and utopianism that we saw in Machiavelli.

Authorizing the Absolute Sovereign

The last chapter of part 1 of *Leviathan* is entitled "Of Persons, Authors and Things Personated." It begins with a distinction between a natural and an artificial person, a legal distinction from Roman law that awarded legal personality to slaves and corporations not considered natural persons. Natural persons speak in their own words, but the words of an artificial person represent the words and actions of another. *Represent*: Here is the first time that this word is used in the modern sense of representative government; it is not in Hobbes's earlier works. It appears as a legal distinction in Hobbes fused into a political distinction, so that natural law in Hobbes acquires a specific character and becomes *natural public law*. Previously—for example, in Thomas Aquinas—natural law was an inclination made specific only in human law, a different type of law. Now natural law becomes specific in itself, yielding legal commands.

Of artificial persons, Hobbes continues, some are actors, some authors, the latter being owners of the words and actions of the actors. What is the relation of actor to author? The actor is owned by the author, who authorizes the actor and makes the actor the authority. This brings us to the trick—is it the artifice or the swindle?—of representative government. The authority is the creation of the author, but it constitutes an obligation to the authority. The relation is not the familiar principal to agent relation that we know with common sense in which the principal is superior to the agent—rather, the reverse: the created is the boss of the creator. Creating an authority institutes an obligation in the author, who has duties to the authority he has created. "Covenants" (a word Hobbes prefers to contract for its Biblical resonance) that set up the authority bind the author, as do any of his acts. Duties arise not from self-restraint nor from one's relation to God, nor from the highest good of man, but in consequence of the authorization of an artificial person. This authorization is done by natural law for the purpose of seeking peace.

Man loses his natural freedom by authorization of an artificial authority. As men are naturally free, so not bound to one another, so they are naturally a multitude—that is, a collection of individuals in the state of nature. A multitude becomes one by representation in an authority, representing one artificial person. This is Hobbes's solution to the ancient problem of the one and the many—whether one precedes many because many are collected ones or whether many precede one because only by comparison can one be defined. For Hobbes, nature is manyness; people are naturally many, which means free, not connected. But because all are many, they are all in the many and are equal. No one is better than anyone else or above the many; there is no quality in the state of nature, only quantity. But equal individuals are potentially one if they can consent to the sovereignty of a single artificial person, or if they can obey the natural law taught to them through their natural right. All are homogeneous individuals, and "man" lacks the ambiguity of classical thought in regard to quality. Are not some men better, hence truer "men" than others? This homogeneity in Hobbes can point toward ultimate selfishness because each looks only to himself or to ultimate conformity and because no one is better than the multitude. Hobbes's individualism, it seems, lacks a moderate middle between too much and too little.

The next step is to see how representation makes the commonwealth, and in chapter 17 Hobbes provides a view of the final cause of commonwealth, "foresight of their own self-preservation and a more contented life thereby." We note that the "more contented life" replaces the virtuous life of the ancients and in his way, of Machiavelli. We also note that "more contented" differs from "contented." Humans can have felicity, according to Hobbes, but felicity consists not in settled enjoyment but in continual progress from one joy to another, which is the opposite. Irrational animals can enjoy their lives because they are not offended with their fellows, whereas humans use their reason to find offense and are most troublesome when at their ease. They will fight one another unless there is a visible common power, for "covenants without the sword are but words." Covenants have no support from nature in the supposed sociability of humanity, so that they must rely on human support—and that support must be *absolute*. To give emphasis to this point, Hobbes speaks of "that great Leviathan" as a "mortal God." Human power has the absoluteness of divine power.

Commonwealth can come about by institution (agreement in an assembly) or by acquisition (the word Machiavelli used to mean conquest). Institution, we shall see, is more unlikely, even utopian, yet serves as the model for understanding the commonwealth, as plain conquest in fact turns out to offer the same rights to conquerors and subjects and the same benefit of peace as institution by law. Or is that benefit the more realistic "peace and common defense" (L 17, p. 121)? In the similarity for Hobbes of institution and acquisition, one notes the absence of elections in his theory of representation, an omission corrected by Locke and later practice. Today we consider a representative government only as one with elections. Elections have become the benchmark of free government because, in the language of Machiavelli and Hobbes, they have two advantages. They provide for venting popular rebelliousness when voting against (Machiavelli) and obedient "institution" (Hobbes) when voting to reelect, transforming "subjects" into citizens. But Hobbes, who demands a single institution of the sovereign as opposed to elections, does not want to endorse even a smidgen of rebelliousness.

How does the "institution" of the sovereign come about? Chapter 18 on that subject begins with the language of representation that is Hobbes's innovation in *Leviathan.* A commonwealth is instituted when the majority of a "multitude of men" give one man or assembly of men "the right to present the person of them all"—that is, to be "their representative." In doing so, everyone authorizes "all the actions and judgments" of the sovereign to be the same "as if they were his own." *As if*: they are not actually your own, but only by a legal fiction. Hobbes specifies that the authorization occurs whether or not you voted in favor; the majority decides and binds the minority. Just by sauntering into the assembly, you are bound to regard and obey the sovereign that results as your own. What do you gain from having your actual opinion replaced with a fiction? You will be able to "live peaceably" and "to be protected against other men." Note that the danger from other men continues in a commonwealth after one leaves the state of nature; to live in a commonwealth is rather a state of protection than simply a state of peace.

The authorization is both horizontal, since it includes all, and vertical, since it sets up a sovereign to be obeyed by all. These two kinds of authorization must occur together. There is some dispute among Hobbes scholars as to whether there is an original democracy in Hobbes's scheme. Is there a democracy before the consent of all (a case of institution) or in the act of consent? This is the paradox of founding discussed above: Sovereigns must have power before they create it. To this difficulty, the answer is in Hobbes's political science, which makes power by conceiving it because a science is not bound by previous experience. In chapter 18 Hobbes fills out the twelve consequences of sovereignty, amounting to the absoluteness of the original right of a single individual in the state of nature: all must obey; no covenant exists without the power to enforce it; voluntarily entering the assembly is submitting to its result; sovereigns cannot injure their subjects; the sovereign is unpunishable, and so on. These consequences are not advantages of absolute sovereignty but rights, each of them necessary to the whole. After numbering them as twelve, Hobbes finishes the chapter with another unnumbered point, an insistence on their unity, for the absence of one will necessarily destroy the whole.[7] He carries the logic of his formula to its unheard of extreme. Hobbes's sovereign is the result of the transfer of power of original man in the state of nature, an extreme of freedom. Absolute power in the sovereign is absolute freedom in his subjects. No wonder *Leviathan* is called a Mortal God; God has been reproduced artificially, his personhood now human, no longer fearsome, now beneficial.

Those who say that it would be misery to live under the absolute power of a sovereign—later liberal philosophers like Locke and Montesquieu—forget that the alternative is to live under the absolute power of men who are equal in the state of nature. It is impossible to avoid absolute power in Hobbes's system, but one can make it beneficent. Chapter 19 is on the kinds of commonwealth, but the main point is that the end of each kind—monarchy, aristocracy, democracy—is the same: to bring peace. Sovereignty is essential; how it is organized is secondary. For Hobbes, all regimes are reducible to one, commonwealth, which is opposed to anarchy, the natural condition of man. He *requires* absolute sovereignty but only *prefers* absolute monarchy. Yet it is interesting to see he prefers monarchy. He has dismissed the bad forms of the three classical regimes—tyranny, oligarchy, and mobocracy—as the same as the good ones when "misliked." Hobbes then denies the possibility of democracy as being an aristocracy of orators who lead the people, so that the choice of the most preferred regime is between aristocracy and monarchy. He decides on monarchy because a man is never more reliable than when he is thinking in private—in contrast to thinking out loud in public, when men put their vanity ahead of their interest. Hobbes prefers monarchy, the form of government that permits a more perfect selfishness, because selfishness is most conducive to the common good. The sovereign's interest is peace for himself and thus also for those he represents.

Civil Liberty in Hobbes's Theory

This self-interest, with an aim toward peace and monarchy, is the doctrine of absolute sovereignty. But as the most radical selfishness authorizes absolute sovereignty, one begins to sense that it leaves, or indeed creates, a sphere for private liberty in which selfishness can thrive in peace. Hobbes's sovereignty is the most absolute to be found in all political theory, yet it also introduces the distinction between state and society to ensure the operation and principle of peaceful and comfortable selfishness. How can this be? Consider that the sovereign is authorized by men acting on their private right of self-preservation; thus, the private is natural, and the public derivative, created by the private. The sovereign power is unlimited, except that the private right of self-preservation is inalienable. A person can consent to a law under which he may be killed as a criminal, but the sovereign cannot ask him to help with his execution. If someone like Sir Thomas More wishes to aid the executioner by lifting his beard, as he did, that is gratuitous. But besides the inalienable right, the sovereign's power is limited by its purpose to secure liberty. In chapter 19 Hobbes says that the sovereign lets custom stand when he does not explicitly change it. This shows that sovereignty outweighs custom but also the limits of sovereignty: what the laws do not prohibit, they permit. With his expansive notion of rule, Aristotle said that what the laws do not prohibit they require. Today, we follow Hobbes when we decide a point by saying that there's no law against it.

More important for Hobbes's doctrine of sovereignty is chapter 21, "Of the Liberty of Subjects." Liberty is defined there as the absence of external impediments to motion, a bodily liberty. Contrary to Aristotle's view, any act of will is voluntary, even if one might think it compelled, as when at sea in a storm (in the example given above) one is forced to throw one's goods overboard to save the ship.[8] Hence there is, for Hobbes, no need for self-control in order to live free, no connection between liberty and virtue. Further, it is then no business of the sovereign to make men good. This liberty of his subjects, civil liberty, is defined by the sovereign; the subjects have only the liberty that the sovereign allows. But if he is passably prudent, or taught in Hobbes's political science, he will allow a wide measure of civil liberty. The more the sovereign prescribes as necessary for common life, the more partisanship he engenders. It is in the ruler's interest as sovereign and also as a private person to keep trouble to a minimum, hence to keep interference in their liberty to a minimum. Civil liberty is of course restrained liberty, as the only absolute liberty is in the state of nature, and very insecure at that. The necessary limits of civil liberty would keep Hobbes from endorsing the extreme libertarianism of today. And since the power of the sovereign is the same in every regime, so too is civil liberty. It is not the characteristic of democracy, as in both classical political science and in democratic thinking of our time. Civil liberty is not political liberty, the liberty to participate in rule; it is the liberty to consent to absolute sovereignty. There is no obligation that does not arise from an act of one's own, which is the consent to obey one's own representative. All duties come from the right of consent.

Chapter 22, with its title "Of Systems Subject, Political and Private," develops the meaning of civil liberty. "Systems" are groups within the commonwealth, with the "political" ones like Parliament or certain corporations, specially authorized by the sovereign. Others, such as the family, are "subject" and not so authorized; they must obey the laws common to all. The latter are private groups, with their status determined by the sovereign. Hobbes is the first political theorist to suggest that such groups are regulated but not prescribed by government. The private groups he approves of are commercial, as described in chapter 24, where he says that "the commonwealth can endure no diet": it can never have too much public riches. The sovereign must assure that private individuals can extend the supply of goods—though such commerce is always regulated, though property is created by the civil law of the sovereign, and though property excludes the right only of other subjects and not the government. Yet the purpose of regulation is to facilitate exchange. "Money is the blood of the commonwealth." Mobility of goods and persons is stressed rather than economic growth, or "increase," as Locke will say. But Hobbes expressly denies Aristotle's thought that economic gain has a natural limit in what is sufficient for a good society.[9]

It is not easy to see how Hobbes's doctrine of absolute sovereignty can be regarded as an advance toward liberalism or even as the founding of liberalism. But if you start from the foundation of rights, you see quickly that rights come before duties, including the duty of absolute (or, as we shall see, not quite absolute) obedience to the sovereign's civil laws. Absolute sovereignty of the public is derived from the private right of self-preservation. Following the thought that rights come first, one can see liberalism in principle, though not in its present practice. Two features of Hobbes's doctrine must be kept clear: the *power* of the public is greatly increased in absolute sovereignty; the *sphere* of the public is greatly reduced to the protection of what is private. In both cases of increase and reduction, the comparison is to the Aristotelian orthodoxy of Hobbes's time and also to liberalism today. For Hobbes, the state must have absolute power, but its purpose is to serve society. Laws have the minimal function of making society possible by supplying the conditions of common life; they do not prescribe what that common life should be. The greatest liberty is to be found in the silence of the laws (L 21).

Yet Hobbes does not escape the risk of absolute sovereignty by reducing its sphere. He needs a good sovereign to see that his task is properly confined to the protection of private liberty—but a sovereign who must be good is not absolute. The sovereign is absolute by natural law, so that every act of the sovereign is in accord with natural law. Since an act of the sovereign is called civil law, every civil law is in accord with natural law. Hobbes says that civil law and natural law are coextensive (L 26). The legality of civil law is as absolute as the political science of natural law is precise. However wrong or foolish any sovereign may be, it is still more wrong and foolish to try to limit the sovereign's power. That is why tyranny is a "misliked" monarchy. Hobbes's political science takes no account of the difference between monarchy and tyranny, and he attacks doctrines of tyrannicide. But Hobbes cannot rest satisfied with this result; justice for him is not "but a word, without substance." So he distinguishes a good law from a just law. Every law is just, but "a good law is that which is needful, for the good of the people and withal perspicuous" (L 30, p. 239). A good law is for the protection of liberty, nothing more; laws are hedges, not principles of action.

Yet isn't this a dubious distinction? Why is a good law better than a bad law? A good law must be more in keeping with natural law, but then it is more just. By the doctrine of absolute sovereignty, Hobbes must accept and defend every law, yet at the same time prefer a good, needful law. He must defend tyranny and he must attack it. We can look at the problem from an individual standpoint: the right of self-preservation. This right is inalienable, meaning that you cannot give it away. If you keep that natural right intact, you find yourself in the state of nature, which is a state of war. So, you transfer it to the sovereign. But you cannot transfer part of it while retaining it for an instance of an extreme situation. Clearly that reservation cannot hold. Whenever the time comes for the sovereign to exercise power, he cannot be sure of that power; nor can you be sure that the sovereign has the power he claims if he can grant exceptions to it. Both the sovereign's power and your obedience are then uncertain. You must conclude that sovereignty has to be certain, without reservations, in order to exist at all. Hobbes makes the necessity of certainty clear when he defines a battle comically as "a running away" on "one side or both" (L 21). In the extreme case of war, the sovereign cannot count on obedience, and his system fails to defend itself. The basic difficulty of an inalienable right is that it does you no good to keep it and you cannot give it away. Hobbes sees he is in trouble, but we cannot relax in disdain, for today we find ourselves in the same predicament. We like and dislike absolute power very much in the manner of Hobbes. We accept that a free society requires the intervention of absolute power to secure liberty for everyone, but we have been no more successful than Hobbes in finding an exact point of intervention where power is sufficient and liberty is secure.

To prevent subjects from harboring reservations to their absolute obedience, Hobbes's justice requires that private individuals not make judgments of good and bad in politics. As civil law is coextensive with natural law, everything the sovereign says is both. Natural law exists, but not as an independent standard with which to judge the sovereign. Natural law is an independent standard for judging subjects, advising them not to exercise their independent judgment in politics. The question that Socrates put, of how I should live, requires an answer to the question of how we should live, which is political. Hobbes circumvents the Socratic question by the method of authorization he has laid down. When you authorize the sovereign over yourself, you sign away your right to ask the question, How should I live? Asking that question presupposes your right to an independent judgment justifying independent action, as in the state of nature. Having signed that right away to the sovereign, the sovereign, if well instructed, will allow you the maximum private liberty consistent with common security. You can answer the Socratic question, but for yourself only. As soon as your private life becomes implicated in politics, you must accept restraint.

Thus the doctrine of absolute sovereignty encourages a privatized life in which subjects touch one another as little as possible. Or as *formally* as possible. This would mainly be a life of gaining private wealth and of commerce meeting trading partners. Not incidentally, it could include a life of science. These would be the more timid, retired occupations at the expense of outgoing, public, honorable pursuits. With some exaggeration one could call this the bourgeois life over the aristocratic or republican lives. Paradoxically, signing away your private right of judging good and bad gives you a more private life in return. In this generally depoliticized life, one political question remains: Rather than ask how good is government, we ask how legitimate is the government? And in considering legitimacy, one must bear in mind that sovereignty can be made legitimate by conquest ("acquisition") as well as institution. The question of legitimacy replaces the question of goodness. Hobbes focused on legitimacy not because he was afraid of making value judgments, but because he wanted to make such judgments more scientific and predictable by confining them to more easily ascertained issues. Does a common power exist? If so, it ought to be obeyed. Even the sovereigns should not ask how to do good for his subjects, much less lead them in schemes of glory; his task is to secure for them a private life of felicity, understood in the Hobbesian sense of chasing one apparent good after another.

In authorizing the sovereign, the subject makes a promise to obey and the sovereign a promise to secure. The system works if the promises hold. For Hobbes, justice means keeping one's promises; that is the central, indeed the only virtue for him. The subject will keep the promise to be just, to be sure, only if the sovereign enforces measures with a sword rather than persuasion. Fear keeps the sovereign's subjects rational and consistent with themselves: a crime according to Hobbes is a self-contradiction, an absurdity, by denying the promise one has made. In making that promise you tell the truth about your intent; this is all the truth necessary. For a contrasting judgment, we can return to Socrates in Plato's *Republic*, where the conclusion that the just is good leads to a search for what the good life is, a search that culminates in the idea of the good, not the idea of justice.[10] For Hobbes, however, justice is not good but a way of avoiding the inquiry into the good that Socrates and Plato thought necessary. For the latter, justice is truth seeking, and that is philosophy; for Hobbes, justice is truth telling and not philosophy, but common honesty.

In the justice of keeping promises, or truth telling, Hobbes's political science seems to contrast markedly with Machiavelli's frank assertion that glory requires the use of fraud. Machiavelli has much of the directness of classical thought because he still speaks of good and bad. He says simply that one cannot always be good; one must mix good actions and bad ones. But one must always appear to be good, and that requires fraud. Machiavelli speaks openly of the necessity of fraud, and not a noble lie, as in Plato's *Republic,* but ignoble lies. Because good and evil must be mixed, Machiavelli is impartial to them, and his political science takes advantage of the mixture of good and evil in the two humors of human beings: those who master others and those who do not want to be mastered. In his view, as seen above, government had to be indirect, accomplishing its ends without stating them directly in claims of why it should rule. Hobbes retains the impartiality of government by avoiding the partisanship of such aims—every government has the same end of peace—as well as the indirectness of representation that denies the necessity of partisan rule. These two Machiavellian features of his political science are secured by a covenant rather than by fraud. The covenant is just and makes justice possible and actual. It is an open and avowed transfer by all persons of the right to judge good and bad. Instead of mixing good and bad, it excludes any judgment of good and bad.

What is the difference between Machiavelli's endorsement of evil and Hobbes's refusal to allow subjects to identify and oppose evil? Hobbes's refusal is certainly not in the spirit of St. Paul's "obey the powers that be," which counsels subjects not to abstain from judgment of evil but from action against it in this world. Hobbes's doctrine is this-worldly and revolutionary against all existing governments not based on consent and representation. Moreover, it relies on fear, the most formidable human passion. But Hobbes finds two fears relevant to politics: fear of violent death and fear of invisible spirits. The first leads to peace, the second to religious partisanship and conflict. Society in his time was a mix of the good fear and the evil one, and Hobbes's design is to make the good fear prevail. Does he not with his theory conceive a disguise for good and bad intended to make subjects believe that the result is self-government, rather than absolute obedience to a sovereign? Is that not fraud disguised as truth, and so all the more a fraud than Machiavelli's frank avowal of the need for it?

One advantage of Hobbes's abstention from distinctions of good and evil, we have seen, is his construction of a sphere of private, civil liberty exempt from the direct rule of the sovereign. But Hobbes cannot be consistent in this. He cannot abstain from identifying two private groups that endanger liberty, which the sovereign cannot leave ungoverned. These are Hobbes's two inveterate enemies, ever the objects of his scorn and satire: the Church and its seminaries, the universities. We turn now to his thought on religion.

Civil Sovereignty and the Sovereignty of Man

Comparing Hobbes with Machiavelli, philosophers so apparently different and so fundamentally similar, refreshes the theme of modern rational control—that rational control is extended for the purpose of increasing *human* power. What of the power of God? Divine power must be kept from interfering with the increase of human power, yet how is it possible to love and worship God, seeking his wisdom and praying for his providence while increasing human power? It seems apparent that increasing human power comes at the expense of divine power. Either one must harshly deny God or find some way to understand God's power as endorsing, in effect subordinate to, human power. This is what both Machiavelli and Hobbes attempt, but while Machiavelli merely suggests such a course, Hobbes actually presents a reworked Christianity in the second half of *Leviathan* that brings divine and ecclesiastical power to coincide with the artificial absolute sovereignty of man. The new rehabilitated Christianity, we shall see, reeks of Hobbes's impudent impiety and strays so far from the original as to be preposterous. What is serious in Hobbes's treatment of religion is his dislike of it as it is, kept barely in check by his respect for its power. To see how the remarkable coincidence of divine power and human power comes about, we can follow the path of Hobbes's argument from civil sovereignty to the sovereignty of man and to the kingdom of God that supports it, then to his conclusion on the relationship of his science to his goal of peace.

To rehearse civil sovereignty for Hobbes, recall that it requires that the sovereign decide all questions of good and bad. There is no right of private conscience to a private judgment of good and bad; if there were, sovereignty would be divided and society would relapse into the state of nature. Men must transfer their own natural sovereignty in that state to an artificial civil sovereign, because to claim to act on your conscience means that you want to retain your natural sovereignty. Hobbes is often accused of neglecting the study of society as it is practiced and as sociologists today would analyze it: he is said to be too abstract. And he is of course abstract, but he does analyze society insofar as it is religious in parts 3 and 4, the second half of *Leviathan*. The objection from sociology could be considered an attempt to recapture the comprehensiveness of political science, including both politics and society, when Aristotle controlled the university. Hobbes's political science is no longer the "master science," as Aristotle called it, but it is still the master in an instrumental sense. For Hobbes, political science is necessary to every good, including all science, as making the peace required for the pursuit of every (apparent) good. Peace is the comprehensive quality for him, because it is necessary and universal rather than good in itself.

Hobbes's political science frowns on the Church for the same reasons as Machiavelli's. The Church makes claims on obedience but cannot deliver security. Instead, it engenders great insecurity by dividing sovereignty. The Church and its priests interfere with the earthly sovereign, and worse, raising tumults and causing wars—above all, the religious wars in England and Europe that Hobbes lived through. Those priests who are not hypocrites living in comfort are fanatics ready to destroy every comfort and all liberty (L 47). The sovereignty of the civil sovereign is necessary to restrain those groups in society that disturb the peace with their "hate speech," to use today's idiom—speech that challenges the absolute character of civil sovereignty. Hobbes's argument arrives at the necessity of the civil sovereign to establish the sovereignty of man over the Church, which surely maintains the contrary—the sovereignty of God over man.

Recall the anti-Christian character of Hobbes's state of nature. The state of nature is not a state of innocence, as in Christian theology; it is a state of war. The state of war is so extreme that each man has a right over all other individuals and to all things. This means that nothing is sacred to man; sin is and has to be necessary to his preservation in the war of all against all. Men cannot afford to be grateful to God and have no reason to be so. Thus, if Hobbes's state of nature is the truth, the Bible's account of the origins of humans in a Garden of Eden cannot be true. Hobbes's science, by which he discovers the new notion of the state of nature, seems compelled to declare Christianity untrue. Because the sovereign is absolute, it is the sovereign alone who decides all questions of good and bad. How does he do this? By science, which requires one to see and follow the truth about the state of nature (L 29, p. 223). Science also tells all men how to escape from the state of nature. And how so? Not by following the commands of God or of God's Church, not by Christian piety or humility, not by penance for one's sins, not by love for one's fellow creatures because all humans have been created by God—the brotherhood of men under the fatherhood of God. None of that. Rather, the solution is the creation of an artificial sovereign made by man on the model of man, by transferring his natural powers to an artificial person, which Hobbes calls a "mortal God."

For Hobbes, science determines what is good and bad; it does not merely counsel but determines ethics, and by doing so it makes ethics more exact and powerful. Therefore, the sovereign must stick to scientific truth: A sovereign has no right to lie and must keep the promise to provide security and establish peace. Aristotle does not agree; he wrote his *Ethics* to persuade ethical people, those he called "gentlemen." For him, ethical problems are decided by ethical people, those who are already inclined to good—not by a higher science such as physics or metaphysics. But Hobbes's sovereign has to know and speak the truth. There can be no appeal to moral experience as for Aristotle, no reliance on any inclination. Nor can the sovereign resort to fables, myths, or private revelations that might be convincing to most people but cannot count as science. Divine revelation, in particular, must be judged by science.

In earlier writings (*Elements of Law, De Cive*), Hobbes tries to establish a natural religion based on reason and completely distinct from divine revelation or Christianity. This would be rational religion unlike any religion known hitherto, but similar to religion based on reason later produced by Locke and Kant, among others. In the second half of *Leviathan*, however, Hobbes attempts a revised Christian theology that accords with his political science but does not come out of it. In chapter 12 of the first part, "Of Religion," he said that the "seed of religion" is in man only, suggesting that it comes, perhaps rationally, from human nature. What is this "natural seed"? Just before, at the end of chapter 11 on manners, Hobbes had mentioned the "fear of things invisible." And what causes this? "That which is common to all men, namely the want of curiosity to seek natural causes" (L 8). People have a "singular passion of curiosity," we have seen, but by being lazy, they misuse it to seek supernatural rather than natural causes. This means that people are not by nature prone to seek natural causes; instead, they find invisible spirits they fear, a fear detrimental to civil obedience and civil peace (L 29, p. 227).

The solution to this lazy but natural habit (not called a vice) is not religion based on this fear or a religion that rejects Christian revelation and looks for less harmful invisible spirits; recall Machiavelli's chicken-men. Rather, Hobbes has a way out of the wrong fear: he contradicts himself. He says that the fear of invisible spirits is not the strongest fear after all (L 14, p. 99). That fear is stronger in present circumstances but it can be overcome by science, the spreading of science, or what came to be called the Enlightenment. Hobbes's doctrine is not merely true; it is *applicable*. The truth of speculation can be converted into utility by practice (L 31, p. 254). To apply his science, Hobbes proceeds to rework

Christian revelation rather than dismiss or ignore it. Is reworking Christianity less hostile to religion, or is it more hostile? It implies that religion itself cannot be supported by science, but one religion, Christianity, can be made tolerable by science. The premise of his undertaking is to agree with Christians that the Bible is the word of God. Hobbes also says that the mysteries of religion are like wholesome pills for the sick that are best swallowed whole (L 32, p. 256).

What, then, must we swallow? God speaks to man, Hobbes begins, immediately and mediately (L 32). With immediate or direct revelation, you cannot oblige another person to believe you. You may say you had a direct word with God, but how does another know this? We go, then, to "mediate revelation," which is through prophets and apostles. But which ones? It would seem that mediate revelation presupposes someone's true revelation. Yet there are false prophets. How are they distinguished from true prophets? Which should one obey? Obey the one who produces miracles? Miracles are often poorly attested, like immediate revelations. In any case, the test of fact is reason: If something couldn't have happened, then, given our limited human knowledge, it didn't happen. One sees the arrogance hidden under Hobbes's apparent modesty. Miracles and prophets being unreliable, one must turn to Scripture. Here, too, is a problem. Scripture is old and diffuse, for Hobbes is early in the tradition of modern Biblical criticism whose premise is that the Bible is to be treated as a human book, not as the word of God. In any case, the Bible needs to be interpreted. Who is the authentic interpreter? None other than the sovereign is Hobbes's answer. Your local sovereign is the sole authority of what is canonical in the Bible.

Who is the sovereign—according to Christianity, according to Hobbes? The sovereign is sovereign over the kingdom of God, which is earth—a real kingdom. The people of Israel chose God by covenant in return for the promised land *on earth*. The kingdom of God ended with the election of Saul when the Israelites repudiated the covenant with God. This was a human decision; God was voted out of office, one could say. Ever since this event, human sovereigns have ruled the earth and will continue to rule it until Christ's Second Coming. Christ's office has three roles: as redeemer and savior in his first coming, as teacher then and now through his ministers, and as King at the Second Coming. Christ is not a sovereign before his Second Coming, which means that his ministers are subject to the human sovereign who is appointed or allowed by God since the election of Saul. When God sent Christ to humans, he did not intend to subvert the Roman Empire or subvert any human sovereign. Ministers of God, appointed by the sovereign, are the Church, of which Hobbes gives a brief and explicit definition. The Church is a meeting called by the sovereign (L 39, p. 321). This definition is buttressed with Hobbes's typical impudence from the Greek word *ecclesia*, meaning assembly.

The effect of this interpretation is to turn the attention of Christians from the First and Second Comings of Christ to the middle period between them when the earth is ruled by humans. Does this mean that the effect is to turn Christians away from the essence of Christianity? No, Hobbes says that the one thing necessary, the *unum necessarium*, to Christian belief is that Jesus is the Christ. Everything else is either implied in this one belief or wrong. The implication is that Christ is the King, hence faith in Jesus means obedience to the King. Jesus is King at his Second Coming, and until then the king is to be found on his local throne. Suppose the local king is an infidel? One should still obey, even if the infidel sovereign requires you not to be Christian or to deny the truth of Christianity (L 43, p. 413). To do otherwise is a sin against Christianity and against the law of nations. Well, then, as a last objection to this analysis, what about martyrs? Must one not accept death rather than deny the true God? No, as refusing to be a martyr, you are not denying the true God, because God has for good reasons known to God installed this infidel sovereign and inspired him with infidel thoughts and policies. One exception remains to this conclusion. One class of people is not only encouraged but required to be martyrs: Christian priests and especially bishops, particularly Hobbes's most prominent critic, Bishop Bramhall (L 42).

Science and Peace

Hobbes's sovereign uses Hobbes's political science to determine questions of good and bad, guided by his promise to provide peace. That is why he makes Christian revelation pass the test of natural reason. The word of God is the word of human reason, and the Bible is by his interpretation brought to coincide with science. The sovereign has no need and no right to lie to his subjects in order to protect the mysteries or fragile truths of Christianity. But has Hobbes in fact told the truth about Christianity?

Is his interpretation really Christianity or just the name? It looks not merely suspicious and sarcastic but even farcical and preposterous. Hobbes uses the distinction between true and false to decide questions of good and evil; he uses science to decide ethics. And since ethics is stated in natural law, and natural law can be summed up as seeking peace, one can say that Hobbes uses science to secure peace. Science and peace are the inseparable elements of Hobbes's system: Science shows how to secure peace, and with peace men can progress in science.

Yet Hobbes cannot quite put them together to make a perfect fit. He cannot make a true Christianity that fits the necessities of civil peace, and he cannot make the "seeds of religion" go away, since they cannot be "abolished out of human nature." Is it that humans, with their fear of invisible spirits, cannot live without religion? Or is there always the risk that certain persons will have the opportunity to cultivate those seeds (L 12, p. 83; 31, p. 253)? Perhaps such dissidents can be prevented by Hobbes-trained officials. Religion can at least be made tolerable and even be made to contribute to peace; science can tame religion but not quite dispose of it. Soon after Hobbes, Pierre Bayle argued openly in his book *Thoughts on a Comet* (1673) that society can be free and moral yet atheistic. This is the belief among liberal democracies today; religion is not needed to support a free society, and a free constitution can and must remain neutral between religion and atheism. Something of Hobbes's hesitation remains, however, since people still find it difficult in public to seem to encourage, much less to avow, atheism. Hobbes thought that people will be religious or superstitious—the difference is up to the sovereign to declare—and so society needs religion. At least for the time being, Hobbes lets on. After some experience with Hobbes's sovereign and his natural law, they may find the need for religion less pressing, absorbed as they are in private—that is, worldly—activities. They will learn Hobbes's version of Christianity, which reduces to obeying the sovereign—no more and no less than obeying the natural law.

Since the chief purpose of natural law for Hobbes is to replace the influence and dogmas of Christianity, it is hard to conclude that his treatment of Christianity is candid. In fact, it looks like Hobbes's regard is tongue in cheek. Rather than recommend Machiavelli's tale of the Roman chicken-men, Hobbes directs his comedy at the scholastic language of priests for using terms like "spirit" as if they meant more than "breath"—in sum, as if there were incorporeal substances, or incorporeal bodies, or bodiless bodies (like God). Yet despite his attack on such metaphorical language, Hobbes uses many metaphors himself, likening laws to hedges, life to a race, etc. He authored the grand metaphor in the title of *Leviathan* itself. He says that metaphors are not downright lies because they assert a similarity by admitting a difference, for everyone knows that a book is not a whale. But can it be said of Hobbes's interpretation of Christianity that it is an admitted metaphor of religion rather than a pretense?

The question arises whether Hobbes was an atheist. It is a question that must be answered with some doubt, for it is difficult to know what goes on in great minds like his. Still, after registering the duty of doubt, one can be fairly sure that he was an atheist. He of course denied it, and his opponents of his day vehemently asserted it. Today, many scholars accept his denial, believing that a philosopher, devoted to truth, would never lie. Perhaps it is the case, however, that to seek the truth one cannot always tell the truth, considering the constant difficulty in "the rough bustling in of a new truth" (L 18, p. 125)? Then let the doubt about the reasoning in Hobbes's mind serve as the reason for doubting his denial of atheism. As with Machiavelli, one can marvel at his audacity but one cannot trust his sincerity. It is much safer to doubt his speaking the truth about religion. Then what about the other side of the equation of science and peace—the side of civil peace? Is this, too, not a failure in candor?

Hobbes's notion of representation, as argued here, is a kind of cloud that hides the primary question of good and bad from our eyes so as to get us to ask about the source, not the quality of authority. Is this also not a failure of candor? Hobbes wants us to ask where sovereignty has come from so that we do not decide its legitimacy by the goodness of its source. All sovereignty is either by institution or acquisition, and Hobbes tries to assimilate the acquisition of sovereignty by conquest to the institution of it by covenant. We must understand being conquered as if the conqueror were providing security so that we will consent to his power. But it seems closer to the visible world of politics to do the opposite, and to understand the institution of sovereignty as a form of conquest. Consent to the sovereign is achieved mainly by fear, and it is only by a trick of Hobbes's science that we could see consent through fear as a voluntary choice.

The factual truth of Hobbes's consent seems again to be Machiavelli's fraud. Hobbes's devotion to public truth is in doubt from both sides—from the side of science regarding Christianity and from that of civil peace regarding consent. Hobbes cannot quite fit together the two senses of absolute sovereignty: the religious (or irreligious) sovereignty of man and the political sovereignty requiring civil peace. He cannot quite "speak out," in our sense today, of intellectual honesty; he did admit that Spinoza was bolder than he was.[11] His devotion to public truth that both discloses science and protects peace is incomplete. More than this, the reservations he holds, the things he does not say, seem to be essential to all the things he does say. Hobbes can be candid about human nastiness in the state of nature because of his theory of the covenant. And he can be candid about the human source of religion because he argues vehemently that his doctrine is true Christianity, indeed the only true Christianity. He believed that it was not necessary to choose between philosophy or science and justice or peace; so he conceived a scheme of public truth that is not imaginary, like Plato's utopia, because it doesn't require the rule of a philosopher but only Hobbes's advice based on every man's self-interest.

Nevertheless, Hobbes stopped short of a realm of complete public truth. The sovereign has no right to lie but apparently he, or at least Hobbes, needs to lie, or at least to use metaphors and pretenses. His devotion to science, great as it is, seems subordinate to his love of civil peace. It was for civil peace that he uses science to remake Christian revelation, and it seems also for civil peace that he does not avow and teach atheism. His science is publicized as long as it supports peace—which is very far—but then is concealed when it no longer supports peace. This fact makes it necessary for us to ask whether science and peace, or science and justice, are after all fundamentally compatible. Is the conflict only marginal and manageable, as Hobbes apparently supposed, or is it fundamental? The latter possibility takes us back to Machiavelli and then to Plato, for we have to wonder whether the notion of intellectual honesty that Hobbes introduces, in which rational control speaks its mind, is itself intellectually honest.

CHAPTER THREE

JOHN LOCKE

(1632–1704)

Daniel Defoe's novel *Robinson Crusoe* begins with the statement, "I was born in the year 1632." This is the year John Locke was born. Defoe's story of a man's isolated life on a deserted isle shows Crusoe in something like the "state of nature" invented by Hobbes and refashioned by Locke, as we shall see. However far from common experience, that story remains one of the most popular ever written. It is peculiarly modern for its study of "one alone" and the rational control he was able to bring to his suddenly dispossessed life, calling for virtues of ingenious self-preservation which Defoe (in 1719) reasonably associates with Locke. Despite Defoe's apparent allusion to Locke's state of nature as possible fact, Locke's main achievement is to have brought modern political philosophy to dwell in England. Having been published after the Glorious Revolution of 1688 displaced the diverse notions of divine right that had been at war in the seventeenth century, his *Second Treatise* offers the example of successful free government. In the eighteenth century Locke's *Essay Concerning Human Understanding* took over the universities, displacing the metaphysics of Aristotle that had given shelter and support to Christian theology. In sum, under the aegis of a philosopher who knew how to qualify and cover over the revolution he led, modernity gained success in institutions, thought, and taste.

Refashioning, rather than inventing, is characteristic of Locke's work. Inventing we have seen in Machiavelli, with his elaborate indirect government and cunning conspiratorial tricks; and in Hobbes, with a revised Christianity never seen before and his state of nature consisting of equal persons holding inalienable rights. Locke's work, though so different in temper, was born from the modern beginnings of Machiavelli and Hobbes, offering nothing shocking like the former and nothing impudent like the latter. Instead of new modes and orders, Locke gave us constitutional government; instead of ruthless acquisition, he offered rights of private property; instead of preposterous religious interpretation, he provided us toleration and wrote a book titled *The Reasonableness of Christianity*. And for this prudence of caution rather than invention, he has been rewarded with signal success and the reputation of a founder. Of the thinkers we study in this book, Locke is easily the closest to today's modern politics and particularly to the Declaration of Independence and the U.S. Constitution.

Locke's Silence on Hobbes

Almost every analysis of Locke's political philosophy begins from or builds to a comparison with that of Hobbes. The main point is usually to compare the state of nature that Locke, following Hobbes, presents—and we shall come to this presently. First, however, is the curious fact that Locke mentions Hobbes only once by name, as "Hobbist," in his philosophical work. Hobbes's work, especially the *Leviathan*, was very well known, if only because it had come under fierce attack—not only for its alleged atheism and its radical revisions of traditional Aristotelian doctrine, but also for the quality and pungency of Hobbes's prose. This was not a book that Locke could have overlooked or ignored, yet he mentions it only once

MAJOR WORKS OF LOCKE

An Essay Concerning Human Understanding (1689): A fundamental work of epistemology setting the origins of human knowledge in experience.

Two Treatises of Government (1690): Published in the aftermath of the Glorious Revolution, the first *Treatise* refutes the theory of the divine right of kings. The second defends the theory of political authority based on natural individual rights, the separation of powers, and the consent of the governed.

A Letter Concerning Toleration (1689): A "letter" that argues for the separation of church and state and opposes religious intolerance as inimical to the aims of both of Christian religion and of civil peace.

Some Thoughts Concerning Education (1693): A method of education designed to instill the independence, self-denial, and rationality needed in a liberal political order.

without discussing it (*Essay* bk. 1, ch. 2, §5). Fresh from having considered *Leviathan* at the end of chapter 2, we may see how it compares with works by Locke. The first part of *Leviathan*, "Of Man," corresponds to Locke's epistemology in his *Essay Concerning Human Understanding*; the second part, "Of Commonwealth," corresponds to the *Two Treatises of Government*; and parts 3 and 4 on religion, to *The Reasonableness of Christianity*: Locke distributes what Hobbes combines. Note especially the difference in the *Essay* and the *Two Treatises* between philosophy or epistemology, or between scientific method and politics. In contrast to Hobbes, Locke puts his philosophy in one book and his politics in another and seems to treat them quite differently—thus creating what has been called "the boundary problem" between the two.[1]

Locke, it seems, is close to Hobbes in philosophy and at some remove from Hobbes in politics. The law of nature, which Hobbes had grounded in self-preservation rather than in the classical search for man's end, seems to be Hobbesian in Locke's philosophy, where Locke attacks the "innate ideas" of morality in the classical tradition. Yet Locke seems to succumb to that tradition in the *Two Treatises*, where he quotes from Richard Hooker. Hooker was a conservative political philosopher of the Elizabethan Age who could be summed up as Thomas Aquinas Englished.[2] Here is a great apparent inconsistency in Locke, over the definition of natural law, yet in its practical results, his political doctrine was much more acceptable and successful than that of either Hobbes or Hooker. Today we honor Locke and forget the other two. Hobbes is of course very well known to political theorists—he is the theorist's theorist—but his politics and his religion are dismissed, offered for display as unworkable. Hooker is totally forgotten.

Does this successful inconsistency mean that Locke, and with him the modern political world, retreat from Machiavelli's radical and shocking beginning? Had he and his followers pasted together modern and medieval doctrine from Hobbes and the political philosopher Samuel von Pufendorf, on the one hand; and from Hooker and the jurist William Barclay, on the other? C. B. Macpherson, an eminent Hobbes scholar and Maple-Leaf Marxist of an earlier generation, liked to say that Locke was "the confused man's Hobbes"—a formulation that does not necessarily imply that Locke himself was the one confused but rather suggests that he appeals to confused readers. Hobbes had restored natural law to modern political philosophy after Machiavelli disposed of it, which was a development, even an advancement, of rational control rather than a retreat from it. Machiavelli's prudence acquired extra reason from Hobbes's science, which offered a new mode of aggressive selfishness in the natural right of self-preservation. In the same way, Locke perhaps made an advance over Hobbes in three practical conclusions of his political science, drawn from his apparently inconsistent attitude toward natural law—namely on limited government, toleration, and especially, property. Locke was the first political philosopher to conclude, after a careful argument, that the principal object of the state should be the protection and increase of property, not merely to the limit of what is necessary for the good life, but without limit. This is a startling conclusion from apparently inconsistent premises; the stodgy Hooker never said any such thing.

It appears that Locke profits from an inconsistency that could not have escaped his notice. Perhaps this was his way of escaping the notice of others, offering his apparent confusion as a way out of their hostile notice. He lived through the time of the restoration of the Stuart kings, followed by the Glorious Revolution of 1688 by which they were ousted and a moderate Protestant succession secured. He had to be careful, and he was. Locke wrote as a deaf person speaks, always repeating himself as if the reader could not have heard properly the first time, avoiding sharp formulations of the kind that Hobbes made so memorable. Seeking not to draw the sort of attention that Hobbes provoked, Locke made himself a very secretive man. He wrote in shorthand himself and recommended that others do so, both for speed "and for concealment of what they would not have open to every eye."[3] He also wrote letters in invisible ink. He did not publish any of his principal works under his own name, except for the *Essay*, his most theoretical and recondite work.

Carrying concealment to surprising lengths, in 1703, the year before he died, Locke wrote to a young friend recommending some books to read. He said, "Property I have nowhere found more clearly explained than in a book called *Two Treatises of Government*"—his own book. In his own library Locke had a catalog, but in his own catalog of his own books, he did not classify *Two Treatises of Government* and *Letter on Toleration* under "Locke," though he did so classify his other books. These two were his political works, riskier than the others. In 1684 John Fell, the dean of Christ Church College at Oxford, was asked by the king to remove Locke from the college. After watching Locke to see whether he was guilty of disloyalty, Fell reported of him that "I believe there is not in the world such a master of taciturnity and passion."[4] In the *Reasonableness of Christianity* Locke remarks that Jesus indulged in "concealment of himself" and used "words too doubtful to be laid hold on against him," that he "perplexed" his meaning" and spoke in parables to convey his meaning with caution (*Reasonableness*, chs. 8 and 9). Since Locke does not object to this sort of deliberate misdirection, it is plausible to think that he may have done the same thing to excuse himself from the danger of being identified as a Hobbist. Evidence that Locke owned and displayed a copy of the *Leviathan* has disclosed that he read Hobbes extensively and knew him well, despite his failure to discuss the relation of his work to Hobbes's.[5]

Locke on Paternal Power

Turning from the contrast between the impudent Hobbes and the secretive Locke, we find what they have in common in the word "power." Hobbes, we have seen, was the first philosopher to use the word in the general sense of quantity we now employ—that someone has more or less power—and thus made power a theme for political science. It is surely a theme for Locke as well. The longest chapter, chapter 21, in his *Essay* is titled "Of Power." Humans need power, it seems. Locke presents them as needy, rather than sinful; as for Machiavelli, people are fundamentally subject to necessity rather than guilty of an original, voluntary sin called the Fall. Locke's *Two Treatises of Government* are about the human need for power and how to satisfy it. The *First Treatise* is on paternal power; the *Second Treatise* on the need for political power, given the failure of paternal power shown in the *First Treatise*. The latter is a critique of Sir Robert Filmer's book *Patriarcha* (1680), summed up by Locke as arguing that "all government is absolute monarchy" on the ground that "no man is born free." The *Second Treatise*, published with the *First*, has its own title page stating its subject as "Civil Government," though its sixth chapter is titled "Of Paternal Power" and considers paternal power within political power rather than rival to it.

It becomes clear that Filmer's book is a defense of divine right on the basis of the Bible. In criticizing him, Locke often refers to "Our Author" without naming him, sometimes in a way to suggest Our Author in another sense. Filmer tried to argue that political authority comes from God and is passed on from father to father beginning with Adam. Paternal power among men is the manifestation of divine power, and it resembles divine power as closely as possible. Locke denies both that political power is derived from divine power and that it resembles divine power. Divine power declares that man is not born free, and Locke hints at his view of this proposition by beginning the *First Treatise* with the word "slavery" and ending it with the word "Adam." The book's 169 sections can be added to the statistics of Machiavelli's book chapters given in chapter 1. One should also observe that in the *First Treatise,* Locke never uses the word "crime"; and in the *Second,* he never speaks of "sin." The Bible makes crime into sin, an offense to God; "civil government" ignores sin and deals with crime, a violation of human justice.

The *First Treatise* is worth careful study for the preparation it gives to the *Second Treatise,* by justifying political power over the divine power that stands behind paternal power. Among its half-concealed niceties of expression is an exact center illuminating its central thesis. In the course of the *First Treatise* (FT §29), Locke states the most obvious inadequacy of paternal power, particularly today. If power comes through generating offspring, why speak only of the father and not the mother? Of Adam and not Eve? Of paternal power and not parental? But it is obvious, too, that the trouble with parental power is that it is split. Father and mother can disagree, come into conflict, and even part ways. What power regulates this typical problem? To regulate the family, such a power would have to be outside the family: thus, political power. And so political power, which controls parental power, cannot be derived from parental power. One thinks of the famous 1961 comedy film *Divorce Italian Style,* which suggests that politics determines marital troubles. Evidently parental power is treated by Filmer, and by patriarchal societies, as paternal power because it comes from God the Father; yet the Judeo-Christian God appears to be above the male-female distinction.

Parental power in the Bible raises a second inadequacy of paternal power that Locke highlights for careful readers of the *First Treatise.* The Bible treats parental power in the fifth of the Ten Commandments, "honor thy father and mother." In America today, students of Locke and citizens generally are more likely to be acquainted with the Fifth Amendment than the Fifth Commandment—perhaps a consequence of Locke's doctrine of political power. The Fifth Commandment makes a basic delegation of power from God to father and mother, awarding them responsibility for paternal or parental power. Is there any difficulty in this award? Consider that the Fifth Commandment is unique among the commandments in its lack of specificity as to any particular behavior. Honor thy father and mother means obey them, but obey them in what? Does one have to obey parents in everything they wish or only in regard to another commandment? If the latter, then the Fifth Commandment would add nothing to the other commandments and grant no power to one's father and mother except that of enforcing God's commands. Parents would have no power of their own but merely serve as God's agents. Or, take the other possibility: Suppose one obeys all the other commandments but disobeys one's parents. Then God would be giving parents a broader grant of power. Or suppose that your parents command you to disobey one of the other commandments. What do you do, then? This was the question for obedience to Hobbes's sovereign when he commands you to be an infidel.

At the center of the *First Treatise* there is a reference to a Biblical passage at Deuteronomy 21.18–21 concerning a son disobedient to his parents. Locke indicates its importance by locating it with precision and intricacy in the central section of the central chapter of the book (FT §61) and within that chapter at the center of a list of Biblical citations (7th of 13). The disobedient son is stoned to death because he was a glutton and a drunkard, a deviant acting against the will of his parents—even though there is no divine commandment against these particular self-destructive habits. To justify the punishment, Rashi, a medieval Hebrew commentator, explained that the son died so his soul could be deemed innocent, before committing the sins he was about to commit. Locke's point is that the Fifth Commandment delegates power to parents more than it crowns them as agents of God.

Machiavelli had called Moses the "executor" of God in *The Prince* (P 6). In the same way, Locke implies with Machiavelli that God delegates power to parents with strings attached; parental power is limited by the other commandments, which sustain the power of God. A person is not made sovereign as he needs to be in order to be sure of his security, his necessity, as opposed to the commands of God or God's necessity. The Fifth Commandment is not a hot topic in our political science, but Locke, following Machiavelli and Hobbes, shows why it should be. The status of political power depends on the sovereignty of human beings to decide their own affairs based on their own necessities. The question of that sovereignty may seem outdated, its discussion obsolete in our secular age, but the point remains theoretically contestable and is still contested in fact by enemies and some friends of liberal democracy who are not convinced by Locke and his fellow philosophers.

Perfect Freedom in the State of Nature

Having now considered paternal power in the *First Treatise*, we are ready to study political power in the *Second Treatise*. At its beginning we are directed to the state of nature first formulated by Hobbes—though this goes unannounced by Locke. The state of nature is necessary to the "right" understanding of political power, and what is it but a "state of perfect freedom." The perfect freedom is "within the bounds of the law of nature," not of God. It is also a state of equality among "creatures of the same species and rank" unless there is "an evident and clear appointment of an undoubted right" by "the lord and master of them all" (ST §4). Note Locke's focus on *undoubted right*. Men are either certainly unequal or equal; there is no middle ground, as in Aristotle, between some who claim their equality (democracy) and others who claim their inequality (oligarchy).[6]

Political power is not to be argued by rival claims; it must be undoubted. Nor are men said to be equal, but only not clearly unequal, and the inequality must not be disputed. The equality Locke sees is in being "born to the same advantages of nature and to the use of the same faculties." Men have the same faculties, but he does not say they have them to an equal degree, which could be disputed (ST §6). Locke is looking for an end to dispute over the ground of political power, and instead of addressing the dispute over equality between the few and the many, he states a ground that ignores it. His political science will put an end not to political discourse, but to the relevance of it to decide the rightness of political power. His notion of equality does not say that humans are actually equal but rests content with the observation that no alleged inequality will be accepted by all. What will be accepted is an equality resting on the failure of any particular inequality to be undoubted.

The doubt of equality one might easily have, based on the observation that humans are actually in many ways unequal, is suppressed for the time being. Locke will later make room in his political science for inequality when he comes to discuss property. He is known as the master and founder of empiricism, the study of facts, but his politics begins from a deliberate distancing from the fact of political dispute. Machiavelli began his *Discourses on Livy* with an account of the fact of political dispute in Rome between the nobles and the plebs; Locke begins the *Second Treatise* by dismissing all such dispute in order to create an equality that is formal and far from empirical. The undoubted right of equality is based on the inability of any inequality to make itself undoubted. In Locke we see the thoughtful origin of the habit of liberalism today to claim to speak only for oneself, for which alone we have an undoubted right. Out of uncertainty comes certainty, out of skepticism that doubts comes dogmatism that has discovered what is undoubted.

If men are perfectly free and equal with an undoubted right, what does it mean to be bound by the law of nature? To answer this question, Locke provides a masterpiece of artful dodging (ST §6) over the duty to others required by equality. One can preserve others "when his own preservation comes not in competition," and must do so "as much as he can." The law of nature is a deduction from a formalized equality of men in the state of nature, but the deduction goes in two opposite directions: If we are equal, we are all *independent* of one another; or if we are equal, we are all *obliged* to one another. How can we understand this apparent contradiction? Every man, Locke says, has a natural power, the natural power to execute the law of nature (ST §§7–8); this means to punish violations of the law of nature. This natural power perfectly expresses the two opposite tendencies of that law: we are equal, hence alike and obliged to one another, hence we have the power to punish violators who endanger others—and we are equal, hence independent of others, hence every man has the power to secure his own life by being his own executive, or executioner, of the law of nature (ST §8). Equality includes everyone and excludes everyone. The natural law is based on what Locke admits is a "very strange doctrine," a law that every man executes (ST §§9, 13).[7] This law, one notes, is not derived from the "judicious Hooker" (ST §§5, 15). So the law of nature is the duty of every individual man to all humanity and the right of every individual man against all humanity.

The question then becomes, Which will predominate, the right against others or the duty to others? Or, what is the character of the state of nature: a state of war, or of peace? This is the question on which every comparison of Hobbes and Locke must focus, and indeed almost all of the many scholarly interpretations do so. Hobbes had said that the state of nature is a state of war. Locke does not say that clearly. To the extent that his state of nature approaches war, his premise as a whole is Hobbesian; to the extent that peace is possible in the state of nature, Locke has reverted to a more traditional natural law that would imply a natural inclination to virtue in humans that would require a less drastic formulation than Hobbes's absolute sovereignty.[8] Which is it, then, in the state of nature: war or peace? Now, Locke, as said above, does not equate the state of nature with war. He writes two separate chapters in the *Second Treatise* on the state of nature and the state of war (chs. 2 and 3), and he says in section 19 that there is a "plain difference" between them and that they have been "confounded," apparently a reference to Hobbes.

The first impression of Locke's state of nature is of humans living amicably in the first ages before civil society, enjoying natural freedom and equality in peaceful coexistence. But the state of nature is not limited to the origins of society; it can also exist between independent governments (ST §14). It is not necessarily pre-political; its definition is "living together according to reason without a common superior on earth" (ST §19). Thus, the state of nature can exist at any stage of political development. What is its opposite? Men living *with* a common superior, which is civil society (ST §87). The state of nature and the state of war are not identical and not opposites. What is the state of war? For Locke, "the use of force without right" (ST §19). In section 19, Locke says the use of force is where there is no common superior, but the example he gives expands the definition. He distinguishes a thief from a robber: a thief you cannot harm because you can appeal to the law, a "common superior"; but a robber you may kill as you desire because he leaves no time to call the police and appeal to the law. The power of the law within society is not always effectual, and when it is not you are in the state of nature and can execute the law of nature yourself.

Thus, for Locke the state of nature is only partly overcome by civil government. Since the "state of nature" describes human nature, one must conclude that civil society never entirely overcomes human nature, though its aim is to do so. Locke says without contradiction, then, that there is war in civil society but that civil society is also a state of peace. When war occurs *within* civil society, as with the robber, it is because civil society has collapsed back into the state of nature. To answer the question, Is the state of nature, in the sense of a pre-political condition, warlike or peaceful? Locke says that it has "great inconveniences" and is "not to be endured" (ST §13) and that it is "full of fears and continual dangers" and that it can be identified with "pure anarchy" (ST §§123, 225). But this might seem to contradict the earlier statement in section 19 that the state of nature is "life according to reason." (One can read section 19 until one's head spins.) The law of nature, one recalls, has two parts: the right to preserve oneself and the duty to preserve others. Will the right conflict with the duty? Locke tries to show that they will not, that an aggressor against me is an aggressor against mankind; when I punish him, I am both protecting my selfish right and doing my unselfish duty (ST §16). The connection between right and duty is through self-preservation, and reasonable self-preservation is the very definition of reasonable behavior. All humans follow the law of nature in that self-preservation is the strongest desire within them, but they don't necessarily follow it reasonably. Most people are not great studiers of the law of nature, and Locke lays great emphasis on the difference between those who are and those who are not (ST §§12, 59, 63, 123, 136). The law of nature is something to be studied and is not merely an impulse to be obeyed. With Machiavelli, we saw the same distinction between spontaneous necessity and necessity as a guide to prudence.

Since most people are not studiers of the law of nature and not "strict observers of equity and justice," it is "not without reason" that they leave the state of nature, which according to section 19 is "life according to reason," an apparent contradiction (ST §123). But the latter statement must mean that the state of nature is a state without civil laws where reason is the only guide, not that men actually do follow reason there and live peaceably. Then despite the initial impression of a "plain difference" between Locke and Hobbes, we have seen three similarities emerge: first, the state of nature for Locke is not war but it is the natural home of war, "full of fears and continual dangers"; second, the source, end, and content of natural law is self-preservation in both Locke and Hobbes; third, civil government is the remedy for the "great inconveniences" of the state of nature and not the expression of the natural sociability of human beings and their desire to live with one another. Yet one must not reject the first impression that for Locke the state of nature is more peaceable than for

Hobbes, for that leads to the real difference between them in respect to property. For Locke, the law of nature permits property in the state of nature—natural property. Hobbes, however, had said that the only natural property a man has is in his body, and even that is up for grabs in the state of nature, where one has a right to everything. For Hobbes, reason in the state of nature dictates a megalomanic desire for power after power. For Locke the same disputes arise out of what seems a more common, less extreme, desire to protect one's property.

Honest Avarice and Liberal Formalism

Locke developed a *theory* of property that is abstract, complex, and even extreme, because he did not want to leave the topic to conventional opinion and common sense. He proposed to make a great change in morality away from these two authorities, which set limits to how much property it was proper to acquire and how private it should be. He wanted to change the ruling opinion that excessive acquisition of property was wrong and avarice was a vice. This view had the support of the classical tradition of political philosophy in its two most conspicuous works. Aristotle's *Politics* maintained that acquisition of property was good only up to the point where a an individual or a country had enough for a sufficient life of virtue; beyond that point—to be sure, difficult to specify—too much was unnatural and wrong. Plato's *Republic* showed that private property itself was a source of injustice and would have to be abolished in a just regime. Machiavelli, we have seen, set no limit to acquisition, as any amount thought excessive might turn out to be necessary in the rivalry of individuals and regimes. Hobbes agreed but stated acquisition in terms of power rather than property.

Locke went further than both his modern predecessors: He found a new moral principle for acquiring property, as opposed to Machiavelli, and he made acquisition more peaceable and less warlike than did Hobbes. Locke's theory made it possible to seek gain without limits and yet, since it made a change in morality, to do so without the shame of avarice. A new category of virtue became apparent—honest avarice. With this theory in charge it was no longer immoral or illegal to seek to become rich. The Bible says that a rich man has the same chance to ascend to heaven as a camel has to pass through the eye of a needle; Socrates, for his part, made his poverty a point of honor.[9] The poor, it seems in these traditional views, are closer either to God or to philosophy. Now Locke's theory did indeed open a new objection to the rich, which was not that they were rich but that they were rich while others were poor. This objection takes for granted his reasoning that being rich is good, and that society might be directed into a "war on poverty," to use a phrase of our time, so that the poor can live the life of becoming rich if not the same life as the rich. This life is no longer regarded as shameful in itself, but instead is recommended for the poor. What was the reasoning that induced the massive change in morality away from a limit to justifiable wealth and toward the pursuit of limitless property?

Before taking up Locke's argument in favor of private property, we need to explore further the formality of the rights Locke establishes and the fundamental this-worldly premise on which they rest. We have seen the formalized equality of humans that Locke uncovers. They are equal not because they are empirically *found* to be equal but because they are *assumed* to be equal by lack of any undoubted proof that they are unequal. From this formal equality, humans have both a duty and a right, but it is clear that the right will predominate over the duty in the "great inconveniences" of the state of nature. The right is to self-preservation, to preserving your individual self. How will you exercise your right? You can do what you please as long as you don't interfere with the right of others, but your right makes you the judge of your own means of self-preservation. Allowing anyone else as judge is handing over your right to him. Self-preservation is also the end for your actions.

There is thus a necessary distinction between the right held by the individual and the exercise of that right by the individual. It is the purpose of government to protect the right, leaving it to the individual to exercise it. This distinction, one could say, is the essence of what is today called liberalism. Liberalism is the form of government that protects rights and leaves it to individuals, or to a society of individuals, to exercise them as they please. The job of government is to protect but not exercise; its end is to protect the individual's end. In doing so it represents the individual, as we have seen with Hobbes, whom Locke follows, rather than ruling individuals. Liberal representative government leaves the choice of exercise open, as opposed to governments that rule and thus direct the choices of citizens. The aim of government is therefore to protect the rights, or the means, of individuals. This is possible only if the means have a certain form or formality.

Rights must take a form that leaves their exercise unspecified. For example, the right of free speech has a certain form to be protected by government—in America today, by the Constitution and the laws made in accord with it—but these protections do not tell individuals what to say. For individuals, the right to free speech is a means to say what you wish; for the government, it is the end. For us today, it may seem that this reasoning makes something simple complicated, but in fact the complication seems simple to us only because it is so familiar. The simple understanding, found in Plato and Aristotle, is that the government rules by uniting ends and means; the government does what it thinks should be done. Liberal government, with its formality, allows citizens to do what they think should be done. It is limited government because it is formal and thus separated from the end it serves rather than imposes.

Justice, under Locke's reasoning, comes to mean the protection of the formalities of rights. It is more important under what we call the "rule of law" to guarantee legal procedures than to produce a certain result—more important, for example, to protect the criminal's rights than to punish the criminal. These rights become, for government, ends in themselves, while for individuals and for a society of individuals, they are means. Yet an obvious difficulty remains: How will the rights of liberal society in fact be exercised? Is it not consequential whether criminals are punished or not? Or whether the poor become prosperous or remain starving? What if individuals hold a belief in divine right and consider fellow citizens who do not share that view to be damned for impiety? Or if individuals hold a belief in aristocratic honor and consider fellow citizens who practice mere self-preservation to be sniveling cowards?

Karl Marx, we shall see, developed this criticism. He thought that the exercise of the right of acquiring property led to the destruction of that right because the few exercise their right in a way that destroys the right of the immense majority. This happens out of necessity under capitalism, not because the few are morally inferior, as we will see in chapter 7 on Marx. Marx concluded that Locke's society of rights is bourgeois formalism. The right to acquire is in actuality a mere formality of law, as in the remark of Anatole France that the law permits a poor man to sleep in the most expensive hotel and the rich man to sleep outdoors under a bridge.[10] For Marx this is the character of bourgeois law. It seems that in liberal or "bourgeois" society the elevation of rights to put means and procedures over ends can always be challenged in light of the end, and that it is impossible to maintain the formalism necessary to liberalism. As in the examples above, the challenge to it may come either from the political Right, concerning honor and religion, or from the Left, concerning poverty. What is Locke's reply to this problem? How does he defend the formalism of his theory?

Locke shows, or allows one to see, that liberal formalism does not destroy freedom but protects it. What is the greatest enemy of freedom? It is not the rich, as Karl Marx and those influenced by him think; it is the wise. It is not the inequality of property but of reason, not the bourgeoisie but those who set themselves up as wise, who most endanger freedom. This includes certain classes of the religious—all those who think they know better because they know God's will. In this thought Locke follows the critique of religion and especially of Christianity that we have seen in Machiavelli and Hobbes, but he expresses it differently, more respectably.

According to Locke, God has given man a strong desire for self-preservation as in other animals (FT §86), and God has given man reason, instead of instinct, to effect his self-preservation. Reason is man's star and compass, part natural, part artificial (FT §58). Reason does not enable man to pursue an end that distinguishes him from other animals but serves him as guide to show him where he wants to go and what he wants to do. Man is superior to other animals because of his reason and therefore has full power to enjoy animals—that is, to eat them—and he had this from the beginning from Adam, not from Noah, as the Bible says. But if man can eat animals because they are not rational, can he eat other humans if they have less reason? Surely not. Rather, can the knowing few rule the ignorant many? Is wisdom a title to rule? Locke says, "We are born free as we are born rational" (ST §61)—that is, we are as free as we are rational, but none is so rational as to destroy the freedom of others.

Recall that Locke says we are equal in possessing the faculty of reason, which means that all men claim to have reason, which means hold the pretension to be wise. To take account of such pretensions is to treat people as rational, which means to let them live freely as they please, within the bounds of the law of nature. Just as in Hobbes, reason is equal because men in their vanity think themselves equal. The democratic premise of liberalism is not really based on reason but on the pretension to reason, though this is not to say that it is unreasonable. For Locke the law of nature is the rule of reason, but not the rule of the wise. For Marx, as for the religious classes of priests and believers that Locke thought to oppose, the few with knowledge are the rulers. In Marx's thinking, knowledge of the laws of history justifies the rule of those few who lead the party of the proletariat. Locke's formalism ignores the inequality of the wise as rulers. As we shall see, it permits the inequality of the propertied, but as rich persons who are distracted from politics, not as rulers. Those who do enter politics are checked by elections, another feature of his formalism, based on the formal right to vote.

Is Man God's Property?

The other preparation for Locke's theory of property is its necessary premise that man is his own property rather than God's property. Recalling the conclusion in the *First Treatise* that political power cannot be derived from God and the doubt raised whether man has an inheritance from God for which he must be grateful, we can ask how this applies to property. It appears that property raises a religious question more fundamental than the question whether some humans have a right to property against other humans. Before we decided whether property is private or social, humans themselves must be justified to hold property—and this is disputable. Is man a creature that belongs to his Creator together with everything that belongs to man? The religious question precedes today's question of "social justice" both in principle and in history. Today the social question is paramount—rich versus poor—but the religious question had to be faced and resolved first. Locke, being the cautious man that he was, both affirms and denies that man is the property of God. He says that man is the "workmanship" of God (FT §53; ST §§6, 56), but he also says that man has property in his own person (ST §§27, 44, 123).

With the workmanship thesis in mind, Locke is sometimes taken for a Calvinist and to be a champion of private property in accord with the well-known Protestant Ethic conceived by Max Weber. Weber perceived that acquisition of property, or capitalism, could be found anywhere, in all countries, but the *spirit* of capitalism demanding *limitless* acquisition was special to the modern West.[11] He noted that capitalists were not pleasure-loving voluptuaries but ascetics dedicated to moneymaking for its own sake. Their devotion was that of Calvinist believers but transformed from the otherworldly to this world. How did this transformation take place? Not through an external corruption outside religion but inside, through an inner transformation of religion: religion transforms itself into non-religion, the non-religion of the spirit of capitalism. Yet is this not Calvinism but corrupted Calvinism? The opening question of the Heidelberg catechism (1563) of Locke's day was this: "Q. What is your only comfort, in life and in death? A. That I belong—body and soul, in life and in death—not to myself but to my faithful Savior."[12] This uncompromising assertion from Calvinism itself had to be denied so that Calvinism could be secularized, and that is the import of Locke's argument, carefully hedged, that humans belong to themselves.

Locke tries to make an inner transformation of Calvinism himself. He deprecates the power of fathers over their children; the father has no right over the child arising from "the bare act of begetting" (ST §65; note the sly joke). The child is not the property of the father.[13] Thus, too, man is made in the image of his maker, and he cannot but suppose that he follows the will of his maker when he seeks his own self-preservation. What is necessary and useful to his being, considering that each man has a self to preserve, cannot but be in accord with God's will. God cannot have property in an image he made of himself any more than a parent can have property in a child. In this way, the two statements for and against man as the property of God can be reconciled. Even if man is the workmanship of God, he cannot be the property of God. Men follow the will of their maker when they regard themselves as their own property, and not being God's property, they have received no property from God. Their only gifts are their desire for self-preservation and the reason to effect it. These are in man's own nature and could not have been withheld by any maker of such as himself. Man is his own property, and this fact proves to be the foundation of private property in the labor theory of value.

The Labor Theory of Value

Locke begins his notable chapter 5 in the *Second Treatise*, "Of Property," from the two aspects of reason and revelation, which come to the same conclusion:

> Whether we consider natural reason, which tells us, that men, being once born, have a right to their preservation, and consequently to

> meat and drink, and such other things as nature affords for their subsistence: or revelation, which gives us an account of those grants God made of the world to Adam, and to Noah, and his sons, it is very clear, that God, as king David says, Psal. cxv. 16. has given the earth to the children of men; given it to mankind in common. (ST §25)

Reason and revelation both say that there was an original, universal common—meaning no private property. But do they quite say the same thing? Locke specifies that in reason "preservation" gives men the right to meat, but we know from Genesis 9 that God gave men the right to eat meat not at first but later in the covenant with Noah. By revelation we learn that eating meat is not included with the original human creation as the consequence needed for human preservation. God's word, then, does not after all, despite Locke's assurance, accord with reason, or Locke's reason, on human necessities. On close examination, Locke takes away the conclusion of his sentence above in the very course of it. He did not have to specify "meat" as a consequence of preservation, but he did. One wonders whether, in his view, God is sufficiently attentive to human necessities (cf. FT §39).[14] Could it be that Locke, like Machiavelli and Hobbes, does not fully share the counsel of Psalm 115 (which he cites) to trust in God?

An original common signifies no property. Locke's definition of property is that which cannot be taken from you without your consent (ST §138). Then how did anyone come to hold property? The argument starts from the exception to this rule: your body (ST §27). No one has a right to your body but yourself, nor, besides this—a crucial addition—to your labor. Whatever is the result of your labor is yours, as long as "enough and as good is left in common for others" (ST §§27, 33; cf. §§34, 36). In this situation, perhaps in early times, it seems that there is common abundance such that you can with your labor—as when taking a pitcher of water from a fountain—take from the common without taking from anyone else (ST §29). The rule is therefore stopping at what is *enough*—not for you, but for others. But why is this property entirely private? It would seem to be part private, but part common insofar as the original common materials found in nature were valuable. Locke, however, estimates that the value added by human labor is 9/10 of the whole, or on second thought 99/100 of the whole; a more sober estimate would indeed be 999/1000 (ST §§37, 40, 43). This is private property without express or explicit consent, hence in the state of nature before there are laws arising from consent. It is naturally private property—private because all value comes effectually from human labor, not from the "worthless materials" of nature, and human labor comes from the human body, which is by nature individual and private (ST §43). Property is not a mixture of private and common but is, rather, entirely private; it belongs not to humanity but to *that* human being who created it. "Who can doubt" what Locke propounds to us, for Locke, we remember, is looking for an "undoubted right."[15]

The labor theory of value was used by Marx to argue for communism, as we will see in chapter 7, but by Locke to argue for private property, because labor is the work of the body—not the understanding of soul—and one's body is the most private thing there is. As opposed to Hobbes, one's private body is not so much motivated toward human society by the fear of violent death as by the creation of value. Man makes value by taking the "almost worthless materials" of nature and turning them into value through labor. Then how much can one man take? Locke's answer is that one can take only as much as doesn't spoil. If you grow more wheat than you can use, the surplus that spoils is not your property; it can be taken by someone else. This is the bourgeois ethic: If a child leaves something uneaten on his plate, his parents say, Think of all the hungry children in the world—finish it! It is worse to waste than to be greedy.

Yet the rule on spoiling doesn't work. It is necessary only if there is a scarcity of perishable goods, but if there is a scarcity then there can be no private property because according to the stated condition for it, there must be "enough and as good" left for others. And if nature gives almost worthless materials, if value is humanly created, then there was no abundance at the beginning of the world. There was, rather, potential abundance and actual "penury." If the spoiling rule doesn't work, scarcity caused men to dispute and conflict over their undoubted but uncertain property. Two things were needed. An invention was needed to reduce spoiling: money. Money changes the situation altogether. Money makes it profitable to own more land than you can farm and grow more than you can eat or barter. After the invention of money, economic inequality grows very rapidly. Money doesn't spoil, and your hoarding doesn't harm anyone. But isn't this unjust? There is scarcity; the original assumption of abundance in "enough and as good" is dropped. Aren't you taking more than your share if you "heap up" money without limit?

No! In the early state of nature, one who took more than an equal share robbed others. Now he *helps* others because everyone gains, even if unequally. Hence one of Locke's famous remarks: "A king of a large and fruitful territory in America feeds, lodges, and is clad worse than a day-laborer in England" (ST §41). Suppressing the thought that the tables have turned between America and Europe, one sees the point that by private gain, humans enable a general increase over the materials of nature. At this stage, when property inequalities are great, property disputes are very likely to occur, and men are "quickly driven into society to protect their property" (ST §123). In society, labor no longer gives title to property, and property is regulated by laws. For Locke, the labor theory of value applies only in the state of nature, not civil society (a difference from Marx). Locke concludes at this point: "The great and chief end of men's uniting into commonwealth is the protection of property" (ST §124). He associates the end of government with something closer to actual experience than the fear of death. In chapter 5 Locke doesn't mention the state of nature and does refer in a general way to actual events in the economic history of Britain, particularly the enclosure acts by which common property was made private.

Government, for Locke, protects private gains that result in general increase. It is not that private property is sacred, for it can be regulated by law (ST §§50–51). Nor is it that private property is justified so as to justify an oligarchy of the rich. For Locke understands property as not merely private but also increasing. Property, of course, cannot increase without spreading as, for example, you cannot make a fortune in wheat except by selling it, and to sell it you must have buyers and those buyers must have money. This is the reasoning by which Henry Ford is said to have paid his workers a wage that enabled them to buy Fords that they had produced.

Locke's goal of increase is what we call a "rising standard of living." It is not an absolute right of the few and damn the rest. Yet, of course, those who profit the most will be the few, today's businessmen. The free enterprise system that Locke presents in sketchy outline also engages the competitiveness as well as the profit motive of the few. In this system, however, spiritedness is engaged in economics rather than politics. Businessmen compete not only to make money but also for the sake of winning a competition. Critics of this system do not so much call it a hog trough as a rat race, decrying competition more than greed. God gave the world, Locke intones, for the "use of the industrious and rational," and not "to the fancy or covetousness of the quarrelsome and contentious" (ST §34). The latter are diverted from politics, where they do damage, and instead make money, with the result if not the intent of general increase. One who works for more than he needs "does not lessen but increases the common stock of mankind" (ST §§37, 46). One who seeks honor more than his fellows, it may be added, is usually a troublemaker.

Let the contentious engage in the bloodless killing of commerce, which they can do only if they have an incentive for reward, with protection of the gains they have made for themselves. For Locke, government takes on the protection of property, because it looks to allow something to men of spiritedness, who desire excess, and thereby to secure their loyalty to the government of liberty and the benefits of their industry. If we distinguish between what is necessary and what is useful to men at large, Locke constructs his system on the utility of "plenty," to use his word. He thinks that increasing property is necessary as well as useful, but useful is what he emphasizes. *Excess is useful*: that is the fundamental thought of utilitarianism, a movement to come in the nineteenth century. Machiavelli stayed with necessity rather than utility, a necessity that anticipates what will be necessary and therefore also seeks excess. But his virtue used prudence and "the art of war" to regulate the quarrelsome and contentious, whom he welcomed more than Locke.

Property and the Body Politic

According to Locke, human property does not depend on human agreement or convention. It is a human right, as opposed to the divine right that Locke discusses in the *First Treatise* when refuting Sir Robert Filmer. According to the Bible, labor is not a right leading to increase but a curse and a punishment imposed on man after the original sin for which Adam and Eve were cast out of the Garden of Eden. The natural right applies equally to all human labor, but it leads to the discovery and implementation of three great conventions that bring about substantial human inequalities and at the same time greatly improve human life after the penury and conflict of the state of nature.

The first of these is *money*, which is necessary to human improvement; without it, private property would be limited, in justice, to the quantity of perishables that would not spoil. With money, inequality in property becomes just, as one who receives more does not take from others. We remember that justice means not taking from others; it does not mean sharing equally or proportionately. This justice is an individual right, not a community right. Community right, we shall see, comes about through the consent of individuals as the servant of those individuals. Money is invented before civil society is formed; no express consent is needed, and labor no longer determines value even though it remains the measure in great part (ST §50). Humans acquire the use of money by "tacit and voluntary consent," without controversy, it seems. This consent does not happen by rational agreement, which would emphasize human rationality, nor does it happen by instinct, which might allow for the gift of divine providence.

Yet there must indeed be controversy over unequal property, and Locke discusses conflict, not merely controversy, in chapter 6 on paternal power in the *Second Treatise*. Here Locke rehearses the arguments of the *First Treatise* and arrives at the distinction between paternal and political power, which is immediately applied to the inheritance of property. Paternal power, it appears, is incomplete because it cannot decide who inherits when a father dies. For this event one needs a power beyond the family—political power, which makes the law of inheritance. *Inheritance* is the second great convention after money. Money permits property to be passed around; inheritance permits it to be passed along, from one generation to the next. So, in chapter 7, Locke says for the first time that the chief end of society is the preservation of property (ST §85). Soon after, property is given an enlarged sense to include life, liberty, and estate (ST §87). Nothing like this was said in his chapter 5, on property. Property, it now appears, is the human good as a whole. The preservation of property is the preservation of the property of all members of society insofar as possible, and this occurs when any number of men in the state of nature enter into society to make one people, one body politic under one supreme government (ST §89). This act of *incorporating into a body politic* is the third human convention. The first two conventions, money and inheritance, provide the impetus toward politics: Man is not a political animal by nature, as for Aristotle.

Locke's notion of the body politic can be defined further. The body politic is a whole whose end is the preservation of property in an inflated sense. External goods are inflated to comprise all human goods. In civil society men consent by majority rule because an act of the majority passes for an act of the whole; the will of society is the will of the majority. In society, men agree to make one artificial body in which each is a member of the whole—not a part but a member of the whole. Society protects property and thereby protects consent, though not because property is sacred and inviolate in Locke's society. You can have your property taken away, but not without the consent of the majority. Property, then, is not merely what supplies your needs and keeps you alive. It is what keeps you *free*. The security of property protects freedom, and freedom is the "fence" to life, marking where one's life is in danger (ST §17). If property has a "fence" in laws and is secure, you are free, and if freedom is secure, your life is secure (ST §§93, 136, 222, 226). The difference between political and despotic power can be stated in terms of property: Political power is power over men who have property at their own disposal; despotic power is over those who have no property at all (ST §174).

Having this crucial role as fence doesn't mean that property is more valuable than life or liberty. Rather, property is the convention that protects life and liberty, for when life and liberty are at stake, they are already in jeopardy. It is better, Locke thought, to elevate the lesser good of property over the higher goods of life and liberty as an early warning system: a danger to property is a danger to life and liberty. But for this seemingly irrational and unjust elevation of property's ranking, one pays a price. That price is an increase in love of gain in Locke's society, the honest avarice spoken of above that typifies bourgeois modernity. A somewhat arbitrary status for property and the propertied results, for it is thought better that the rich to be on top by majority consent than have anyone else rule without majority consent. Property is therefore an effectual whole, such that when any one person's property is taken without consent, Property as a whole with a capital P is attacked. The people as a body can see or can be brought to see clearly that an invasion of property right is the sign of coming tyranny. All can read the warning. In the nineteenth century, "property" was often awarded a capital P, a development of which Locke would approve. Today gun ownership seems to offer a similar, exaggerated status as protection to life and liberty, like Locke's notion of property, only with advantage to the poor as much as the rich. But whether guns actually provide or detract from security remains an issue, just as property became an issue after Locke in the rise of socialism and, we shall see, the thought of Karl Marx.

Thus, property in Locke. With property, Locke offers an alternative to the political ambition that combined so dangerously with religious zeal in his day. Still, political ambition does not entirely disappear into the search for material gain, and Locke's government turns out to be stronger than one might expect simply because it is limited. How does Locke manage the ambition of those who love honor more than gain, and who, he says, need to govern competently, without tyranny? The answer has two parts: constitutionalism and toleration.

Locke's Constitution

Since not all the ambitious few will be deflected out of politics into business, Locke must see to it that they serve the majority. Those who love honor do not serve the best of men, as Plato's guardians serve the philosophers in the *Republic*, yet they do maintain their inequality by seeking honor above ordinary folk. Locke, like Hobbes, is fundamentally democratic in basing his political science on the equality of rights, but he is more amenable to the desires of some to rise above others, and he does not subordinate all honors to the decision of the sovereign. For Locke, those desirous of honor will indeed serve the majority, as the rich spread their wealth to the many, but in so doing they will serve themselves as well. In present-day terms, Locke argues for equality of opportunity rather than equality of result, and not only because it is freer, but also because those who love honor—and they do exist—will moderate the democracy of majority rule with justice for themselves. He does not simply deny the oligarchic view that those who contribute more deserve more—he democratizes it.

Freedom to excel, or simply to exceed, sets those in business to compete against one another, as will be seen of intellectuals, and the same holds for those in politics. The famous rule of James Madison a century later, "ambition must be made to counteract ambition," appears in Locke's constitutionalism. The problem for both is how to keep government in check through competition within it without weakening it. Locke sets about this task by distinguishing himself from the absolute sovereignty of Hobbes (though of course without mentioning him). He says that "absolute, arbitrary power" is no remedy for the evils of the state of nature (ST §137), for such power would put men in a worse condition than one in which they at least have the liberty to defend themselves. It follows that absolute monarchy, which by some (William Barclay is mentioned, not Hobbes) is counted the only government in the world, is no government at all (ST §§90, 166, 239). So then, which form of government does Locke recommend?

What Locke does *not* recommend is to limit the sovereignty of government. In one paragraph he makes one of the most emphatic statements of sovereignty ever composed. The power of government, he says, extends everywhere to all controversies, however private, and to all parties, however protected or secluded (ST §87). Instead of limiting sovereignty, Locke draws a distinction between absolute power and arbitrary power; the first is necessary, the second not. The distinction appears suddenly in a later paragraph after several uses of "absolute" and "arbitrary" together have lulled the reader into thinking that they always belong together. To explain why they do not, Locke uses an example in "the common practice of martial discipline." The preservation of the army and "in it the whole commonwealth" require "absolute obedience to the command of every superior officer." It is "justly death," Locke warns, to disobey or dispute the "most dangerous or unreasonable" command of a sergeant that might bring sure death. This "blind obedience" is necessary to the end of preserving the rest of the commonwealth, but that same sergeant "cannot dispose of one farthing of that soldier's estate or seize one jot of his goods," which would be arbitrary taking of his property without consent (ST §139).

The entrance of military necessity in Locke's argument is one decisive stroke. He had been assuring us that passage from the state of nature to the commonwealth would bring "peace and safety" and preservation of rights (ST §134). Now we find more realistically that war continues nonetheless with enemies perhaps in other commonwealths, requiring the duty of blind obedience as part of the safety of one's rights. Note, too, the contrast with Hobbes, who allowed for the inalienable right to save one's skin by running from battle. Locke takes the part of every stupid sergeant and saves not the life, but the farthing of every poor soldier's property. He does this not because he favors the rich but because the power of government is necessary for the preservation of society. Though society is artificial, it has a "fundamental natural law" consisting of its own preservation (ST §134). All rights of the members of society must be consistent with the preservation of society: One cannot hold any right that would, in the opinion of the government, destroy society. The power of the whole exerts its sovereignty over all individual members—in the military, this sovereignty transforms right into duty. Locke's peace does not indulge pacifism. How, then, does Locke ensure that the absolute power of government not be used arbitrarily? Two means are offered: rule of the majority, and the supremacy of the legislative power in combination with the separation of powers.

The majority acts as a check on government on two occasions. First, the majority institutes the form of government at the beginning of society, as it has naturally the whole power of the commonwealth. Its power is absolute but not arbitrary because all men are equal in the state of nature. Majority rule is just since each individual counts as one. This majority is an "original democracy" that entrusts the government to another group (ST §132); this entrusting (to a group, not one person) is not a second social compact, however, but an act of the majority government. As well as at the beginning of society, the majority intervenes at the end of society, in case the government should be dissolved after it has violated the rights of the people, for whose protection it was entrusted with power (ST, ch. 19). This revolutionary situation also resembles the state of nature: the majority is protection against arbitrary government when men are close to the state of nature. Locke calls this an "Appeal to Heaven"—that is, to war (ST §168). Most people are not inclined to revolution and have to be stirred to action by a few (an instance of Machiavelli's two humors of the active few and passive many).

At other times, the majority will not intervene; thus, the ordinary protection against arbitrary rule, while the government is in operation, is the principle of legislative supremacy as expressed in the separation of powers. The majority does decide in elections to the legislature but depends on the power of the legislature rather than on its own action outside the government (ST §§132, 154, 176). What is legislative supremacy? Locke says that a form of government is decided according to where the legislative power is placed. Note that he says *legislative power*, as we would today, following Locke, not the *laws*. Legislative supremacy means the supremacy of the power to make laws rather than the supremacy of any particular laws considered more sacred than others. That is how legislative supremacy can be made consistent with absolute sovereignty. It is not that certain laws are untouchable by humans, as, for example, the higher law asserted in Sophocles's play *Antigone*, in which Antigone appeals to the higher law of Zeus against the decree of the king. Locke does not care for Antigone's sort of appeal to heaven; he offers the rule of law in the modern sense of the law-making power, so that laws are "settled, standing, rules," not whimsical and made for the occasion (ST §87). Laws are required to be published, and they do not have a required or determinate content. Yet this is not enough; it would simply imply an all-powerful Congress or Parliament—a legislative body—that might act arbitrarily.

One must return to the act by which the commonwealth is "constituted," which Locke calls its "original constitution" (ST §§149, 153–154). Here we find "constitution" in our sense, a verbal noun from "constituting." Locke's constitution seems to come from existing institutions such as king and parliament, but unlike Aristotle's constitution or regime of the rule of one, few or many, in which those who make the laws are rulers, his legislative power is subject to the laws and must hold elections. For Locke the legislative *body* is distinct from the legislative *power*, which includes the king, with his power to veto legislation. "Power" has the generality of Hobbes's notion, by which a body has an abstract, quantitative amount of power; Aristotle's notion of power, by contrast, pertains to the quality of a body (such as a pig's power to grunt). With Locke's notion, one can separate a mass of power into different powers—the legislative, the executive (including the judiciary), and the federative (handling foreign affairs). Given the separation of powers and the requirements of elections to the legislature, it is difficult in Locke's constitution to decide who rules—this is always Aristotle's primary political question. Is it "we the people" or their representatives, and if the latter, which part of the government? Or does Aristotelian rule disappear from sight in the separate, constituted institutions of government?

Locke's endorsement of legislative supremacy would seem to imply that there is no check on the legislature, but he qualifies this theory by adapting it to actual institutions in England at the time, no doubt as one of the "well-order'd commonwealths" or "moderated monarchies" he refers to (ST §§143, 159). Since the legislative power is not merely Parliament but the king in Parliament, the king is much more than a mere executive in the strict instrumental sense of executing someone else's will. Locke gives the English monarchy executive powers that well exceed the meaning of the word. The king's veto is a legislative power (ST §152); the federative power goes together with the executive (ST §148); the executive has the power to convoke the legislature (ST §156); it has the power to correct the malapportionment of the legislature (ST §§157–158); most important, it has the power of prerogative (ST §159). All these powers "fortify" the executive to the point where it is equal or even superior to the legislature.[16]

Thus, despite the theory of legislative supremacy, the actual practice of the separation of powers in the English monarchy produces a check on the legislature and enables Locke to refer to the "supreme executive" (ST §152). To pass a law, it appears that you must send it through two or three separate bodies. The legislative power becomes what is today called the legislative *process*; that process is what is supreme. The government is therefore sovereign, but the various parts or stages in the process must agree so that no one of them is sovereign alone. Locke's constitution delivers what he promised in the distinction between absolute power (good) and arbitrary power (bad).

Locke on Toleration

Continuing with the inequalities that flourish in civil society, after property and politics are those of mind and speech. Together with businessmen and politicians, Locke must provide space for those now called "intellectuals," who in his time were clerics zealous for faith, "quarrelsome and contentious" for religion rather than worldly honor. Locke must lift the burden of harsh religious penalties that weighs on free speech and hampers free inquiry. He must open the way for the advance of modern science led by modern scientists and not incidentally ensure a safer existence for philosophers like himself. In fact, Locke lived at Oxford under constant surveillance and then escaped the threat of Catholic enmity from the court of James II by fleeing to Holland in 1683–1688. All this he did in *A Letter Concerning Toleration*, published in 1689, the same year that he published his *Two Treatises of Government* and *Essay Concerning Human Understanding.*

The *Letter* had been published from the Latin, *Epistola de tolerantia*, in Holland in 1685, addressed to a Dutch friend. It was then translated and published in England after the Glorious Revolution in 1688 that dislodged the Stuart monarchy and under Whig leadership brought a new monarchy eager to end the religious enmities of the Civil War. The translator was not Locke but William Popple, a friend and radical Whig, whose work Locke acknowledged and maintained were his in the four defenses he made thereafter against the attacks it provoked. The *Letter* was this very careful philosopher's most direct entrance into politics, narrowly framed without reference to the new political situation or to his own place in it.

Two characteristics suggest a broader intent beyond its immediate (though important) occasion. First is Locke's reference near the end (60) of the "Principle of Persecution for Religion" as his target, a very general issue. Second, the assertiveness of his argument is remarkable—he frequently says "I say" something, even on one occasion exclaiming, "I beseech you." At the same time, Locke frequently anticipates the response in opposition to his affirmations, sometimes impersonally as "it might be alleged," and sometimes personally as "you'll say." The *Letter* is in fact a dialogue. It might therefore be taken as an imitation, perhaps an improvement on, another dialogue with the same target, Plato's *Apology of Socrates*. Locke's *Letter* is a private conversation, not a public defense of personal conduct like that of Socrates, and it does not feature Locke as Plato's dialogue dramatizes the charges against Socrates. Locke does treat the same problem of religious persecution but, unlike Plato, offers a political remedy, a "Law of Toleration" that would bring peace not only among religions but also between reason or philosophy and religion.

While Socrates provides religious disguises in the Delphic Oracle and his own demon to stand as his authorities, Locke starts the *Letter* with an assertion of his own: "I esteem . . . toleration to be the chief characteristical mark of the true Church" (7). He offers no Biblical citation to support his estimation but moves to consider the essential character of Christianity, his comparable authority to the two divine inventions of Socrates. Christianity, he says, is not striving for "power and empire" over others; it is rather warring against one's own "lusts and vices." Christianity is a kind of warfare, but against oneself so that one can love others—though they have vices too, making love difficult. In fact, the intolerance of Christian sects for one another shows that they love themselves and war against others. This world is not ruled by love or by the "charity, meekness and good will" that Christian doctrine requires. Sectarian anger revealed in "the infliction of torments" and "all manner of cruelties" belongs to the kingdom of this world, not the kingdom of God. Politics is full of anger and force rather than love, a truth that Christianity attempts to deny in doctrine but follows in practice. Locke's dutiful beginning from Christianity results in the criticism that its exercise is hypocrisy. Instead of relying on Christianity, he is obliged to "esteem" matters for himself in order to correct it and bring it to practice toleration.

As if Locke's estimation were now decisive, he proceeds to "esteem" further that it is "above all things necessary to distinguish exactly the business of civil government from that of religion" (12). As we saw with the "undoubted right" of self-preservation seen in the *Second Treatise,* we now receive an exact distinction to decide the ancient question of state and church provided by John Locke. What is it? The "civil magistrate" (government) executes the laws that protect rights, particularly the right to property, but refrains from the salvation of souls or correction of the mind. The latter belongs to each of us. "All the life and power of true religion" consist in being "fully satisfied in our mind that [the profession] is true" and that "outward worship" is pleasing to God. Note that Locke speaks of the life and power, not the truth of true religion. In short, for his purposes in the *Letter*, true religion is what is taken as true. Locke affirms and esteems, and his readers decide in their own minds. Both are opinions, not truth. Locke's opinion satisfies him, and he recommends a similar satisfaction to his readers and to the public, rather than a quest for truth.

The exact distinction between magistrate and society is that the former cares for "civil interests," what he calls ("I call") "life, liberty, health and indolency of body" together with the "possession of outward things," otherwise known as property. This concern ought not "in any manner to be extended to the salvation of souls" (13). What, then, of public education in the true principle of toleration, of the kind that takes place today in liberal democracies? One sees again the exaggeration necessary to Locke's exactness, as well as the hostility to public education in his work *Thoughts on Education*. And what is the relationship between mind and soul? It seems that the satisfaction of one's mind is decisive and takes charge of one's soul, and that any inclination toward God has been expelled from the soul. It follows from Locke's exact distinction that the church is "a free and voluntary society," or on second thought is "absolutely free and spontaneous," yet for this reason quite powerless to enforce its commands, or rather "exhortations" (16).

A church has the power of excommunicating wayward members but must reckon without the power of the magistrate to attach any penalty to this resolution. Locke declares this conclusion from this limitation: "For there is no civil injury done unto the excommunicated by the Church minister's refusing him that bread and wine in the celebration of the Lord's Supper, which was not bought with his but other men's money" (20). Here is a beautiful illustration of the relative strength of this-worldly government and otherworldly love. If an excommunicated person had paid for the bread and wine that was denied him, the excommunicated would then have a justified claim of compensation to the magistrate. In Locke's profane description of the Mass, we get a sniff of Hobbes's more brash impudence regarding the sacraments of Roman Christianity.

What does the duty of toleration require from priests or ministers? These are described as "those distinguished from the rest of mankind" by "some ecclesiastical character" or "however else dignified or distinguished" (24). Locke himself might be among those described last, who are not churchmen, and he surely gives himself over to exhortation in this part of his *Letter*. Locke the philosopher speaks in his own name to society. Unlike the magistrate, he has a care for the minds of his readers, whom he must persuade by the reasons that appeal to them, if with a spice of irreverence. Locke ends the *Letter* by stating four things that the magistrate cannot tolerate, despite the exact distinction that excludes him from governing the mind or soul of citizens. First, he cannot tolerate an opinion contrary to the "moral rules . . . necessary to the preservation of civil society," rules "condemned by the judgment of all mankind" as endangering "their own interest, peace, reputation" (49–50). He does not name the rules, but he omits religion from what is endangered. Second, those sects "who upon pretence of religion" challenge the authority of civil government, including a prince or a king, have no right to be tolerated by the magistrate (51). Third, a church that delivers its believers to the service of "another prince" cannot be tolerated. This item would seem to refer to James II, who apparently wished to bring his subjects under the protection of the Catholic French king, but instead Locke refers to a "Mahummetan" (Muslim) who would have divided loyalty (52). "Prince" could have several meanings, including the Pope to whom Catholics hold obedience. "Lastly," he says, those cannot be tolerated "who deny the being of a God." Taking away God even in thought "dissolves all," perhaps because their oaths cannot be trusted. Besides, such atheists can have no pretense of religion by which to claim the privilege of toleration (52–53). Does this mean that all atheists have to do is to confine their atheism to their thought while claiming a *pretense* of religion?

Then, having said this is the last of four exceptions to toleration, Locke adds a fifth. He asks whether assemblies or conventicles of religion should be tolerated by the magistrate since they are "nurseries of faction and sedition" interfering with civil authority. But he concludes that if these meetings were to issue a "law of toleration" binding all churches to tolerate one another and "teach that liberty of conscience is every man's natural right," this would remove all causes of complaint and tumult and bring peace. All churches would then be "obliged to lay down toleration as the foundation of their own liberty" (53). After all, then, the magistrate does have care of souls by arranging for a law of toleration obliging all churches and by teaching the necessity of such a law. Locke's argument for toleration based on religion stealthily becomes an argument against religion, should it endanger moral rules, induce obedience to another prince (whoever that might be), or fail to accept toleration as its foundation. But this is just what Locke has said that Christian churches do without fail. His condemnation of atheists, which today would be found intolerant, comes with an escape hatch. At the end of the *Letter,* Locke seems to authorize the magistrate's care of souls if it is done properly in accordance with his own argument. On the whole, the *Letter* shows the assertive Locke in contrast to the cautious Locke of the *Second Treatise.* In the latter he quotes the traditional authority of Richard Hooker and makes no novel legal proposals, apparently confining himself to a description of features of the English constitution. In the *Letter* he puts himself forward, speaking in the first person, arguing with only himself, and offers a novel law claimed to establish by itself a hitherto unknown peace between civil and religious authority.

How goes our theme of rational control in the political philosophy of Locke? We have certainly seen reason in control. From Hobbes,

Locke borrows the state of nature, a condition that sweeps authority away from all tradition, superstition, and prejudice, allowing human reason to build on a minimal foundation that owes nothing to irrational conventions and beliefs, thus to construct its own rational powers and features without compromise. For Locke, as opposed to Hobbes, these features are concentrated in the newly prominent status of property that sums up all human goods, when property itself is declared the end of society. Also in contrast to Hobbes, Locke presents a rational constitution, though bearing a strong resemblance to the English one that was fought over in the civil war of the seventeenth century, and a rational solution of a new principle, of toleration, that violates Hobbes's notion of absolute sovereignty. Locke's important differences from Hobbes bring him much closer to the politics of today's liberal democracies and thus justifies Locke as our founder of liberalism. Locke's fundamental similarity to Hobbes in the concept of the state of nature, natural rights, self-preservation, and government by consent, calls for the rather grudging title of first proto-liberal to Hobbes. And while honors are being awarded, let us not forget Montesquieu, the "celebrated Montesquieu" of the American founding, who wanted to surpass and even eclipse Locke as the better founder of liberalism, and succeeded in part.[17]

Locke shares in the fundamental character of modern political philosophy, seen so far in Machiavelli and Hobbes, of lowering the standard of morality in order to achieve a more rational result. In Machiavelli this "downgrading" was learning how to be not good, and in Hobbes it was a recovered morality by comparison with Machiavelli, but a morality of self-preservation much lower than that taught by the ancients. Locke accepts this lower standard from Hobbes, and adds to it a more elaborated hedonism, setting pleasure ahead of good. But he adds a notion of duty to "the rest of mankind" to Hobbes's settled self-preference, though that duty is often in name only when it competes with one's self-preservation.

Machiavelli's concept of indirect government is clearly at work in Locke as well—the exercise of control by government indirectly so that government does not appear to rule or oppress its subjects. Locke's grand concept of Property allows men to acquire private property and become rich rather than rely on their virtue or public spiritedness or sense of duty to achieve a good life. Less control yields better control, as with arguments made today in favor of relying on "the market" rather than a directed economy. The same indirectness is used in Locke's constitution, with its separate powers rather than single source of rule to gain control. His idea of the rule of law does not attempt to specify directly what are good, rational laws but rather to establish a legislative power, checked by the other powers and by elections, to make laws that will be more readily obeyed than specific laws that are imposed. Toleration, too, has an indirect character. It is better with toleration to sustain a more or less free market of ideas than directly to impose good or sacred ideas and practices. With Locke, Machiavellianism finds its way into the self-government of liberalism.

CHAPTER FOUR

JEAN-JACQUES ROUSSEAU

(1712–1778)

WE HAVE DEFINED MODERNITY as based on the belief that man is alone, free of any obligations to God or to nature. Men have been given very little and they owe very little or no gratitude. On the contrary, they are very needy; whoever made man botched the job or never finished it. They made men needy and neglected to supply those needs; man has to provide for himself, guided by human necessities. This we have called a project of rational control carried on for humans and in this world. Man's freedom turns out to be the freedom to answer his own needs with his own arms.

To do this, to concentrate on human necessities, men have to address controversies regarding things above their own needs. They must consider how to address controversies over human *ends*—about religion and the good life. These are typically called "metaphysical" questions because they are beyond ordinary human science concerning necessities. In the course of history and political science, it appeared that there were two ways of dealing with inconvenient controversies: One could settle them or set them aside (bracket them). One could settle on a single official religion that was nondescript and undemanding or have no official religion at all. The first solution attempts to be inclusive of all religions or all civilized religions; the second offers no comment on religion. Both ways have difficulty with religions requiring human sacrifice, then being discovered in the new world of America. These practices can neither be included as official nor allowed to unofficially exist. It appears that one cannot address controversies over human ends without considering issues above men. It had always been supposed that men, in their gratitude, should somehow devote themselves to things above men. But if the next world doesn't matter, then differences over it do not matter. Modern societies may either settle religion or set it aside, but it seems that both ways assume a general stance hostile to religion.

Encountering Rousseau

At this point we encounter Jean-Jacques Rousseau, who confronts modernity and questions its faith in reason. The reason of modernity takes its power to motivate from unreason, from fear and the desire for self-preservation. Rousseau rejected these lowly means and advanced the thesis that progress in science and civilization does not bring progress in morals, as Hobbes and Locke had supposed, but rather retrogression. His treatise on education, *Emile*, tried to keep a boy from being corrupted by

MAJOR WORKS OF ROUSSEAU

Discourse on the Sciences and the Arts (1751): The "First Discourse" made Rousseau famous as the earliest major defector and critic of the eighteenth-century Enlightenment.

Discourse on Inequality (1755): The "Second Discourse" traces inequality from an apolitical state of nature through the formation of society.

Discourse on Political Economy (1755): The treatise that prefigures Rousseau's later arguments in the *Social Contract* and introduces the "general will."

The Letter to M. D'Alembert on the Theater (1758): An essay on the relation between politics and the arts.

Julie, or The New Heloise (1761): Rousseau's epistolary novel, one of the most popular and influential philosophical novels of the eighteenth century.

The Social Contract (1762): Rousseau's central work of political theory that establishes the foundations of political right on the sovereignty of the people and its "general will."

Emile, or On Education (1762): The treatise, identified by Rousseau as the most comprehensive of his writings on political philosophy, that considers the opposition between the innocent and apolitical character of human nature and the moral requirements of society.

The Confessions (1769) and ***The Reveries of the Solitary Walker*** (1778): Rousseau's late autobiographical writings on the "goodness" of human nature and the fundamental tension between the individual and society.

the society that Hobbes and Locke had left free. He invented the notion of *bourgeois* to describe liberal society that was to torture liberalism ever after. Like his modern predecessors he was a revolutionary, but he was less cautious and more democratic; he became a hero of the French Revolution that came soon after him. He departed from liberal self-preservation to examine himself in several works of confession toward the end of his life, questioning and judging himself in a manner to compete with St. Augustine's *Confessions* and to earn from Edmund Burke the label of "philosopher of vanity." Even if so, he was also the master of paradox, and his writings glow with surpassing force and vivacity.

Now in the eighteenth century, Rousseau was able to see that in all the ruling intellectual circles of Europe, modernity was no longer merely imagined and advocated but established. Not all regimes were modern, but modern regimes led the others. Even the ancien régime in France was rationalizing itself before the French Revolution in 1789.[1] Above all were the curricula of the universities. Hobbes had said that Aristotle controls the university (L 1, 46, 47); by the end of the seventeenth century John Locke controlled it—or, to exaggerate somewhat, it was Hobbes through his student, Locke. The ancient writers were not displaced entirely, though the Romans were favored over the Greeks in accordance with the modern preference for size and power. Nor was Christianity destroyed, but it was enervated, made tolerable, and made reasonable, in the sense of Locke's book *The Reasonableness of Christianity* (1695). This was not true everywhere or for a majority of Christians, but it was true of the leading lights. Christianity was not rejected or replaced but it was desensitized, made "latitudinarian," or as we say, with a big tent. It was no longer *the* authority in morals. The pious frown of the common priest or preacher had begun its transformation into the fixed, all-consuming grin of the modern cleric.

Moreover, and most significant, actual modern regimes—Holland and England—existed that were grounded in modern principles. They had adopted religious toleration, encouragement of commerce, constitutional government, and protection of individual rights. When these principles were established, they faced the test of their claim to represent progress. Of course, they were improvements on the Dark Ages, the "Kingdom of Darkness," as Hobbes called it. But were they better than the ancients? This was not so easy to demonstrate. It was not enough to say that modern *principles* were better than those of the ancients, though misapplied, because the superiority of those principles was supposed to be their realism—that is, their greater applicability to the world of fact. It would be disastrous to discover that realistic principles did not work and thus were not realistic. One would have thrown away the highest principles of the good life in order to be sure of self-preservation, and then not even achieved that. It is surely better to fail with the highest principles than with the lowest. It was therefore necessary to prove not the possibility but the actualization of modern principles. Had there been progress defined as the further "relief of man's estate," in Bacon's phrase?

This is just what Jean-Jacques Rousseau questioned in his *First Discourse, Discourse on the Sciences and the Arts*, his first publication (1751). In it he aims to show that moral progress is not the same as intellectual progress in the sciences and arts. In fact, the two kinds of progress work in inverse proportion—the more intellectual, the less moral. The rise of modern science has brought decline in modern morality, and the value of the whole modern project is questioned and denied. Later, in the *Second Discourse* (1755), Rousseau carries his analysis further. He shows that man is perfectible, and capable of infinite progress, but also of infinite degradation. Here is a challenge to the whole idea of rational control, presuming that science is good for us. The range of Rousseau's writings is remarkable, running from the two discourses, to works on politics and on education, on the theater, a novel, and personal confessional works, together with plays, writings on music, botany, and political economy. His influence on the rest of his century, and especially on the nineteenth century, was colossal.

None today would be considered a disciple of Rousseau, but everyone is affected to the extent of his depth by the movements that emerged from his pen. The list includes nationalism, in which the nation appears as a pre-political unit; romanticism, expressing the solitary genius and the lover; socialism, in which society owns all or the most important property; anarchism in defiance of all government; historicism, for which human nature is made in a historical development of accidents; evolutionism as development in gradual stages; revolutionism as the overturning of illegitimate government in the French Revolution and thereafter. In the twentieth and twenty-first centuries, Rousseau can be seen behind the division of the Left and Right in politics, for and against the bourgeoisie—which Rousseau invented by distinguishing bourgeois as town dweller from citizen as the free founder of self-government (SC 1.6, p. 173n). I once gave lectures on Locke and Rousseau to an audience of judges: all those appointed by a Republican preferred Locke, all those by a Democrat loved Rousseau. Yet no one can love or reject Rousseau in every regard, for he is too contrary or too wise not to supply checks to all the passions he enthuses.

Rousseau Versus Hume

In Rousseau's *First Discourse,* a writing he later criticized as "at best mediocre" (FD, p. 5), one sees Rousseau at his youngest but also, perhaps, at his most comprehensive. His works as a whole reveal within them a basic distinction between those that regard politics as a serious solution to the human problem and those that do not. The *First Discourse* combines these two aspects and can be seen to anticipate most everything Rousseau later says. It consists of a critique of politeness, the courtesy that is the main attribute of modern behavior, and a defense of the frank and honest morality that politeness wants to replace. To understand the, to us, rather surprising importance of politeness, it is helpful to consult the *Essays, Moral, Political and Literary,* of David Hume (1711–1776), first published in 1741. One essay of Hume's, *Of the Rise and Progress of the Arts and Sciences*—precisely the topic of Rousseau's *First Discourse*—was published in a 1742 edition of Hume's *Essays,* nine years before. It is as if Rousseau were replying directly to Hume, although he was also criticizing other modern writers such as Locke, Shaftesbury, Hutcheson, and especially Montesquieu. Montesquieu had taken care to praise the virtue of the ancients but he took his stand with the moderns when he "paid homage" to modern times and endorsed the authority of "Today" over that of yesterday's tradition and the greatness he admitted in the ancients.[2] Among and yet somehow above all these defenders of modernity stood Voltaire, august master of the French *philosophes,* the maître d' of the Enlightenment. Yet Hume provides the most convenient summary of the modern ideas Rousseau opposed.

In his essay *Of Civil Liberty,* Hume praised that modern invention for refraining from the imposition of ancient virtue and confining itself to the restraint of dangerous passions. Civil liberty limits government and citizens alike; as the rule of law does in Hobbes and Locke, such liberty makes it possible for a free state to be large and diverse, and also to be, not a despotic but a "civilized monarchy," like France. Hume legitimizes the very monarchy that the French Revolution was to dismember in 1789. Then, in *Of the Rise of the Arts and Sciences*, Hume addresses the relationship between progress and forms of government. He argues that by providing security, civil liberty becomes the nursery of the arts (of manufacturing) and the (intellectual) sciences, a process that occurs gradually and does not require the leadership of a great legislator or founder. Such progress occurs by "emulation," in which neighboring and independent states or diverse regions of a large state compete and copy one another. Once established, the arts and sciences are easily transplanted elsewhere. Republics favor the growth of science; civilized monarchies favor the "polite arts."

Explaining this distinction, Hume contrasts the ancient republics with the civilized monarchies he saw in Europe and England. Republics nourish the genius necessary to science, but the ancients with the vehemence of their philosophers fashioned schools, like the Platonists, featuring "blind submission" to the master of each, amounting to "a servile philosophy" in all. Under the Church, in later centuries these sects disappeared and were succeeded by the "Peripatetic philosophy" (of Aristotle), "to the utter depravation of every kind of learning." After the discovery of civil liberty the faults of ancient philosophy could be seen behind the domination of Aristotle, both of them too assertive. The modern republic requires that men who want to "be successful" look down to gain the votes of the people; they must be useful. But modern monarchy teaches people to look up to the monarch, like the royal courtiers, and thereby become "agreeable." The strong taste of republicans is abandoned for the "refined taste" congenial to monarchy—hence the political cause of "modern politeness," "civility," and "gallantry." Gallantry is both generous in its deference to one's companions and natural by serving human sociability and correcting those few with disagreeable natures through "refined breeding." Hume concludes that "the company of virtuous women" polishes the mind with feminine modesty, delicacy, and decency. These are the polite arts.

In his essay *Of Commerce* (1752), Hume returns to the contrast between ancient and modern states, again giving advantage to the modern. Suppose there is a successful state that has used the security of its laws to bring more wealth than needed to subsist: What should it do with the surplus? Should it maintain large armies and fleets like the ancients or seek "luxury" (prosperity), as do modern states? The moderns choose luxury, which lessens and checks the ambition of their rulers, for luxury is both the cause and the effect of free government. Luxury withholds the energy of private persons from the support of the state, as with the "industrious and rational" of Locke's regime of property, who make money rather than pursue political glory. The false policy of the ancients was to enlist private persons in public service; they failed to realize that the public is better served indirectly through incentives rather than directly through an appeal to public spirit, which increases the power of the state and encourages wars. In Hume's formulation we note again the indirectness of modern politics.

Rousseau's *First Discourse*

Rousseau begins his preface of *The First Discourse* by showing how little impressed he is by the "Enlightenment" he lives in the midst of. This was rational control out in the open: the assertion of the *philosophes* in France (but including Hume) to claim to rule society, not from the closet or by means of a conspiracy like Machiavelli, but boldly and undisguised in their own name. These characters are many or fashionable, and though calling themselves "free thinkers and philosophers," they would have been as eager for religious persecution in an earlier age as they are against it now. "Philosophy" was just the current rage—that is, not real philosophy but trendy opinions: "One must not write for such readers when one wants to live beyond one's age." There we see Rousseau's ambition as a philosopher who seeks a life beyond his time but in this world. It is still a claim to rule, and not for just a single age.

Then Rousseau introduces himself as an honest man addressing the "truly learned" (*vrais savants*). He is a nobody, a hick, before the awesome Academy of Dijon (a town in Burgundy known today for its mustard). How will he have the nerve? He is defending virtue, and doing so before the virtuous. Here, in a paradox typical of Rousseau, he states the problem of the whole discourse, because he shows that virtue and learning are opposed. How can he defend virtue before learned men? How, too, can he deny his own learning? He is far above the people he pretends to defer to. What can Rousseau contribute to virtue with his own learning?

Rousseau begins part 1 of his discourse with a paragraph of ironic praise for the emergence of science, first out of nothingness and then out of "scientific jargon" worse than ignorance, apparently of scholasticism. Science takes men out of themselves and gives them to the universe, but the grandest feat of science is to come back to the knowledge of man; it seems that taking man out of his obscurity did not help him. Rousseau here gives a hint of his program for himself. He is superior to the scientists of the modern Enlightenment because he brings science back to bear on man. Does this mean that he restores man's original obscurity? We can recall Cicero's remark about Socrates that he took philosophy from the heavens and brought it down to cities and men. After the fall of Constantinople to the Muslims, refugees brought literary works to Europe, from which followed sciences, and the arts of thinking and writing, to the effect of making men more sociable. These works inspired not knowledge but the "desire to please one another with works worthy of their mutual approbation" (FD, pp. 11–12).

This new sociability is based on the needs of the mind as it expands, but they are moral rather than intellectual—or rather immoral because they put pleasure ahead of virtue. The sciences, letters, and arts, more powerful than laws and government, spread "garlands of flowers over the iron chains burdening men," causing them to lose their original freedom. Such is the civility or politeness surpassing Athens and Rome in modern times. For Hume, decent politeness presented in his elegant sentences was a great advance of the moderns over the simple rudeness of the ancients, but Rousseau passionately argues the contrary. For him politeness is merely the appearance of virtue and in fact is veiled hostility rather than true sociability. The essence of politeness is diplomacy, which is practiced with enemies: "The good man (*l'homme de bien*) is an athlete who enjoys competing in the nude" (FD, p. 13). Far from shrouding himself in diplomacy, the good man is perfectly open about his loves and hatreds. Rustic morals show on rustic faces so that the appearance is the reality; sophisticated morals are disguised and unmanly, based on fashion rather than firm opinion and aimed at pleasing others rather than oneself. Politeness in morals produces conformity, and polite people are dullards trying to be brilliant. Rousseau goes as far as to call them a "herd" (*troupeau*), anticipating Nietzsche's condemnation of herd morality.

Corrupt politeness, Rousseau continues, does away with self-trust or confidence, hence with sincere friendship. You cannot know yourself until you know how others esteem you, but you cannot esteem others unless you know yourself enough to judge them and the value of their esteem. Politeness is opposed to self-knowledge and to esteem: one thinks of two psychologists meeting, the first asking "how am I?," the second replying "you are fine, how am I?" The vices of politeness are worse than those of rudeness; Rousseau turns the table on Hume for his praise of modern civility. Thus, politeness indulges in blasphemy instead of swearing, disparaging others instead of boasting, slandering enemies instead of insulting them, and rather than expressing national hatreds it forswears patriotism. With politeness, one disputes at length without ever stating an opinion and replaces rude ignorance with the sophisticated pretense of knowing it all (a peculiar Harvard trait).

What do these bad effects cause in the rise of the arts and sciences? Rousseau gives five examples of societies with a high development of arts and sciences whose citizens had corrupt morals: These are Egypt, Greece, Rome, Byzantium, and China; note the lack of any modern nation of Europe, though the corruption of China is said to be "before our eyes." The presumed target of his potent denunciation of politeness would seem to be France, which is not mentioned, and England, the exemplar of liberalism according to Locke, Montesquieu, and Hume, is also missing. His third bad example is Rome, where Rousseau damns a "crowd of obscene authors," one of whom (Ovid) he quotes on the title page of the *First Discourse.* His denunciation is not without exception or nuance, as we shall see in the *Second Discourse.* Then he lists five good examples of countries that put virtue above progress: the Persians; Scythians; Germans; Romans, when poor and ignorant; and apparently the Swiss, though they are not named. Rome is mentioned in both lists as after and before its corruption by Greek philosophy. No reference is made to Christianity, which offers a new, otherworldly virtue opposed to the frankly this-worldly virtue that Rousseau extols—and which, rather than attacking Greek philosophy, had captured it to serve its otherworldly virtue.

Rousseau's contrast between the bad and the good regimes is resolved, surprisingly, into the single contrast between a virtuous Sparta and an Athens corrupted by philosophy. He delivers a paean to the "happy ignorance" of Sparta as opposed to Athens, "the abode of politeness and good taste, the country of orators and philosophers" (FD, p. 17). He admits the brilliance of Athens but denies the value of "astonishing works that will serve as models in every corrupted age." Yet there is an exception to be found in "some wise men" who resisted general corruption in Athens and denounced it. Speaking of Athens makes one think of Socrates, who was killed by Athens. Rousseau quotes from Socrates's defense of himself in Plato's *Apology of Socrates*. One almost forgets that ugly Socrates would have been exposed at birth in Sparta or killed long before he reached the age of seventy in Athens, where he was permitted to speak in his defense. Rousseau changes Plato's text to suit himself, having Socrates reject the wisdom of "artists" instead of "artisans," as Plato has it. The consequence of introducing the contrast between Sparta and Athens, and then of extolling an exception to Athenian corruption who denounces it, is to align himself with Socrates. The contrast in Hume between ancient coarseness and modern politeness is replaced by Rousseau posing as a new Socrates who claims to love Sparta. The "some wise men" who resist corruption turn out to be Socrates as misquoted by Rousseau from Plato; Cato the Elder in Rome, who is not quoted; Fabricius (a Roman consul in 282 BC celebrated for his patriotic morality), in whose mouth Rousseau places an entire made-up speech; and Rousseau himself, who finishes the first part of the *First Discourse* with a fine rhetorical flourish in support of the "happy ignorance" in which we were left by nature:

> Peoples, know once and for all . . . that nature wanted to keep you from science just as a mother tears a dangerous weapon from the hands of her child, that all the secrets it kept hid from you are so many evils from which it protects you, and that the difficulty you find in educating yourselves is not the least of its blessings. (FD, p. 20)

Rousseau wishes men had left alone the secrets of nature—a surprise for us moderns. He agrees with Francis Bacon that nature has secrets she withholds from man; she is not intelligible, not open, to man. But he disagrees with Bacon that this makes nature the enemy of the human to be conquered. Like a mother, nature has a benevolent purpose in keeping her secrets. Rousseau is in accord with the modern understanding that science consists in discovering nature's secrets; nature is closed and does not wish to be understood in its manner of being, yet she does this for a moral purpose. Intellectual progress works against nature to conquer nature, but morality has the support of nature. The usual modern view in Hobbes and Locke, as well as Bacon, Descartes, Spinoza and others is that nature is the enemy of *both* morality and science.

Nature is thought to be unintelligible; it does not disclose itself in ideas or essences, as Plato and Aristotle supposed. Nature obstructs science: we make progress in science only by discovering the secrets she withholds. Scientific experiments "vex" nature (Bacon's term) by removing objects from their usual positions, as did Galileo by theorizing the action of gravity in a vacuum and Hobbes by finding the "state of nature" outside society.[3] Nature is also the enemy of morality. Look what happens to the just person; according to Hobbes, he is lost without an absolute sovereign that is humanly created. In this usual view, science and morality cooperate against nature, using human constructions in science and humanly contrived institutions in politics and morality. But Rousseau declares here that nature is the friend of morality by being the enemy of science.

Thus, it would seem that Rousseau compels us to choose either science or morality. If we choose morality, we must enforce ignorance by maintaining political control over the sciences and the arts. We must believe in something like creationism because it says that nature was created for our good, and not believe in technology that exploits nature by exposing its disadvantages and hardships, such as cloning human beings to avoid the troubles of natural birth. But if we choose science, we run the risk of an explosion as human morals worsen as human power grows. This looks like a choice between primitive obscurantism, called "happy ignorance" by Rousseau, and nuclear or climate catastrophe. Does Rousseau have a solution for this agonizing choice? We shall see. It is enough now to emphasize the problem he raises. There is hardly any issue today more fateful than the question of whether modern science is the friend of politics and morality, as Hume says, or the enemy, as Rousseau says. It is easy to say it is both friend and enemy, but which of the two prevails? It is hard to be consistent today, for example, on abortion and the environment. Those on the Left interfere with nature in allowing abortions, but leave the environment untouched in its natural beauty; and those on the Right let nature take its course in births but exploit the environment.

For Rousseau, science shows itself to be the enemy of man by constructing a morality of politeness. Since the relation he finds between science and politeness is not obvious, let it be explained. Intellectual progress, or progress in the sciences and the arts, proceeds through the use of human constructs, such as Hobbes's sovereign and, as we shall see, Rousseau's social contract. Following the necessity of human ideas, hypotheses, constructions, or "connections of names" (Hobbes) as opposed to natural forms, ideas, or essences, Rousseau agrees with modern science. But what happens when these constructs are applied to politics and morals? What we get is universal rules for human behavior, in which men are asked to measure themselves by other men. Universality is the key—not the best example or one's own instinct, but a universal rule. In this view, men do not have any measure within themselves, no natural self-respect or virtue. Nature leaves men naive and proud, two qualities that traditional (or Aristotelian) ethics endorsed to a considerable extent. Yet according to Hobbes, woe comes to one who measures himself by his own opinion of goodness or pride. One must always look to see what the other is doing, and if one does, one sees that the universal basis of human behavior must be fear rather than pride.

Hobbes expresses his universal rule in a reversed version of the golden rule: *don't* do to others what you would not have them do to you (L 14). Note the essential indirectness of Hobbes's version: look at the other person because you cannot be good unless that other person is. For Hobbes, and for moderns generally, morality is other-directed. Now Rousseau tries to show how this rule, which Hobbes states very abstractly in Latin, actually plays out in social manners. The answer is politeness. Politeness means don't *behave* toward others as you wouldn't have them behave toward you. The essence of politeness, therefore, is waiting: wait until you see what others do. At the table, wait to see which fork to use.

Politeness consists in the crucial pause, the hesitation, the elegant inhibition. Whereas impolite persons are always first, they are always doing what is polite to do a little bit later and perhaps elsewhere. They act on their opinions of themselves and their own needs without reflecting on what others will do or how it will look to others. Hobbes seems so impudent, and Hume and Montesquieu so elegant, but the impudence and the politeness are connected. The universality of modern science, applied to morals and politics, yields the formality of modern manners in which pleasing others takes precedence over the moral quality of self-assurance.

Rousseau, one could say, argues on behalf of the typical American—naive, proud, and always smiling.

In the second part of the *First Discourse* Rousseau comes to a defense and description of the morality he shows to be endangered in the first part. He begins by saying that all the arts and sciences have their origin in the vice of human pride. Agreeing here with Hobbes, he points to swellheaded people who did not know how to keep to their modest pursuits. If everyone did their job, there would be no philosophy and no need for philosophy. Besides their origin in vice, the arts and sciences have defective objects: the object of the arts is luxury; that of jurisprudence is injustice; and history is a record of tyrants, wars and conspiracies. Moreover, the arts and sciences have dangerous effects. They nourish laziness, for scientists are useless citizens. Worse, they feel compelled to attack public spirit and to bring religion and patriotism into disrepute. In this they are worse than useless because they produce luxury, which destroys good morals and ultimately even good taste. Artists wish for applause, and to get it, they will lower themselves to the taste of their time, which they proceed to corrupt. The prime example is Voltaire.

Further, while cheapening virtue, the arts and sciences give too much distinction to talents. Talents were a theme in eighteenth-century writers—for example, with Thomas Jefferson, who spoke grandly of an "aristocracy of talents."[4] He did not mean by this a Platonic elite of the most virtuous people, philosophers, but rather a lesser elite similar to what is meant today by a meritocracy. For Rousseau, talents refer especially to facility in making money unnecessarily and generally to everything agreeable rather than useful, everything specialized rather than common. One mustn't forget that the natural equality of people in the state of nature, shown by Hobbes and Locke, establishes not only the natural right of self-preservation but also legitimizes through the social contract the natural distinctions of talents and the resulting inequality. Locke, in particular, was for equality in the state of nature and at the same time said that the "industrious and rational" few should be permitted to heap up money without limit. Thus, as today, equality of opportunity always produces inequality through unequal talents. Rousseau, strongly for equality but unlike egalitarians today, saw that equality of opportunity requires enforcement of simple virtues as distinct from sophisticated ones, and severe virtues as opposed to the agreeable ones for which Hume spoke. Attractive as his arguments are, and remain today, his message speaks to liberals and conservatives but is disconcerting to both. To liberals concerned with equality, he says to aim at virtue; to conservatives concerned with virtue, he says to aim at equality.

Such are the dangerous effects of the arts and sciences. Is there a remedy? Only, it seems, by an alliance of philosophy and morality when philosophers appear who are willing to defend morality. They would be sophisticated people ready to defend and adopt the simplicity of "vulgar men to whom heaven has not imparted . . . great talents" (FD, p. 35). "O Virtue, sublime science of simple souls," Rousseau exclaims at the end of the *First Discourse*. His last words contrast "two great peoples: that the one knew how to speak well and the other to act well." These are the Athenians and the Spartans. Rousseau the philosopher takes his stand with the city that never allowed philosophy and against the city where philosophy thrived as well as the philosophers of his time in the so-called Republic of Letters. The latter, however, did not consider themselves joined to a particular people but took a public stand as a "republic" above all peoples. Rousseau made himself the loquacious philosopher of Sparta, the defender of good morals (*bonnes moeurs*). He also left a half dozen bastards in various orphanages—but let us not hastily accuse him of hypocrisy. He was both spokesman for the vulgar and scientist-philosopher, and perhaps morality is only for those who are tempted and corrupted by immorality. It is characteristic of Rousseau that he never summoned the discretion to keep quiet about this possibility.

We move now to the *Second Discourse*, where Rousseau goes beyond morality and politics to seek their origin in history.

The New Idea of History

At this point occurs a critical juncture in the history of modern political philosophy as rational control. With Rousseau's *First Discourse*, a crack has opened in that notion: Intellectual progress in the arts and sciences, that is, the advance of reason, has not been accompanied by moral progress. Rational control brings more of the first and less of the second, and the easy, obvious superiority of the moderns typical in Machiavelli, Hobbes and Locke is denied. This is trouble enough, but in Rousseau's *Second Discourse* the crack deepens as reason itself comes into question and, under his scrutiny, encounters the facts of history. Reason is not in our human nature. It does exist, according to Rousseau, but it is acquired over history—and as it is acquired, it brings corruption along with civilization. How can there be rational control if reason, the standard by which modern political philosophy judges morality and politics, cannot be relied upon? Rousseau liberates men from reason and its corrupting civilization. The first attempt at rational control by Hobbes and Locke, whom he criticizes explicitly, is a failure. Yet despite these devastating discoveries he does not give up on rational control: human beings make themselves over history. Rousseau's *Second Discourse* is the hinge of modern political philosophy and of this book, by which reliance on reason is replaced by reliance on history. After Rousseau, modern political philosophy centers on history and its rationality in Kant, Hegel and Marx, or the contrary in Nietzsche.

What, then, is the idea of history? The answer will become clear or clearer as we proceed, but some preliminary notion is needed. Can we think of history as a thing, like a frog or a cigar? What is problematic about history requiring us to have an *idea* of it? Look at the phrase "sense of history," often used to describe what some callow intellectual lacks. Sense of history is not like a sense of smell; there must be some problem concerning it. Normally, it means an awareness of different ways of life at different times or places other than one's own. Those with a sense of history are not parochial; they know when the time is ripe or more likely, when it is not. The phrase "sense of history" makes History (with a capital H) the judge of human affairs. People say today that History will decide, not philosophy. Philosophy considers what is permanent and eternal and asks how important humans are in that light. History assumes that humans are important and that what happens to them is of central and ultimate concern, never mind eternity. When History is judge, philosophy is bent to its will and made subordinate. Or is this a decision by philosophy, such as Rousseau's?

Let us return to the idea that history is a thing—this is what is new. The view of the classical thinkers was that the facts of history are not knowledge. Facts come and go; they are ephemera and knowledge is of permanent things. Facts had to be invented. Locke and Hume spoke of "matter of fact," and Hobbes spoke of fact as opposed to imagined visions. We take fact for granted when we appeal to facts to decide a question, but they were conscious of the newness of fact. Machiavelli did not use "facts" as we do but he began the sense of history with his notion of effectual truth. If truth is in the effect of a notion, of how it works out, then history as the sum of effects is the truth. Moral truth, as well, is "according to the times," for Machiavelli. "Fact" and "effect" come from the same Latin word *facere*. The ancient historians, whom Machiavelli advised to be studied, did not share the modern idea of history. To them the history of Rome, for example, was the series of accidents that happened to Rome; it was not Rome itself. Herodotus, Thucydides, Livy, and Polybius thought the history of their subject was worth writing about: the Greeks and Barbarians, the Peloponnesian War, or Rome. The modern historian would never say that the Peloponnesian War was the greatest war ever, as did Thucydides; such a claim would be lacking precisely in a "sense of history."

In our contemporary view, certain historical events might be taken as more important than others, but only because they are more historically important, not because they reveal the truth of things more than other events. For modern historians, all history is equally history and everything historical deserves to be covered. Unimportant events become important by their continuity with important events. History consists in continuity; its periods lead into one another. Even contrast of periods—for example, medieval versus Renaissance—can be understood as part of continuity, for what did not happen is part of what happened. Two apparently contrary aspects of History can be identified in this brief sketch: that History is a thing (or to be fancy, a dimension of reality) and that it is continuous. Somehow these two aspects must be brought together and unified to make History with a capital H.

Rousseau is the key philosopher in the discovery of History.[5] History was clearly present in theories of prescription central to the political philosophy of Hume and Edmund Burke. Prescription is a right to property or usage that can be acquired if it is exercised for a long time—in the beautiful phrase of the jurist William Blackstone, "time whereof the memory of man runneth not to the contrary." But Rousseau went deeper, not so far as Hegel's philosophy of history but far enough to prepare it. In the *First Discourse*, we have seen, he attacked the idea of progress in which Hume put so great stock and at the end presented a choice of evils between primitive obscurantism against science and moral corruption with science. Rousseau seems to have had two solutions for this dilemma: a political solution, particularly in the *Social Contract,* and a nonpolitical one in his autobiographical writings. Neither is presented in the *Second Discourse.* Instead, he attempts to prepare both solutions by transcending the distinction between science and morality.

Rousseau shows that it is necessary to go beyond morality to its origin, which he must do, of course, with the aid of science, thus overcoming the opposition between the two. In Plato's *Republic,* Socrates made a defense of justice, yet to do so he went above justice as normally understood to defend it as the wisdom of philosophers. Rousseau, with a similar task, does not go above morality to something higher but goes back to its origins, to the condition of pre-morality. He had shown in the *First Discourse* a contrast between the simple morality of Sparta and the sophisticated, corrupt morality—not so much of Athens but of contemporary France, his true target. Simple morality, however, is still morality, and Rousseau takes us back in time to the simpler condition *before* morality to explain morality from its origin: this is the modern scientific method of reducing the complex to the simple and then reconstructing it from its simple elements. He does not follow the method of Socrates, who instead of descending to the simple ascends from the imperfect to the perfect or the best.

A first look at the *Second Discourse* reveals a surprising number and variety of preliminaries, making it very thoroughly introduced. There is a graphic picture of a Hottentot "savage" rejecting civilized garments so as to "return to his equals," then a title page with Aristotle's statement—in agreement?—that nature must be found in what is good and not what is depraved. Both of these, indeed all of Rousseau's references, deserve to be inspected by a careful reader. Following these is a dedication to the republic of Geneva, next a preface, a notice from Rousseau instructing careful readers to study the footnotes (an earlier translation of the work by G. D. H. Cole included this notice but omitted the footnotes), a statement of the question that the *Second Discourse* will address, and at last the text, but with an introduction to its two parts. The first part is about man in the state of nature and the second is about how man escapes the state of nature. We will proceed through these two topics, as with the *First Discourse,* and conclude with comparisons between Rousseau and Socrates, as well as Rousseau and Hobbes and Locke, his inadequate predecessors in describing the state of nature.

Hasty readers skip the dedications of philosophic texts, thinking them of no account. But a dedication supplies an indication of an author's intended audience and of what he thinks he can convey of his purpose to that audience. Or is that too complicated? The author tells what the book is about insofar as that audience can and should know of it. This dedication is very odd: Here is a discourse that culminates in the assertion that politics is a necessary evil because it establishes an artificial inequality among humans, yet this one is dedicated to Rousseau's hometown, Geneva, and stated in terms that seem to exaggerate its freedom from corruption—to put it mildly. This discourse on "natural man" begins with a reference to the honor that only a virtuous citizen may render to his fatherland. But on examining Rousseau's praise of Geneva, it seems to disappear in if's and qualifications put in the conditional tense. He also states demonstrable falsehoods, such as that Genevans were happy and uncorrupt, untouched by prodigal manners, their women simple and virtuous—all things denied by Rousseau elsewhere or known to be false by him. He even delivers a eulogy of his father as "the virtuous citizen to whom I owe my being," supplying him "the tender instruction of the best of fathers" (SD, pp. 47–48). This of the man who deserted both his son and his fatherland. But it was perhaps the "virtuous citizen" that he wanted to describe rather than actual fact.

What does Rousseau mean by giving lying praise to his father and fatherland? He is about to make an inquiry into the root of morality, from which morality will be shown to derive. But morality that is derived is no longer valuable simply for itself, as moral conduct wishes to be. The moral person does not have a nonmoral motive derived from outside morality, such as self-interest or pride. With his fulsome description, this is what Rousseau provides. He reminds us that his inquiry, which will not justify his words of praise, must be brought back to morality as it is today, practiced by people as they are today. The study of "natural man" must improve knowledge of the duties of the civilized human, the citizen; in transcending the opposition between science and morality, he must come back to the problem it presents. We do not have "natural man" today. Our politics may be necessarily *evil,* but politics is also a *necessary* evil. If one insists on calling it evil, one will make it worse than it has to be. It is a question whether Rousseau, with the wide and various influence of his works, kept to the standard of responsibility he shows here. In his condemnation of political evil, did he not loose passions and yearnings that he had no sufficient way to control? Rational control calls for prudence and moderation, as well as rationality.

The preface to the *Second Discourse* begins with a promise to take up "the most useful and least advanced" of all human knowledge, the study of man (SD, p. 51). Rousseau's subject is the "source of inequality." His title page reads "On the Origin and Foundations of Inequality Among Men." The question proposed by the Academy of Dijon was, "What is the origin of inequality among men and is it authorized by natural law?" Rousseau reduces the academy's question to the "origins and foundations" of inequality, then reduces that to "sources." The source is the foundations, and since "natural law" is dropped, its relevance is doubtful. Natural law almost disappears from Rousseau's thought; it is almost replaced by history. Now, why is the study of man difficult? The difficulty is in distinguishing what belongs to the original constitution and what has been added by "the sequence of time and of things." This sequence is very familiar to us in the word not used but fundamental to today's natural and social science: evolution.

Hobbes had claimed in the introduction to *Leviathan* that the reader can verify what Hobbes said by looking within himself. Thus, for Hobbes, civilized man still has natural passions, and the state of nature is a recurrent threat to man. Rousseau says that it's not so easy. Human nature, having lost its original simplicity, is now nearly unrecognizable. It is partly artificial, partly natural—a paradoxical expression showing that somehow the nature of man must have changed, since the meaning of "nature" is that which doesn't change. The further we depart from "natural man," the harder it is to know what it is. Men began as equal, as equal as animals are equal. The source of inequality must then be in the changes that have happened to man. This difficulty has not been appreciated, still less understood, so that natural right and natural law have been misunderstood.

Rousseau drops "natural law" from the question he poses because natural law will now have an entirely new complexion. He is making the first adequate inquiry into human nature because his is the first adequate inquiry into the sequence of changes that have happened to man. He discusses three previous treatments of natural law by the ancient philosophers, Roman law, and the moderns. The ancients he dismisses because they contradict one another; they did not seek a definition on which all could agree. The Roman jurists lumped man and animals together and therewith spoke of what nature describes rather than prescribes. Modern writers do distinguish animals from men as moral beings, but to do so they offer metaphysical principles that only few understand.

Rousseau says that natural law must be recognizable to all who submit to it so that they agree. Understanding must include those who do not easily understand and do not reflect. Hobbes's inverted golden rule, which is indirect because it depends on calculation from one's own interest, will not fit the bill. So, setting aside "scientific books," Rousseau says he believes he perceives two principles that precede reason and so speak directly to us because they affect us at the animal level: these are the fundamental desire for well-being and self-preservation (what he later terms love of self or *amour de soi*) and "a natural repugnance to seeing any sensitive being, and principally our fellow humans, perish or suffer" (SD, p. 54). It seems that there are sensitive beings recognizable without reason. Rousseau's paradox is a natural law arrived at by treating men as brutes. Such is the nature of the inquiry and the demand, for which one must construct what Rousseau calls a "hypothetical history."

That was the preface; we are now ready for the introduction (of four pages) to the first part, containing striking passages not easy to understand that challenge scholars and translators. Rousseau finds two kinds of inequality: natural, or physical; and moral, or political. The latter depends on convention established or authorized by humans; the former has its source in nature, which is not a source. Rousseau denies that one can speak of a source for something political or moral in nature: to inquire as to whether there is any essential connection between natural and political equality is to pose "a question perhaps good for slaves to debate in the hearing of their masters" (SD, p. 61). So much for Aristotle's discussion of natural slavery in his *Politics*. The question, then, is "to indicate in the progress of things the moment when right replacing violence, nature was subjected to law." The implication is that, though there may be a connection between law and nature, law entirely replaces nature and so eliminates "natural law." Then comes a famous statement: "The philosophers who have examined the foundations of society have all felt the necessity of going back to the state of nature, but none of them has reached it" (SD, p. 62). These are the modern philosophers, and their mistake has been to put *social* ideas into the state of nature, where they do not belong. Their second mistake, connected to the first as will be seen, is that they failed to consider the passage of *history* in the state of nature.

We arrive at the challenging passage in which Rousseau explains the method of his inquiry. Rousseau says:

> Let us begin by setting aside all the facts, for they have no bearing on the question. The research that may be undertaken in regard to this subject must not be taken for historical truth, but only for hypothetical and conditional reasoning more appropriate for clarifying the nature of things than for showing their genuine origin and similar to the reasoning our physicists employ all the time with regard to the formation of the world. (SD, pp. 62–63)

He adds that religion orders us to believe that God made men unequal, but it doesn't forbid making conjectures about what humans might have been if left to their own devices.

What does it mean "to set aside all the facts"? No wonder the passage has aroused so much dispute. First, it means setting aside all the so-called facts in the Bible. As argued in chapter 2 on Hobbes, but partly concealed here by Rousseau, the modern state of nature is entirely incompatible with the Bible. Second, there can be no facts about the state of nature because no one would have had the time and security to record it and, as Locke said, no one could write at the time (ST §101). And third, most important, Rousseau is using the scientific method of "our physicists," which is the hypothetical and conditional reasoning set forth by Hobbes. Hobbes had said in chapter 7 of *Leviathan* that men have no absolute knowledge of past facts and science must proceed with "if . . . then" propositions. Rousseau means something similar; he will produce a hypothetical and conditional history of man that shows, by separating the natural from the artificial, how man *must* have developed. This is the construction by hypothetical reasoning of the typical history of man. One must set aside facts about men as they are now, because men now are far removed from their original nature; one must set aside facts in the sense of what today's science of anthropology might tell us about the actual sequence of human societies or "cultures" in its lingo. This sequence is just a matter of chance. What is not a matter of chance for Rousseau is the sequence of stages in human history—for example, that men have to acquire reason before they can acquire morals.

Some say that this passage offers only an ideal type, a hypothesis that Rousseau does not necessarily believe but only adopts and uses—which would mean that Rousseau does not describe the nature of man in his *Second Discourse.* He does say that the state of nature no longer exists and perhaps never existed, but he insists that it is necessary to know it correctly in order to judge it correctly. One cannot know whether it ever existed on the Hobbesian ground that there can be no absolute knowledge of particular facts, but it matters a great deal whether it *could* have existed and how it was. Rousseau cites facts throughout the *Second Discourse,* especially in the endnotes, to indicate that the state of nature was a fact. Why else would he mention orangutans? The difficulty is that knowledge of the state of nature cannot be arrived at through the study of facts; the problem is harder than Locke thought. Locke remarked that you would not say that Xerxes's army (of Persians) were never children because we never hear of them except as grown-ups (ST §101). But for Rousseau, men have changed much more through history than they would have changed by natural growth from child to adult. Locke's remark shows him to be relying on the fixed human nature described by Aristotle even as he departs from Aristotle's notion of limits on acquisition that accord with human nature. Rousseau is more consistent, more Machiavellian, and more radical.

The Sequence of Accidents

We have reached the first part of the *Second Discourse.* Rousseau begins with "man" as an animal, taken bodily as he is now. It would be well for him to have had evidence of bodily changes also—not just Darwin's 1859 theory of evolution about a century later—but evidence from comparative anatomy not available to Rousseau. In his notion, the human animal has super-animal gifts and no artificial faculties. What is he? "The most advantageously physically organized" animal. Though the simplest human, he is the most complex animal. Organized for what? That is left open, though Rousseau does say that man's eyes look to heaven, not just to self-preservation (SD, p. 63). The human animal needs food, drink, sleep, all of which he receives from fertile nature. Nature is more fertile than the artificial fertility of agriculture according to Locke. The condition of its fertility is that there are just a few men living dispersed. Man is by nature vegetarian, though Rousseau notes the fact, given emphasis by Aristotle, that man is not forced to eat any particular food. Aristotle gives this fact a teleological significance: it shows that mans is freer than other animals, free for political life, while Rousseau connects it to man's advantageous organization that frees him from instincts. Man is neither naturally proud, as Hobbes had it, nor naturally timid, as for Montesquieu.[6]

In this state, man has three natural enemies: infancy, old age, and disease. None of these is so great as to cause disorder and conflict. Rousseau's hypothetical reasoning is necessary to make these points, since no actual facts exist for the time, only facts about men as we know them now. Regarding disease, he reasons that the life of reflection and thought is almost assuredly contrary to nature because it makes the body soft. Perhaps he could have reasoned the other way, from hard body to soft mind, that the life of primitive savagery fails to develop the mind; therefore, it is contrary to nature. For does not "develop" mean *fully* develop as to what a thing or being is when complete? In this way man would be defined by his perfection and end. But Rousseau doesn't go this way: His theory will not rest on reason as the difference between man and other animals; he will explain that difference rather than begin from it. At this point we arrive at the moral and metaphysical aspect of man in the state of nature, who has thus far been a well-organized animal. Rousseau cannot deny such differences from other animals, as was seen in his criticism of other modern political philosophers. They explained the moral character of man with a theory that required a philosopher to understand it; hence they could not explain a natural right that is recognizable and direct.

Rousseau says that every animal is an ingenious machine, and man is the same—but with one difference. With other animals, nature operates the machine, but "man" contributes to operations "in his capacity as a free agent," with freedom rather than instinct (SD, p. 71). Man is free to resist nature and is conscious of it; "the sentiment of his power" is the only thing not explained by the laws of nature's mechanics. Freedom, not reason, is the distinguishing feature of man—the freedom to resist nature and to refuse to fulfill his natural function. Here is a difficult thought: How can you refuse to be a man when the act of refusing is what defines you as a man? Perhaps with a bow to the force of this difficulty, Rousseau drops freedom as the criterion of humanity and picks up *perfectibility*. Freedom requires a metaphysics to show how one can escape nature, which was just what earlier modern political philosophers had failed to produce.

To say that man is perfectible is morally neutral; it is the faculty by which humans perfect themselves to an enlightenment that includes both virtues and vices. Perfectibility is to be nothing specifically or originally human, and yet to have the capacity for everything. There is no natural inclination to become better and more fully human. To use Plato's term, there is no *eros* to higher things, no teleological notion that man has a definite end. For Rousseau, man is something special but nothing definite. The something special is the process through which man perfects himself. If men had a definite end, they would have a definite nature to be fulfilled. They would be reasonable creatures rather than free, and would be as free as they are in order to be reasonable. Perfectibility of man means that there is no perfect man; man is like next year's car, always more perfect and never perfect—so as to make room for yet another year's model.

Rousseau said of Hobbes and Locke that they maintained a hidden teleology. They rebelled against Aristotle's view that man has a natural end but they kept the notion of a fixed human nature in the state of nature from which men escape. In the state of nature, men have the same nature as when they are civilized and are capable of the same reasoning. According to Rousseau, the vanity and acquisitiveness of men are not natural but social. Indeed, all passions are social, which means artificial. Men acquire passions in the process of perfecting themselves; passions are not natural. Hobbes and Locke import these artificial passions wrongly into the state of nature. Actually, passions appear later in the state of nature and cause men to fear that state and join society only at the last stage of it. The mistake of Hobbes and Locke was to overlook the passage of time in the state of nature, during which men change from asocial to social; this happens within the state of nature, not by passing from it into civil society. Hobbes and Locke argue that men reason their way out of the state of nature, convinced of the advantages of society and following the law of nature that is the law of reason. Rousseau says that men were social beings only at the last stage of the state of nature, and their nature included both reason and fear at that time. He exposes the hidden teleology of Hobbes and Locke as opposed to the open teleology of Aristotle. They relied on the nature of man to solve the human problem, but this is inconsistent with their view that nature is unfriendly to man. They were not entirely faithful to the modern project of rational control, whose principle is that men must rely on men alone. Rousseau shows that man relies on himself only if he makes himself rather than fulfills a human nature he has not made.

Aristotle says that men are by nature good, and so they join into the polis; Hobbes and Locke say that men are by nature bad, and so they join civil society. But if you rely on man and not on nature, as Hobbes and Locke wanted, men must be neither good nor bad by nature. They must be perfectible, and in the course of perfecting themselves, they make *themselves* good and bad. Rousseau said that the modern, state of nature philosophers did not go back far enough. If you do go back far enough to original nature, you find that men are neither good nor bad, so that one must abandon the modern principle that nature has left men in a predicament. On the contrary, nature has left man in a good state with all natural needs satisfied, for if he had been left in a bad state, he would have a natural inclination to civilize himself—which means that the work of civilization would not have been entirely his own. It must be that men are left in a good state, then, but there's a catch to it. The good state is still animal, not yet human. Humans are made human by perfecting themselves so as to become human. There is a fine distinction between the goodness of nature and the good—or rather, excellence and virtue—achieved by perfectibility, but Rousseau's thought depends on it. In making themselves human, men make themselves both good and bad, in keeping with the ambivalence of progress shown in the *First Discourse*. Perfected humans are capable of crimes, which is not the case with animals.

For Rousseau there can be nothing in nature, including human nature, that inclines men to improve themselves. Human reason is perfected by the passions, and passions are created by needs; yet at this stage men have no needs. One must conclude that reason is not natural to humans. The early moderns, Hobbes and Locke, had used reason against nature; natural law consisted of rules of human reason. Rousseau points out that one cannot rely on rules of reason—that is, progress in intelligence shown in the sciences and arts—because the discovery of truth is not necessarily good for humans. Thus, when you go back far enough, you see that reason is not part of human nature. Language is not necessary to man in the early, pure state of nature. Rousseau wrote an *Essay on the Origins of*

Languages to which this part of the *Second Discourse* could be compared. The savage is not sociable yet not miserable; he has nothing within himself to take himself out of the state of nature. Contrary to Hobbes, man has a natural pity, an innate repugnance to see a fellow human suffering, but this doesn't make man sociable. It doesn't attract one man to another but only makes one reluctant to harm another. Nor, still contrary to Hobbes, does man have a natural vanity—in Rousseau's term *amour propre*—based on comparisons with others. Man has only an *amour de soi-même* based on the sentiment of his own existence. Nor does sex make man sociable, Rousseau says, now in agreement with Hobbes and Locke. That physical desire is only for the opposite sex in general, not for any particular person. One can doubt this assertion that in the vernacular, all cats are gray in the dark. There seems to be something natural in the choosiness of human sexual attraction.

Here in the early state of nature, men are equal because they live like animals. They may of course have unequal faculties, but these are not yet in operation. They come into use only when men start to perfect themselves. Since men cannot perfect themselves by any inner inclination, they must do so *in response* to natural accidents they meet. The paradox is that the more men make themselves, the more they must do so in response to accidents external to them, which are the only way they can be disturbed and forced to perfect themselves. The idea of man's creating himself leads to the necessity that he is subject to his environment. The highest creativity is not to think and plan ahead but only to react after the fact. Thus, man is determined not by human nature with its inclinations (called teleology) but by history. Rousseau perfects modern political philosophy by saving it from inconsistency. Is he himself reacting to external conditions or is he improving it by employing the reason in the great mind he received from nature?

The second part of the *Second Discourse* considers how this creativity by reaction comes about. Human perfectibility happens, and has to happen, by increments, for it cannot skip or leap ahead in great advances by relying on the capacities of human nature. Man gradually makes himself as he is forced out of his animal beginning. Historical continuity replaces Aristotelian teleology toward an end, and history replaces human nature. The stages to this development can be discerned in the three sections of the second part: society, property, and government.

Society comes about by accident as humans encounter difficulties in nature while population increases. When more people live closer together, competition is bound to arise. Yet the first stirring of pride came when humans compared themselves to other animals and realized their own superiority, giving them confidence needed to survive in unforeseen circumstances. The first human act is the self-discovery of freedom, that humans are free from instincts, which itself makes them still more superior. As population increases, families are formed; the competition among men arises, for which elementary rules regulating conduct are established. With families comes property and leisure, hence language; as families are forced together, a larger association forms—a nation.

A nation is characterized by a way of life, formed unconsciously out of common experience, not by a founder or a government. The nation is a crucial way station between the asocial human at the beginning of the state of nature and political man at the end. Rousseau needs some way to explain how men come together that does not depend on a deliberate social contract consciously reflected on. He wants to avoid the mistake of Hobbes and Locke that requires men to be philosophers before they can become civilized. When Rousseau's social contract comes—indeed a deliberate project—men are no longer individuals in the state of nature. They have been formed into nations. This is the first appearance of a pre-political nation in the history of political philosophy. Previously, as by Machiavelli, it was thought that the creation of a nation requires a founder such as Theseus or Moses, performing a political act (P 6), but now, for Rousseau, the nation becomes the basis for politics rather than a result or creation of politics. Later theories of nationalism owe much to this fundamental step of Rousseau's.

The nation stage of the state of nature is an equilibrium of indolence and primitive activity, "the youth of the world," Rousseau says (SD, p. 97). This is where the "noble savage" lives, partly human and not yet political. (That phrase, often heard, does not occur in Rousseau, but is not misleading.) Politics comes as a consequence of disputes over property, as for Locke. Accidents force men out of the natural equilibrium between their desires and capacities, and in response they invent the sciences of metallurgy and agriculture, which bring surplus wealth. Men have leisure to use their talents, until now lying dormant, and large inequalities of property result, producing divisions between rich and poor that lead to frightful disorders and perpetual conflicts. From these comes government. Government is an invention of man, but Rousseau says more precisely of rich men to protect themselves from the poor. This third stage of the state of nature will be discussed shortly with Rousseau's politics.

In the *First Discourse,* Rousseau aligns himself with Socrates as the defender of morality, but this requires that he reconcile his science with Socrates's morality. He could have done this by following the way of Socrates, by showing that justice requires the search for the idea of justice, thus justifying morality through philosophy: philosophy as the perfection of man. In this way, men differ from other animals by having reason, which culminates in philosophy. Philosophy justifies and also criticizes morality, like Rousseau's science. But Rousseau did not accept this way; it is not realistic. As he says in the *Second Discourse,* "While it may belong to Socrates and minds of his stamp to acquire virtue through reason, the human race would have ceased to exist long ago if its preservation had depended only on the reason of those who make it up" (SD, p. 85). Rousseau wants preservation, not perfection. Men are perfectible but not by that in which they are perfect, their reason. The perfection of reason is confined to a few, which makes reason a weak reed. Rousseau is willing to sacrifice the highest for the sake of what is feasible. For all his criticism of modern morality with its elaboration of politeness, he remains within the modern scheme: the relief of man's estate rather than the *summum bonum.* Not only does he accept modern philosophy, but he radicalizes it. For the sake of their own purposes, Hobbes and Locke cannot be accepted; they tried to be critical but they were not critical enough. They wanted a feasible political philosophy but did not succeed. Their mistake was to retain a vital remnant of ancient philosophy in the special status of man in nature as the only reasonable being. Next we turn to how Rousseau teaches men to create their own social contract, their own politics, using reason and recalling man's animal nature, but without any help from *human* nature.

Rousseau and the Limits of Politics

Are there limits to what can be achieved in politics? Here, too, Rousseau presents a critique of the moderns and a striking half-return to the ancients. The theme of the ancients is the tension between the life of the mind and the life of society, followed by a reconciliation between them.

Philosophy is a challenge to all things taken for granted, which means especially the prejudices of one's own society. The tension is inevitable, and the question becomes whether it discloses an unbridgeable gap between mind and society. The political philosophers—Plato, Aristotle, Xenophon and others—said it does not; the pre-Socratics, Epicureans, and to some extent the Stoics, said it does. This issue was submerged in modern thought, most evidently in Hobbes, who tried to introduce a methodical philosophy or science that would do away with the need of societies to live on prejudice. Even Plato's *Republic*, the best city, had a myth for the nonphilosophers to live by and concluded that this city was a cave of planned ignorance. But Hobbes had a scientific simplification of ethics to live by that is both true (or as we have seen, close to truth) and easy to live by. Truth cannot only be understood by the few but made understandable by the many, who can learn "the easy catechism of the rights of man."[7] Thus the tension is relaxed; philosophy is no longer a danger to society because society is capable of living according to these truths (or semi-truths).

With Rousseau, however, the issue of the tension of mind and society returns to view. Rousseau, as we saw in the *First Discourse*, was dissatisfied, even disgusted, by the view that society can be based on truth, or that society can be enlightened. This was the meaning of the Enlightenment that was fashioned in Rousseau's day. His treatment features the sort of paradox one expects of him: he offers a political solution in the *Social Contract* that appears to reproduce the ruling character of Aristotle's citizen and an opposing nonpolitical solution for the artist independent of politics. We first study the political solution.

Politics, as will be recalled, appeared late in the second part of the *Second Discourse* after the creation of property and of society, in the sense of an unconscious "culture" or nation. When property has been created, the rich usurp it from the poor and the poor engage in banditry. The right of the stronger (the rich) opposed the right of the first occupier (the poor). Rousseau agrees with Machiavelli that the poor, as weaker, are not morally superior to the rich. Both sides misbehave and a horrible state of war ensues. Rousseau agrees with Hobbes that the state of nature is a state of war, but not always, only at the end. Humanity is at the brink of ruin because it could not return to the early state of nature to recover its innocence. The necessary result is government, the happy invention of some rich men wishing to protect their property against the poor. The social contract is a fraud of the rich, and it is irrevocable because the presence of one society requires all others to form societies. All live under civil societies, the law of nations, and the natural humanity or "commiseration" of a "few great cosmopolitan souls," such as, we may suppose, Rousseau himself, who loves the whole human race (SD, p. 103).

Note what happens to pity in the *Second Discourse*. The first men have pity, we have seen, at the sight of the suffering of others of the same species. Being so affected, however, does not make them sociable; it does not make them need others or even help others. Needs come through a long succession of accidents that throws men together, and when men need each other, they no longer have room for pity. They do not look on other men as fellow members of the species but as instruments. When property disputes break out, pity has much less power. And after the social contract is made, pity for fellow men is transformed into patriotism for their own country; pity stops at the national boundaries except for the few rare souls. In politics, pity is tempered by the vanity of one's preferences for natives over foreigners. Politics is a mixed blessing in the *Second Discourse*, where Rousseau explains the origin of inequality; but in the *Social Contract*, where he shows more particularly how society and right might be created and inequality diminished, he never finds a place for pity and never denies that the social contract is a fraud of the rich on the poor. Nevertheless, Rousseau presents his political science in the *Social Contract*, which is the only science that he provides. There must be something special about that science, either that it does not have the defects of the other sciences and arts or has them in significantly lower degree.

The *Social Contract* was published in 1762, the same year as *Emile*, Rousseau's great treatise on education. It has four books: the first on the social contract; the second on its implications; the third on government; the fourth on policies of government. It is an abstract work, especially the first two books, in contrast to other political works of Rousseau on Poland, Corsica, and Geneva that are more specific. Without a dedication to any person or regime, it begins with the bald statement: "I want to inquire whether there can be any legitimate and reliable rule in the administration in the civil order, taking men as they are and laws as they can be." Men as they are: How is that? In the *Second Discourse* Rousseau says that men as they are now are very much changed from how they were originally. They have changed their nature gradually over time and are now ready for politics at the last stage of the state of nature—thoroughly corrupted but capable of receiving the best laws possible.

At this point it is useful to pause to consider an interpretation of Rousseau that does not accept the force of this opening statement and hence does not emphasize the limits of politics. This interpretation began from Immanuel Kant, who we shall see was astounded by Rousseau, and it can be found best in Ernst Cassirer's *The Question of Jean-Jacques Rousseau.*[8] In this view Rousseau resolved the problem of the two *Discourses* that showed men becoming corrupted as they were perfected in the *Social Contract.* This work provided a political cure for corruption that overcomes and transcends the paradox of intellectual progress and moral retrogression; it is the fundamental work that supersedes the *Second Discourse.* In the analysis presented here, this is a mistake. It overlooks the fact that Rousseau declared his most important works to be the two *Discourses* and the *Emile,* omitting the *Social Contract.*[9] It is true that the *Social Contract* offers a political cure, and that political science has a special status for Rousseau, but the cure is not complete and political science takes its departure from the last stage of the state of nature. Thus, the *Social Contract* remains bound by the results of the *Second Discourse,* and Rousseau remains faithful to the lowered moral expectation of modern political science that we have seen so far. That reduced morality of self-preservation has the scientific advantage of certainty, as shown in the phrase "legitimate and reliable rule" of Rousseau's opening sentence quoted above. Our analysis will consider the two signature terms of Rousseau's political science, "legitimacy" and "general will," and then proceed to see what legislation it proposes.

Here is the memorable beginning of chapter 1, book 1:

> Man is born free and is everywhere in chains. He who believes himself to be the master of others fails not to be a greater slave than they. How did this change come about? I do not know. What can make it legitimate? I do believe I can resolve that issue.

Man is or was born free (the French bears both meanings) and yet is everywhere in chains, which are forged by men for men. All are caught, master more than the slave, since the master is caught by his needs and enjoyments—a slave in the suburbs. Men make their own slavery, and one cannot blame it on nature as did Machiavelli, Hobbes, and Locke. Rousseau does not know how the change took place any more than in the *Second Discourse*, which presents only a hypothetical history. But he shows how it can be rendered legitimate. Rousseau says as plain as it can be that he makes the chains legitimate rather than strike them off. The history of man is irreversible. In the *First Discourse* Rousseau says that civilization puts garlands of flowers on "men's chains," and in the *Second Discourse* he says that the social contract is a fraud of the rich on the poor. Rousseau will make the fraud legitimate but no less a fraud. Rousseau's notion of legitimacy has the taint of Machiavellian fraud but, in common with Hobbes and Locke, the nicer name of "contract." As against them, Rousseau is more candid about the drawbacks of a contract and also more careful to address them.

Next, what makes the chains of society "legitimate"? Rousseau had said "I shall always try to join what right permits with what interest prescribes, so that justice and utility are not always at odds" (SD, p. 163). Socrates had said something similar, that justice and utility are different but must not be separated, but he argued from regard to what is best. In the *Republic* he shows that the best justice is possible if not feasible, so that the best justice and greatest utility are the same at the highest level—not merely united. Rousseau starts at the lower level of interest. "Men as they are" need government to put an end to the war at the last stage of the state of nature. Men are responsible for that war, as well as for the chains they need to emerge from. Their interests have been forged by themselves. Self-interest, for Rousseau, means not only the interest of the self but also created by the self. Then, if you want to join right to men's interests, it would seem necessary that right come from man and only from man. Rousseau says that the right he is looking for comes not from nature but from a convention. This he shows in chapter 2 regarding the most ancient and natural association, the family. Family is natural, but one cannot argue from that fact about family to society. Rousseau makes a sardonic remark about King Adam and Emperor Noah: Adam was sovereign because he was alone, not because God created him first. The basis for natural rule in the family is the right of the stronger, and this works in the family because the father loves his children. Why does he love them? Because they are his own—which is not true of ruler and subjects.

Rousseau proceeds to argue against the right of the stronger: "The stronger is never strong enough to be forever the master unless he transforms his force into right and obedience into duty" (SD, p. 166). This possibility of transforming force into right does not depart from the statement in the *Second Discourse* that society and its political rights are formed by a fraud, because the "right" into which force could be transformed here is still understood as a form of force. Force *to be strong* must transform itself into right. Then Rousseau says that if force makes right, you would switch allegiance to the new bully on the block as soon as that bully replaces the old one. Such disloyalty might seem unjust, but is it? "Force" might mean something besides the ability to win fights by means of dirty tricks. Suppose it was athletic prowess: When a new wrestler joins the team and is stronger than everyone else, would he not be given the first place—or in tennis, be put at the top of the ladder? Or suppose it is intellectual power. When some new thinker arrives on the scene, are we not obliged by *natural right* to read his books, sing his praises, follow his train and join his band? Rousseau is opposing not so much the conventional might of the bully as he is opposing the idea that natural gifts are the sources of duty and right. Instead of distinguishing the deserving force of the natural best from the bully, Rousseau discards both as illegitimate. There is no natural authority, a conclusion confirmed by chapter 4 on slavery.

At the end of the *Second Discourse,* we have seen, Rousseau tells us that there is natural right in the state of nature. But in society he makes right totally exclude nature: "Because no man has any natural authority over his fellow human, and because force produces no right, conventions remain as the only basis of all legitimate authority among men" (SD, p. 167). Then he says in the title of chapter 5 that it is always necessary to go back to the first convention because only convention makes right or duty or justice in society. Conventional right replaces natural right, civil liberty replaces natural liberty; neither is derived from nature. Conventional right comes from man alone; it is his own and it owes nothing to nature or anything external. Natural gifts like intelligence do not provide a title to rule in society. Thus "to render legitimate" means to make one's own. Men make force into right by making their own right—despite the favor shown to the "few great cosmopolitan souls" in the *Second Discourse.*

Moving now to chapter 6 of book 1 "On the Social Compact," we encounter Rousseau's signature notion of the general will. He first tells us where "men" are:

> I assume that men have reached that point where the obstacles that interfere with their self-preservation in the state of nature prevail over the forces that each individual can use to maintain himself in that state. Then the primitive state can no longer persist, and the human race would perish if it did not change its manner of being. (SD, p. 172)

This statement directs readers to the end of the *Second Discourse*. Then Rousseau states the problem:

> "How to find a form of association that defends and protects the person and goods of each associate, with all the common force and by means of which each, uniting with all, nonetheless obeys only himself and remains as free as before." Such is the fundamental problem to which the social contract provides the solution. (SD, p. 172)

Note that each person is to remain as free as before and *not freer*, as he does in the Kantian interpretation. He is to be as free as he was just before joining the association; Rousseau is not comparing social man with natural man in general, but as he was just before becoming social. He continues: "The clauses of this contract are so completely determined by the nature of the act that the slightest modification would render them null and void." They require the "total alienation of each associate with all his rights to the whole community" with no reservations (SD, pp. 172–173). Now, why is this required by the nature of the act? Hobbes and Locke said nothing quite like this. But for Rousseau, the nature of the act is the making of conventional right entirely disjoined from natural right—the two are mutually exclusive. You must give up to the community everything that would give you a claim by natural right—the claims of your strength and character—and of course everything you may think is yours, your property.

The alienation produces the association, which is complete and leaves nothing for private individuals within it, and "since each gives himself to all, each gives himself to no one." The association is a moral and collective body receiving its unity, collective personality, life and will—the general will—from the same act as makes it an association. Society and right are made at the same time by the same act; by the alienation of everything that belongs to them, men make a sum of forces with one motive, a greater might with right. The total alienation in the social contract is the solution for the otherness, the lack of integrity, the dependency of most men. In the *First* and *Second Discourses*, men are held to be degraded because they compare themselves with others; they measure themselves by external standards and they follow the morality—if it deserves the name—of politeness. Polite men are afraid to be good, afraid to be natural, always looking to the other fellow for their guide. Rousseau says that by carrying this dependency to an extreme, you can cure it, at least politically. By alienating everything, you create a community that is not dependency because it is all yours. Or it is as much yours as anyone's. You belong to it because it belongs to you, and it belongs to you because you made it. You are a citizen, not just a bourgeois, a town dweller. The far-reaching footnote mentioned above explains that "the true meaning of the word [citizen] has almost entirely vanished among the moderns." Rousseau has split Locke's civil individual into citizen and bourgeois, with the consequence that the bourgeois was venomously rejected from the Left by Marx and from the Right by Nietzsche.

The act of the social compact constitutes the society for Rousseau. No end is outside the act; men do not create a community because they want it to attain a certain goal. They do it to express their freedom—that is, to overcome their subjection to things outside them, their nature and their own external standards. All right is said to be conventional in society, not at all natural. Then what is the guide for making conventions? If natural right cannot guide men, what guide will they use when exercising their freedom? Rousseau's answer is freedom itself. Men make their freedom for the purpose of expressing their freedom in a contract; they use their freedom for the purpose of expressing their freedom; they make a convention for the purpose of making conventional right. The guide for freedom is not anything extraneous to freedom, which is to say that the guide for man is in no way extraneous to man. Machiavelli had said that men must exercise their will in accord with necessity, and in doing so adopt and appropriate the power of necessity as their own for the sake of their virtue. Princes of necessity impose their form on the peoples they master, bringing them freedom from ecclesiastical tyranny. Rousseau expels necessity from the act of making a compact by means of the general will, "a form of association" adopted freely that democratizes society in freedom for all. Yet Machiavelli's necessity lives on in the development of the human race by accidents of history that we have seen in Rousseau's *Second Discourse*. There, as with Machiavelli, freedom appears not in the voluntary pursuit of a goal but in response to new and urgent necessities.

At this point it may be helpful to compare Rousseau with Hobbes and Locke, or to make it simpler, with Hobbes. Rousseau seems to say something new with the magnificent sparkle characteristic of his writing and thinking, but isn't this the same old social contract of seventeenth-century liberalism? It is indeed the old social contract but now revised with a new argument, new implications, and new political consequences.

The new argument is that Rousseau says that right and nature exclude one another—in society. Hobbes had said there is a natural right of self-preservation that remains in society in two ways. First, it means that each person authorizes a sovereign by natural law, which says to keep your promises to obey the sovereign and everything he commands. Every positive law must be obeyed. Hobbes says that natural law and positive law are coextensive (L 26). Rousseau says, to the contrary, that they are mutually exclusive. So direct a contradiction is not often encountered in the history of political philosophy. Further, for Hobbes natural right remains in society through the right of resistance, we may recall, to the executioner. As we shall see, Rousseau denies this. So, for Hobbes you do not leave nature entirely behind when you join society; you continue to have a relation to the state of nature. Every once in a while the state of nature pops up, as when you hear the footsteps of the executioner approaching. Rousseau says that when you enter society you leave nature behind; self-preservation remains the most important end but not by nature, only as the aim of the social contract that will be included in whatever the general will decides and must be freely accepted (SC 1.6, 2.4). There is no teleology for Rousseau, open or hidden. The necessary presence of natural right in society that we see in Hobbes constitutes lingering, hidden teleology.

The difference over natural right is reflected in the argument for making the social contract in Hobbes and Rousseau. For Hobbes, men make the social contract by reasoning about the nature of reason. What is reason? Its fundamental principle is noncontradiction. When you make the social contract, you promise not to contradict yourself, not to go back on your word. Hobbes says that injustice is like absurdity; it is denying what you have made your own. For Rousseau, men make the social contract by free exercise of their capacity for freedom, their capacity to make themselves. The social contract is an invention of reason, part of the perfectibility of man discussed in the *Second Discourse*. For Rousseau, the key word is freedom; for Hobbes, it is reason.

Then what are the implications of Rousseau's new argument for the social contract? The free exercise of freedom is expressed in the general will. The general will has no particular content. Hobbes's society aims at self-preservation, *commodious* self-preservation, as does Locke's. Rousseau does not say this—why not? That is for those who make it to decide. No doubt it must include self-preservation, but Rousseau, or the political scientist, cannot prescribe the content of the general will. That is why the discussion in books 1 and 2 of the *Social Contract* is so vague and abstract; nothing can be said to hinder the freedom of the men making their own standard of right. The general will consists in the act of generalizing through reasoning, as distinct from avoiding contradiction in Hobbes. Because the general will generalizes it cannot be wrong, since the standard is right because men make it so generally. To generalize it must prevent contradiction by avoiding the exclusion of someone's will rather than insisting on consistent reasoning. Or is generalizing the same as consistency? An error could occur only in the form of the contract, if the form were not general. Men cannot have freedom in politics without generality; so a man who refuses to obey the general will must be "forced to be free" (SC 1.7, p. 175). This is the most famous, or notorious, of all Rousseau's paradoxes. A man who wants to make himself an exception must be forced to be free. No one can be free unless all are free, and this requires a general will. In our reluctance to accept this proposition, we recognize the limits to freedom in politics.

The general will is distinct from the will of all, which is a mere addition of particular wills (SC 2.3). This would be the social contract of Hobbes to which all men consent *as individuals*. Rousseau insists on more than consent; one must *alienate* everything and make a society as a free act, not as a means to the preservation of a self that retains its right to consent. This can occur only if everyone forgets himself as an individual in the act. An individual becomes man in the social contract only when he is completely social, because only then is he as free as he can be: He has made himself out of himself through society. Of course, a man is not completely free when he is completely social. One must not forget that Rousseau is making our chains legitimate; he is not striking them off. Here lies the vital difference between Rousseau and Marx. A last implication of Rousseau's social contract is that there can be no partial societies within the society, for they would destroy the generality of the community. He does not mean that all groups must be destroyed, only those that challenge the generality of the community. We shall see which group in particular fails this test.

What are the political consequences of Rousseau's dichotomy between nature and right? A list would include the following. First, there is no right of resistance to government, as we have seen in contrast to the thought of Hobbes. There is also no right of revolution, as with Locke. For Rousseau, the community can at any time disband itself or change its government, but this must be a general act, not a protest of a part of the community on account of individual grievances. Second, there is no representation in politics. With Hobbes (in the *Leviathan*, ch. 16), the sovereign represents "natural man" in society, but for Rousseau this is inconsistent and impossible. Men must make their own laws if laws are to be just. They cannot make them indirectly through a representative. Yet the distinction between sovereign and government in Rousseau, by which the sovereign chooses the government to execute its laws, means that the government is indirectly the will of the people when engaged in executing. Third, there are no limits to sovereignty in Rousseau. He has none of Hobbes's hesitations on this point, arising from the continuance of the right of self-preservation in society, and he is very far from Locke's notion of limited government in regard to the sovereign, though limits do exist in the government executing sovereignty. Fourth, there is no tacit consent in Rousseau's formulation, though one can presume consent from universal silence when the people could have opposed a law (SC 2.1). Tacit consent is a presumption that a person would have *reasonably* consented in a situation from which he receives benefits, like the advantage of security from government. One can presume upon someone's reason but not upon his freedom. Freedom has to be exercised for oneself. This would be Rousseau's criticism of the liberal theory of John Rawls, which relies on a reasonable representative to supply consent rather than actual voters.

Fifth, Rousseau's state must be small and homogeneous. Its citizens must trust one another if they are to alienate everything to the community and receive back everything from the community.

Such is the general will, its argument, implications, and consequences. But as one might perhaps expect, it is too general. It must be particularized by legislation, as happens in books 3 and 4 of the *Social Contract*. Rousseau is both more abstract than Hobbes and Locke and more concrete than they are. The general will is general to a particular people living in a particular situation, and they cannot receive mere generalities as the basis of their social contract. Its form is universal but not the content it invites and requires. Thus, the general will has a particular content, and it varies and must be created by each particular people. That content cannot be specified by the political scientist, the outsider, as Locke (and Montesquieu and Hume) specified the life of a free society as commerce. This does not mean that the general will does not need specific content, but rather that it must be specified *for* that people *by* that people. Yet this includes being specified by a legislator *within* that people. Rousseau, a political scientist, cannot specify the content of the general will, but a legislator of that people can do so. The legislator guides that people to laws and even uses religion to make it receptive, pretending that laws have come down from on high, although all are equal in having to alienate everything in the social compact.

Rousseau has stirring words to describe the character and the work of the legislator:

> He who dares to undertake to establish a people's institutions must feel that he is capable, so to speak, of changing human nature, of transforming each individual, who by himself is a complete and solitary whole, into a part of a greater whole from which the individual receives, as it were, his life and his being. (SC 2.7)

If changing human nature—"so to speak," for Rousseau does not take ownership of this expression—is the challenge, how is it that the legislator does not invade the sovereignty of the social contract?

> The legislator is in every respect an extraordinary man in the state. If he must be so by his genius, he is no less so by his office. It is not

> magistracy; it is not sovereignty. This office, which constitutes the republic, is not part of its constitution. It is a particular and superior function which has nothing in common with the human realm. For if he who has command over men should not have command over the laws, so neither should he who has command over the laws have command over men. (SC 2.7, p. 191)

"Nothing in common with the human realm" appears indeed to say that the legislator's office is at odds with the principle of the social contract. Rousseau goes so far as to quote Machiavelli's assertion that there was never a "maker of extraordinary laws for a people who did not have recourse to God" (D 1.11.3; SC, p. 193n). "Sublime reason exceeding the grasp of vulgar men" recalls the natural right of the ancients, the rule of the wise. But this wisdom is not likely to emerge, nor is it likely to be agreed to by vulgar men.

Hence Rousseau turns to the legislator's guidance in the creation of mores (*moeurs*). To the three kinds of law that he lists—political, civil, and criminal (note the absence of natural law)—Rousseau adds a fourth, the mores, or customs, of a people, which are so important that their creation is the chief work of the legislator. Among the mores the chief one is a civil religion, described with two features. The first is an open critique of Christianity for dividing the sovereignty of the state and preaching a harmful and submissive spirit to the people (SC 4.8, p. 270). In place of Christianity Rousseau wishes to inculcate a religion of simple dogmas, positive and negative, of which the only negative is denying the principle of intolerance. In these two things, the legislator and the importance of mores, Rousseau is closest to the classical political philosophy of Plato and Aristotle. He adopts their concern for the way of life of a people as a whole and their view of a legislator as the founder of a way of life. But he adapted these two features to a system that is fundamentally different from theirs. Plato and Aristotle thought that political life is natural to man, though with hedges and hesitation, and Rousseau thought that the state had to be created by man. With his concern for the legislator and the mores, he tried to ensure that men create a general will successfully, with eyes open to the circumstances and variations of peoples.

We are now in a position to answer the question with which Rousseau's political argument began: What is different about political science, as compared to other sciences and arts, which are degrading? Political science is generated from within. It is not only a human standard, made by men, but also, unlike the other sciences, a standard whose content is the essence of man, his freedom. The general will is the only truly human measure of man, made by man out of man. It is the general will that renders our chains legitimate. But is this enough? Rousseau is not satisfied with legitimate chains. They are enough for most, but not for the rare few who love humankind.

Rousseau's *Reveries*

We have seen limits to Rousseau's political solutions. In the *First Discourse*, politics is limited because it must either stand in the way of scientific progress or allow moral corruption. In the *Second Discourse* we encounter a still more radical limitation on politics. Politics cannot achieve human goodness precisely because politics is based on morality. Morality is the recourse of men who have lost their natural goodness and who must therefore be content with fraud made legitimate in the *Social Contract*. To repeat the question above, is there not some way, though not political, to save both the natural goodness of men, their premoral compassion, and their humanity—their reason and their science? This possibility is presented in Rousseau's *Reveries of the Solitary Walker* (1778), his last work. This book is part of Rousseau's confessional works, his *Confessions* (1769) and *Rousseau Judge of Jean-Jacques* (1776), and it is a defense of natural goodness as represented in the reveries of the artist (poet?) against the intrusion of political control. As befits Rousseau's love of paradox, one can also find among his works, contrary to the *Reveries*, a defense of morality against artists in his *Letter to D'Alembert on the Theater* (1758). Finding his consistency through his paradoxes is the challenge Rousseau sets to his readers. He inveighs against useless citizens in the *Letter to D'Alembert* and exclaims in *Emile* that "every idle citizen is a rascal"; yet he admits in the *Reveries* that, though he has doubtless done less evil than any man in the world, as a "useless" citizen he has done very little good himself.[10]

With just a glimpse of the text of the *Reveries*, one can see two points of interest, the notion of alienation and the beginning of romanticism. Rousseau begins the *Reveries* with the statement that he is all alone on earth, having no longer a brother, neighbor, friend, or society but himself.

Everyone hates him and plots against him. All are strangers to him. Then, it remains for him to find out about himself. This is the other way besides the general will to escape otherness: the first is to alienate yourself to the general will of the community; this one is to alienate yourself from others. Alienation in both senses refers to something strange that used not to be strange, your property or a friend from which and from whom you are alienated. Your former friend is not simply a stranger, but only now. Your situation used to be familiar but has become strange.

The alienation of existentialism was stated in the works of Jean-Paul Sartre and Albert Camus in postwar Europe: *I* am alienated from the customary world around me, which now appears strange to me. I may call myself "stranger" as did Camus, but only because I look strange to others. In fact, I am alienated from them. Rousseau puts it the other way; it is *others* who are alienated from me. He might think that the existentialists are still moralists who are too much concerned with others' opinions. He might think the same of the revolutionists of the late 1960s. For him, it is the bourgeois who is alienated, not the hippies who in their excessive morality reject the bourgeoisie. The bourgeoisie is alienated through its very civilization, its very morality. Rousseau is innocent; he is not responsible for his present state; the bourgeois are strange to him, not he to them. Only Rousseau, solitary Rousseau, can make contact with the primitive goodness of man; it is the rest, the vast majority, who are alienated.

How can one find natural goodness in the midst of civilization? Rousseau says that civilization is not only compatible with natural goodness but also required to rediscover it in the form of philosophy. Once natural goodness was naturally available instinctually without any effort of philosophy, but today one needs wisdom to recapture it. One needs to read and understand the *Second Discourse*. The difference between early man and civilized man is that between the noble savage and the romantic, who needs philosophy. Rousseau is a political philosopher, thus a politically responsible citizen-romantic, once again a notable paradox. As romantic, he is a sincere rebel without a conscience, walling himself in a romantic or sublime landscape. He has pity for the men he meets, and perhaps love for some of the women he becomes involved with, but he avoids any permanent connection. He lets himself go to reveries, which seem to be between dreams and thoughts.

He allows and receives the passage of images through his soul, for the activity of the philosopher is not natural to man. Early man was more interested in images than in truth, and philosophy is needed today only to recall the nonphilosophic nature of man. In this state of partial recall, Rousseau prefers plants to animals. Plants are the clothing of the earth. They are easily and tirelessly imaginable in contrast to animals, which excite one's pity and get one involved. He is not interested in the stars; wonder is completely lacking in his dreams. Man is the center and Rousseau proves it by studying lower things that can be munched. The solitary walker is the complete man but he is completely nonpolitical. Rousseau of course, unlike his romantic followers, realized in other writings that this view is impractical by itself. Even a solitary walker needs a tranquil society that will leave him at peace. This society will necessarily make its demands on him and exact its price from him as from everyone else. Rousseau, who has been accused of totalitarian sympathies, was fully aware of the extent of these demands. But it seems to be his highest solution to bring the life of man in a full circle back to his origin in the nonhuman.

This conclusion may be suggested. If we wish to maintain our belief that there are limits to what men can accomplish in politics, we must look either to the very beginning of man, with Rousseau and with Machiavelli; with Hobbes and Locke in their apparent diversity; or to the end of man, with Plato and Aristotle. There is not enough comfort in the middle among the facts of civilized life. The advantage of the older way is that Socrates, unlike Rousseau, engages in philosophy in the city and brings his philosophy down to the city. Rousseau seems utterly to divide the philosophic few from the nonphilosophic many, and the reason is that he has abandoned the conception of a common human nature.

CHAPTER FIVE

IMMANUEL KANT

(1724–1804)

In Rousseau we find the turning point in the rise and fall of rational control, where nature, particularly human nature, yields to history. Modernity began in Machiavelli with a critique of nature as the standard for human choice. Nature was an unreliable guide because it left room for chance or fortune to spoil the success of any human who followed it. The nature of a thing is its good, according to the ancients, but it does not always achieve its good. Above all other examples for Machiavelli, men cannot be counted on to be good, and those who rely on the goodness of others easily "come to ruin." But if human nature was not good, it was at least reliable when this failing was taken into account. Nature and fortune taken together, as Necessity with a capital N, could be mastered by men, forcibly making their own guide. Necessity combines nature, previously thought (by Plato and Aristotle) to be unchangeable, with fortune, always blamed for its fickle changes from good to bad and bad to good. Necessity in Machiavelli's presentation enabled *control* of nature, which is reliable change for the good. Necessity gives both a direction toward which to move—progress—and a motivation to act toward that vague but promising end. Hobbes and Locke formalized Machiavelli's necessity of prudence into a science of rights and institutions and a morality of utility.

Rousseau did not abandon necessity. Quite to the contrary, he extended necessity from a motivating guide in philosophy to a necessary "sequence" in history. Humans became human without a guide before them but in response to "accidents" interpreted by the philosopher Rousseau. Rousseau used philosophy to contribute to human progress in its late stage, after human nature had evolved without reference to philosophy. Rousseau first explained the creation of reason and then showed how to use it. He did not presuppose philosophy while expounding it; he showed how philosophy came to be through history. The remaining four philosophers in this book follow Rousseau by basing their systems on history rather than nature. They were all German and wrote in German. The first of them, Immanuel Kant, said at the beginning and at the end of his masterwork *Critique of Pure Reason* that he had made a revolution in philosophy comparable to the Copernican revolution in astronomy. Certainly he believed the fundamental change he set down, called *criticism*, overturned for good all previous philosophy. But whereas Copernicus seemed to diminish human importance by denying that the universe revolved around the Earth, Kant seemed fundamentally to raise the status of human beings, to the extent that they are "rational beings," to a higher level beyond any dependence on nature than ever before. This he did with his thesis of the "spontaneity of the understanding," to be discussed.

MAJOR WORKS OF KANT

Critique of Pure Reason (1781): Kant's "First Critique" aims to determine the limits and the range of theoretical and empirical reason, with a critique of traditional metaphysics and a theory resting on the distinction between a priori and a posteriori knowledge.

The Groundwork of the Metaphysics of Morals (1785): The work that establishes a foundation for morality on the basis of reason alone, independent of human desires or facts. It advances the concept of the categorical imperative, a universal and unconditional command of reason to all rational agents.

Critique of Practical Reason (1788): The "Second Critique" applies Kant's theoretical principles to morality and against consequentialist and utilitarian theories to reach a moral basis for the dignity and free will of the individual.

Critique of Judgment (1790): Kant's "Third Critique" examines the nature of aesthetic judgment and argues that beauty is based on universal conditions.

Religion Within the Limits of Reason Alone (1793): Kant's chief work on religion, which aims to reconcile religious belief with a moral philosophy accessible to human reason.

"Idea for a Universal History with a Cosmopolitan Intent" (1784), *Toward Perpetual Peace, A Philosophical Project* (1795) and "On the Common Saying: That May Be Correct in Theory but It Is of No Use in Practice" (1793): All essays discussed in this chapter.

Immanuel Kant

Kant was born and died in Königsberg (a port city now called Kaliningrad in Russia). He never traveled from that city and was both educated and taught at its university. He was a man of odd habits and unvarying daily routines dictated by his strict morality and confident beliefs. Yet for morals and politics, he spoke for the "cosmopolitan point of view." He was so sure that other rational inhabitants could be discovered in our solar system that he said he might bet everything he had on it. That bet would be his whole philosophy. Though himself an opponent of all actual revolutionizing because it required one to conspire and thus to lie, he was a revolutionary in philosophy. His three critiques, or at least the first one, the *Critique of Pure Reason,* is required reading beyond any other work, including Plato's *Republic,* for every student of academic philosophy today.

Yet that work will not be read for our treatment of Kant. Readers will note that less space is devoted to Kant and his successors, writing in German, than to the earlier modern political philosophers, who mainly wrote in their native languages. Hegel said that he "wished to attempt to teach philosophy to speak German," a sentiment too parochial for Kant, who nonetheless taught Hegel by writing in German. Kant had a subtle relationship with Machiavelli. He openly denounced Machiavelli's immorality and actually accused all morality prior to his own as tainted with Machiavellianism because it was impure. Previous morality was impure because it offered some advantage, above all happiness, to those who followed its dictates, thus adding an incentive but detracting from morality itself. Yet Kant also continued Machiavelli's enterprise. He carried Machiavelli's attack on nature as the guide for human action to a new extreme, and he shared Machiavelli's regard for the utility of doing evil and carried that to a new extreme in historical necessity as well. With these strictures in mind to calculate Kant's debts, one may still consider the true language of modern political philosophy to be Machiavelli's splendid Italian.

Kant's Moral Idealism

Machiavelli had what appears to be a direct contrary in Kant's thought to his doctrine of the necessity of evil. That is the doctrine of moral idealism associated with Kant's name. "Kantian morality" is a phrase not as likely to be heard as "Machiavellianism," but an educated person needs to recognize the outstanding modern alternative to Old Nick. To begin with, moral idealism is not dependent on utility. It's the real thing: being good when there's nothing in it for you. Before Rousseau, modern morality was very dependent on utility; it was almost the same thing. With Hobbes and Locke natural right is seeking self-preservation, your own preservation, together with the preservation of others, as Locke says in his beautiful phrase, "when your own preservation comes not in competition." This is selfishness, but *enlightened* selfishness, long-run selfishness. Recall Hobbes's strictures against the fool who says in his head, and sometimes with his tongue, there is no justice. This fool is refuted by showing him that he cannot count on other people to be such fools as to allow him to break his promises with impunity. And if utility is at the core of morality according to Hobbes and Locke, it is the slogan of the odious Machiavelli: where the act accuses, the result may excuse. Never mind fratricide; think of the consequences—the founding of Rome and the glory of Romulus, which is utility beyond utility.

It is only human to find this doctrine base, even revolting. Are men like other animals, made only for self-preservation? Men have their own peculiar self-preservation by this doctrine beyond that of animals—self-preservation with comforts. Think of the easy life in the suburbs, where homes come equipped with all major appliances, "mod cons" in the British expression. All is designed to mollify the soul with substitutes for passion, concentration, and hard work. Doesn't this improvement on animal instinct suggest that humans are capable of more than preservation? If we can be comfortable animals, why can't we be human? Kant created the doctrine of moral idealism, not so much, as we shall see, to vindicate human nature as to demand that humans rise above their mere nature to the level of rational beings unconcerned with utility yet held enslaved by modern realism.

We have seen, to be sure, that from its beginning in Machiavelli, modern realism contained a strong element of idealism. Recall that modern realism began with the observation that man is free: God and nature have given him nothing to be grateful for and man is not born indebted to a grander person or force than himself. The realism of modern political philosophy consists in the proposition that men must turn their attention to their own necessities, the human necessities of self-preservation. Yet this very realism implied a hidden idealism that man can climb out of his predicament by his own efforts. The conclusions of Machiavelli, Hobbes, and Locke, which seem so tolerant in the face of evil, are counteracted by the inspiring task of building a new society and teaching a new doctrine. Now on the other hand, in the moral idealism of Kant, as we understand it so far, an element of realism can be seen. It is true that we are revolted at the morality that can be reduced to suburban self-preservation. But we do not like to think that our morality will sink away unnoticed in the universe, without consequence, as we "come to ruin." We like to think, and need to think, that it has a place in the economy of things, that however little a moral hero like Martin Luther King Jr. spent his life seeking utility, his life will not prove useless. In the doctrines of the Christians and the ancients, morality was rewarded by God in the afterlife and by nature in this life, and immorality was punished in hell or by having to live in the company of vicious rascals and gangsters like yourself—so to speak, in Las Vegas.

Today, however, the reward of morality is different; it is not from God or nature but in History. One who follows moral duty and does not live by mere expedience will go down in History as a profile in courage. History will vindicate him. This realistic side of moral idealism can be found in Kant, particularly in the essay about to be considered, "Idea for a Universal History with a Cosmopolitan Intent" (1784). Kant is a modern philosopher who rebelled against realism, but he also came back to it. Besides his notion of "History," and unsatisfied with a vindication of the moral person only in this world, Kant developed an argument supporting the immortality of the soul. He held an old doctrine in this regard as well as the new one in this writing on which we shall concentrate. As to the new doctrine, you can easily surmise that the desire of moral idealism to be free of utility may conflict with its desire to be rewarded in History. If a moral hero—which for Kant refers not to any particular human being but to every rational being—is confident that he will be vindicated from insignificance by History, isn't he in fact thinking of himself, indulging in the thought of his utility that spoils his moral idealism? Somehow we humans need both the elevation we receive from morality and the assurance that after all our morality will be vindicated in fact, not merely posited in imagination.

Kant's philosophy deserves a much fuller study than it receives in this book, and readers should take advantage of the *Prolegomena to Any Future Metaphysics* that Kant provided as an introduction to his system. This book pursues the theme of rational control and in its second part, the turn to reliance on history, which Kant develops from Rousseau. He is primarily a moral philosopher, though this would be contested in favor of his theory of knowledge for which he is best known and most studied. His three great critiques with their formidable titles—the *Critique of Pure Reason* (1781), *Critique of Practical Reason* (1788), and *Critique of Judgment* (1790)—are surely not bedside reading, but to tell a secret, they are not as difficult as many think. Kant's thought is complicated because he tries to put everything together in a system; once one learns his terminology, one finds that Kant is not as problematic or as subtle as the ancient philosophers. Kant is less difficult than Plato. But these two points—that Kant is primarily a moralist and not so difficult as Plato—will be left for proof on another day. His writings on morality are *The Metaphysics of Morals* (1797) and *The Groundwork of the Metaphysics of Morals* (1785); and on religion, *Religion Within the Limits of Reason Alone* (1793). The three essays on politics and history to be analyzed here would be termed minor works if Kant were a minor writer. But Kant is a major writer, hence incapable of writing a minor work. This is a third axiom we won't prove.

Rousseau and Hume in Kant

The two greatest influences on Kant were Rousseau and Hume, as we can see from acknowledgments he makes to them himself. The most striking is one in which he criticizes the contemplative life dear to the classical philosophers and gives the credit for his discovery to Rousseau:

> I myself am an inquirer out of inclination. I feel a complete thirst for knowledge and a greedy anxiety to make progress as well as contempt for every progress. There was a time when I believed that this would all turn out for the honor of mankind and I despised the vulgar who know nothing. Rousseau straightened me out. This illusory preference disappeared. I learned to honor every human being and would regard myself as much less useful than common day-laborers if I did not believe that this consideration would give value to all others by establishing the rights of mankind.[1]

Note Kant's moral motive to do honor, and the phrase "straightened me out" (*Rousseau hat mich zurecht gebracht*), a vigorous statement on behalf of the unwise, nonphilosophic multitude. This attitude can be found in Rousseau's *First Discourse* (1751) in the contrast between moral and intellectual progress and in the *Second Discourse* (1759), where reason and morality are both found unnatural to man but morality is closer to natural goodness (SD, pp. 69, 147).

Then what is to be done to defend morality, given the incapacity of reason? Science is on the scene and in power; *philosophes*—the intellectuals of the later eighteenth century—are in charge of educated opinion. The great Enlightenment is at full speed on its way to more and more progress, bringing along with it less and less virtue. Against the immorality of philosophy, the only defense is better philosophy to counter the danger from within. Rousseau had attempted to do this, and Kant takes over to try to improve on Rousseau. What he did was to address the speculative premises of morality. It had been supposed before Kant that morality has certain speculative premises outside morality that are necessary to defend it. Kant does not abandon the notion but resolves it in a manner he declared definite. Three speculative premises to morality were in question: the immortality of the soul, free will, and God. All were not part of morality but said to be required for it, and modern political philosophy cast doubt on all.

The immortality of the soul, already discussed as under attack by Machiavelli and denied by the materialism of Hobbes, was said to assist men to be moral in this world because they would be rewarded or punished in the next world. Free will was required to prove that the voluntary action of moral persons is possible, for if actions are determined or forced on men, they cannot be the result of moral choice. That premise was challenged by the determinism of Hobbes's political science. As for the existence of God, moral duty to other men was held unreliable if it was not also duty to the divine. How would the rights of man be secure if men were not held sacred as creatures of God? This premise was taken up by Locke. Rousseau wavered on all three. In the *Second Discourse* he presents a materialistic, atheistic determinism that denies them, but he also includes in *Emile* a section on "A Profession of Faith of a Savoyard Vicar" that is certainly heretical to Christianity but contains alternatives to these denials. Instead of materialism, the Vicar offers immortality of the soul; instead of determinism, freedom and conscience; and instead of atheism, deism (a rational God). It is unclear which Rousseau believed;

perhaps it was both, each for a different audience. And in the *Second Discourse,* as we have seen, he dodges the proof of freedom by speaking of perfectibility.

Kant did not address the problem of speculative premises of morality through Rousseau, but through Hume. Hume might seem to have left room for human freedom with his skepticism about causality, but he applies the notion of necessity to actions of the mind as well as to those of the body. Even though the link from cause to effect is mere habit for Hume, the habit in the mind forms of necessity.[2] Yet Kant said in a famous remark that "David Hume . . . first interrupted my dogmatic slumber."[3] The speculative premises could be called metaphysical questions, and what Kant attempted was not a new proof of them to make a new metaphysics. What he did in the *Critique of Pure Reason* was to question the very existence of metaphysics. The result, however, was not to deliver mankind to skepticism and cynicism but rather to establish morality as the sole certain knowledge that humans can have, indeed that every human being can have. The metaphysics of philosophers trying to prove the premises of morality dissolves in contradictions that Kant called *antinomies.* But the morality of an ordinary person—even of a child—is solid. It is all the more solid and all the more *moral* because it has been freed of the speculative premises of morality.

To explain this stunning result, it is time to take up some of Kant's fundamental terms. What follows will be puzzling to those who have no acquaintance with Kant's system and simplistic to those who do. We can start with four terms describing judgments (propositions). *Analytic* judgments have the predicate (what is said about the subject) implied in the subject. It's not a tautology but an implication. For example, man is a mortal animal; think man, and you think mortal animal, nothing new. In *synthetic* judgments, the predicate is not implied in the subject; one has to look to see, for example, that a dog has four legs. This character applies to judgments of both science and common sense. *A priori* refers to judgments known before experience, and *a posteriori* to judgments known after experience. Now, according to Kant, Hume's philosophy means that no judgments are synthetic a priori. All judgments are either analytic (judgments of reason) or synthetic a posteriori (called by Hume "matter of fact"). Synthetic a priori judgments would be those in which the predicate is connected to the subject, not implied in the subject but connected of necessity. There can be no synthetic a priori judgments from experience because a priori means prior to experience.

Another way to say this is that there is *no necessary experience*. Although Kant ultimately argues for the existence of synthetic a priori judgments, he agrees with this initial premise. No necessary experience means that, for example, it is not necessary for a dog to have four legs in order to be a dog, or not necessary for a human being to have a tongue. One may, in fact, encounter a three- or five-legged dog, or a human without a tongue. One could have the mind of a human being in the body of a Wookiee (in *Star Wars*), for science fiction is based on Kant's acceptance of Hume's argument. No necessary experience thus means that there are no natures within nature; nothing has to be as it is. The enterprise of Machiavelli that denies reliance on nature but accepts necessity is now extended to deny necessities. "Necessity" turns out to be a temporary stopping point between nature and chaotic experience, as was indicated by Machiavelli himself. According to Machiavelli, there are no natural forms, but forms are imposed by humans for their convenience or necessity on matter (P 26). This is preparation for Kant's more radical step, which goes beyond Hume and elaborates Machiavelli's vague statement in a system of Kant's own invention.

Kant goes beyond Hume and does find a synthetic a priori. He finds it first in cause and effect. One cannot find causality from experience because experience is always only up to now. To repeat, there is no necessary experience and nothing has to be as it is. Many events go unobserved, and things (fortune) could change at any moment. Causality also could not be a posteriori because experience is not necessary, only probable, as with Hume's reduction of natural necessity to habits of the mind (see also Machiavelli, D 3.46). Causality could also not be analytical, because cause must precede effect and not be contained within it. So Kant developed a notion of the spontaneity of understanding that is original with him. He finds the synthesis of cause to be made by the understanding spontaneously. The synthetic a prioris as a whole are the necessary conditions of experience. One cannot have experience without certain necessary forms and categories by which to have it—for example, space and time. Sense data are meaningless by themselves, and they become experience only through interpretation in which the understanding actively projects into the chaotic data of experience. Knowing is not receiving, as had always been supposed (except by Machiavelli), but is, rather, projecting. Interpretation is effected by the spontaneous act of the pure understanding. *Pure* is a technical term of Kant's, meaning "uncontaminated by anything alien"—the pure understanding uncontaminated by anything it understands but confined to the qualities or means by which it understands. It is knowing that does not know any object—that is, nature or natures—to be known. It projects without assuming any potentiality in what is to be known. It does not know what is understandable or fit or suitable or to be expected. If one sees a dog, one does not know whether it can bark of even whether it is a dog. Things do not have a look suggesting their nature. All that sort of preliminary understanding is subject to the fact—the fact of facts—that experience is only up to now.

There is no necessity in the nature of a dog that requires it to have four legs, but one cannot see the dog without implying the necessity of space and time. There is no necessary experience but there are necessary qualities to have the experience of seeing the dog. True necessity is thus possible, with universal validity and evidence. Yet science can become actual only from sensible objects. In order for a possible object of experience to become actual, sense perception is required. There is no knowledge of non-sensible beings; there is no supra-sensible being such as a form or an essence. There is no knowledge of God or of the soul. The so-called knowledge of invisible essences Kant calls the "transcendental illusion," which is the belief of reason that it can know the essences of things. *Transcendental* characterizes the knowledge of possible experience—the transcendental dialectic and analytic. The knowledge of beings and things is the knowledge of the *phenomenal* world; one cannot know *noumena*, the essences or things in themselves. Again, one cannot know that a dog must have four legs, or that a swan must be white, or a crow black.

Pure Morality

Yet there is one essence one can know. One can have a purely rational knowledge of the thing in itself that is utterly independent of experience. This cannot be theoretical knowledge, which always depends on experience or possible experience. Practical knowledge, however, the knowledge of duty or the moral law, can be known as a thing in itself or a *noumenon*. You should always do your duty, regardless of experience; you can know what it is without considering experience. Now the moral law requires freedom, and perhaps also God and the immortality of the soul. Therefore, metaphysics is possible as the knowledge of justice, the soul, and God, but only in practice and because they are implied by practice. One cannot know them theoretically or speculatively. We see the crucial importance of morality for Kant; philosophy serves morality, as for Rousseau. The *Critique of Pure Reason* serves to protect ordinary people and their morality from metaphysicians:

> So far . . . as our Critique limits speculative reason, it is indeed negative, but since it thereby removes an obstacle which stands in the way of the employment of practical reason, nay threatens to destroy it, it has in reality a positive and very important use. . . . To deny therefore that the service the Critique renders is positive in character is like saying that the police are of no positive benefit inasmuch as their main business is mainly to prevent the violence in which citizens stand in mutual fear, in order that each may pursue his vocation in peace and security.[4]

Kant the policeman against metaphysical gangsters! And if philosophy serves morality, morality returns the favor to philosophy. For the *Critique* shows that a moral metaphysics is possible, which is speculative metaphysics from a moral point of view.

Yet philosophy does not merely protect, but improves morality. Kant's philosophy makes possible a pure morality—morality with a new power never attained before: "Pure morality has an influence on the human heart so much more powerful than other incentives."[5] "Heretofore morality has been comparatively ineffective because it has never been purely expounded." Kant compares pure morality to simple beauty and empirical morality to painted coquetry.[6] What is pure as opposed to empirical morality?

Pure morality is valid without reference to facts outside of morality, particularly without reference to human nature. According to Kant, the study of man is scientific only with regard to man as a phenomenon, not as noumenon. The study of man as phenomenon is psychology, which cannot describe the nature of man, as man is in himself. Psychology studies man *up to now* and cannot speak of him as he must be. Today, for example, feminism, using Kant's formulation, argues for facts that establish gender neutrality as opposed to natural or biological differences of sex; women do not have to be as they have been and are. The only knowledge of the essence of a human is practical, because one has knowledge of the moral law by virtue of giving that law to oneself. You are in the position of God: you must know what you are doing, assuming that you use universal laws. Hobbes had said that one can only know what one makes, and Kant adds that the law one makes must be rational and universal. But the moral law is true only of moral matters; in theoretical matters, you cannot penetrate to truth about your own essence. You cannot know whether you will obey the law that you set for yourself; you might falter or fail. Since the knowledge of the moral law is a priori, it has no reference to the facts of experience, which are a posteriori. Kant agrees with feminism that there is no certain definition of woman, but he would add that this impossibility frees women, in questions of morality, from the burden of having to think as women. Women can think as rational beings in accordance with the moral law.

Pure morality is done for its own sake, not because you are self-interested or sociable or independent, or noble, or any kind of creature or being. It is not morality for the sake of any incentive or to fulfill any possibility or potentiality, or in general for the sake of happiness. Morality and happiness are separated. Here Rousseau enters into Kant's thesis:

> But the well-being of a state must not be understood as the welfare of its citizens and their happiness, for happiness can perhaps come to them more easily and as they would like it to in a state of nature (as Rousseau asserts) or even under a despotic government. (*Metaphysics of Morals*, in *Practical Philosophy*, p. 461, Ak. 6:318)

This great thesis of Kant's has a source in Rousseau. The view of Socrates and his tradition was that the happy life is the virtuous life. A despicable criminal cannot be happy if only because he has to live his life with others like himself. But Kant makes a radical separation of happiness and virtue so that virtue cannot be tainted by considerations of what makes people happy. Rousseau had prepared this in the *Second Discourse* when he said that savages or pre-savages can be happy without being virtuous.

Kant disregards all reference to facts of the state of nature or to the escape from it, which for Rousseau necessarily affect morality. He makes not only Rousseau but Socrates, Plato, and Aristotle, all of whom argue for the supremacy of good over pleasure, seem to be tantamount to hedonists: each of them makes concessions to human nature and experience from which Kant's argument relieves him. For Kant, all previous morality with its speculative premises and its alleged facts is either plain or varnished hedonism. His morality is perfectly *categorical* as opposed to *hypothetical* (more Kantian terms). By hypothetical, Kant means morality with a conditional *If*: If you want to be reasonable, or to preserve yourself, then say you are sorry for a fault or slight. Kant rejects this morality because it is sordid; it depends on something outside itself, whether self-preservation in the case of the moderns or a healthy soul for the ancients. Previous philosophers spoiled morality by making it *empirical*, basing it on facts. True morality is perfectly categorical—without exceptions, limitations, or hesitations. Kant lifts morality above the concern for facts, the "ought" above the "is." Today's distinction between "is" and "ought" is quite different, because it says that science is concerned only with the "is" and not with the "ought." This distinction leads to dismissive cynicism and lazy relativism, neither of which applies to Kant. For Kant, there can be scientific knowledge of facts and supra-sensible knowledge of values (not a Kantian term), based on morality that is rational because it is pure and pure because it is rational.

Pure morality, then, is both less sordid and more powerful than empirical morality. This is true by contrast to all previous morality, whether Machiavellian or not. It is more powerful because it sets no limit to the demand it places on human nature. Having no limit means that pure morality is necessarily impossible. It necessarily calls for more than facts or circumstances permit. It is an *ideal*, in the modern sense of a goal that is unattainable. Our human nature and our circumstances hold us back, yet the ideal remains as a goal we can only approximate. Pure morality gets more because it asks for more; it does more because it knows that ideals are impossible to attain. By aiming at the impossible, one achieves much more than by gauging the realities in the manner of Machiavelli. Thus Kant's morality is more realistic than realism. It is certainly more powerful. In the twentieth and twenty-first centuries one sees all kinds of ideals. Even materialism, in the form of Marxism, becomes an ideal, a cause for which one must sacrifice (and millions were killed for it). We are very idealistic today, thanks in good part to Kant, but are we more moral?

Vindication of Pure Morality in History

Pure morality is impossible morality, yet we can hope for its realization. Must we not hope, or have some foundation for this hope? The principal foundation for hope in Kant is the immortality of the soul, but that says nothing about realization on earth. He set down his thought about realization on earth in an essay, "Idea for a Universal History with a Cosmopolitan Intent," published in 1784, three years after the *Critique of Pure Reason*. Cosmopolitan intent is moral intent. If there is a moral duty to become a citizen of the world, there is also a duty to look at history from a cosmopolitan point of view or to contribute to the establishment of a world commonwealth. One's duty is to be a citizen of the world because pure morality is universal and has no relation to facts, so that there is no basis for preferring one country over another. By contrast, Rousseau's general will is not a universal will but suited to a particular community.

Kant prefaces the essay with a note to say that a newspaper report of a scholar visiting Kant misquoted him and he now corrects the record. Writing this essay was accidental rather than planned by Kant, which suggests that the topic of history was not of central importance to him. History, for Kant, exhibits both scientific necessity and morality, which requires free will. How can necessity and freedom be combined? History is the narrative of human actions, of actualizations of free will. But free will is not scientifically observable. All that one sees are phenomena that are determined according to general, natural laws, not by free will. Kant could say that a completed natural science in which everything is explained, though of course impossible, could predict the actions of an individual human being as accurately as astronomers predict the motions of the moon.

Yet free will must be present in history. Among the facts of history, consider the statistics on marriage and on suicide, the former virtuous, the latter a vice, according to Kant. Here is an obvious choice: marry or kill yourself! No one could possibly confuse marriage with suicide. All men see the necessity of this choice and act freely. Yet there are strange regularities in the statistics. Despite free will, it is possible the phenomena of marriage and suicide will be regular. How can we resolve this problem? Perhaps by considering aggregates, not individuals: determinism one can predict in the former, free will one cannot predict in the latter. This is not satisfactory and Kant was not satisfied, but it shows the difficulty of philosophy of history for him. How can one find room for morality in a necessary sequence of cause and effect? Now how does history proceed in this regard?

> The means that nature uses to bring about the development of all of man's capacities is the antagonism among them in society as far as in the end this antagonism is the cause of law-governed order in society . . . man has a propensity for living in society . . . he also has a great tendency to isolate himself and he therefore anticipates resistance everywhere. . . . Now this resistance awakens all of man's powers, brings him to overcome his tendency toward laziness, and driven by his desire for honor, power, or property, to secure status among his fellows. (UH, pp. 31–32)

History proceeds by antagonisms of competition and rivalry, by "unsocial sociability," not by simple progressive enlightenment but from premorality to morality on a path of immorality in which men resist one another. Again, we see how Kant derives his principles from Rousseau and, to anticipate, how close he comes to Marx. Moral progress occurs not by moral means—but given that, then, is it really morality? Kant of all people must deny that the end justifies the means. Do men become more moral or merely more civilized in displaying their immorality? The competition that produces these antagonisms among us results in a development of capacities. This is once more something new in Kant, prepared by Rousseau, and developed further by Marx. For Locke, and for Adam Smith, competition is for comforts and luxuries, not for the improvement of mankind. Kant edifies liberalism: Competition is not for sordid gain but to make the best of oneself. He concludes that competition and antagonisms have in fact brought progress in freedom, enlightenment, and peace. Kant even argues that increase in the debt burden raised for fighting wars will make war unlikely (UH, p. 37).

In this writing of Kant's, history appears as natural theology. It offers a "comforting view of the future" in which a "justification of nature" becomes a notion of providence that is not a "perfectly rational objective" but "brings us to the point of hoping for that end only in another world" (UH, p. 39). The status of the philosophy of history would seem to be no different from the teleology of nature; it is a "regulative idea" in the service of a theoretical explanation. When science looks at a living thing, it needs the idea of purposiveness as a regulative idea to instruct it and to enable it to study that being. Science needs the idea that a bee wants to make honey. It cannot prove that idea since science must be deterministic and mechanistic. But does this reasoning apply to the study of history? The theoretical study of history does not need any such regulative idea. One can explain war perfectly in terms of the motives of the actors and their circumstances. There is no need to assume for the understanding of war that there is an underlying perspective of which the actors are unaware. Instead of a regulative idea, the philosophy of history must be justified as a postulate of moral or practical reason, such as this one for Kant: We are obliged to act morally, thus to recognize the rights of man, indeed of every man. One must therefore have moral concern for the political order that recognizes the rights of man and one must work toward that end. But there is one obstacle to revolutionary activity in support of the moral political order. That is the prohibition of lying, argued in Kant's *Metaphysics of Morals* (pp. 552–554, Ak. 6:429).

Lying to another or to oneself is a dishonor to the equal dignity of every human being; it is treating another or oneself as a means and not as an end. Now, revolution requires conspiracy against the immoral, imperfect order, which requires lying, and lying for Kant is absolutely forbidden: it is said to be the "greatest violation" of one's duty toward oneself. Then can one hope for a just political order? A sensible person would be tempted to say no, but one must look at history philosophically—that is, approach it with the a priori premise of a possible teleology of nature toward justice and peace. Kant sketches a trend of history and does little to prove it, particularly the laughable idea that the expense of modern war will help prevent future war. This trend is necessary and yet has a moral end; necessity and morality converge. The convergence must not come about through the work of morality, for that would interrupt the system of necessity, but rather through amoral or immoral actions and passions of greed and injustice. Moral progress must not be caused by the intellect, given the dichotomy between moral and intellectual progress argued by Rousseau. And we have learned from Machiavelli that immoral passions are more reliable than reason and morality.

The trend of history for Kant, however, does tend to bring about the just political order, not the success of a prince as *uno solo*. Here lies the great achievement of Kant: He accepts that the goal of modern political philosophy is to require a deliberate lowering of moral standards but replaces this apparent necessity with a lofty and demanding morality of human honor and dignity. The trouble is that Kant must insist that one never *sees* morality; all we see is legality. We see people obeying the political and the moral law, but we do not see their motive for doing so. Kant's reluctance to elaborate a philosophy of history in this short, accidental essay reflects his overpowering intent to retain the difference between morality and legality, or between genuine sincerity and outward conformity.

Kant's A Priori Justice as Perpetual Peace

Kant's *Toward Perpetual Peace, A Philosophical Project* (1795) is an essay on politics, and the "Idea of a Universal History" is a short essay on history. Neither is a theme of Kant, who characteristically studies morals, not politics, and the ahistorical premises of morality rather than its vindication in history. Yet these short, atypical writings are very revealing because they show his principles in action. Kant's sophisticated theories are meant to be applied. He wrote another short essay "On the Common Saying: That May Be Correct in Theory but It Is of No Use in Practice" (1793) in which he tries to refute that oft-heard slogan. Kant's theories are meant to work—or to be put to work—and it is particularly illuminating to see how he thought they would work or were working. He says repeatedly that he has not produced a new morality, but rather a new way of looking at morality. His new formulation of a priori morality, not based on facts or on human nature, is decisive because now, for the first time, morality will work. His statement is generally true of modern theories of morality; they are theories *about* morality, not new notions of what it is to be moral. Compared with Aristotle's *Ethics,* modern theories hardly discuss morality. Aristotle supplies a list of moral virtues or claimed virtues and considers whether each is truly a virtue, what kind of virtue it is, what its degrees and qualities are, what its corresponding vices are.

No such discussion can be found in modern theorists like Descartes, Hobbes, Spinoza, Locke, Hume, or Kant, all of whom create new formulas of virtue. Each discovered a new formula that for the first time would make virtue work. Since they are formulas, rather than empirical studies of virtues praised and vices blamed, they tend to narrow the virtues they consider to one, and that one a social rather than an individual virtue. Of these Hobbes and Kant fix on justice as the single outstanding virtue that orders all other morality. Both understand justice as keeping promises. For Hobbes justice is keeping promises made in fact to a sovereign, but for Kant justice is a priori; it is a categorical promise made not to actual human beings but to all rational beings. The promise is that one will behave as a rational being and not claim an exception for oneself as human beings tend to do. Kant's morality is above all directed against the exception—the person who claims to comply with the rules most of the time but needs one small relaxation so that he can murder a nagging wife or a faithless husband. Kant admits, as if to Machiavelli, that human nature is corrupt, that humans are made of "crooked wood," hence that they are not in fact rational beings. But human weakness can never be an excuse; one's moral duty is to think and act as a rational being.

Then, supposing it is true that a priori morality may be desirable for one's private life, what about politics? Isn't the enforcement of morality acceptable for private life within a state—we do have policemen—but does it apply to international politics? Can states follow the rules of rational, a priori morality in regard to other states? Can there be a policeman for the world? If not, why should the state not take care to be moral at home, but behave as a criminal gangster in foreign policy as do other states? Machiavelli, we have seen, denies any difference between domestic and foreign policy, as both are criminal. To be sure, morality can be self-defeating if it leads to instability, but for him the purpose of the stability arising from morality is to enable an imperial country to digest what it eats. After a time, an empire is ready for new ventures of aggressive immorality. Kant, opposing Machiavelli, also denies that difference but instead of lowering the higher (more demanding) morality tries to raise the lower (less demanding) and make relations among states resemble domestic policy through a proposed world government. While Machiavelli tried to show that one's domestic friends are always potential enemies, Kant tries to show that one's foreign enemies are potential friends. His essay *Perpetual Peace* is his true answer to Machiavelli. He makes it clear that "extraordinary means"—Machiavelli's euphemism for criminality—are never necessary as exceptions to a pure, universal, categorical morality that from now on will direct all states.

Perpetual Peace has the same ambiguity as the "Idea of a Universal History." In the latter, morality needs to be vindicated in history, but when that happens, something is subtracted from it. In *Perpetual Peace* Kant tries to meet the challenge of Machiavelli both on the level of self-interest and above that level in a parallel argument.

Preliminary Articles

Kant's essay *Toward Perpetual Peace* takes the form of a peace treaty composed of preliminary and definitive articles, for what is to be done when the "treaty" is introduced differs from when it is completed. The essay has the form of a legal document, as suits a universal morality that applies everywhere and at all times, but most laws do not distinguish in this way between what can be done first and what must wait for completion. The foreign policy of the United States and most contemporary liberal democracies share Kant's universal legalism and the half-prudent hesitation in doubt of its universality that is responsible for this distinction. One can go further to suggest that the foreign policy of liberal democracies cannot be well understood without a careful reading of Kant's *Perpetual Peace,* beginning with its mix of utopianism and prudence. He himself begins the essay with a rather perfunctory preface that anticipates a mocking reception from worldly-wise politicians who look down on empty theoreticians. Though he is aware of his doubting addressees, he does not really respect them. He writes for rational beings on the basis of a priori morality and he is aware of the—flattering?—appeal of his arguments to the human beings he demands to be rational.

The essay presents six preliminary articles. In the first preliminary article, Kant declares that peace means real peace, not a truce but an end to all hostilities and the establishment of perpetual peace. The treaty must eliminate all future causes of war, for which any tacit reservation would mean bad faith and an open reservation would be no peace. A priori morality is all or nothing; it does not depend on favorable circumstances because it does not depend on circumstances. The second article says that no independent state can come under the dominion of another state; each state is legally protected as a moral person. The third article requires that standing armies be totally abolished in time—not right away. Standing armies mutually incite war from one another as each state pursues an arms race. At some point one state will think it has sufficient advantage to break the peace and start a war. The fourth says that national debts shall not be contracted with a view to external friction among states. Previous modern philosophers, particularly Montesquieu, had wanted to facilitate commerce because it led to peace, but Kant learned from Rousseau that commerce has a hostile aspect. The fifth preliminary article declares that no state will interfere with the constitution of another state, but in case of civil war there is no state but anarchy, and intervention in this event is not interference. To this one may remark that in human affairs every universal rule has exceptions; they can be waved away by making the rules categorical, but they will return through loopholes like this one. Recent experience and ancient histories show that it can be quite easy to find or incite a civil war that justifies the intervention of a foreign power to bring its desired peace.

The sixth article denounces "dishonorable stratagems," a revealing point (PP, p. 320). These are acts of war like the use of assassins, poisoners, breach of surrender that would lead to a war of extermination. But this is a consideration of interest, not honor. One could make the reverse argument that one's interest is a matter of honor, as did Winston Churchill in criticizing England's abandonment of Czechoslovakia in 1938. Kant continues this remark by saying that "war is after all only the regrettable expedient for asserting one's right by force in a state of nature" where there is no power to adjudge a war unjust. But does that decide the issue? What of a state that uses assassins and spies (spies are liars)? Would that not be conducting an unjust war? Kant wants the certainty of law in his argument, which is in the form of a legal treaty. He cannot introduce questions of honor and justice that would be disputed. His argument could not explain the reluctance of decent nations in our day to respond in kind to terrorists and guerillas. Why not admit that judgments of justice can have an effect even in the absence of a competent court? Kant's answer is that an imperfect justice that is contestable justifies war and makes perfect justice in perpetual peace impossible.

Kant's treaty makes all states legally equal; each state is a moral person because a state is required to fulfill one's moral duties. There is no superior or inferior among states, which today is still the premise of international law and of the United Nations. Following Kant, interference with another state (articles 2 and 5) is called aggression. This is the right of self-determination, but in Kant it comes with the proviso that self-determination requires a free, republican constitution (the first definitive article). The situation today is that self-determination does not require a free constitution and is enjoyed by the worst and most powerful tyrannies. Their right of self-determination has the effect of protecting them in their infancy when they could have been crushed. At the end of the preliminary articles, Kant shows his awareness of the difficulty implied in the distinction between preliminary and definitive articles, which is that one cannot establish international morality all at once (PP, pp. 320–321). He says that articles 1, 5, and 6 are strict, but 2, 3, and 4 may be delayed, even though they are only preliminary. Then he says that states do not have to give back any territory taken previously, for such possession is justified by "public opinion"—an astounding exception. The United States will not have to return Texas to Mexico. Kant sees that the one country that adopts his international morality (and takes the United Nations seriously) will be at great disadvantage. So he makes allowances and provides leeway in or toward the momentous change. The change must be gradual, but if it is gradual, will it ever arrive? It would seem that all would have to adopt it at once, in Machiavelli's expression, "with one stroke."

Definitive Articles

The first of Kant's definitive articles in *Perpetual Peace* is that every state must have a republican constitution. This is a constitution to which one could have given consent even if one has not actually consented. A more empirical moralist or political scientist would discuss how to bring about consent with a nation, or a civil religion, or an education, as did Rousseau. But Kant's morality is a priori, and the republican constitution is for rational beings, and as we shall see, also for another kind of being. He describes a republican constitution in a typical paradox: the more popular or democratic, the less republican it is. A democracy will be despotic because the majority is sovereign over the minority, whereas a republic is the form of government in which all consent to be governed by whoever decides—and monarchy will decide best. Perhaps this odd Kantian formula of republican form that is monarchical in execution as opposed to empirical democratic rule is not so far from American democracy today, when accused of being subject to an "imperial presidency." It also resembles Rousseau's distinction of the sovereign general will from the executive government that serves it and the legislator who establishes it.

The second definitive article introduces the very influential notion of a league of nations. The law of nations, Kant says, is founded on a federation of free states. It might seem that his argument for republican government would call for a world state to match the universality of the moral law. But peoples do not want that, Kant allows. The duty of man to join the state cannot be extended to a duty of states to merge into one world state. But this judgment is of course not a priori; rather, it corrects an a priori judgment with an empirical one. If all states retain their sovereignty, then the league could be prevented or ended by just one member with a sovereign veto. This situation reveals what has been called the open secret of Kant's notion of perpetual peace: it is unachievable, *eine unausführbar Idee*, as he says in the *Metaphysics of Morals* (p. 487, Ak. 6:350). One must conclude with Kantian strictness—or with Machiavelli's effectual truth—that perpetual peace as an idea is actually in fact perpetual war. If so, how can it be a responsible policy? Warfare might be more civilized in the eighteenth century than in the twentieth or twenty-first, but that is an a posteriori judgment. Civilized behavior during war, one might add, is probably due more to the self-respect of a nation, based on the opinion of its own superiority, than to its equal moral sovereignty in the Kantian scheme.

At the end of the third definitive article, Kant takes up the problem of feasibility. He refers to the progress by which a cosmopolitan idea of right has spread (PP, pp. 330–331). It is not enough to say that perpetual peace is the dictate of moral reason and therefore required, as in the phrase "you ought, therefore you can" (*du sollst, denn du kanst*). The dictate has a guarantee, as explained in the first supplemental article. Nature will guarantee peace, it says. But it is quite ambiguous. If perpetual peace is morally demanded, we are entitled to consider whether the mechanism of nature will achieve the morally required end. But if nature did achieve its end through mechanical necessity, there would be no room for human freedom and moral satisfaction. Still, the mechanism of nature gives us confidence in the possibility of true peace. The chief disaccord among nations comes from diverse religions, and these are about to be replaced by (Kant's) rational religion. Moreover, the agent of universal harmony is the enlightened spirit of commerce that engages nations with one another and holds them to peace for the sake of mutual advantage. The bad effects of religion and the good effects of commerce are not a priori, however, hence not a part of the a priori political philosophy that demands a league of nations.

In this context we find a famous passage so very expressive of Kant's moral politics: "The problem of establishing a state, no matter how hard as it may sound, is solvable even for a nation of devils (if only they have understanding)" (PP, p. 335). It is true that the good moral condition of a people is to be expected under a good constitution. But then why isn't it the requirement of a good constitution to make a good people, rather than intelligent devils? Why does the good constitution secure only external freedom? Because if it could secure a people by the necessity of mechanical causation, its goodness would not be freely achieved and hence not moral. Morality has to be freely legislated as a categorical law for oneself. Any good effects from education may be helpful but are not decisive; they are external to morality and do not guarantee it. No one can make another person moral, or even be sure that one's own self is moral as the result of a successful categorical law passed by and for oneself. For all you know, you might be an intelligent devil yourself.

After the preliminary and definitive articles of the treaty for perpetual peace, and the two supplements to them, there are two appendices of great interest. The first is on the opposition between morality and politics, where there are two points to note in Kant's argument. First, reason can state a person's duty but it cannot foresee one's destiny. The only certain guide to morality, as seen above, is morality itself. Second, Kant turns to the strong point of the realists, the Machiavellians, that the factual basis of right will always be force. Kant admits this but denies the doubtful conclusion drawn by the Machiavellians that force will never bow to right. Karl Marx, on the side of Machiavelli, said that the bourgeoisie will never abdicate. Kant replies that the Machiavellian politician does not know the possibilities of man but knows only ordinary human behavior. The possibility of acting morally is realized by the moral politician as opposed to the political moralist (PP, p. 340). The first interprets the principles of political prudence to make them morally coherent, and the second fashions morality to suit the statesman's advantage. Here Kant delivers politics to the Machiavellians. Politics is the realm of legality, which is the external freedom of intelligent devils, while morality is the realm of true freedom. They can be combined only when morality gives the law to politics, which is possible according to Kant. This formulation of the problem is very popular today: Morality is clean, and politics is a dirty word used for reproach. No one will try to insult a politician by calling him moral, but calling him "political" will do for immoral.

Kant accepts Machiavelli's view of the problem, that morality is imaginary and politics is real and based on fact, but what Machiavelli rejects as imaginary he accepts as a priori rational, a possibility open to every human being. Plato had set forth utopian politics as the standard, human possibilities being derived from facts of human nature, above all the fact that philosophers exist. The trouble is that the possibilities may exist only in what philosophers say, or in speech. But since Kant's a priori morality disregards facts, the moral statesman can disregard facts and consequences; morality does not have to be prudent. The moral statesman can expose the maxims of prudence as immoral and hypocritical. He can confront the political moralist and expose everything short of pure morality as deceitful and immoral (PP, p. 340). Today's moral language often reflects Kant's position, as when people speak of one action as moral and the opposite as prudent. For Kant, "prudent" is always a subtraction from morality rather than an addition, as for Plato and Aristotle. For the latter morality is in need of prudent direction toward favorable and away from unfavorable circumstances. One modern political philosopher, Edmund Burke, a contemporary of Kant, disagreed when denouncing the French Revolution: "Circumstances . . . give in reality to every political principle its distinguishing color and discriminating effect. The circumstances are what render every civil and political scheme beneficial or noxious to mankind" (1790).

The second appendix addresses the right that is established between morality and politics. There is one certain criterion—note again the love of certainty in modern political philosophy—for the morality of public right or law, and that is whether it is publishable. A moral law is one that can be universalized, and the test of universal is whether a claim can be published. Kant qualifies it because a decidedly superior power has no need to conceal its criminal excuses. Restated, it says all measures that stand in need of publicity to reach their end agree with politics and right combined. What does that mean? This criterion would apply against Machiavellian politicians—for example, Machiavelli himself.

Machiavelli's immediate political purpose, stated in the last chapter of *The Prince,* was to unify Italy in order to liberate it from "barbarism." How this was to be done was shown indirectly earlier in the work by his treatment of conquests from which one could infer that it would be necessary to exterminate princely houses and eliminate republics (P 3–5). These were immoral means necessary to the end that Machiavelli craftily both conveyed and concealed but did not *publish* in the sense of make it obvious.

According to Kant, a right of rebellion is impossible because it could not be publicly defended. It is not that such a defense would bring suspicion on the defender; rather, the moral authority of law could not be conferred on an attack against law. A law could never be made to give a right to rebel against the law—a contradiction. With Locke there is a right of resistance in his principles, but it remains in the background and could not be stated as a public right in the constitution. Kant implies that there might be a right to rebel against a usurper, but not against a legitimate king who is governing tyrannically (PP, pp. 340–341). But this is another instance of Kant's reliance on a posteriori experience rather than a priori morality.

Other difficulties in the criterion of publishing can be found. Kant proves that it would be imprudent for a smaller power to publish its policy against a larger one (PP, pp. 349–350), but would it be unjust? Also, is it true that unjust maxims cannot be defended in public? Or that a maxim that stands in need of publicity cannot be unjust? "My country right or wrong" is unjust according to Kant, but will it necessarily lose an election? A doctrine of religious intolerance is unjust according to Kant, but it would not be indefensible in an intolerant country. In his debate with Abraham Lincoln in 1858, Stephen Douglas said that in a contest between a crocodile and a "Negro," I am with the Negro; but in a contest between a Negro and a white man, I am with the white man.[7] Lincoln pointed out the injustice of this statement but Douglas won that election (though not the one in 1860). Some unjust doctrines stand in need of publicity in order to succeed, such as holy wars of religion or Hitler's genocide of the Jews or Stalin's of the kulaks.

What is the presupposition behind Kant's criterion of publicity that distinguishes moral policies from immoral ones? It is that the people are moral. This is also why republics are peaceful; they are dominated by the people, who are peace-loving because they have to fight the wars, while kings can afford to be warlike from the safety of their palaces (or is it, rather, that "uneasy lies the head that wears the crown"? From Shakespeare, *Henry IV* 3.1). And where does this presupposition come from? From Machiavelli, the first philosopher who uttered it (D 1.58). One could say that the very writing of Kant most opposed to Machiavelli rests on a proposition first set forth by Machiavelli, a proposition that is in no way a priori. As for Machiavelli, that proposition prevents full disclosure of his thought and requires that politics be hidden, use fraud, and center on conspiracy, so for Kant the same proposition validates publicity and forbids secrecy and conspiracy. Thanks in good part to Kant, secrecy today has a bad name because it is usually regarded as a harbor for evil rather than a recourse for the good. Yet even in a democratic country today, there is one place in politics where secrecy is regarded as the unquestioned privilege of good people. This is not a government secret service, nor is it the ladies' room; it's the voting booth. The seat of sovereignty is protected by secrecy, for the sovereign is the person or the group that watches over others but is not watched itself. The sovereign decides privately what it will do and say publicly. Kant knew this as well as did Hobbes, but he never admitted publicly that the consequence of forbidding secrecy is abolishing all government. Modern political philosophy had to await Karl Marx to assert in the name of Enlightenment what Plato had said against the spirit of the Enlightenment—that since human justice is imperfect, all politics requires secrecy and lying. Machiavelli did not invent this truth, but under the name of human necessity, he exaggerated it and rejected the possible justice that might be gained by lying.

Strict and Stern

Kant, we have seen, continues the desire for certainty that is so characteristic of modern political philosophy. Machiavelli began it with his adoption of necessity, both urgent and foreseen, which resolves the problems of living as one ought; Hobbes, Locke, and Rousseau maintain it with the "undoubted right" of a contract fixed and decided under the pressure of fear. Kant finds a new moral version of certainty made voluntarily in making laws for oneself, and he brings it to a peak in the categorical a priori of morality without exceptions. A priori morality distinguishes a human being, with all its diverse qualities and circumstances, from a rational being, which is the same everywhere because it does not depend on the facts that define and constrain a human being. That is why it can be categorical rather than hypothetical, and thus perfectly certain. Because it disregards the facts or consequences of a moral action, a priori morality is based purely on goodwill rather than the good it intends or hopes for, which would taint morality by making it depend on that intent, thus rendering it hypothetical rather than categorical. Pure goodwill has no regard for others' reaction to one's actions, which means no regard for politeness. Once again we find the Rousseau in Kant, the opposition of Rousseau to Hume's praise of politeness discussed in chapter 4. With the purity of his goodwill, Kant puts the limited, constrained politeness of people who are "nice" in the same basket as those who are oblivious of others or even vicious to them. To sum up: the desire for certainty makes Kant strict, and his strictness makes him stern.

The Kantians of today tend to soften or abandon his sternness, but without the examples of his a priori morality, Kant is nothing more than the nice guy he would firmly dismiss and despise. We have seen his insistence that lying is immoral and that secrecy in politics, let alone revolution, are morally impossible even though their prohibition would condemn even George Washington. We have seen, too, that the perpetual peace of his argument, since it is unattainable, amounts to perpetual war, and thus exposes any nation that expects or seeks it to the deceits of its enemies. The infinite approximation of an impossible ideal, we shall see, was defined by Hegel as "bad infinity," whereby those of goodwill seeking impossible goals are led to the ruin Machiavelli pronounces for this error. Two examples of Kant's stern morality regarding capital punishment and marriage show the practical consequences of not considering practical consequences. One further example from Kant's essay "On the Common Saying: That May Correct in Theory but It Is of No Use in Practice" (1793) illustrates his provision for how a priori morality is applied to the political issues of who votes and how government represents the people.

Justice must not be rewarded, Kant says, since its purity would be spoiled if it were done for the sake of an end or a consequence, but injustice must be punished. Punishment must be inflicted neither in anger nor to deter other injustice but to respect the "honor" of the doer of injustice as a moral person who acted voluntarily. A murderer must receive the "special honor" of capital punishment equal to the deed, and Kant makes a remark frequently quoted against him, and made here to honor his a priori morality: "Even if a civil society were to be dissolved by the consent of all its members . . . the last murderer remaining in prison would first have to be executed." If not, the people might be regarded as "collaborators in this public violation of justice" (*Metaphysics of Morals*, p. 474, Ak. 6:333).

So much for murder, but what about sex? First, we note the article "On Defiling Oneself by Lust," the "unnatural lust" that is "contrary to morality in its highest degree" and that "is considered indecent even to call [by] its proper name"—which Kant does not supply (*Metaphysics of Morals*, p. 549, Ak. 6:425). Prostitution is also rejected as unnatural, for it is "hiring a person for enjoyment on one occasion" in which the prostitute "would be surrendering herself as a thing to the other's choice." The only natural way to have sex is within marriage, which is defined in an almost indecent manner. Marriage is a lifelong contract in which two persons of opposite sex "make use of the sexual organs and capacities of one another" (*Metaphysics of Morals*, pp. 426–428, 495, Ak 6.277, 6.360). It is made natural by the possibility of having children, but this end is not part of the definition. The end might not be fulfilled, and the definition, to be certain, must cover all cases. Also, to specify the end in the definition would detract from the moral freedom of the couple to find happiness as they will.

Two features of Kant's discussion of marriage interest us today. The first is the equality of husband and wife—their equality as moral beings, but not as persons with equal authority in the family or with the same duties and capacities (p. 428). The shame of having a child outside of marriage is the mother's and must be punished (p. 477, Ak. 6:336). And to treat a woman as a prostitute is to treat her as a *thing*. To use someone as a means to an end rather than as an equal moral person is to make him not a slave or servant but a thing no different from an item of nonhuman property. There is no middle between moral person and thing, no place for Aristotle's moral virtue that is resplendent yet second to the intellectual virtue that Kant, with his three mighty critiques, has criticized out of existence. For when moral virtue is the highest virtue there is no other basis to judge the world but whether the rational capacity for morality exists and is respected or not. All is either the thing in itself or a thing in a mechanistic system.

The essay "Theory and Practice," in which Kant defends the practical relevance of theory, is in part a review of a book written by Christian Garve, critical of Kant's moral theory. Like the two essays we have studied earlier, "Theory and Practice" is not a major work but reveals difficulties in Kant's theory by addressing objections to it, in this case from common sense. In opposing Garve's objections, Kant turns the table on common sense and sustains the moral wisdom of a child over the experience of an expert. In another well-known passage, he declares that "a child of say eight or nine years" would know enough to resist the temptation to be compassionate and not to violate the duty of a trustee. Even if no harm were done and much good could be accomplished, the child would choose to obey the law rather than redirect an inheritance to a needy person who deserved it more (TP, p. 288, Ak 8.286). The child's innocence would protect it from the errors of the sort of experience that seem to confer wisdom but actually spoil it (TP, p. 289, Ak 8.288). The purity of moral theory is illustrated in the unthinking reaction of a child against the temptations of empirical morality based on what makes for happiness. Moral theory in practice reflecting the lack of practice, exposing the weakness of common sense.

How do moral persons come together in politics? Kant takes up the question in a part of "Theory and Practice," where he contrasts his answer with that of Hobbes. Instead of depicting abstract individual human beings, Kant distinguishes the human being in three aspects: the freedom of every member, the subject as equal, and the citizen as independent. These aspects are interesting because he gives substance as he explains them in regard to Hobbes's abstract human individuals, as well as to his own moral persons. Human beings are free to seek happiness after their own fashion, but to do so they must be mature, unlike the eight- or nine-year-old child who knows morality so well. Equality in subjects has nothing to do with rich and poor but it is hostile to inherited rank. Kant's equality means that every member of society must be permitted to rise as far as "his talents, his industry, and his luck may bring him." Kant pronounces that a person "can be considered happy . . . provided he is aware that, if he does not reach the same level as others, the fault lies only in himself" (TP, p. 294, Ak. 8:294). His equality as a moral person needs the support of a society with free institutions permitting him to "get ahead" in the American sense. He is happy when, with the full permission of society, there is no one else to blame but himself. One of Aristotle's moral virtues is the right amount of anger, neither insensitive nor irascible, needed perhaps to prompt the moral person's awareness of his advantages.

Citizens must have a character enabling them to be independent; each man must be "his own master" in order to vote. Dismissing women and children as obviously dependent, Kant awards an independent character to those with property or with a skill or art by which they produce something that can be transferred and sold to another, as opposed to having only one's labor to offer to another, like a domestic servant, a shop clerk or a laborer. To clarify his point, Kant says that a barber would not be a citizen, but a wigmaker—even one fashioning the wig with the client's own hair—is indeed qualified as citizen (TP, p. 295n, Ak. 8:295). Though Kant admits that it is "somewhat difficult" to determine which human being is his own master, "independence" in this way is visible, whereas the pure goodwill of the moral person is not. As visible, it is merely a probable instance of genuine freedom to which Kant's critique of reason denies us certain access. It makes sense, common sense, that a republic needs independence in its wigmaker citizens, who protect it from surrender to tyranny. But is Kant entitled to the use of common sense, which he excludes from knowledge of morality? In fact, he does not trust the independence of citizens in a representative government. Departing from Rousseau, who requires that each individual citizen be asked whether he agrees to the general will, Kant only obliges a representative legislator to consider whether the people *could* possibly have agreed to a proposed law. It is his duty to regard it as just even if he knows that they are in a mood where they would probably not consent to it. Here is the anticipation of democracy led by a vanguard with better knowledge of the people's will than have the people.

To excuse Kant for his untoward judgments because of his time would be to invoke the empirical morality he abhors. He does not go wrong because he is prejudiced but because of his attempt to escape all prejudice, especially the prejudice of reason itself in the transcendental illusion. His denial that we can know the nature of things leaves him at the mercy of deterministic science aided by probable guesswork, both of which he condemns as merely "up to now." His desire for certainty, resulting in his moral purity, led him away from the questions of philosophy that he despised as "antinomies." In *Perpetual Peace,* Kant denies that philosophers can be kings (PP, Second Supplement, p. 338, Ak 8.369). Philosophy can be misused and therefore it cannot be the highest activity; only the goodwill cannot be misused. Though Kant said that "the class of philosophers" should be permitted to speak publicly, he loosed morality from the sovereignty of philosophy and made moralism king over men.

CHAPTER SIX

G. W. F. HEGEL

(1770–1831)

Common to us now is a high school course in world history, presenting for study a series of civilizations or cultures. Each of them makes its own diverse contribution to humanity as a whole, known as the "world." We have seen that word, actually a term, in Machiavelli understood in contrast to the other world known as intelligible by philosophers and as the next, heavenly world by Christianity. Machiavelli's "worldly things" (*cose del mondo*) that he says he knows have no order or organization that make them a whole but instead are divided into various sects of religions or opinions (D Let. Ded., 2.5). World history, however, is one thing, a whole, with civilizations in an order of succession, a rational ordering. To show that rational ordering so as to make the world a whole is the achievement of G. W. F. Hegel. Even more, to make himself the author of World History (with capitals) is his crowning contribution to world history, for in doing so he makes world history aware of itself.

Rational control is the idea of modernity, this book argues. That idea was endangered by Rousseau's discovery of history in the evolutionary development of man. In Rousseau's *First Discourse* it appeared that scientific progress—rational control—was made at the cost of moral degeneration, a bad bargain for humanity. There was, for Rousseau, a self-sufficient world freed of the frowning supervision of the classical heaven and the Christian God, visible and empirical rather than invisible. But the sequences of history did not amount to a rational world that would be a rival to the nonhistorical critique we have seen from Machiavelli to Locke of this world of premodern thought. Kant, we have seen, addressed the problem in minor writings with a half-hearted claim that the phenomenal world of history could be posited, though not proved, to be rational. Hegel came to the rescue of rational control in the predicament left by Rousseau and

Kant, and, taking the bull by its horns, showed Kant to be wrong, and history to be a rational liberation of humanity in its own, self-made world. In his *Philosophy of Right* (1820), Hegel presents the articulation of the rational state at the end of world history. In his lectures on the *Philosophy of History* (1837), he outlines the development of cultures to the end, or completion, of world history. After Hegel, one finds a critique by Marx of Hegel's version of World History, supplying a more rational account of history through the succession of class struggles within states. And at last, Nietzsche comes to spoil the party and put an end to Hegel's notion of a rational end. Rational control in its original version was inseparable from freedom. In Machiavelli's *Mandragola* there was liberation from the old morality in the prudent reason of a plan of seduction and Messer Nicia's

MAJOR WORKS OF HEGEL

The Phenomenology of Spirit (1807): The consequential text that develops human consciousness from sense perception to absolute knowledge, and examines the dialectic of successive shapes of mind or spirit (*Geist*) that arise, such as the "master-slave dialectic."

The Science of Logic (1816): An account of dialectical logic, in which contradictions emerging from posited categories yield new concepts, that expresses the German idealist principle that thought and being constitute a single, active unity.

Encyclopedia of the Philosophic Sciences (1817): A teaching manual that presents an abbreviated version of the *Science of Logic.*

The Philosophy of Right (1820): Hegel's major work of political philosophy argues that freedom can only be attained through participation in a rational ethical community. He develops three spheres of right: abstract right (*Recht*) of noninterference; morality (*Moralität*), based on Kant's moral philosophy; and ethical life (*Sittlichkeit*), which integrates abstract right and morality with rational political order.

Lectures on the Philosophy of History (1837): The focus of the present chapter; versions of the original lectures were delivered in 1822, 1828, and 1830, with a compilation based on notes by Hegel and his students published in 1837.

Lectures on the History of Philosophy (1833): Not to be confused with the former, these lectures, delivered between 1805 and 1831 and compiled posthumously in 1833, present a systematic historical analysis of philosophical development from Chinese, Indian, and Greek thought to modern German idealism.

cuckoldry. Nietzsche maintained, to the contrary, that freedom means above all freedom from rational control and so founded the "postmodern" movement known to us today.

Hegel left two kinds of writings: books he composed, and compilations of lecture notes either by him or collected from intelligent students. The former are tightly and densely stated in a manner that reworks common words and phrases into a system, such as his main political work, *The Philosophy of Right*. He wrote an *Encyclopedia of the Philosophic Sciences* to work out and display his complete system, in which nothing is as it is given and every expression has a rational reformulation bestowed upon it in order to lock its place in reason made triumphant. To read any of these books, one must wave goodbye to everything familiar and set forth into a foreign land where home becomes a distant and unnecessary memory.

The second kind of writings is made for the classroom and is considerably more accessible, and one of these, the *Philosophy of History*, I have chosen for analysis. As well as easier to follow, this text best fits the theme of this book's philosophic history of rational control. One could almost say that my book's theme is identical to Hegel's, but for the fact that mine addresses the philosophical antecedents to Hegel's philosophy rather than the world-historical events Hegel chooses to explain. Hegel's system gobbles up its predecessors as if they were not needed. As Hegel says in one of his most famous phrases, "The owl of Minerva takes flight in the dusk," the goddess of wisdom takes flight only when events have prepared her reflection.[1] Philosophy cannot see ahead and is confined to what it can see in retrospect. In this fundamental thought, Hegel stands alone as the first philosopher able to see the rational whole of human history. To understand what he saw is one the best reasons for reading this book—and, of course, the primary source, Hegel's *Philosophy of History*. To see why Hegel found it necessary to study events and to foreclose all philosophy but his own, we go back to the modern turn to history before Hegel.

Actualizing Freedom

The argument of this book has been that the owl of Minerva took flight at the dawn of modernity, when Machiavelli fashioned his plan or plot to change the world through modern political philosophy. Let us refresh that argument. What did modern political philosophy teach? It was reason and freedom: reason to control human lives, and freedom as both the means of releasing reason from its traditional shackles and as the goal reason pursues. Freedom uses the idea of necessity, most clearly in Machiavelli, to control the chance that has always intervened to thwart human happiness. If one wanted to characterize generally the difference between modern and premodern or ancient political philosophy, it would be that moderns stand for freedom and the ancients for virtue. Why do the moderns say that men are free? It is because they are free from God and from nature; they have no natural obligations. Nature is not a friend to men; it doesn't supply them with things they need and doesn't even guide them to find the things they need. As nature is not a guide, the whole idea of natural right, the central feature of classical political philosophy, is cast into doubt. That idea, though rejected at first by Machiavelli, is picked up for rescue by Hobbes and based on the nature of human reason, the only natural guide.

Human reason becomes the solid foundation for everything else, as in the formula of Descartes, "I think, therefore I am." A similar foundation can be found in Hobbes, so that in using human reason, men can escape from their nature, from their neediness, from the nasty necessities of pre-civilized life. Natural right remains in an attenuated form as nature teaches human reason the negative truth that men must escape from their nature. Men are not only not born with natural gifts for which they must be grateful, but instead they are born with great needs that must be met. In our day one hears the complaint that every American child is born with millions of dollars in national debt, as if this were the burden of an original sin. This is Hobbes's and Locke's idea of man: life is a burden to us; we have to expend our lives to make a living. There is no reason to be grateful. With this fact the modern regimes of England and Holland that served as models of free, constitutional government were still in thrall to necessity. Now Rousseau changed this picture fundamentally, as we have seen. He pointed out that reason is not so reliable a foundation. Reason is not such a friend to man as Hobbes and Locke had supposed. It was created to control passions that were not in man's originally good nature, and in controlling them, reason used force that much diminished man's original freedom, while at the same time adding to the number and strength of the passions it controlled. Hence came the perverse consequence of moral danger from rational progress that we have studied in Rousseau's *First Discourse*.

Man has come so far from original freedom and goodness that the nature of human reason is no longer a simple guide to follow. Yet if man's original nature is good, the possibility is raised of a return to nature—not a return to its primitive cocoon, but a higher reconstruction of nature in an otherwise corrupted society. This would be a return to nature after having been alienated from nature. One thinks of the Tahiti paintings of Paul Gauguin, a nineteenth-century artist who went primitive among the twisted inventions of modern art in Paris. Rousseau held to the view that man's nature was originally good but denied that reason was capable of recovering it as it was when original, simple, and complete. Since reason depended on accidents for its development, it did not fully control itself. Thus, since man was not fully responsible for the alienation brought by reason, he could not reverse its progress and overcome his alienation. In politics he could render his chains legitimate, but only with the aid of conventions unguided by human nature as introduced by a legislator who might or more likely might not arise. Rousseau agrees, therefore, with the modern philosophers before him that there is a catch to human freedom. Man is born free but his freedom is devoted to supplying human necessities. Either man must continually escape from the state of nature—because there is no perfect escape from it, as with Hobbes and Locke—or he can never finally recover it, as with Rousseau. Machiavelli, of course, invented the notion of necessity that keeps the prince awake at night. In short, men have freedom but can never escape necessity; they can never move from the realm of necessity to the realm of freedom.

Kant agreed with this summary of human imperfection. For him, humans always live in both realms. They are free as rational beings and unfree as human beings, having a nature like crooked wood, as he says. That is why perpetual peace is only an ideal that can never be realized but only approximated. According to Kant, necessity and freedom are not two kinds of actions, like making a living and reading a book. They are two aspects to every human action. Every action, however necessary, has its aspect of freedom. One is always free to step from necessity into freedom by giving a categorical moral law to oneself. Necessity remains but we are free to reject it: that is Kant's peculiar position. Alexander the Great was a great man as a phenomenon, but as noumenon he was a knave.

We come now to the philosopher Hegel, who removed the catch that caught and held human freedom. Hegel discovered the way to actualize human freedom. In this he was followed, but otherwise faithlessly, by Marx (to be treated in chapter 7). He developed the philosophy of history, going beyond Kant, by showing that freedom can be achieved. Not only is it that the moral can be vindicated in history and that there are signs of moral progress, as with Kant. Hegel shows that the realm of necessity is overcome by the progress of the spirit (*Geist*), of freedom and reason.

Substance = Subject

We can find an introduction to Hegel's system in the few pages that introduce *The Philosophy of History*, the book of his lectures, which is the text for our treatment of Hegel. The theme of this book and the path followed so far prompt a brief return to Machiavelli, who began the "world" of Hegel. Machiavelli's "worldly things" are not natures or essences but necessities mixed with chance that can be managed with prudence, sometimes even with "great prudence" or philosophy (D 2.26.1). Human reason contends with nature, which for him is "chance custom" rather than rational and intelligible, with the aim to conquer or "acquire" nature for human advantage. Yet chance remains, not fully rationalized: Machiavelli's "Italy," based on his analysis of Rome and freed from barbarian exploitation, does not amount to Hegel's rational Germanic state in which nothing could be otherwise than reason makes it. History does have "the cunning of reason," in Hegel's phrase, meaning that reason uses apparently irrational means to arrive at its rational end. Machiavelli likewise spoke of the necessity of fraud, which is the tool of the prince, rather than impersonal reason. The highest cunning is supplied to history by Machiavelli's tendentious interpretation rather than found in history itself. Hegel is closer to him than he appears, but Hegel has a system to abolish "chance necessities," and Machiavelli retains them, with his eye on room for human virtue. Hegel's system is a more radical, yet also a more open and public version of Machiavelli's conspiracy. Unlike Machiavelli, the master conspirator, Hegel reveals himself to be in charge.

How is the world to be understood? Hegel distinguishes understanding, which he disparages because it works merely toward exposing contradictions, from reason, which dialectically combines those contradictions.

Machiavelli's *Discourses on Livy,* for example, would be for Hegel an attempt of reflection that abstracts from the facts of Livy's *History* but wrongly assumes that those abstractions are universal rather than merely Roman. For Hegel, reason considers Rome as a stage in World History, to which Rome makes its own special dialectical contribution. Hegel states at the beginning of his *Philosophy of History* that "reason governs the world": "Reason . . . is *substance* and infinite power. [It is] itself the *material* of all natural and spiritual life and the *infinite form* that activates this its content" (PH, pp. 79–80). Reason is omnipotent; it is not only form, which would be nothing new in metaphysics, but also matter—so that reason is not limited by its dependence on the matter it forms. This point is made long before by Machiavelli, but he does not state so directly that everything is reason (P 7). Instead of referring to Machiavelli's effectual truth as opposed to wishful imagination, Hegel refers to the common popular belief in God's providence that combines God's knowledge with power to effect it; this belief supplies a nonphilosophic analogy to his principle (PH, p. 83). He says flatly, against Socrates (who claims to follow the Delphic Oracle), that "this belief" is contradicted by "our principle."[2] When reason governs, there is no need to respect the power of the belief in God's providence, as had Machiavelli (who spoke of "our religion") and Socrates, who recognized and conceded to it. Hegel will not admit the mysteriousness of providence, however, because it would mean that the power of reason is abandoned to chance. What he has to acknowledge is not "to be regarded as a presupposition" but attained in world history, "a result that is known to me because I am already familiar with the whole," here stating that he knows as much as God (PH, p. 80). Hegel's knowledge represents the total conquest of chance or fortune by reason in what Bacon had called the "conquest of nature."

For Hegel, nature is not unchangeable and chance is not variable, because both are subject to reason, which moves through history, changing its definition while eliminating chance: "Reason is thinking that determines itself wholly, freely: nous." This is the same as the plan of Providence. Freedom is based not on ignorance, as in doing what one pleases—which gives its cause over to chance—but on knowledge that allows one to exist depending only on oneself. How does reason overcome the separation of nature from oneself? How does Hegel overcome the obstacles of both nature and fortune to one's freedom? Not by the violent rape of Lady Fortune, as with

Machiavelli (P 25), but reasonably and without counselling violence while relying on the violence of others, we shall see. Machiavelli was not a violent man himself but contented himself with praising violence. For Hegel, it is not that the prince conquers nature but that he allows nature to conquer itself. As opposition to man, nature is matter with a gravity of differing parts that seek unity in a central point. Seeking unity, matter is not merely receiving form but finding it for itself. Its own logic of separateness would destroy itself in self-contradiction as made of exclusive parts, except that parts make up a unity.

And what is unity without matter? The form, or the form of forms: oneself. So matter moves on its own to the form that it implies and that brings it out of the self-contradiction of separate matters or natures into the unity of form and matter that is human reason (PH, pp. 86–88). Hegel's reason, therefore, is not merely abstract but, as he says, "concrete." Abstract would be form without content, separated from its matter, as in the phrase "free speech," in the sense of saying what one pleases. But free speech is free in a concrete sense only when it is rational and voluntary, and not constrained by error. It seems that only a philosopher in Hegel's time was capable of free speech.

Hegel's notion of substance has been traced to Baruch Spinoza (1632–1677), a modern political philosopher contemporary to Hobbes and comparable with him, who returned to favor in the German Idealism in the nineteenth century of which Hegel was the master. Spinoza posited that God is not a personal God but that God is God's creation, his works, not just a person. God's creation then amounted to a universal substance often called "pantheism," or today "monism." Its doctrine differed from the speculative metaphysics of Thomas Aquinas, designed to prove the existence of a personal God, which Spinoza declared to be impossible. Spinoza's metaphysics, shown in his *Ethics* (1677), featured a deductive "geometric manner" that Hegel and others adopted. For them God is not outside the world, and since we possess adequate knowledge of the essence of God as the first cause of everything, we can go down the line to prove a certain point deductively. Spinoza called the theme of philosophy "substance" and tried to prove that there was only one substance. His idea was adopted and improved in German idealism by the German philosophers Johann Gottlieb Fichte and Friedrich Wilhelm Joseph Schelling, then perfected by Hegel. In the *Critique of Pure Reason,* Kant, too, had worked out deductively a table of categories of the pure understanding rather than empirically taking them from ordinary speech, as did Aristotle.

Spinoza's substance had been divided into infinite attributes of which we humans have access to two—cogitation and extension—according to the first book of Spinoza's *Ethics*. Such a slipshod procedure is denounced in German idealism as dogmatic, using a new definition of that derogatory term. Dogmatic is whatever is taken as given rather than deduced. Nature and God are condemned as dogmatic sources of things given and thus as causes of intelligibility. Intelligible distinctions must come from the human understanding by deduction; they must not be imposed on humans by an external source. Only so are humans both rational and free. Hegel's *Science of Logic*, beginning from nothing and deducing everything, is the height of the manner Spinoza had called geometric. Deduction makes for abstruseness. German idealism does not like examples, because examples depend on common sense, which is knowledge one already has without deduction. In the preface to the first edition of the *Critique of Pure Reason*, Kant disparages examples and says that an argument is clearer without aids to clarity (A xviii). Kant himself uses examples—the child in the *Metaphysics of Morals* and especially the famous "four examples" of his *Foundation for the Metaphysic of Morals*—but he keeps them to a minimum. He leaves doubt as to whether these examples provide clarity or aids to clarity. Either way, his readers are grateful for them.

Social science shows this tendency today when it calls a study of Luxembourg or San Marino a "case study," rather than an example: Such a study has to be a case of a larger system, instead of an example of a small country. Science isn't science unless it is complete in a system, which is a whole created by deduction rather than by appeal to what is obvious. A human being has one nose and two eyes; why isn't it one eye and two noses? To deduce an answer would seem to be more difficult than necessary. What is the meaning of example? An example is an appeal to something outside the deductive system, a given of some kind that is needed to pull the argument to its conclusion. An example signals a difficulty in the deduction, either a rhetorical difficulty, when one needs to overcome the resistance of an audience, or an inherent difficulty in the argument. In classical political science, Plato and Aristotle willingly offer abundant examples because their philosophy depends on the intelligibility of nature, rather than a system.

Reading Hegel's *Philosophy of Right* is like crossing a desert in which examples are as rare as oases and as welcome. But in Hegel one should be suspicious that when one sees an example, it may mask a difficulty where the argument strains and needs outside help. Examples are oases of nature in a desert of deduction. One can take this as an example of an example. An example sets up a proportion: An example is to Hegel's philosophy as an oasis is to a desert. It implies the intelligibility of nature in analogies. But modern rational control wants a system that depends on nothing outside it: no givens, no dependency, perfect freedom in the ambit of one's own reason. That is the meaning of "system," as noted before, of which Hegel's is the masterpiece. Is that a system of human reason in general or one's own reason by itself? Nietzsche will have an answer not favorable to Hegel's apotheosis of human reason.

Hegel's system would be the universal substance that is the object of knowledge, but what of the subject that understands? Here, in the suggested equation of substance and subject, one encounters Hegel's view of Kant. According to Hegel, it seems, Kant discovered true metaphysics without knowing it; he discovered the importance of subject. To simplify, Kant's "subject" is the spontaneity of the understanding. The world as we know it, whether as science or common sense, is the work of the human mind. The mind brings order into the chaos of sense data from the senses that it receives, and understanding is a project, or a projecting, of the mind into the world. Yet since this understanding was the work of the human mind, Kant believed it was not the understanding of the true world. The true world, the noumenal world, is not accessible to us as theoretical humans. Now Hegel observes very simply that the understanding which creates the phenomenal world cannot be part of the phenomenal world. If it were, the phenomenal world would be explained by itself. One could not have a psychological explanation of science because psychology, as a science, presupposes science. Every psychological explanation of this sort fails to explain the *psychologist*. Was Freud suffering from an Oedipus complex when he devised the theory of the Oedipus complex? Was Machiavelli's theory of effectual truth itself an effectual truth of his humanist education? Was Hobbes in fear of violent death when he constructed his theory of that passion?

Hegel's point is that the understanding of the phenomenal world is not part of the phenomenal world; it is in the noumenal world. The organizing, legislating, projecting mind is the absolute, the thing-in-itself. Subject is the absolute; mind understood as the spontaneous understanding is the absolute. Today, many who live under what they consider pluralist democracy and fear the despotism of any single principle have an allergy to the word, but the absolute was a special term of German idealism. It is not something above human reason but can be found by simple analysis of the world. Analysis of the mind and its acts shows that the hidden ground of everything is mind. Even a rock is mind. It is non-mind in its stolid stupidity which has to be understood in terms of mind. It is not intelligible in itself but only as alienated mind. Why do objects offer themselves to the human mind? They hold mind in themselves. Kant's critique of metaphysics focused on the proof that if the human mind tries to think about the principle or ground of anything, it becomes entangled in contradictions, a dialectic of contradictions. When Kant used the term "dialectic" he referred to the collapse of reason, the transcendental dialectic resulting from "antinomies." In cosmology, for example, the first principle can be proved to be that the universe has no beginning or that it has a beginning. Human reason collapses when it reaches the highest principles of speculative metaphysics.

At this point Hegel leans in to say, "Kant, you dummy, you have the solution to the problem in hand." The essential contradictoriness of reason can be the vehicle of reason and its instrument. Contradiction on this level proves the necessity of going to another level where contradiction can be overcome. Kant's antinomies in the dialectic of reason are fundamentally equivalent to the antagonisms in history of which Kant made much use. These were the moral or amoral antagonisms in his philosophy of history that are bringing about the just society. While for Kant dialectic indicates the collapse of reason, for Hegel it is the triumph of reason. Then it must be that the mind essentially develops; the mind doesn't merely project, as for Kant. Kant's analysis of pure reason and of the understanding is part of the analysis of the thing-in-itself, the noumenal world. The noumenal world is mind and things understood as works of the mind, objectifications of mind. For Hegel, the mind must essentially develop so as to overcome its contradictions.

History is the mind in development. Things-in-themselves are not inaccessible or accessible only as a moral postulate, as they were for Kant. We can see them by looking at history intelligently, which means history as the process of mind. Mind is not the individualistic ego of Descartes or the self of Hobbes, Locke, and Rousseau—with all its accidents and foolishness. Mind develops in the acts of a society, or what Hegel calls the people (*das Volk*). Subject is finally the spirit of a people or nation. Note that since mind develops, the word *Geist* can also be translated as spirit, as is done here. It is often best represented in an individual, a world-historical individual, but it is not essentially individual. Substance seen as equivalent to subject is the development of national spirits in their entire sequence. History, the process of mind, must be rational. Two consequences follow from this.

First, this process is necessary. The follies and crimes of vulgar history are necessary. Early stages of history did not simply miss the truth; Hindu, Chinese, Greek, Roman—all had something valuable to pass on. This cosmopolitan outlook is common today, particularly when combined with the equality of cultures, which was definitely not the case for Hegel; yet, for him, all of them are equally necessary as stages of development. The follies and crimes make the noise of history, he says, while reason silently progresses in the background. Second, the rational society in which reason is fully developed, must be fully actual: Freedom is actualized. If a rational society could only be infinitely approximated, as for Kant, it could never be actual. There is no infinite process, and Hegel can develop a teleological doctrine—a doctrine of purpose or end of things—of the whole with a clear conscience. In the unfolding of the mind, the process is teleological as the whole is fully manifested to itself. The whole process must be completed, for if it were not, one could never prove its rationality. Some last-minute tragedy might intervene; something might happen on the way to the Forum to disrupt the fullness of human life. That is why Hegel opposed in Kant what he beautifully called "bad infinity" (*schlechtes Unendlichkeit*)—the discovery that perpetual peace means perpetual war, that morality can never be visible or provable.

A quick comparison of Hegel's teleology with Aristotle's very different notion may be helpful. Aristotle could also be taken to say that mind is the absolute, but nature to him does not mean that mind rules over nature. Mind meets with nature and grasps it, a meeting that is possible because nature is intelligible. But if nature is intelligible, nature must be distinct from accidents, qualities, or aspects that could be otherwise, such as the warts on Oliver Cromwell. Nature intends an end but does not always achieve it, as with acorns that do not sprout into trees. In the case of man, the end of a complete and perfect human being may not be achieved or ever achieved. Nature, as distinct from accident, allows nature to serve as a guide for human choice in the face of accidents; nature is not everything that exists. Aristotle's teleology requires the sacrifice of the omnipotence of nature, because to say that nature is intelligible is to dethrone Zeus, who was both mind and power (*Politics*, 3.13, 1284b). No rational society can exist, according to Aristotle. Every society is subject to accident, hence every society needs a Zeus to be an authority over measures not justifiable by reason.

To the contrary for Hegel: The political meaning of the end of history is that the rational society exists, and exists now. What is it? It is the society of the rights of man recognized and accomplished in the French Revolution. According to Kant, the French Revolution, though accomplished with "misery and atrocities," inspires spectators with "a wishful participation close to enthusiasm."[3] Hegel accepted this judgment, exclaiming that after the revolution "man stands on his head . . . a glorious mental dawn. All thinking beings shared in the jubilation of that epoch" (PH, Sibree, p. 447).[4] Taking responsibility to speak for all thinking beings, Hegel added the actualization of human freedom presented in his *Philosophy of Right*. Since the French Revolution was resisted and its influence corrupted, it was not enough for Hegel merely to recognize it. There had to be a structure that would make the revolution permanent, a government capable of protecting rights, requiring certain inequalities explained in that work, together with a distinct "civil society" to maintain the difference between public and private, and an independent civil service to keep government well advised and impartial.

What Is World History?

World history is the demonstration, or working out in stages of history, of a rational Christianity. It is not easy to see how much of Christianity Hegel believes or how he believes, but what follows is an attempt. The book we use, *The Philosophy of History*, is a translation of Hegel's lectures collected by students, which must suffice.[5] World history, we have seen, is not the mere application of Hegel's thought but the working out of his metaphysics, and the most essential aspect of his metaphysics, as well as the most complete and brilliant flowering of the modern philosophy of rational control we study in this book. Here is Machiavelli and his successors brought to a rational end rich in insight and colored with beautiful descriptive reasoning. Yet where are Hegel's predecessors in the philosophical formation of modernity? Strangely enough, these preparatory philosophers from Machiavelli to Rousseau are covered up by their completion, their laurels removed and their names unmentioned. For Hegel, modernity is not explained in a book of political philosophy such as this one, but in a book of historical events and their analysis. Modern political philosophy, insofar as it ends with Hegel's solutions for all vital problems, puts an end to political philosophy. After Hegel's splendid idealism, noxious weeds take over, especially the two most imposing of them—Marx and Nietzsche—who succeed Hegel and take him apart. The need for political philosophy revives and its modern ambition calls for an effort of reexamination.

What is it that Hegel completes? Modern political philosophy demanded a new morality and politics beginning from Machiavelli's "new modes and orders" and continuing through the Enlightenment and idealism. Machiavelli's legislation (P 15, 25), intended to free human beings from dependence on God and nature, culminates in Hegel's system, in which reason cancels every natural distinction and makes its own replacement for God. This recovery of the world from the spell of "invisible spirits"—to mention Hobbes's contribution—results in the denial of the other world or at any rate the denial that it is relevant to this world. The morality that overcomes nature overcomes God, and this is the work of world history according to Hegel. "Overcoming" for Hegel is *aufheben*, "overcome" is *aufgehoben*; it means to cancel, preserve, and transcend. As with an unsatisfactory boyfriend, one first "cancels" him, then preserves the idea of boyfriend, and at last transcends the original with a new one. The word *overcome* will also be found in Nietzsche. Hegel is the greatest overcomer because he connects the Christianity he destroys with the modern morality he preserves. As we shall see, this is not just a dead, spiritless deism but an actual incarnation—not the passion of Christ, but of reason.

Three kinds of history are set forth in the introduction to the *Philosophy of History*: original, reflective, and philosophical. Original history is written in the spirit of its time and does not adopt a point of view above its relation of events. The best cases of such histories cited by Hegel are those of Thucydides and Caesar, in which the author was a participant in the war described (today's best example would be Winston Churchill). But if not a participant, the author does not step out of the world of action. Such history could be poetic, as distinguished from mere tradition; some representation and imagery may be used. Hegel remarks on the speeches that Thucydides ascribes to the individuals he discusses, but he omits mention of Thucydides's claim to have produced a possession for all time. This might have induced an interesting comparison of Thucydides's claim for himself with his mind and Hegel's declaration of World History's absolute moment in his philosophy of the development of mind.[6] Today one could write a history of the Peloponnesian War, as did Thucydides, but it would not have the same feeling for the war in its time, which was his time. Our time limits the empathy we can feel for a time long past, however appreciative one may be of its virtues and deeds. Can one truly preserve the particularity of time past? But one can understand a universal principle, and that is what Hegel finds in the second kind of history.

Reflective history is universal and abstract. The spirit of the author differs from that of the actors. Livy, for example, came too late to sympathize with the actors of early Rome. Hegel lists different kinds of universal history: the pragmatic kind, consisting of moralistic critics of the past living in the present, who watch from the sidelines and overlook the difficulties in satisfying moral demands; modern (nineteenth-century) critical history that cares nothing for the original spirit of deeds and documents but seeks accuracy regardless of importance, for which Hegel had great contempt; and abstract history, the history of ideas.

Philosophical history combines the central element of both original and reflective. The content of original history is the individual: individual human beings or nations. Reflective history uses universals for content, using names but only as examples. What the reflective historian intends is universals, in which no names appear and the individual is not important as such. Even the scientific historian, whose concern is with the minutest particulars of individuals, works from a conception of universal science and seeks to establish a scientific historiography. The English historian of the eighteenth-century Sir Lewis Namier exposed the daily contacts of great men such as Edmund Burke, but he did so in order to prove that human motivations are petty. He could have made the same point with a study of Napoleon; for him, Burke was just an example and Namier's account was a case study of a universal. Philosophical history offers universal history with names to be seen in the table of contents: China, India, Persia, etc. The universal of reflective history is beyond history, where it loses the individual. Philosophical history preserves the individual and has no case studies, for its instances are no longer examples; they are essential elements in the progress of history, now World History.

Then philosophical history is concerned with individuals—but which ones? Which individuals *contain* the universals? How does one distinguish world history from mere history not essential to World History? Such a distinction would be scorned by historians today, but it can be defended from a commonsense point of view. What is world history? Is it the wars between the mercenary armies of Italian cities that Machiavelli mocks, in which nobody gets hurt? "World-historical" would mean something affecting all inhabitants of the earth; an example of the 2020s would be the COVID virus. A remedy exists, a remedy from modern technology. Modern technology comes from modern science—and where did that come from? From Galileo, Newton, Einstein. And that came from where? From the Greeks, who discovered science as a rational account of the whole. Then the Greeks are a world-historical people. Hegel's procedure is more complicated, but it arises from an obvious fact—that the world has been conquered by the West. That was already true in Hegel's day, still more in ours. Hegel may seem to be parochial and ethnocentric for the West, but his concern is based on the hard fact that all nations seek to imitate the West in its military technology if not in its ideas. For, as we shall see with Marx and Nietzsche, and as we know from the wars of the twentieth century, the West became divided against itself. So far as the West could be identified as the only civilization with science or philosophy, the West proved to have a divided mind. Hegel was the one who identified science as belonging to the West, particularly arising from Greece and landing in the Germanic mind—rather than arising in Greece by accident, for which he can be accused of ethnocentrism. Yet he had a proof for his claim, which included giving credit to non-Western civilizations for their contributions to the rise of the West.

How, then, does Hegel begin? Which is the first historical people? The first people with a history is the people that keeps records. Hegel notes the ambiguity in the word *history* in German (also in English) between the account of events and the events themselves. This we must regard, he says, as no mere accident, as a people would not keep records if there were no events deserving to be recorded, nor would they keep records of events not worthy of recording. It is not the case that records might be lost, or as Machiavelli suggests, suppressed by any new "sect" wishing to destroy the memory of the old regime (D 2.5). In his optimism, Hegel declares that only a people with a state and a constitution would think itself capable and deserving of leaving a record (PH, pp. 115–116). This situation makes for a distinction between prehistory and history, as today in the difference between archaeology and anthropology—but the distinction for Hegel is made by written records, not by language. Thought appears only when language is written. If thought and language were the same or essentially connected—as is implied by the Greek word *logos,* which means both speech and reason—then thought would have occurred in prehistory, which is impossible for Hegel. For him, reason makes itself known in history and could not depend on anything taken from prehistory; there is no oral history, as practiced in our time. And within history in the time of the Greeks, Plato shows Socrates to have philosophized without having written a record of it such as Plato supplied in his dialogues.

What is known as the Socratic tradition must trace its origin to a man with no publications to his credit—or discredit. From reflection on this fact, it appears that philosophy is not essentially written; but, for Hegel, philosophy, to be philosophy, must be preserved in writing. This is a consequence of the truth, according to him, that mind develops. Furthermore, the recording depends on the existence of a state with a constitution that sponsors the recording, by which philosophy is no longer a private act but constituted as a public memorial. The development of philosophy requires that it be made by and for a public authority. Philosophy is not essentially critical or subversive but expressive and sustaining of the mind of its time. It does not use the discovery of unchangeable nature as opposed to changeable convention to give itself life for the ages.

The paramount prehistorical continent is Africa, because it remains prehistorical (in Hegel's day). This is the old state of nature we have seen, now made actual: Africa is man's natural condition as prehistorical. Hegel explains Africa after a few pages on the world's geography, for world history takes place in separate locations with diverse geographies. Kant, with his distinction between human being and rational being, would be comfortable with rational beings that are not human. His distinction inspires science fiction and creatures who are rational but not human; Kant would be confounded by the discovery that the only rational being is here on Earth. Hegel makes the development of rational being identical to the history of man on Earth, and he would be confounded by the discovery of rational beings elsewhere. He even dismisses the new world, America, as "the land of the future" and concentrates on the old as the arena for the development of World History (PH, p. 193).

What do we see in Africa? When studying a nation, Hegel directs our view to what would most impress a tourist. He scorns the recondite; he shows us the big, obvious things—the sights—in a nation. No complicated fieldwork is needed, such as an anthropologist of our day would insist on. He is a higher version of our political scientist in comparative government, who carries with him a carpetbag filled with jargon that is commonly composed of turgid, structural concepts made in imitation of but very distant from Hegel's high-minded categories. For Hegel has no less scorn for the humdrum as for the recondite. He does not categorize nations by the kind of tool they used, as if some future archaeological expert would announce that the United States was a power lawn-mower culture. It is true that a tool, whether from the Stone or the Iron Age, contains an element of mind, since it helps to overcome nature. But Hegel turns our attention to what is held to be highest in a nation. What is remarkable about Africa is that nothing is held higher than man. Hegel remarks on sorcery and its use by magicians, in which man tries to command nature and thereby escape nature. Sorcery is a tool after all, helping man to rise from his natural condition as a slave. In this way, out of the absence of freedom, Africa begins the rise to freedom. Its features are slavish: fetishes, the worship of the dead, cannibalism, slavery, and courage. These qualities show man to be the highest creature—and yet, therefore, to have no reverence for man: man is the most edible treat. They are summed up in a certain constitutional despotism that is both derived from and limited by the power of violent subjects. Africa shows the natural human condition as absolute injustice, where blacks learn freedom from their slavery. Slavery becomes a phase of education for man: "It was not so much *from* slavery as *through* slavery that humanity was emancipated"—a theme to be seen in the work *Up from Slavery* by the black American educator Booker

T. Washington (PH, Sibree, p. 407). But in Africa, people had no conception of mind, Hegel says, which would manifest in their appreciation of themselves. Africa is unhistorical, undeveloped mind.

What distinguishes the first historical nation, China, is having a history. By contrast with India, China has the oldest, most continuous writings, and its historians were high functionaries revered for their work. But China and India were dead ends as cultures, for both were lacking in self-consciousness. The beginning of World History was in the writing of it, not by the actual contact of peoples; we do not learn by reading the records of other nations. If we could, there would be no need for history to develop the mind: Nations could make history and philosophers could develop the mind. Writing is necessary for Hegel's philosophical history, though not for unhistorical philosophy. If philosophers want to communicate to later philosophers, writing is necessary, but they would have to write for other philosophers rather than, or in addition to, later peoples. Hegel's philosopher, namely himself, writes from the end of history, where problems have been solved, so that philosophy does not have to disguise its discoveries but only explain to the world what the world has accomplished. No secrets or enigmas or aporias are to be found in Hegel, only abstruseness. His philosophic history is history with content, with names. But if names are to develop philosophy, they must touch each other. This means, as said above, that geography is crucial for World History. He restates Aristotle's proposition that civilization is possible only in temperate lands, but then goes far beyond that to consider particular features such as continents, mountains, rivers, etc.

The geographic basis of World History is mere nature. Geography imposes mutual exclusiveness on mankind, but the idea of freedom crosses oceans and mountains and enables thought to overcome its separations. The idea of freedom culminates in the Germanic nations that become most powerful and master the world, a process of "globalization" that is neither simply commercial nor simply exploitative. Geography is the space of man, which means of thought, so that in the dominance of Germanic nations, space ceases to be a determinant of World History. Not only is reason unbounded by space but also by time, since the appearance of the Germanic nations is the end of history, the absolute time. Man loses or overcomes his natural perspective of space and time by working through history. Kant's phenomenal man becomes Hegel's noumenal man. In the briefest summary, Hegel's philosophical history develops by means of the actual contact of peoples from the substantiality of freedom in the East to the discovery of mind or spirit in Greece, in which the point of contact is the Persian war; to the Roman world, in which the plastic individuality of Greek freedom becomes the abstract universal personality of Rome and Roman law, through the Roman "liberation" of Greece that expressed the crushing destiny of Roman power; and to the Germanic world, whose destiny is to bear the Christian principle, not merely as the substance of Christianity but producing it freely from subjective self-consciousness—where the point of contact is Christianity.

Christianity makes the transition between the Roman world and the Germanic, having been born within Rome and flourishing after the fall of Rome. This is the most interesting point of contact for us because it supplies the transition from ancients to moderns. If Hegel can surmount this division, the others would not be so difficult. For the one between Greece and Rome, one could find virtue in the abstract universality of Roman law rather than regard Rome as mere decline from Greece, and for that between Greece and the Orient, one could see freedom in Eastern despotism rather than regard Greece as the sole source of Western civilization. The period of Christianity between the Roman world and the Germanic, between the ancients and the moderns, is known as the Middle Ages. Hegel is the philosophic source of the concept "medieval," which is taken for granted today. "Medieval" was used sparingly in the seventeenth century, more often in the eighteenth, to refer to a hiatus between ancients and moderns, but Hegel uses it strictly in the sense of a transition that permits a dialectical development from the ancient to the modern world. The concept was a great invention for Hegel as the middle of World History. Not only is the opposition between ancient and modern overcome because it is seen as a development, but also it presents a new view of Christianity.

With this view Hegel opposes the very analysis of the present book. The quarrel between the ancients and the moderns is not in Hegel as it is presented here: the classical political philosophy of Plato and Aristotle vs. the modern conspiracy of Machiavelli and his followers. What is notable in Hegel is that World History is the development of mind but not of the history of philosophy, for philosophy as the owl of Minerva always comes too late to be the cause of an effect in history. Hegel recasts the Greek discovery of philosophy (by Thales)—which saw it as the distinction between nature and convention—as the discovery of self-consciousness without mention of "philosophy" or "nature." Hegel calls it the Greek discovery best represented by Socrates, as if he were the hero rather than the critic of the Greeks. When Hegel comes to the modern age there is no mention of Machiavelli and his new effectual truth, but rather a discussion of Machiavelli's rival in rebellion against the Church, Martin Luther: "The essence of the Reformation [is that] man is in his very nature destined to be free." Thus it was the Reformation, not the Renaissance (though the latter appears as "attention . . . again directed to the ancient Greek literature")—and it was Luther, not Machiavelli, who brought modernity into World History (PH Sibree, p. 410). Machiavelli, too, had shown how to "interpret" Christianity according to virtue rather than idleness (D 2.2.2), but his appropriation of the Church was political and conspiratorial. By contrast, Hegel openly adopts and adapts the Church as a stage of the development of reason. In doing so, he finds the cause of the "universality" of modernity "after the terrible night of the Middle Ages" to be in religion directing itself and not in a new Machiavellian politics that redirects religion against itself. He praises Christianity as Machiavelli never did for having "rendered humanity free," using the Church as its instrument (PH, Sibree, p. 411).

Machiavelli attacks Christianity and the Church openly in his *Discourses* and subverts it with his blasphemous interpretations. Because he puts politics to the fore, he praises the use of fraud and uses it liberally himself (D 2.13). Hegel, we have seen, does not use fraud himself but attributes its use to reason, "the cunning of reason." As Prince Rational himself, Hegel exposes reason in advancing its cause through such apparently irrational instruments as the Church and Christian doctrine, now "interpreted"—as Machiavelli would have it—as reason's fraud, not his. Hegel himself takes the high road, and instead of interpreting the high as low with Machiavelli, he interprets the low as high, unreason as the cunning of reason. Hegel shares Machiavelli's view of rational control and can be said to belong to the succession of modern political philosophers we have studied in this book. Both Machiavelli and Hegel believe in the power of reason to give effect to itself, but Machiavelli, having given focus to "worldly things," was the first of the two, however excused as he was from World History. In chapter 15 of *The Prince*,

Machiavelli attacked the ancients for their devotion to truth that ended in an imaginary republic or principality—that is, a truth that cannot make itself actual in the world as we experience it. This truth is subject to the chance that hinders its every advance and prevents its final success. Machiavelli came up with the "effectual truth" and made himself the prince of his enterprise: He left a role for Lady Fortune that was also room for human virtue, and he claimed it for himself. The first word of his *Discourses* is "I" and the last is "greatest." Hegel comes at the end of Machiavelli's enterprise, now understood as the absolute marking the end of World History, where the prince is subject and his principality, together with his republic (in his *Science of Logic*), is substance.

The difference between Machiavelli and Hegel, and between the beginning and the end of rational control, is the greater role for politics and for political philosophy in Machiavelli. For Machiavelli politics leads the charge and exploits victory, by acquiring and maintaining; for Hegel, politics follows culture obediently with no "modes and orders" of its own. The result is to place culture over politics in the peoples of World History; culture becomes the motive force of history. Politics is subordinate to culture, which means to religion, because religion is higher than politics. Politics is no longer the master science of Aristotle that subordinates all other sciences; nor is it the sect that commands this-worldly religion of Machiavelli. Machiavelli and other modern political philosophers through Rousseau regarded Christianity as one of the two great enemies of human freedom (the other being Aristotle, forerunner of Christianity). Kant made a move against this hostility when he praised the purity of Christian morality.[7] Hegel went further in finding the Middle Age, dominated by the Church and Christian doctrine, as the crucial stage of human freedom between ancient and modern. Its division between sacred and secular had to be overcome, a change prepared but not made in the Reformation that initiates the modern time.

The geographical basis of the new status for Christianity is to consider it to be a part of the West. The Jews play a role in this transformation. They are the only people mentioned twice in Hegel's World History, under Eastern despotism and again under the Roman world in the West. Christianity appears under the Roman world and not as something Eastern. Thus it is through the Jews that Christianity becomes the link between Eastern despotism and Western freedom by which we today in our loose unconscious Hegelianism speak of the Judeo-Christian tradition. Hegel contrasts Western civilization to Eastern but not as in permanent, fundamental opposition. A college course in Western civilization now includes the Judeo-Christian heritage in amicable company with the Greeks—quite a change from earlier philosophers of freedom such as Hobbes and Montesquieu. Denizens of the Middle Ages, of course, did not know where they were. They understood their spirit as essentially the same as the ancient, with the addition or subtraction of Christian divine revelation. Their philosophers were mostly Platonists or Aristotelians or both, facing a challenge that did not present itself to the ancients—the challenge of monotheistic revelation, inspiring a church with a status independent of politics.

Hegel shows how philosophy and revelation can be reconciled in a rational Christianity. The main tenet of his rational Christianity is a necessary Creation. Thomas Aquinas also held a rational Christianity, but with the provision that God is omnipotent, so that by his will he could or could not have created the world. For Hegel, God had to create the world of necessity. In the introduction to his *Science of Logic*, Hegel says that the book is a description of the world prior to its creation by God. This is what he knew—or thought—to be true. The rational creation demonstrates that the necessary victory of mind in logic would be incomplete without its concrete incarnation in World History. The beginning is poor, and the end is rich. History is the activity of God, for God is not at rest as Aristotle supposed. The activity of God must be shown as actual in the world: Creation is necessary and the philosophy of history is necessary to Hegel's logic.

The activity of Christianity is a movement from the idea of the incarnation of God as man, which is embodied in the separation of sacred from secular, to an altogether secularized Christianity that contains the truth of incarnation. Christianity brings God to this world, thus creating a distinction within this world. In Hegel's account, Christianity becomes part of life on earth and is no longer understood as opposed to *this* world. This means that the Church and its priests no longer have an independent status and do not enjoy sanctuary. In one of his *Jena Aphorisms*, collected in the notebooks of his early years, Hegel says that reading the daily newspaper is a civilized man's version of morning prayer.[8] The editorials with their pieties and platitudes serve as sermons to start the day and provide security in the world instead of in God—perhaps by purging one's grievances instead of confessing one's sins. But wait! In a rational society there won't be any justifiable grievances or mortal sins. It is hard to assess whether Hegel was a Christian believer or not. If he was, his faith was Protestant, not Catholic. His followers split on the issue, the Left Hegelians claiming that he was an atheist, the Right Hegelians, that he was a believer. A rational Christianity exists in a rational society, which means no more debate with the ancients over his justice and theirs, and no more issue taken with Christian revelation. Hegel accepts the universality of freedom, as opposed to the ancients' reservation for the status of the wise over the many, and he secularizes the incarnation of Christ in the development of World History.

At the end of the introduction, Hegel brings the sovereignty of religion over politics to the fore (PH, pp. 209–210). Religion is the essence of a people, not its rulers. For the ancients and for the moderns from Machiavelli to Rousseau, religion is seen as an instrument of rule, so that the kind of religion reflects the kind of politics. These moderns, most notably Rousseau in his *Social Contract,* criticize Christianity for not being subordinate to politics (SC 4.8). For Hegel, however, a rational Christianity leads to a politics without rule in which *all* are free and "the antithesis of Church and State vanishes" (PH, p. 109). There is no rule because there is no irrationality in principle, no partisanship but only accidents and misdemeanors. A rational society could decay, but not in such a way as to challenge an old principle with a new one. These difficulties can be handled by an educated bureaucracy such as Hegel defines in his *Philosophy of Right.*

One might conclude that this happy situation, all problems having been solved, does away with the need for philosophy. This is not Hegel's conclusion. He says that the mind does its own work, making its own "creation" and its own world history, vindicating God's justice in a "theodicy," but it does this for itself. At the end of his book, Hegel says "the mind is only that to which it makes itself; therefore, it is necessary that the mind presupposes itself" (PH, Sibree p. 457). What remains is to understand "God" in quotation marks, or as mind. The philosophy of history must return to the *Logic* as its presupposition. For this, one still needs philosophy for contemplation, as Hegel asserts on the last page of the *Philosophy of History.*

G. W. F. Hegel

Immoderate Politics

What are the *political* consequences of a view that finds an end to politics? Kant and Hegel sought to replace earlier liberalism that rested freedom on formal rights, secured by government and exercised by citizens. There may be a tendency that citizens, given opportunity and incentives, will use their freedom sensibly to maintain their freedom, but there is no necessity, no guarantee. Kant and Hegel sought to supply that guarantee, Kant with hesitations; and Hegel, criticizing Kant for stopping short of certainty, without those hesitations. But it turns out that seeking certainty is harmful to good sense in politics. The idea of rational control, seeking ever greater certainty and necessity, yields immoderate rationality—in Kant, a critique that separates reason from the world; and in Hegel, an extension of reason that leaves nothing to chance and embraces the whole world. Too little responsibility in the first, and too much in the latter.

Let us return again to Kant, with a view to Hegel's critique. Kant says that men are moral only when morality is pure—that is, without regard to the consequences of actions. Why is that? Regard for consequences means regard for what one has to gain from an action, and thinking of what one gains taints the morality of the action. In such a case, you are seeking to gain for yourself or your group or your country rather than, or in addition to, acting morally on others' behalf. Now, if one considers morality without reference to consequences of actions, one must do so also without reference to motives, for motives look to the consequences. Exclude consequences, and you exclude motives. Kant makes interesting remarks about motives. Motives are private and can even be unconscious; you may not know why you are carrying out an action. The moral person's motive might be unconscious selfishness. Hence one cannot be certain that anyone's motive is moral. One cannot be certain even that any moral person has ever existed: Kant anticipates the psychology of the unconscious, "depth psychology," of today. By ignoring the motive of actions, Kant can save morality from all psychology, including depth psychology. Whatever one's unconscious motive, man's dignity consists in the possibility of consciously ignoring his selfish interests. Morality consists in ignoring what is one's own; as we have seen, morality for Kant is the universal reason of a rational being.

The possibility of acting as a rational being is enough, for one cannot know whether the possibility becomes actual in any particular case. The rational being knows the noumenon of man but not whether any human being lives up to it. The rational being knows, or at least postulates that he knows, the essence of a rational being in his self-legislation. This is the extent of his self-knowledge. But, since he must act as well as think, he must come into contact with the world of phenomena. This fact makes for difficulties in Kant's scheme. The moral person must act to bring about *moral* society, but all his actions can at most bring about *legal* society. One can see the actions of humans but not their motives; for all we know, they might be the intelligent devils in the essay on *Perpetual Peace* that Kant claims could run his legal constitution. In sum, the moral person cannot know whether he is making others moral. If he tries too hard, he is guilty of paternalism; if he does too little, he is guilty of neglect. In this alternative we can spot conservatives of our time, wary of paternalism; and liberals, who fear being guilty of neglect.

The moral person must recognize that morality is more likely and attainable in a legal society; so he should try to bring it about. But how? Suppose he is by himself in an illegal and hence presumably immoral society. He cannot conspire with others to reform or revolutionize his society, because he cannot lie or use violence against the illegal or immoral institutions he lives under. The moral person achieves his morality only by self-legislation that disregards his own self, which means only by taking himself as a rational being. His morality has to be universal and can make no exceptions. He cannot distinguish a necessary from an unnecessary evil, nor a noble lie from an ignoble lie; he cannot weigh moral alternatives. He cannot hoodwink a tyrant and become a revolutionary against an illegal society. All he can do, and this he must do, is *wish* for a revolution in an illegal society, but he must not act for it. We know what Machiavelli thought of wishing for imaginary republics or principalities, but we also remember that Kant alleged solid grounds for his wish based on the very sort of historical analysis that Machiavelli provided against mere wishes. By the immoral or amoral antagonisms in history that Machiavelli said made Rome strong and free (D 1.4), the rational or legal state is established. Recall the double life of Alexander the Great, according to Kant.

This is not a tenable view. It was hypocritical of Kant to be glad for a revolution—the French Revolution—that he could not have entered into.

He took refuge in his own tender conscience, which rejects lying and violence, and then let others do the dirty work. Allowing violence by others is not really nonviolent; it is sanctioning the violence of others if done for a moral motive. This is just what the moral person is not allowed to do. Such a person thinks he is pure but his purity depends on the immorality of others. And not only does this person hypocritically proclaim his own purity but he also forces the authority he confronts to get its hands dirty by using violence openly and admitting to its own immorality. This is the confrontation politics we have seen in Kant's essay on *Perpetual Peace* and is visible today. With nonviolent protest, one can force the authorities to use violence, which means forcing them to be immoral. Kant was the first philosopher not to fear moral passion and the first to encourage it. His immoderate morality applauds the immoderate immorality of others. Kant was surely a more moral man than Robespierre, but his doctrine could not explain why. This was the beginning of Hegel's criticism of Kant—but also one that could well be applied to himself.

For Hegel, morality is not such a secret as is declared by Kant and his theory. One does not have to probe into unconscious motives to see whether the moral person is secretly immoral. In fact, as we see in Hegel, moral is as moral does. Those who are moral show themselves in speeches and deeds, above all in politics. It is not a question of politics versus morality, as Kant presents it. Politics is the theater of morality: morality cannot be esoteric. You can say that you believe in God and privately disbelieve, but you cannot deny your morality in public and still privately believe in that morality. You can be an atheist in the closet, because God's existence is not affected by your affirming it or denying it. But a moral principle is affected if you deny it publicly; your denial makes it less effective and harms it. Hegel says there are conscientious people in all societies and at all times (*Philosophy of Right*, §140). It is possible to be conscientious and a cannibal. Those Aztec priests, busy cutting out the hearts of prisoners, who can doubt they thought they were right to do so? They thought they were doing their duty, wrongly to be sure, but still they were conscientious. Religious persecutors were very conscientious; so, too, were slave owners. The former believed they were agents of God; the latter could be decent to their slaves while never doubting the rightness of slavery. Kant posited that conscience cannot err, but only because, as universal, it is strictly formal. Conscientiousness as formal, if not as strict as Kant's, can always be found regardless of content. Today we like to speak in praise of someone as "principled" without specifying the principle. But the content of the principle has to be right, according to Hegel, in order for one to be truly moral.

Both of Hegel's criticisms seem right: that morality is not a secret and that formal morality is not enough. But Hegel goes beyond them to the conclusion that the rational society is actual. The right content of morality not only needs to be combined with the right motive but the two have now been combined in moral and legal society. How does rational society become actual? By stages that conflict with one another, not by the gradual Enlightenment of reasonable people. Hence World History is not the home of happiness; the great passions responsible for progress always go too far. When man attempts something, it is not so much like building a house—the architectural motif of modern philosophy that we have seen in Machiavelli (P 2) and Hobbes (not build on sand), but rather the burning of a house, Hegel says, for revenge (PH, pp. 94–95). This is an act that usually has unintended consequences. Freedom does not build itself by easy stages, managed by moderate persons, as if according to our contemporary theories of political development. Men always go too far; they induce a reaction that also goes too far, as passions carry men beyond their intention. Human freedom builds itself as men see events pass beyond their control. Hegelian man is in charge of nature and history—the acme of rational control—on condition that no single actual man ever accomplished anything without going further than he intended. If passions are stronger than intentions, they are stronger than any contemplated ends. Thus practical, political men such as Caesar and Napoleon are the heroes of World History, not philosophers. Their particular aims involve or contain the great issues of World History, but to actualize these issues, "History," for Hegel, needs the great passion of great egoists. It is necessary that the actualization of freedom proceed by stages in which freedom is partial and "overcome" in the next stage.

The "cunning of reason" that we have encountered describes the use of persons as the means of reason (PH, pp. 128n, 186, see also pp. 4, 16). It is the morbid craving for power of History's great—let's use the right word—tyrants. Men, in using reason, have no consciousness of the idea of World History: If they are practical, they don't have this idea themselves, and if they seek philosophers for guidance, they cannot get it, because philosophers are always too late. Men of conscience are found in every age, but they are not likely to be heroes of World History. They are too scrupulous to achieve anything, says Hegel in agreement with Machiavelli. Hegel is not Machiavelli but he uses Machiavelli's insight without endorsing his immorality. Doesn't this smack of the hypocrisy he accuses in Kant? The moral person stands on the sidelines and deplores the means while he cheers the end. In the very act of denying, even denouncing, such moral hypocrisy, Hegel seems to show it himself. What is the difficulty in this conflict between Kant and Hegel? To keep morality pure, Kant separates it from law, and to show morality in success, Hegel identifies it with law. What Kant and Hegel share is the belief that freedom can be made actual—that is, a rational society constructed in which men are not and will not be irrational. They can live freely without trouble or challenge, and without need of either courage or moderation.

CHAPTER SEVEN

KARL MARX

(1818–1883)

KARL MARX was born in Trier, Germany, to Jewish parents who converted to Lutheranism. His education was more like that of a graduate student today than any we have seen so far in this book. He went to the universities of Bonn and Berlin and fell in with a group of radical Young Hegelians. Marx wrote a doctoral dissertation on the ancient materialist philosophers Democritus and Epicurus, introducing materialism to Hegel's system on his way to crafting his own theory of historical materialism. The communism he came to espouse opposed the utopian theorists of his time, Charles Fourier, Henri de Saint-Simon, and Pierre Proudhon, whom he criticized unsparingly. It also differed profoundly from the communism of Plato's *Republic* and Thomas More's *Utopia*, which were designed to support a life of philosophy. Marx's communism aimed at abolishing the capitalist division of labor, which exploits the productivity of the proletariat class and imprisons and disfigures men in one cramped dimension of life. For its thought as well as the power it retains in our time, Marx's communism owns a major station in the history of modern rational control.

Any study of Marx should begin with an acknowledgment of Friedrich Engels (1820–1895), Marx's faithful and modest friend whom he met when living exiled in Paris. Engels always subordinated himself to Marx, but he outlived the great man and was able to edit volumes 2 and 3 of Marx's great work, *Das Kapital*, after Marx died. He coauthored with Marx *The Communist Manifesto* (1848), perhaps the most powerful political pamphlet ever composed. Engels also wrote *The Dialectics of Nature* to address an aspect of Marx's thought where it might be considered inadequate and in need of support. Rejecting the philosopher's contemplative life as he did, Marx had little to say of the sort of friendship he enjoyed with Engels, leaving it unclear how much he was partner in thinking and how much a collaborator in a worldwide conspiratorial movement to revolutionize human life.

A survey of Marx's works finds a definite break between the early and the mature Marx, which our discussion will respect. The early Marx is Marx *der Philosoph*, still in the ambit of Hegel, with whom Marx struggled,

MAJOR WORKS OF MARX

THE EARLY MARX

"On the Jewish Question" (1843): An essay that criticizes fellow Left Hegelian Bruno Bauer for confining his critique of religion within liberalism.

Economic and Political Manuscripts (1844, first published 1932): Drafts of an unfinished book known for Marx's conception of capitalist alienation, critique of liberal political economy, contrasting humanism and historical materialism, and his early account of communism.

The Holy Family: Critique of Critical Critique (1845): Marx and Friedrich Engels's critique of the idealistic historicism of the Left Hegelians, in which they promote the historic role of the proletariat.

The German Ideology (1845–1846, first published 1932): A set of works in which Marx and Engels develop historical materialism and argue that political institutions and ideology are mere superstructure to a given economic stage of development.

The Poverty of Philosophy (1847): A critique of Pierre-Joseph Proudhon's *Philosophy of Poverty*, attacking his utopian socialism.

THE MATURE MARX

The Communist Manifesto (1848): Marx's famous work, discussed in the text.

Capital: A Critique of Political Economy (Das Kapital), vol. 1 (1867): Marx's magnum opus analyzes the structure, origins, and decline of capitalism. The unfinished volumes 2 and 3 were published by Engels only after Marx's death.

The Eighteenth Brumaire of Louis Napoleon (1852): An essay that analyzes the 1851 coup by which Louis-Napoleon Bonaparte became head of the Second French Empire

The Civil War in France (1871): A pamphlet by Marx as the official statement of the Communist International on the struggle of the Paris Communards in 1871.

Foundations of a Critique of Political Economy (Grundisse) (1857–1858): First published in 1939, the *Grundrisse* is often described as the rough draft of *Capital*.

against whom he rebelled. Here is Marx the humanist, a thinker who still fascinates intellectuals on the Left living outside Marxist regimes. In this humanism, the human being emerges with splendor as a "species being." The mature Marx is the economist and social scientist, the Marx of dedicated Marxists and of regimes in which Marxist economics is official, if not always (or ever) followed. Present interest in Marx's ideas looks to his early work, to his humanism—as opposed both to the economics, now generally abandoned because it was flawed and did not work—and to the Leninism that perfected the original temporary dictatorship of the proletariat of Marx's science and made it permanent. What could not be accomplished automatically, as it were, by the operation of laws of economics has had to be done through tyranny. Humanist neo-Marxism introduces Marx as a political theorist when, according to both the early and the mature Marx, politics is the last relic of alienation that will be abolished together with capitalism. In this book a more radical view of the mature Marx than is usual will be presented and its failure not taken for granted; the later, wider influence of Marx will not be examined.

Marx is the only one of our eight moderns held as an official state philosopher by regimes today. As self-named living schools of philosophy, of the eight only the Kantian, Hegelian, and Marxist establishments remain. The others survive only as adjectives describing aspects of their thought, except for "Machiavellian," which covers everything human and modern. In keeping with our theme, Marx will be studied for what he contributes to modernity and its history. To arrive at the radical substance of the mature Marx, where politics is abolished, it is better to start from the early Marx who is less self-contained, critical of liberalism, less scientific, and more revealing.

Marx's Critique of Liberalism

A general view of liberalism as Marx faced it will be useful before turning to his early critique of it in "On the Jewish Question," for his critique is also a radicalization of liberalism to its extreme. His critique is to the narrow selfishness of liberalism and appeals to the interest of the whole. In doing so, Marx continues the "actualization" of freedom from idea to historical fact that we have seen in Hegel and extends it to the removal of necessity from freedom. For Hegel freedom and necessity were together in the rational state whose laws were necessary to define freedom correctly and rationally. But the laws still were enforced and had to be obeyed; necessity was necessary as an accompaniment of freedom. With Marx, the state with its powers of enforcement disappears. How does this happen? Through necessary laws of history by which capitalism must yield to communism. Necessity removes itself from human life by necessity.

Looking back to Machiavelli, we see necessity set forth as the instrument of human virtue and freedom. In the critical sentence in chapter 15 of *The Prince*, Machiavelli says it is necessary to choose *according to* necessity. Those who choose according to imaginary regimes they wish for will "learn their ruin rather than their salvation." That unfortunate choice is possible, indeed generally taken for granted in Machiavelli's time, so that it takes a Machiavelli to point out the mistake. Marx, however, points out what is going to happen necessarily; his laws of history will do the work done by Machiavelli, who is reduced to an agent of those economic laws and denied the status of the glorious founder of "new modes and orders." The difference between Machiavelli and Marx is that Machiavelli wants freedom in the company of human virtue and glory, which Marx finds superfluous. Machiavelli, the inventor of necessity as the goal of politics, is by Marx's reasoning no longer necessary. Yet Marx's theory is in the spirit of Machiavelli's enterprise of making freedom through necessity; it is indeed the completion of his enterprise, at which time necessity can be tossed aside and freedom lived without restraint or any inhibiting memory of restraint. We shall see that according to Marx, at the end of history, men can forget history.

One can combine Marx's critique of liberalism with his extension of it: remove necessity in the interest of the whole, of *human* wholeness. Thus the triumph of the human over necessity—which means over nature understood as necessity—becomes visible. It is first a triumph over religion, now shown to be a myth of divine powers over us; religion is no longer a necessity to which we must conform. It is, second, a triumph over politics, the realm in which men conflict and struggle. Liberals (here including Machiavelli) had supposed that politics is necessary in order to resolve such conflicts, but the removal of necessary conflict puts an end to politics. The end of politics for Marx is peace, as in Hobbes and Locke, not a noble end, as in Kant and Hegel. To achieve peace, one must remember that human beings have individual interests, which when given freedom, will conflict—the famous argument of James Madison in *The Federalist* No. 10. Politics according to liberals is then limiting and restraining human freedom for the sake of peace, because of necessities. Liberal politics creates a realm of freedom, which is limited but productive, versus natural freedom, which is unrestrained but disastrous. Marx says that humans can rise above this distinction; religion and politics are not necessary to the human condition. Necessities can be mastered if we learn that religion and politics are *human* creations, neither necessary nor natural to us. They are human creations that appear not to be ours but rather over us; they are ours in alienation. When we humans see what we have done to enslave ourselves, we shall have conquered our alienation and returned to ourselves. In what follows, I consider the overcoming of religion mostly in Marx's early writing "On the Jewish Question" and the overcoming of politics in *The Communist Manifesto*, the text that declares his maturity five years later, at age thirty.

"On the Jewish Question" turns out to be a brilliant critique, not of Judaism or religion, but of liberalism. It sets the stage for the Marxism that came soon after but could stand on its own for the depth and power of its analysis. It is in appearance a critique of religion but it becomes a critique of the political liberalism that protects religion, not on behalf of some other politics than liberalism but against all politics. In a longer book, one could compare Marx's writing with the thought of Baruch Spinoza, surely the greatest modern expert on the Jewish question and a contemporary of Hobbes who wrote in defense of liberal politics. Marx, however, does not return to the seventeenth century to contest Spinoza; he begins from the situation of his own time after the death of Hegel in 1831. This writing is a critique of Bruno Bauer, a Left Hegelian. Hegel had claimed to have secularized Christianity, as his statement of the modern rational state reconciled the Bible with the world; Christianity in this view was no longer preoccupied with the other world, but now with this world. After Hegel's death a split arose between Left and Right Hegelians as to whether Christianity survived this reconciliation, the Left Hegelians asserting that it did not and that Hegel was an atheist. Atheism came to be the topic of the day; no longer a devious stance to be concealed in the closet, it was accepted and held as an honorable conviction (JQ, p. 32).

Marx begins his critique by laying down the views of his opponent, Bruno Bauer, who had himself criticized the special claims of Jews in demanding emancipation from state-authorized intolerance. Such a demand by Jews, said Bauer, made them egoists; they should work for the emancipation of humanity. They wanted Christians to give up their religious prejudice, but were these Jews giving up theirs? They should have made their demand as men, not as Jews. Jews must emancipate themselves before asking others to emancipate them. How should they do this? Simple—they should make religious prejudice impossible by abolishing religion. Jews and Christians are different stages in the development of the human spirit, which when recognized will be seen not to be opposed. Science enables them to see their unity as human beings (JQ, p. 28). Thus, according to Bauer, the Jewish question can be solved by removing the contradiction between religious prejudice and political emancipation, which says that a Jew cannot be a citizen. Man should be emancipated from religion in order to be a citizen: Man must give up religion, and Jews must give up Judaism. Bruno Bauer, it would seem, goes very far against religious prejudice by abolishing religion, but Marx says that he did not go far enough. He should have asked what kind of emancipation is needed; Marx says that it must include emancipation from politics. By criticizing the Christian state, Bauer stops short of criticizing the state itself.

Marx says that for guidance on the Jewish question, one should not look to France and Germany, where it is considered a theological question; rather, one should look at America, where the state is not religious and the question is treated as secular. But in America religion remains in force because, quoting Tocqueville's *Democracy in America*, Marx says that "no one in the United States believes that a man without religion can be an honest man" (JQ, p. 31). One should not see religion as the cause of secular narrowness and social exploitation as does Bauer, but rather as a consequence of exploitation by the state that permits it. Political emancipation from religion is incomplete without human emancipation from the state. Marx does not adopt the liberal view that the state should be neutral to religion; he insists that the effectual meaning of the state's "neutrality" is atheism. Liberalism is a contradiction between an atheist state and a religious majority that in practice overwhelms its atheism. Marx here overlooks the concern of the liberal theorists—Hobbes, Locke, Kant, and especially Spinoza—that the religious majority be educated gradually and indirectly into religious indifference, which in time would amount to atheism, in practice if not avowed in theory.

Marx disregards the difference between the liberal religion and the old-time religion supported by the Church and the clergy. He rejects the liberal distinction between the state and civil society that wants to define the citizen as universal and his private life as egoistic and bourgeois (JQ, p. 34). In this liberal "dualism," the species life of man is opposed by his material life, which means that his species life is unsocial and therefore incomplete (JQ, p. 39). The contradiction between Jews and the state is part of the more general contradiction between civil society and the state that must be overcome. For Marx there can be no First Amendment that in the U.S. Constitution protects religion because the right to the free exercise of religion, along with other rights protected by the liberal state, allows and avows the egoism of the bourgeois against the universality said to be the principle of the state. The so-called rights of man, evidenced in the constitutions of Pennsylvania and New Hampshire, are actually rights of bourgeois man hostile to the universal, species life of man (JQ, p. 40). This conclusion applies not only to religion but also to all individual rights of private property, equality, and security. Egoistic man is the presupposition of politics and the state, for instead of freeing man from such private, egoistic pursuits, the liberal state awards man the freedom to engage in them.

Marx quotes Rousseau in *The Social Contract* on the need to alienate man's natural freedom to the state, calling this "the transformation of human nature." But Rousseau says the transformation is only "as it were," since it may be good politically but not good for the natural freedom whose value he wants to preserve against political transformation. Marx quotes but ignores that reservation of Rousseau's; it gets lost in his condemnation of the egoistic individualism of liberalism. Natural freedom is replaced by the concept of "species being" that his theory will define and make actual (JQ, p. 46n). For this we must take up the *1844 Manuscripts*, where Marx replaces liberal dualism between state and society with a new description of the wholeness of man.

The second, shorter part of "On the Jewish Question" might seem to be a surrender to common anti-Semitism, for Marx finds the secular basis of Judaism in the practical need for money. But his analysis does not blame Jews. The Jew, he says, is a haggler, a negotiator, as is characteristic of modern capitalistic man. As money gains power in the world, Christians have become the same as Jews; now everyone "Jews you down" when making a deal. Judaism reaches its peak in the concept of civil society in the Christian world. For Marx, Christianity makes all natural, rational, and moral human relationships external to man, because they are dependent on God. Judaism operates on this sort of alienated man, making him commercial and transforming alienated man and nature into alienable, saleable objects. In practice, the Christian egoism of eternal happiness becomes inevitably the material egoism of the Jew.

In all of "On the Jewish Question," it is amazing that Marx makes no reference to the philosophers of liberalism and quotes only liberal declarations of constitutional rights, Tocqueville on alienated honesty, and Rousseau in one of his points of difference with liberalism. Instead, Marx stays within Hegel and explains liberalism within the Hegelian categories of state, and civil society as the expression of religion. Liberalism and modernity in this view are secularized Christian egoism; the concern for the salvation of one's own individual soul has become the egoism of pursuing individual rights. A later, truncated version of this outlook can be found in Max Weber's celebrated argument that finds the spirit of capitalism in the Protestant ethic. One can also get a hint of the honesty or probity that will be promulgated by Nietzsche in Marx's bravado atheism, though Marx makes no mention of this or any other virtue. History, or Hegel's interpretation of World History, has made it possible to say what it used to be necessary to conceal. It is not Hegel but Marx the Left Hegelian that can attain and proclaim the effectual truth of religion. Have we not heard of the effectual truth somewhere before Marx?

Species Being: Materialist or Humanist?

"Species being" (*Gattungswesen*) is to succeed bourgeois egoism. The expression occurs several times in "On the Jewish Question," but Marx, having adopted it from Ludwig Feuerbach's *The Essence of Christianity* (1841), does not explain it. In the *1844 Manuscripts* Marx comes to an explanation that considers what makes the human species distinctly human (hence, humanist) and what makes it economic (hence, materialist), but he leaves it unclear how these two can be combined in defining species being. Marx begins from Feuerbach, author of the concept. Feuerbach's materialism derived from his atheism rather than concern for economics, but Marx had been studying liberal political economy and found it useful to extend materialism from hostility to the soul to the positive satisfaction of human needs. These manuscripts were apparently material for a book that was never completed and were not published until 1932. They show Marxist economics, the vital essence of Marxism, in its moment of genesis out of Hegel's philosophy and Feuerbach's critique of it. You won't find "species being" in an economics textbook these days, not even in a Marxist version, but in these manuscripts we see the philosophical basis in that term for Marx's turn away from philosophy to economics.

Contrary to theology, Marx says that in accordance with political economy, he proceeds not from the fall of man into evil but from an "actual economic fact," a fact about production:

> The worker becomes all the poorer the more wealth he produces, the more his production increases in power and range. The worker becomes an ever cheaper commodity the more commodities he creates. With the increasing value of the world of things the destruction of the world of men proceeds in direct proportion. Labor produces not only commodities; it produces itself and the worker as a commodity—and does so in the proportion in which it produces commodities generally. (MS, p. 71)

With a devaluation of the human world comes an increasing valuation of the world of things—a reminder of the woeful summation of history in Rousseau's *First Discourse.* This would have to be a fact in order to make a sound beginning, but Marx goes on with his analysis of the alleged fact. The object produced by labor, its product, now stands opposed to labor as an alien being, as a power independent of the producer; the product in fact becomes the objectification of labor:

> The laws of political economy express the alienation of the worker in his object thus: the more the worker produces, the less he has to consume; the more value he creates, the more valueless, the more unworthy he becomes . . . the more ingenious labor becomes, the duller becomes the worker and the more he becomes nature's bondsman. (MS, p. 73)

This is a good statement of the alienation political economy conceals in failing to examine the direct relationship between the worker and his product. Alienation can also be seen in the process of production, by which the worker's product becomes external to the worker, not a part of his nature. He feels homeless during his work and at home only during his leisure time. His work is forced labor not for the satisfaction of need but to satisfy others' needs. Work is self-sacrifice—working for another to whom one belongs.

This definition of work would properly be alienation from the true human condition only if alienation could be overcome, if "necessity" in Machiavelli's broad sense was exaggerated and wrong. Aristotle has it that work is for the sake of leisure, and recreation for the sake of work, to recharge your batteries. Thus a hierarchy exists from recreation for the sake of work, which is for the sake of leisure, the highest human activity.[1] But Marx, wishing to overcome necessity, has work or production as the highest activity. As the result of alienation from his production, the worker feels himself freely active only in his animal functions of "eating, drinking, procreating" and feels himself in his human functions nothing but an animal: "What is animal becomes human and what is human becomes animal" (MS, p. 74). The worker's animal functions are human but when separated from all other human actions they become ultimate ends, hence animal. Are they then classified as recreation, or are they redefined as productive? Perhaps it is the latter. Perhaps Marx understands all possible human activities as productive so that recreation and leisure become work, and work loses its character as necessity by contrast to them. In comparison with Aristotle, work gets a promotion by Marx from means to end, from necessary for leisure to the highest human activity, productivity. Necessity and consequent alienation were always recognized, as in Machiavelli's notion of necessity, which alienates man from the easy way out of his troubles and problems posed by his wishes and imagination. Marx did not discover alienation; he discovered the possibility of overcoming it.

To overcome necessity requires a certain kind of human being, Marx shows—a "species being." While for Machiavelli necessity always means my necessity versus yours, Marx's species being does not have an essential concern with individual needs because those needs can be satisfied. If there is no necessity, there is no individualism arising from an urge to think of yourself. Man becomes a species being in the double sense that the common or the community becomes his object and that he treats himself as "universal" and hence as a free being. He does not need to think of himself as an individual and of others as competitors. Kant spoke of the rational being, Marx of the species being for whom the body is not overcome or resolutely ignored as with Kant, but the body whose needs are satisfied. Then, what is a species being? Are animals like the (endangered) spotted owl also species beings? No, man is more universal than an animal. An animal is an organic being as is man. But man—omnivorous man—lives from the whole of nature so that nature becomes man's inorganic body as the means to life and his life activity; man eats from nature but also uses what he doesn't eat. So, nature is man's inorganic body, a closer relationship than with his environment, as we say today. In our science of ecology there is no special status for man; man is more an endangering species than an "endangered" one. Yet if nature is part of man, as for Marx, man is part of nature. Alienated labor makes the natural species life into an individual life as the end of species life, thus requiring attention to one's individual needs. Under alienation labor appears as the means to an end and species being is lost. But in truth, labor is the end; man's productive life is his life activity, his being, his species being. Well, then, produce what? And for what? Anything is the answer. If one's being is to produce, one cannot specify what one should produce, and production becomes an end in itself, not for the sake of products. In specifying the product one becomes enslaved to it, alienated by it. President Jimmy Carter was a peanut farmer before he turned politician; it's as if he ran for president as a species being to escape being identified by his mode of production.

This is Marx's "humanism." Man differs from animals, and is not himself an animal, because he is universal by using all nature; all nature becomes man's "inorganic body." Man uses animals, and they become part of his inorganic body. But can't man use his own body? What is the difference between his organic and inorganic body—between living and dead matter? How can *life* be crucial for Marx's humanism if life is shared by men and animals? Why should there be a privileged status for the human body over other bodies, as in the distinction between organic and inorganic? We need something else, and that is conscious activity. Other animals produce hills and hives, like ants and bees, but "one-sidedly, while man produces universally . . . an animal produces only itself, while man reproduces the whole of nature." Man produces not by the standard of his species but of every species, hence freely and "according to the laws of beauty" (MS, p. 76). Man differs from an animal because he is conscious. Aristotle defined man as a political animal, a rational animal, and a pairing animal, but still an animal. Marx has man as no longer an animal because he is conscious. Conscious of what? Of himself as producing anything, the whole of nature, which is *reproducing* the whole of nature. Note that reproducing is not producing; it is producing what is already produced—having a baby as opposed to bringing out a new product. It would seem that the highest production is reproduction of the whole of nature, and that nature is not inert or chaotic but is divided into species with a plan of its own. It would then seem that the common in communism needs to be ordered by the highest being—the one that is the universal species being. It is typical of communism, we shall see, that it wants to have excellence without aiming at it. Here the species being aims at all beings, yet all includes the highest, though not designated as highest.

Moreover, does consciousness come before production? There can be production without consciousness, as in a beehive, but man is conscious of what he is going to produce. A plan or mind precedes production, not instinctual necessity. How is this consistent with materialism? Marx adds that alienated labor to a particular product alienates man from his own body, his nature, his mental life, "his *human* being," which means alienation from other humans (MS, p. 77). Is there species life without "species consciousness"? An individual says, "This is my matter, not yours." How can this be overcome? Two minds can think the same thought, which is possible between friends, but in the whole species? For Marx, it is not simply thinking but producing—thinking in the process of producing. He is in a dilemma: If he departs from life to thought, he loses the relevance of his economic analysis. Man is no longer alienated simply because he has to work. But if Marx stays with "life" as the definition of man, how can man deserve to appropriate the whole of nature? What is so special about man as such? It appears that Marx has to choose between his humanism and his materialism. Yet there is one further step to consider in his argument.

Well-Rounded Productivity

Man conquers or "appropriates" nature, but in doing so he returns to nature. The difficulty is that when man appropriates nature, man is above nature, but in returning to nature, man puts himself within nature. This is the problem stated above of nature as man's inorganic body. In a new passage, Marx says man corrects nature but in doing so stays natural: How? Through society.

> The human essence of nature first exists only for social man, for only here does nature exist for him as a bond with man. . . . Thus society is the consummated oneness in substance of man and nature—the true resurrection of nature—the naturalism of man and the humanism of nature both brought to fulfillment. (MS, p. 85)

Before, Marx had spoken of reproducing the whole of nature; now he says that "the individual is *the social being*" (MS, p. 86). Nature is not merely reproduced but resurrected by the passage of the individual from egoistic to social. Reproducing the whole of nature distinguishes man from the rest of nature, which lacks this ability; resurrecting brings man back to nature as its peak or culmination, which occurs when men bond together as social. The resurrected "oneness of substance" is material and humanist together through human society.

To show how far the individual is lost in the social Marx dismisses the importance of the fact of individual death: "Death seems to be a harsh victory of the species over the definite individual and to contradict their unity. But the determinate individual is only a determinate species being and as such mortal" (MS, p. 86.) Here comes a point of attack on Marxism by existentialism and particularly by Martin Heidegger, for whom the human is characterized as "being toward death." How can the awareness that every individual dies be so easily disposed of? Marx's optimism leaves him indifferent to the cost in lives of the revolution he espouses. Moreover, his attitude toward death is matched by his misdescription of love. He claims that "the relationship of man to woman is the most natural relation of human being to human being" (MS, p. 83). But human love is for a particular individual man or woman. With his casual dismissal of romance in his species sex, Marx eliminates the choosiness of humans in their loves. Both death and love are problems for the species being.

Marx denies that man's five senses are individual. They are so for egoistic man under the regime of private property but society emancipates those senses from their individual, utilitarian life as mere means and corrects them so that they are not used for competition and conflict with fellow humans. The complete emancipation of all human senses and qualities makes man social without a hierarchy by which some can claim precedence over others. The result is that good qualities do not have to be protected against bad qualities; society can have both universality and excellence together without a trade-off that forces a choice of one or the other. Marx's overcoming of the superficial utilitarian view of humanity in these early writings has attracted anti-bourgeois youth to his cause despite his later praise of the bourgeois capitalist revolution and his general rejection of romantic idealism. He soaks up for himself the attitudes he attacks in his enemies.

For Marx, man becomes wealthy in his needs, and not just in one need or two, but in all of them. A need that can be satisfied does not press on an individual like Machiavelli's relentless necessity to acquire, and satisfying all one's needs in society makes a full life of wealth, free of necessity. Man becomes a well-rounded whole, even though needy. He has a healthy relationship with nature, since he needs nature and admits it. Alienated man comes back to his nature, as this is the humanism of nature, nature's highest development out of its egoism. Therefore, man cannot have been created, for a created being is dependent on his creator. Man is his own cause, which can only be if man existed from the beginning: To ask about it is to presuppose yourself. Man is the absolute being, the highest being. Marx was forced to abandon this view after 1859, when Darwin's theory of evolution was published, but he shows here what he would have preferred and what its logic required. Marx speaks here of a circular motion of man returning to his nature: How, then, can history have created man? Nature and history are in tension: Does history serve nature, explaining how nature is alienated and returns, or does history make nature, declaring what nature is? Marx's early writings needed a recharge in the economic laws of history that made his name. These economic laws will explain the evolution of man and serve beyond Marx's intent to supply a response to or substitute for Darwin's theory. But the tension is in Darwin and remains in Marx.

To grasp Marx's place in the history of modern political philosophy, let's return to the preoccupation of Machiavelli and his liberal followers with necessity. For them, necessity stands for the necessity of concern for what is one's own—my necessity. This necessity did not enslave humans, as one might think, but actually liberated them from their enslavement to "imaginary republics and principalities" of the classical philosophers and Christianity. Concern for one's own became the basis for a new politics of self-preservation that liberated the body from the tyranny of the soul. In theory the soul might seem to be the palace of human virtue, but in its effectual truth it was the agency of scheming, unbelieving priests. To oppose such corrupt abuse, a realistic modern political science made promises of great results in peace and prosperity to come from "self-interest well understood," to quote the phrase of a later liberal, Alexis de Tocqueville.

The liberal use of one's own selfishness necessarily brought with it a demotion of public spirit and devotion to the common good. This did not mean that liberals did not care for the whole. On the contrary, given the liberation of selfish interests, it was vital to show how they could be controlled to produce a common good. To do so was the work of modern constitutionalism inspired by the pithy principle of *Federalist* 51: "Let ambition counteract ambition." As we saw when discussing Locke, there were some men of higher caliber than required for the ordinary working of the system who had to be conscious of the whole, "studiers" of the law of nature. Such were the American founders Madison and Hamilton, inspired by Locke and Montesquieu and followed by Tocqueville. These modern founders, or founders of modernity, fashioned republics, that if not entirely devoid of virtue, as with Kant's republic of devils, nonetheless gave primacy to the honest self-interest of citizens, based on one's own body. Following Machiavelli, who does not use the word "soul" in his two principal works, *The Prince* and the *Discourses on Livy*, these liberals opposed the philosophy of the ancients, who founded politics on the soul. More than all other works of political science, Plato's *Republic* went so far as to promote the interest of the soul over the body in a city ruled by philosophers and dedicated to justice, defined as communism in defiance of one's own. Justice could mean communism only in a city ruled by those who because they were philosophers were without selfish interests. Such justice would surely be rare, perhaps indeed impossible, but it would be the model regime for political science. After Thomas More, who invented the term, that regime came to be called "utopian."

Now Marx discovered, or believed he discovered, that, contrary to Plato, the body could be liberated without conceding to the power of selfishness.

He brought forth communism that would be established not on the basis of Plato's imagined republic and invisible ideas, but on real—bodily—interests. And for everyone, not just for philosophers. Everyone could become not a factor in a liberal system of selfish interests, but consciously part of what is common. Rather than living as a fragment determined by one's interest, or as a philosopher above it all, one could live a whole life. A whole life means not selfish and not one-sided. Man can live a whole life not in bourgeois society—for the conflict of men's selfish interests, which Marx called class conflict, can be abolished. When that happens, the state can also be abolished and therewith all politics in the sense of political conflict. The state is succeeded, in Marx's phrase, by "the administration of things," a phrase that hardly describes the "Gulag Archipelago" of prison camps under the Marxist Soviet Union. In considering Locke's liberalism, a connection appeared between private property and constitutional government. Marx sweeps them away because both are tainted with selfishness. How does he do it? How does he restore the wholeness of man in communism without resorting to Plato's philosopher-kings? To answer, one must look at the partisanship displayed for all the world to see in *The Communist Manifesto.*

The Proletariat

The Communist Manifesto, written and published in the revolutionary year of 1848, is a political statement, not a work of political philosophy. Composed by Marx and Engels, commissioned by the Communist party, it is addressed to workers under the name of the "proletariat." The word comes from *proletarius,* a Roman term for the lowest class of citizen with little or no property. This taste of the ancients helps to turn Marx's analysis away from the false promise of liberal equality. *The Communist Manifesto* is not addressed to all men because it is the authors' doctrine that ideas take effect only when they appeal to interests, which for them always mean selfish interests. There is no basis on which to address all men, no common good at present to which one might appeal, and the authors do not disguise their partisan allegiance as one might do if there was any possibility of persuading readers to a common good or a self-interest well understood. Marx and Engels issue a defiant manifesto whose arguments are meant to shock their enemies and rally their friends. The extraordinary power of its rhetoric can still be felt by every reader, whether inclined to agree with it or not, but its extraordinary character is not only in its rhetoric.

The Communist Manifesto is more than an ordinary party pamphlet because the Communist party is not an ordinary party. Up to now every society has consisted of classes and displayed class struggle. This judgment includes modern bourgeois society, which has not done away with class antagonisms despite its professed intention, as we have seen in Hobbes and Locke, of bringing peace out of a state of war. Despite the institutions of government and property designed to bring peace, bourgeois society has established new classes, new conditions of oppression, and new forms of struggle in place of the old ones it claimed to have dispelled. Yet bourgeois oppression is fundamentally new, not merely a new variety. All previous oppression was caused by scarcity, not by the malice of the oppressors, malicious though some of them were. Now scarcity has been abolished by the wondrous achievements of capitalist production, which has been so successful that the greatest problem today is not lack of production but overproduction. The bourgeois economy in fact suffers from crises of overproduction, a unique phenomenon in human history that clarifies the present situation. The old excuse for oppression, scarcity, no longer applies because scarcity has become abundance. Abundance has been made actual by capitalism, meaning that the old excuse of necessity arising from scarcity is gone. Machiavelli's principle of necessity, so far as it rested on scarcity, is obsolete.

The new oppression is pure inhuman exploitation because it treats man not as a slave or a beast but as a thing. Capitalists do not even try to humiliate the workers they oppress because that would be acknowledging their humanity. They consider labor itself as a commodity to be bought and sold like other things. Locke had developed a labor theory of value, but in the *Second Treatise* he says that what belongs to me is the ore I have dug, the grass my horse has eaten, and "the turfs my servant has cut" (ST §28). But, for Marx, that is not my labor; it is the labor I bought from my servant. This difference is the essence of capitalism: the difference between my labor and the labor I buy. My labor is my own; that is the principle of justice under capitalism. But capitalism doesn't live up to its principle when I buy the labor of my servant. The price of labor is what will keep the servant alive, but in buying his labor, I acquire his labor power, which amounts to more than his subsistence. The difference is the *surplus value* and the profit of the capitalist. The capitalist tries to increase the productivity of the worker and thus his exploitation as much as he can (see *Capital*, p. 351, for the explanation). Why the capitalist pays only a subsistence wage is a longer argument in Marxist economics.

Marx takes Locke's labor theory of value and perfects it, or so he thought. Locke would no doubt have allowed the employer to take the product of his servant's labor because the employer provided the capital. In his view, the labor theory of value strictly applies only in the state of nature, not in civil society (ST §50). In civil society, the seeming necessity of capital to human value made it impossible to understand all value as based on labor; the clerk in a supermarket is not paid as if he owned the supermarket and contributed its capital to the business. Capital fundamentally represents not need, but the desire for excess and the excessive desire of the rich for more than one needs to live. The rich owner seeks a kind of commercial glory in an enterprise that reminds us of the Machiavellian prince transformed into the Lockean businessman—one of the industrious and the rational few.

Marx's great problem, therefore, was to overcome the necessity for capital and to show that capital is really labor, congealed labor held by the capitalist. If this were shown, capital would not be a distinct or independent factor in human value, nor would the capitalist, with his excessive desires for riches and glory, make a necessary contribution. Given this fact, the capitalist is nothing but a pure exploiter. Marx could then deny the Machiavellian desire for endless acquisition, or more common wants and preferences (the term economists now use), and show how human value is based only on true needs. As it is based on needs that can be satisfied, society need not be selfish. The real selfishness comes from the excessive desires of the few rather than from the ordinary person who wants only a decent quantity of goods but whose thinking may be infected by the few who want more. Marx said against Locke that the day laborer in England is not better off than the savage king in America (MS, p. 100), and even if he were, the vast inequalities of wealth under capitalism caused and justified by the necessity of capital revive and intensify the old war of the poor against the rich.

Hence again, Marx had to understand capital in terms of labor, and this he did in his major work whose suitably convenient title is *Das Kapital*. For this is his major work, and one has to have read it carefully before claiming to understand Marx. Capital is *the* human problem because capital represents human selfishness—what might in economics be called the demand curve. Marxist economics explains everything from the supply side; the labor theory of value as perfected by Marx proves that man is essentially a producer, not a desiring being or a consumer. Here the Marxist Old Left differs from the New Left of consumerism, just as the working class differs from bargain seekers and health devotees.

Marx has found that capitalist exploitation is new because for the first time it is pure and utterly unjustified. He found this by social, political, and economic analysis beginning from his observation that all society suffers from class conflict and that the present class struggle differs only in the extent of its oppression and exploitation. Yet instead of being resigned to the situation as an unfortunate fact, or not so unfortunate as did Machiavelli, he becomes indignant at the wholly unnecessary oppression under capitalism. Marx the philosopher sees that the problem of scarcity has been solved and is moved out of contemplation into action: "The philosophers have only interpreted the world in various ways; the point, however, is to change it" (*Theses on Feuerbach*, 11, p. 145). The philosopher becomes an empirical social scientist as he sees through objective analysis that all oppression can be ended. This is the crucial premise: not that it exists but that it can be ended. Unlike previous philosophers, Marx is moved to action by his analysis—to *The Communist Manifesto*. Unlike today's social scientists, he makes value judgments right and left, to be sure mostly left, though it is important to remember that communist heresies included infantile leftism as well as senile revisionism (on the Right).

These value judgments, however, are not based on ideals or on values asserted against the facts; they emerge from the analysis of the facts showing that capitalism as a whole is oppressive. Marxist social science, as opposed to today's bourgeois social science, thinks in terms of wholes. The latter fears making judgments of good and bad, believing that such judgments imply black and white distinctions. For this social science, there are no essential distinctions made of wholes; everything is a matter of degree and a shade of gray: nothing to get excited about. Against this, Marxist social science posits that capitalism is essentially different from communism. There is no neutral "social system," but rather class antagonisms, and there is no seamless continuity in history. Unlike Rousseau's sequence of accidents, Marxist history is a dialectic of revolutions that moves through stages, and the stages are not the development of Hegel's spirit but are defined economically by modes of production.

Thus we see that the partisanship of Marx and Engels in *The Communist Manifesto* is justified by what they thought they saw in capitalism—pure exploitation that can be overcome by the revolution of the proletariat. The bourgeoisie is the unnecessary class; the proletariat is the universal class. For the first time capitalism reveals the possibility of a class not based on exploitation: a society of communism ruled by the proletariat. Since the proletariat is unlike any previous class, the party of the proletariat is partisanship for all of mankind. The cause of the proletariat is the cause of man, and the justification for this party pamphlet is confirmed. But what is the cause of man, or what is man whose cause we must support? To begin an answer, two further questions arise: Why is this cause the final cause of man when history is complete? And what role does politics play in the end of history?

Consciousness and Politics

In the *1844 Manuscripts* Marx says that man is distinguished from bees because he has an idea of what he wants to build before he builds. Man is social like bees but, unlike them, is a *conscious* producer. In the *German Ideology* a year later (1845–1846), Marx and Engels again address the problem of consciousness in the materialist conception of history, but with less of Hegel's philosophical terminology. "Consciousness" in this text appears as the production of ideas, said to be a social product like other production because material life comes before thinking:

> The first premise of all human existence and therefore of all history . . . [is] that men must be in a position to live in order to be able to "make history." But life involves before everything else eating and drinking, a habitation, clothing, and many other things. The first historical act is thus the production of the means to satisfy these needs, the production of material life itself. (GI, p. 155–156)

In a longer passage that bears careful consideration, they say that consciousness, which is not animal, is at first merely "concerning the immediate sensuous environment," and is "at the same time" consciousness of nature, which first appears as a completely alien all-powerful force "with which men's relations are purely animal and by which they are overawed like beasts; it is thus a purely animal consciousness of nature (natural religion)." It seems then that animals have some consciousness after all, and of nature as "natural religion," whatever that might be (GI, p. 158).

The passage continues confusingly to say that the restricted relation of men to nature determines their restricted relation to one another, and the latter determines the former. At this point men have "mere herd consciousness" that is "sheeplike," except that consciousness takes the place of instinct. Men then develop through greater productivity and the acquisition of new needs, discovering the division of labor, "which was originally nothing but the division of labor in the sexual act" (GI, p. 158). (We set aside the sexual division of labor for later treatment.) But true division of labor only arrives with the division between material and mental labor, after which consciousness can emancipate itself from the world and become theory and philosophy (GI, p. 159). To sum up, on the one hand, consciousness is as old as man because it is what distinguishes humans from animals. It may be herd consciousness in a sense, but what true herd has a natural religion? On the other hand, Marx and Engels want to say that eating comes before ideas, that economics comes before religion or philosophy. In the introduction to *The Communist Manifesto,* Engels puts economics first. He says that its basic thought is that "economic production and the structure of society of every historical epoch necessarily arising therefrom constitute the foundation for the political and intellectual history of that epoch." If man is defined as a conscious producer, then how can he produce consciousness? How can man produce what defines him? What he produces comes after man exists, so how could it define him? This is Marx's difficulty.

Supposing this difficulty is overcome, or setting it aside, we can compare Marx's view of the classes in society to see what makes it distinctive. For Plato in his *Republic,* the primary distinction is between the class of philosopher and the class of nonphilosophers, the first being the only class truly entitled to rule. For Machiavelli, as we have seen, class is based on two humors: those desiring to master others and those desiring not to be mastered. This is the situation faced by the prince, whose mastery is seen by Machiavelli as the most pressing human requirement. Both Plato and Machiavelli, with their different understandings of class, expected that classes, and therefore class conflict, will continue as long as man exists. But Marx, who bases class on economics, thought that when the economic problem was solved as he had accomplished, class conflict could be abolished. For when the essence of man is productivity, the essential science of man is economics.

What, then, of politics? Politics comes into play in a subordinate or instrumental role, helping to usher in the new universal society. Marx and Engels say in *The Communist Manifesto* that the bourgeoisie sets the proletariat in motion. The proletariat becomes a class and consequently a political party, and it claims that the role of the communists is to represent the proletariat as a whole, independent of nationality (CM, p. 484). Politics, one could say, is economics made visible. The Communist party represents the proletariat not in the Hobbesian sense of having been authorized by consent, but in the sense of making visible the facts that already exist. This does not require that the proletariat consent to being represented by the Communist party, and Marx and Engels do not claim that it does or admit that it should. Nor do they promise consent under communist society, nor have communist countries practiced or promised consent. They hold elections, but for the purpose of expressing solidarity, not for individual consent. Consent is tied to the selfishness of the bourgeoisie, and bourgeois consent is unworthy of man.

Man's essence is conscious social productivity. But this is an essence, an idea: How do we know that this is the final true idea? Ideas are rooted in history. How do we know that history is not an infinite process, and this idea is not merely a product of our times, one that will be abolished when history moves to some new stage now unknown? The Marxist Georg Lukács raised this point in his book *History and Class Consciousness* (1923). What is history? Here enters the Marxist concept of alienation, by which history is alienation. Man begins as man, then becomes alienated from himself, and then overcomes his alienation and returns to himself. We have seen alienation in Rousseau and Hegel: It means not that things seem strange and alien to us, but that things once familiar to us are now alien. An example is money; money begins as an instrument of man to increase his freedom by allowing him to store goods and trade them. Then, however, men treat money not as an instrument but as an end. They spend their lives seeking money and become slaves to what was originally their instrument of freedom. Human products in general lose their identity as products and come to be goals of production or external forces. In this way man comes to be alienated from himself and his productions take charge of him; they no longer appear as *his*. He no longer recognizes himself in his production.

The purpose of Marx's writings is to bring the proletariat to see itself in capitalism—to see that its labor is the source of all value, especially of surplus value, and thus to overcome alienation. We know that man's essential productivity is the final truth about man, therefore, because man returns to his beginning when he recognizes this idea. If productivity were utterly new to man, we could not be sure that history might have other new stages or infinite stages. History is not infinite, not in the sense of increasing progress, always bettering itself, nor in the sense of cycles of good and bad times with infinite renewal, as in Plato and Aristotle. History is cyclical, but there is only one cycle—of course, a cycle with improvements. As with Machiavelli there are no problems without solutions. The man who returns to himself after having fully exhausted the possibilities of alienation is a much higher, more perfect creature than he was in the beginning; but still it is a return. If there were no beginning of unalienated man, there would be no guarantee of man's end: the beginning guarantees the end.

Freedom in Communism

The end of man is communism, and it is now necessary to conclude the study of Marx with a discussion of his few but very significant words to describe it. Man's essence is productivity, we have seen, and this is man's freedom to rise above, to overcome, to conquer his environment or nature. This freedom carries on the movement of modernity begun by Machiavelli to bring rational control to human life as the remedy for religious tyranny supported by corrupt tradition, prejudice, and superstition. These irrational forces drew inspiration from the classical philosophy of the ancients that rested on an understanding of nature as the permanence of things. Human nature gave us the natural desire to know, said Aristotle as the first words of his *Metaphysics*, but it also gave us stubborn resistance to learning and wayward yearnings to distract it that prevent philosophy from coming to power and bringing relief. In declaring that the point of philosophy is to change rather than interpret the world, Marx gave a perfect summation of the modern movement begun by Machiavelli.

To change the world it is necessary to overcome the power of nature, which sets limits to change, validates unreason, and prevents progress. That is the general definition of modern freedom. Marx is a member of Machiavelli's army of followers, marching in the proud *Aufheben* battalion of German Idealism that he likes to mock, yet from which he cannot escape. While Machiavelli invented necessity to replace nature, German Idealism sought a way to find an alternative to necessity—Kant's moral freedom—or to rationalize it in Hegel's World History; Marx discovered communism as a historically necessary return to nature, now without the limits to human freedom that it set, according to the ancients. Plato's "communism," with its abolition of the family and private property and with its denial of the relevance of the sexes, might seem reasonable in Socrates's presentation, but it was not really possible except in speech; it came to be known as utopian—that is, nowhere. Marx's communism, based on historical necessity and vehemently opposed to the utopian socialism of his day, is presented as "actual," if somewhat over the horizon. It is bound to come after the coming revolution. When we see what it is, the most normal reaction might be to dismiss it as against human nature. Marx will try to show that its description and its coming realization are, despite what you might think, reasonable.

To gain momentum into Marx's argument, it is well to oppose it once again to Locke. For Marx, humans are defined by conscious productivity. Supposing man has this capacity and this freedom, the trouble is that as soon as you use it to make something, you become partial or one-sided to the extent that you are devoted to that *one kind* of production—for example, the breeding of rabbits. As soon as you make some particular thing, that thing becomes property, and property is mine or yours. Property is private in virtue of the division of labor. According to Locke, however, human labor makes value from the "almost worthless materials" of nature. But labor, making value, produces goods that are scarce, and scarce goods belong to those who perform or purchase the labor. Labor proceeds from human bodies, so that property made by labor is private, as are bodies. Men make property to overcome the penury of nature, but one never escapes nature entirely; one never escapes scarcity; one never leaves the realm of necessity. Property expands freedom, but property is private, attaching to each man or each man's body. Human freedom is limited by human selfishness. This means that human freedom works against itself when it results in property. My property is opposed to yours means my freedom as opposed to yours. And since property is unequal, so is freedom. More freedom for *this* person means less freedom for *that*. Property may increase human freedom in sum, but it doesn't increase it to an equal degree in each person. That day laborer in England may be better off than a savage king in America, but not in every respect. He pays for the comfort of his dependence and suffers from a lack of wholeness.

Marx wanted to eliminate this problem in productivity. When human freedom issues in property, it is limited by the necessity of selfishness—but it can be purified and necessity satisfied. Pure productivity is having the power to make goods without reference to their result as property. There is no end that would imply human selfishness, such as the end of self-preservation in Locke. If there is no end, there is no conflict; an increase in human productivity adds to human freedom with no limitation or reservation. Pure productivity occurs on two occasions: before you have made anything, because you have merely potential; and after you have acquired the ability to make anything—without concern for scarcity, and hence without regard to any end that might limit you. This is communism: Man produces for man, because no man produces for any particular man.

For this situation, Marx gives two formulas. The first is from his *Critique of the Gotha Program*, written in 1875 and published by Engels in 1891: "From each according to his ability, to each according to his needs" (GP, p. 531). Here Marx implies that there is a balance between ability and needs; abilities as a whole are equal to needs as a whole, but not in any individual human being. Every human being would give freely with his own abilities but without regard to his own needs. No individual incentives would apply; no one would make a name for himself because he contributes more. There would be no problem of justice in communist society, indeed no political problems at all. Would this work? Isn't there a correlation between abilities and needs that isn't necessarily selfish? One can agree that the best scholars don't need the limousines and resort vacations they have now under capitalism, but shouldn't the best scholars have access to the best libraries as well as access to each other? Shouldn't the best athletes have the use of the best facilities? And so on.

Moreover, this formula—from each according to his ability, to each according to his needs—implies that men are not equal; some have abilities, some needs. Aren't those with abilities going to feel alienated to those with needs, and vice versa? It seems that the result would be a society divided into patrons and clients that would easily descend into a society of patronizing and servility unless this were prevented by considerable force. All relationships would be characterized by alienation. Perhaps this formula refers to the early stages of communism, though in the passage of the *Critique of the Gotha Program,* Marx says that it belongs to a higher phase.

In addition to this later passage, however, Marx and Engels had offered another, more radical formula in *The Communist Manifesto* in 1848: "An association in which the free development of each is the condition for the free development of all" (CM, p. 491). This formula has no reference to capacities that would imply limits to man's productivity. No one is free unless all are free, and all are free if they develop together. Without reference to capacities, "each" now implies that each individual will come to have a balance of abilities and needs, not merely a balance in society as a whole. This would happen only if all develop together. Then what does "free development" mean? Develop to what? Not to any particular capacity that would imply a limitation, but rather free development to anything—back to pure productivity. Each would be well rounded, not partial or one-dimensional (as the Marxist Herbert Marcuse explained), but each would be a whole. Note that one is not required to be excellent in any capacity because excellence requires devotion and devotion subtracts from wholeness. For Socrates in Plato's *Republic,* to perform a productive art was not just to do the job in any way, but to do it well. Doing it well requires devotion, and devotion makes you one-sided rather than whole. Socrates shows that one can only combine devotion and wholeness in the life of a philosopher, who is devoted to the whole of excellence. Marx lets go of excellence in the hope that wholeness can be brought within reach of all:

Hence the famous passage from the *German Ideology*:

> In communist society, where nobody has one exclusive sphere of activity, but each can become accomplished in any branch he wishes, society regulates the general production and thus makes it possible for me to do one thing today and another tomorrow, to hunt in the morning, fish in the afternoon, rear cattle in the evening, criticize after dinner just as I have a mind, without ever becoming hunter, fisherman, shepherd, or critic. (GI, p. 160)

If you wish to be a critic, you can be one; you don't have to be good, but you have to be good enough so that your wish is not frustrated. Otherwise you are alienated. But who wants to be a mediocre critic? It must be that unequal capacities are not natural to man. It must be that they can be equalized to prevent alienation when confronted with unequal talent or ability. It must be true that intelligence, for example, is acquired and not inherited. The genetics of Trofim Lysenko, Stalin's biologist, who pronounced that inherited genes were a "bourgeois invention," must be on the right track.

Speaking of human wholeness, one thinks immediately of sex and of Marx's remark mentioned earlier that the division of labor "was originally the division of labor in the sexual act" (GI, p. 158). The division of labor is the essence of partiality and alienation in Marxism, and now it seems originally to be sexual, rather than economic. Then "free development" of each and all would have to overcome division of labor in the sexual act. Why not? Why should male human beings be satisfied with what John Locke called "the bare act of begetting" (ST §68)? How can a male be considered a whole, a species being, without the satisfaction of giving birth to a child? The possibilities now of being transgender or of indulging in polymorphous perversity are only steps in the right direction of abolishing bourgeois sex roles.

We see how far Marx's principle carries. To see the difficulty in it, consider the following. Man is the producer. He makes his own needs by changing his wishes. The less he stays with one wish, the more well rounded he is as a human being. In making his own needs, he makes himself. But what does he make of himself—anything? If he is to be a pure producer not limited by any good or end, so it would seem. Yet we learned that capitalism is inhuman because it treats a human being as a commodity, a thing. A human being is not a thing. As a producer, he is above the things he produces; as a conscious producer, he is above other animals.

Yet it seems possible for a human being to make himself into a thing or an animal. It is possible for a human being to degrade himself, exploit himself, dehumanize himself—for example, as a lazy, cud-chewing consumer. Note that fisherman, hunter, and shepherd are all producers, and the very kind of producer that emphasizes the superiority of man among animals. What of the lout, the footpad, or the parasite? If the human being is a producer, don't we have to avoid these unproductive occupations? Therefore, our productivity must be limited to productive occupations, precisely to avoid alienation. If that is so, then we still have choice between productive and unproductive paths; our lives are not determined by necessary laws of history. We still have a choice as to the best life and hence have need for philosophy. Empirical social science, including economics, is not enough by itself to ponder our choice. It is not a mistake Marx makes to find constraint in a life determined by the division of labor and to look for the satisfaction of wholeness. To desire to transcend the limitations of one's sex is also not unnatural, if only by being married to the opposite sex. But we must consider human wholeness with an eye to excellence.

Man as the producer of man must produce an excellent man, at the least an excellent producer. This philosophic pondering must be in keeping with the dignity of man as above (other) animals in order to aim at something noble. Marx's theory did change the world, as he wished. It was adopted by the Communist party he founded to unleash a world revolution that killed and enslaved hundreds of millions of human beings. This very sobering result reminds us of Machiavelli's noble war against nobility and his philosophy of effectual truth. It seems that the effectual truth of eliminating choice is a surrender to force and violence. But we are not finished with Machiavelli's modernity, as it can also be applied to the question of nobility Marx passed over. We are led out of Marx's theory of free development to the philosophy of Nietzsche, the opposite critic of liberalism from the Right. Liberalism's reliance on human selfishness can be challenged on the Right for being ignoble, as by Nietzsche, just as for lacking community, by Marx on the Left.

CHAPTER EIGHT

FRIEDRICH NIETZSCHE

(1844–1900)

Friedrich Nietzsche was born into a Prussian Lutheran family. He was named for the king, and his father was a pastor. But his father died when he was four years old, and he grew up in a household of five women, including his sister Elisabeth, who after his death edited his book *Will to Power.* Nietzsche went on to excel in preparatory school and at the Universities of Bonn and Leipzig, where he studied theology and classical philology. During military service he suffered a severe chest wound and returned to Leipzig, becoming a friend of the composer Richard Wagner and an enthusiast for the philosophy of Arthur Schopenhauer. Receiving unstinted praise from his professor at Leipzig, Friedrich Ritschl, Nietzsche was awarded a professorship, without a doctorate, at the University of Basel at the age of twenty-four. This evidence of early promise, however, hardly prepared the academic world for the explosive brilliance of his first book in 1872; *The Birth of Tragedy* at once catapulted him to fame and overturned the field of his fame, classical philology. From this moment he was the Nietzsche of renown who challenged the thoughts and conventions of all modernity.

The philosophy of Nietzsche, ever a surprise treat, deserves a preview that sets it in place on the path of modernity. The theme of this book is the rational control that characterizes modernity in its rise and fall. Rational control from its rise is an idea of the application of reason to revolutionize the life of human beings as individuals and in politics in order to liberate them from the unreason of prejudice, tradition and superstition. This idea was begun and maintained by philosophers and has an internal history of rise and fall from Machiavelli to Nietzsche. What Machiavelli began, Nietzsche brought to an end—and with both a bang and a whimper: modern rational man proved to be what he called the "last man."

MAJOR WORKS OF NIETZSCHE

The Birth of Tragedy from the Spirit of Music (1872): Nietzsche's first major work examines the birth and decline of ancient Greek tragedy through the contrast between two principles of art: the "Apollonian" (ordered individuation) and the "Dionysian" (dissolution and intoxication).

Untimely Meditations (1873–1876): A collection of four essays that criticizes contemporary German culture on the themes of history, philosophy, and art. The essays include "On the Use and Abuse of History for Life" (1874), as well as "David Strauss: The Confessor and the Writer" (1873), "Schopenhauer as Educator" (1874), and "Richard Wagner in Bayreuth" (1876).

Human, All Too Human: A Book for Free Spirits (1878): A collection of aphorisms criticizing metaphysics, religion, and morality, this work marks a shift from Nietzsche's first period toward a more skeptical, positivistic, and scientific approach.

The Gay Science (Die fröhliche Wissenschaft) (1882): A key work of Nietzsche's "middle period," this book advances the declaration that "God is dead" (*Gott ist tot*), the idea of *amor fati* (love or affirmation of fate), and the concept of "eternal recurrence" (the thought that all events in life will repeat themselves infinitely). The title refers to the Provençal expression (*gai saber*) for the art of writing poetry.

Thus Spoke Zarathustra: A Book for All and None (1883–1885): Among Nietzsche's most famous and ambitious works, *Zarathustra* develops the ideas of the last man, the *Übermensch* (Overman/Superman), the death of God, and the will to power. It differs from Nietzsche's other late writings in its poetic, allegorical, and quasi-prophetic form.

Beyond Good and Evil: Prelude to a Philosophy of the Future (1886): Written in part as an exposition of *Zarathustra*, this work offers a critical examination of the "will to truth" and the history of philosophy, religion, and morality. Nietzsche introduces the concept of "master-slave morality" and criticizes the dualism of traditional moral systems.

On the Genealogy of Morals: A Polemic (1887): A theory of the origins and development of fundamental moral concepts: guilt, responsibility, and the distinction between good and "evil." Nietzsche argues that modern morality has been shaped by historical processes that have worked both to deepen humanity and to repress the creative impulses of life-affirming human instincts.

Ecce Homo: How One Becomes What One Is (1888): Nietzsche's late autobiographical work, a deeply personal and enigmatically ironic reflection on his life, writings, and philosophical development. The title *Ecce Homo* ("Behold the Man") refers to the words of Pontius Pilate in presenting Jesus to the crowd before his crucifixion.

Whatever the accidents of history that helped give rise to modernity and to bring about its crises, its internal, philosophical history consists of the arguments we have seen by which the modern philosophers attempted to cure the faults of their fellows earlier in the conspiracy, and at the same time to maintain the integrity of the singular modern idea, given motion and variety by its devotion to "new modes and orders." Along the way modernity, in newly formulated stages from one author to the next, disposed of its foundation in reason and delivered itself to history. It became more and more radical in its proposals of greater freedom to the point of abolishing politics in Marx, and at the same time more savage in self-criticism as it undermined its foundation. Hegel seemed to save reason with resort to history, but for him reason always came too late, only after it had been handed its next stage of development by the passions of world history. His beautifully constructed rational state was not timely but temporary, standing now like an abandoned castle visited only by curious tourists. With Nietzsche modernity came to free creativity openly hostile to reason and, while returning to philosophy's function as vanguard, was critical of all previous philosophy, modern as well as ancient. He liked to repeat the phrase "modern ideas" decorated with quotation marks.

How did modern philosophy descend to Nietzsche? Machiavelli came first. In *Mandragola* he showed a liberation from irrational control that was also a submission to necessity, a strange form of liberty in which one has no choice but to submit. He left it unclear whether rational control was for the sake of liberation, or liberation for the sake of rational control. Liberalism, led by Hobbes the almost-liberal, came next in a form that combined liberty with necessity. According to liberalism, if one wants rational control and liberty, one must keep them distinct through the formality of rights. Liberal rights distinguish the protection of rights, the task of government that applies strictures of laws and measures necessary for a free society, and the exercise of rights, which is the choice of individuals and the groups they choose to form. The formality of a right permits a distinction between state and society. The state protects rights, and individuals in society exercise rights. This means that the definition of a right does not decide how it must be exercised but leaves that open for free choice. The right of free speech, for example, does not tell you what to say—apart from necessary exclusions like slander and causing a riot. But the distinction between state and society in liberalism allowed irrational opinion still to exist in society and even to flourish. For Marx in "On the Jewish Question," this result was intolerable. He had been shown by Hegel that the formality of reason versus liberty must be overcome and made actual, so that liberty would be assured and not left contingent on people's capricious or stubborn choice. Reason and liberty must be made to coincide by stages of historical necessity by which each stage defeats the one before it and loses to the one after. It is an ingenious scheme called "dialectical," even though history's answers are given in events, not speech. But suppose this plan should be accomplished?

The result would be to make life uninteresting with nothing to do, lacking challenge and risk, and the excellence necessary to act when an acceptable result is not automatic and expected. The last stage in Hegel's reason and Marx's communism would not have to be reached for its character to take effect in thought and behavior. Without stirring and striving for progress, boredom would set in—a phenomenon unknown to premodern civilization. In the nineteenth century it was expressed in a single French word, *ennui.* Gustave Flaubert's *Madame Bovary* is about a woman with a boring husband; Conan Doyle's Sherlock Holmes gets bored between his cases and turns to drugs when his remarkable and odd intelligence is not at work. Drugs provide artificial excitement by means of a deliberate throwback to primitive societies where drugs accompany activity rather than substitute for it. The drug problem in modern life arises as rational control turns against itself, having forgotten the sweetness of life and the pleasures of virtue, to say nothing of Machiavelli's triumphant *virtù*. At this point Nietzsche's "last man" comes to view. "We invented happiness, say the last men, and they blink" (*Zarathustra*, pt. 1, "Zarathustra's Prologue," §5).[1] This is modern man with nothing to do; bored with himself, he hangs around malls, has little pleasures for the day and for the night, but honors health. The drug problem is considered a health problem.

This is Nietzsche, the philosopher of excitement, a thrill to read. But please try not to fall in love with him. In one of P. G. Wodehouse's novels on the brainy manservant Jeeves and his less endowed gentleman Bertie Wooster, Bertie suffers in the company of an unsatisfactory girlfriend who wants him to read Nietzsche. Jeeves remarks with his frosty disdain: "Nietzsche is fundamentally unsound, sir."

FRIEDRICH NIETZSCHE

The Just and the Noble

Nietzsche is a philosopher of morality, and a careful, wary approach to his thought requires a broader look at morality to see what modern rational control has done to the duality of the just and the noble set forth by the ancients. For the ancients, morality consists of these two components—just and noble—visible today in the difference between what is expected and what is admired. What is expected is paying your taxes; what is admired is hitting a home run to win the ball game. The expected is useful, but the admired is above the useful. Useful is what the law requires and admirable is "beyond the call of duty," like the phrase on a soldier's medal, describing conduct at risk to one's life and fortune. In the movie *High Noon,* the hero (Gary Cooper) who comes to the aid of justice when no one else will is noble for his service but disgusted by the cowardice of those ordinary citizens whom he serves. The noble is subservient to the just but regards itself as superior (see the scene with Jeeves above).

Consider the drama in book 1 of Plato's *Republic.* The subject chosen by Socrates is the question of what justice is, and his answer is attacked by Thrasymachus, who declares that justice is the interest of the stronger. Thrasymachus is embarrassed by Socrates and falls silent, but the two youths in the party, Glaucon and Adeimantus, are dissatisfied with the result and ask Socrates to prove that justice is worthy of choice for its own sake and not merely as a means. Glaucon and Adeimantus are not crooks or gangsters who hate justice, but they are fascinated by Thrasymachus's argument because they feel the opposition between the just and the noble. As noble or potentially noble youths, they feel disdain for mere justice, which demands the expected and forgets the admirable. Socrates leads them to construct the best city, of which the characteristic institution is communism. For them, as for spirited youths today, communism has the appeal of nobility but also combines nobility with justice. The nobility of communism is in the sacrifice of every privilege that is unearned or undeserved; its justice lies in its promise of rewarding each according to merit (which is Plato) or needs (which is Marx).

The just and the noble are allied in communism, but Socrates says that the only possible rulers for such a society are philosophers. Philosophers are the only human beings willing to sacrifice the highest and most powerful human desire, which is to rule other humans. They are noble and they receive the reward of ruling the best city, and since their philosophy is about the forms or ideas that are the cause of order in nature, their rule that allies the just and the noble is according to nature. Now, Machiavelli and Hobbes agreed that this alliance was possible, but they held that it was supported by human nature only, not all nature, and was inspired by fear rather than noble honor. In Machiavelli, there are two humors: one of those who want to master others and the other of those who do not want to be mastered; they can be combined with a common fear, differently felt. In Hobbes, there is the state of nature, which humbles the proud and drives men to create their own artificial sovereign. To do so is an act of nobility on behalf of all mankind against their nature, not of special noble founders. These writers are fundamentally egalitarian, if not entirely so. They are generally hostile to nobility and try to make it compatible with the common good of "humanity," as in Machiavelli; or with justice, as in Hobbes. They recognize the noble but subordinate it, preferring sociable virtues to eminent virtues, as David Hume said with typical Scottish understatement.

Kant tried to raise the just to the level of the noble, and he reintroduces the noble to modern political philosophy. Rousseau prepared the way for this attempt, but with his ambivalent notion of amour propre, he was still wary of the proud. Kant, by making justice independent of its consequences, made every human being a universal legislator for all rational beings—surely a noble office beyond ordinary legislators. Justice is allied with nobility by philosophy according to Kant, but by *practical* philosophy, which does not require that one be a philosopher. Justice has no support in nature, which is what makes it noble, although it turns out that justice needs to be vindicated in history. Hegel allies justice with nobility in history, but only at the end of history. World-historical individuals are noble without being just, and the rational state is staffed by bureaucrats, not by world-historical individuals. And Marx? For him also, the just is allied with the noble in communism, but unlike Plato his version does not require philosophy. In his communism each gives according to his ability, which is noble, and receives according to needs, which is just. The noble is denied when it means exploitation by the ruling class and is then re-created under communism when it is demoted to harmless whims. But the noble is featured in the militancy of revolutionary struggle on the way to communism. The "struggle for peace" of the communist slogan is not peaceful and is devoted to punitive justice. It shows more Nietzsche than Marx.

Nietzsche presents a doctrine of creativity, itself an assertion of nobility bringing along a train of ideas familiar in the twentieth and twenty-first centuries: the self, the id, the Protestant Ethic, the fact-value distinction, charisma, sublimation, depth psychology, activism, existentialism, perspectivism, etc., to fill a postmodern carpetbag of concepts for sale. Nietzsche's creativity can be understood as the dissatisfaction of the noble for the just, who are always seeking to level and equalize, either ignoring or fearing what is best. In modern political philosophy there is the special difficulty of defending the noble because of its concern for the universal and the exact, which favors the just over the noble. Rational control is habit-forming and prefers the unquestioning routine of average folk. Nietzsche makes his way in this defense through the problem of history as it has come to be in the course of modern philosophy we have followed after Rousseau. The problem of history shows Nietzsche as he saw himself in his situation.

History and Nihilism

Coming back to the comparison of Marx and Nietzsche, one finds no evidence that Nietzsche read Marx, but he seems to know him nonetheless. Marx argued for communism, but not with an exhortation. He showed with an analysis of history that communism was bound to come, and that when it came it would solve the age-old problem of injustice and oppression. The solution is made known by Marx's economic analysis, showing that the oppression by the bourgeoisie is unjustifiable, and that the revolution of the proletariat must abolish this unnecessary exploitation. The proletariat is the universal class, and its cause is the cause of man. Now this economic analysis has not held up, and it cannot be said by any reasonable person that the bourgeoisie contributes nothing to human value and the proletariat everything. It follows that the proletariat is just another class that can oppress like all classes; its triumph does not introduce a new era of freedom. Marx's analysis of history ends not with a solution but with a problem: history is not the cyclical return to freedom from alienation. The same criticism could be made of history as it appears in Hegel.

After Hegel history does not seem to provide a guide for humans, much less a guaranteed solution, yet all seem to have no other guide besides history. We today, still locked in the problem, like to say "history will decide" but what does that mean? It means that historians will decide. People used to say that God will decide, and this meant that the priests will decide. Historians are the priests of today. God is dead but history is alive—and not reassuring. What standard will historians use to decide? If it comes from history then you need a philosophy of history from Hegel or Marx, but both of these are regarded by historians today as eminently unhistorical. Both considered that history has come or will soon come to an end. Yet if the standard comes from outside history, then the historian is not the one deciding and you must deny the central importance of history. But all the nonhistorical definitions of man and his freedom have been discredited, or so it seems. They do not account well enough for the changes in man. The central fact of human life, we say, is change—which means history is on top. History discredits everything outside history yet finds no definition of man in history.

In an early tract, part of a larger work, *On the Advantage and Disadvantage of History for Life* (1874), Nietzsche quotes the renowned historian of his time B. G. Niebuhr: "History . . . has at least this one use, that one knows how even the highest and greatest spirits of humanity do not know how accidentally their vision adopted the form through which they see."[2] He calls this a superhistorical viewpoint that reveals how history robs itself of seriousness, for why should one study history if it is nothing but a series of accidents? This is our problem and our danger. Nietzsche called this danger nihilism and gave it a succinct definition: "Nothing is true, everything is permitted" (*Genealogy of Morals* III, §24).[3] The communist society of Marx, the well-rounded life of wholeness without excellence, would be nihilism for Nietzsche because this wholeness would require that there be no choosing, no rejecting, no high and low, no conflict. He made a general attack on modernity and modern man, not only on communism or socialism, though these for him would be modernity at its worst. Modernity, for him, is an attempt "to unbend the bow" (BGE, preface). Man is a bow, which when taut, can send an arrow farther than he knows, but the idea and program of modernity is "to reduce tensions." One hears that phrase in individual psychology and also in politics and society. The idea is worthy only insofar as it demands an effort to achieve, as in the phrase "struggle for peace" that used to be heard from the Soviet Union and its partisans. The struggle for peace means war, requiring sacrifice and nobility, but should this struggle be achieved, its value would be destroyed. In fact, it was clear that during the Cold War communism was attractive only where it did not triumph, or in the effort to force others to accept it. One would not exaggerate to say that the only vitality of communism has been in its point of resemblance to Nietzsche.

Revolutionary from the Right

What does Nietzsche mainly aim at? He tells us himself:

> Gradually it has become clear to me what every great philosophy so far has been: namely the personal confession of its author, and a kind of involuntary and unconscious memoir; also that the moral (and immoral) intentions in every philosophy constituted the real germ of life from which the whole plant had grown. (BGE 1.6)

The drive for knowledge is not the "father of philosophy" but rather morality, which he later equates with politics, asserting that "genuine philosophers . . . are commanders and legislators" (BGE 6.211). It is sometimes said that Nietzsche is not a political philosopher because he has nothing to say about political institutions that might be commanded or legislated. Yet he does comment on left and right from his high altitude. That altitude, as he says, is not above morality and politics but a standpoint from which to make his personal confession a command to modern men. In this fundamental point he is part of Machiavelli's team of rational controllers, however uncomplimentary he proves to be about the power of reason and especially science.

In Europe between the 1860s and 1880s, it was liberalism versus conservatism, with socialism at the extreme of liberalism. Nietzsche had much in common with conservatives but was not a conservative: "Whispered to the conservatives: what was not known formerly, what is known, or what might be known today, is that a reversion, a return in any sense or degree is simply not possible. We physiologists know that, yet all priests and moralists have believed the opposite" (*Twilight of the Idols*, §43).[4] We cannot go back, as liberals like to say, and Nietzsche is not a progressive on the Left, but a revolutionary on the Right. Before him, atheism was the mark of a progressive on the Left. Followers of Hegel were said to be Left or Right Hegelians according to whether they thought Hegel's thought amounted to the victory of reason over religion or the culmination of reason in religion. But Nietzsche said that God is dead, meaning that any ideal was dead, especially God (*The Gay Science*, §125). "God is dead" also means that God was once alive but could not survive God's being a fact of history—that is, of human invention. Nietzsche was an atheist on the Right who believed that Christianity was too egalitarian, rather than the source of hierarchical inequality. Atheism on the Right appeared as fascism and Nazism in the twentieth century long after Nietzsche's death. Nietzsche would not have approved of their civilized barbarism, but they admired him, and he remains the most important intellectual source for those vicious movements. Followers of Nietzsche today should beware of the company they keep.

The extremes of both Left and Right hate each other but touch each other in their atheism. Together they have been the worst regimes, guilty of the most colossal crimes known so far in human history: the Nazis in Germany and the Communists in Russia and China. Besides atheism, Marx and Nietzsche have in common a world revolution that looks to the past—Marx to original communism, Nietzsche to the Greeks—but with the understanding that the past cannot be recovered. Both look to a finite future rather than an infinite goal, and while Marx looked forward to a radically socialized view of human life, Nietzsche's prospect was for a life radically individualized. As opposed to Marx, there is no program of action in Nietzsche, and it was easy to pervert Nietzsche's individualistic view to fashion a political program of fascism and Nazism. Early in Marx's life, as we have seen, he reached the conclusion that philosophy must be transformed into empirical social science. Philosophy was not needed to interpret the world because the world was changing inevitably to foreclose any choice; for Marx, philosophy is overcome by social science. Nietzsche took the opposite course. He never supposed that philosophy could come to an end or that choice could be overcome by inevitable necessity.

Philosophers are often given their own history, as when their works are divided by history scholars into early, middle, and late. Plato's dialogues are so organized but done so without a word of authorization or hint of encouragement by Plato. The case is different with Nietzsche, who does speak of three periods, divided according to his changing interests rather than by unconscious juvenility, maturity, and senility imposed on philosophers by scholars seeking for the psychology under the intent. The first period is defined by studies emerging from Nietzsche's education as a classical scholar, 1872–1876, when classical studies were captured and directed by critical history. At this time Nietzsche was attracted to Richard Wagner and Arthur Schopenhauer, against whom he revolted for his second period, 1878–1882. Here, with *Human, All Too Human* (1878), he made an apparent surrender to scientific positivism, which says that truth is what scientists discover. After this move he revolted from positivism, which he soon concluded was nihilism. His third period on overcoming nihilism, 1883–1887, was the time of his greatest works, *Thus Spoke Zarathustra* (1883–1885) and *Beyond Good and Evil* (1886). *Zarathustra*, Nietzsche said, is the vestibule to his final work, which would have been called the *Will to Power*, but which he never wrote. Parts of it were put together by his sister Elisabeth Förster-Nietzsche after his death and published under that title. *Zarathustra* is an amazing work—hard to understand and said to have been written in forty days. Nietzsche wrote *Beyond Good and Evil* to explain it, he said, and then wrote the *Genealogy of Morals* (1887) to explain that.

Since Nietzsche, as opposed to Marx, does not think that philosophy can come to an end, what is it that distinguishes his philosophy from all previous philosophy? Here is what he says:

> All philosophers have the common failing of starting out from man as he is now and thinking that they can reach their goal through an analysis of him. . . . Everything the philosopher has declared about man is, however, at bottom no more than the testimony as to the man of a very limited amount of time. Lack of historical sense is the common failing of all philosophers. (*Human, All Too Human*, §2)[5]

He does not note that his remark is reminiscent of Rousseau's criticism that the picture of man in the state of nature of Hobbes and Locke does not go back far enough. For him, this means that there cannot be a *true* thought; truth itself becomes radically questionable, and there being no true good, he presents himself as an immoralist. He discussed history in his first book, *The Birth of Tragedy* (1872), referring to the plays of Aeschylus, an event that suggests the death of tragedy occurring soon after with Socrates.

Socrates, in Nietzsche's view, changed human history by introducing theoretical man, the man who stood for comprehensible nature and the value of knowledge. His rationalism led to optimism, for the rationalist believes that reason is virtue and virtue brings happiness. Eventually, in the modern age rational optimism leads to the notion of universal enlightenment that makes all men happy under a world state combining socialism and science. With this reasoning, Nietzsche makes Machiavelli's founding of modernity unnecessary: Socrates's rationalism is for him the same as Machiavelli's, as all philosophy is moral and political in nature. Nietzsche has hopes for a great future, surpassing even Greek tragedy.

History is the theme of *On the Advantage and Disadvantage of History for Life* (1874), the second of his four *Untimely Meditations* (1873–1876), mentioned above. Nietzsche here questions the assumption of thinkers after Hegel that it is necessary to study universal or world history. History, he says, requires a horizon—that is, a limited horizon—and it is abused when this necessity is denied. When we teach ourselves from a cosmopolitan viewpoint, we attempt to avoid the conclusion that everything is historically relative, as Hegel did by assuming that his time was the absolute time or as Marx did through a theory of alienation and return. Those after Hegel did not find this assertion of an absolute time tenable; they asserted against him that the historical process is unfinishable. Men make progress in thinking, but reality recedes from them: infinite progress in science matched by infinite mysteriousness in the object of science. Even the idea of progress is historically relative. In *On the Advantage and Disadvantage,* Nietzsche finds three kinds of history: monumental history of the great; an antiquarian history of nations; and critical history, the new kind that is critical especially of itself, as with Niebuhr. This last kind is the one that interests him, and he says that it yields a truth deadly to life. Critical history dissects life with its "greedy curiosity" and "systematic torture"; it paralyzes the mind, for no one will strive for a goal that is historically relative and has no truth (*Advantage and Disadvantage of History for Life,* §1, p. 14; §7, p. 40). Is such history even true? Nietzsche grasps a deeper truth that life is creativity. Examining universal history, one sees that it consists of acts of creativity that bring new ideas into being—a creativity threatened by relativism and nihilism.

In our time a symptom of the decay in Nietzsche's idea is the degenerate "creativity" used to describe the business of an advertising company or a college course in writing, by which it becomes an example of foolish, optimistic rationalism, rather than the cure for nihilism. One can state the problem as follows: Creativity arises out of relativism, yet it must rise above relativism. It must mean something more than a fluffy pretense of greatness within reach of all, the grade inflation that results from relativism. This means that some things and some people are not creative, which in turn means that there is such a thing as the capacity to create. Machiavelli "decided to take a path as yet untrodden by anyone" (D 1.pr); Shakespeare did not need to take a course in creative writing. It also means that "the goal of humanity cannot be at the end of history but only in its highest specimens" (*Advantage and Disadvantage of History for Life*, §9, p. 53). If there is a capacity to create, can that capacity be created? If it cannot be created, then there would be something that is not historically relative: those endowed with that capacity would not owe their creations only to themselves but to their capacity, to their nature, to nature generally. If creativity rises above relativism, it must end in some principle above creativity—call it nature—that cannot be created. Nietzsche was far from being unaware of this problem: One could say it is the theme of the book we shall now study, *Beyond Good and Evil.*

The Will to Truth

This will be a brief study with stops to consider selected passages, the kind of looking over that, though not mere summary, necessarily suffers from overlooking much that a longer study would reveal. Beginning with the title, one notes that "beyond good and evil (*böse*)" is not "beyond good and bad (*schlecht*)," a distinction from Nietzsche's *Genealogy of Morals* to be discussed. Then the subtitle*: Prelude to a (einer) Philosophy of the Future,* where the "a" in fine print instead of "the" should be noted. Today the indefinite article is commonplace, as in John Rawls's book *A Theory of Justice,* where it signifies a becoming modesty. With Nietzsche it is an opening shot at the usual claims of philosophy for the truth. Then we come to a preface (*Vorrede*) to the book that as a whole is a prelude (*Vorspiel*) and find a startling notion to suppose:

> Supposing truth is a woman—what then? Are there not grounds for the suspicion that all philosophers, insofar as they were dogmatists,

> have been very inexpert about women? That the gruesome seriousness, the clumsy obtrusiveness with which they have usually approached truth so far have been awkward and very improper methods for winning a woman's heart?

We do remember that Machiavelli spoke of fortune as a woman who likes to be "beaten down" by young men (P 25), whose youth excuses their clumsiness and produces results.

Nietzsche imagines truth as a woman less tolerant of pushy, assertive types who favor a direct approach. Contrary to the skepticism of our time, he assumes that women have a special character distinct from men's and that no one objects to this assumption. Supposing, then, that Nietzsche knows what a woman is, what does he mean by supposing truth is a woman? If truth is human like a woman, truth is not a god, nor is it God. If every man wants or has a woman, truth is every man's and truths like women are diverse. Truth insists on an indirect approach; she must be wooed, not commanded—but also impregnated? Truth is not above human convention as previous philosophers—the dogmatists—have supposed. Plato, with his ideas or forms, is the prince of the dogmatists, the one who stands for eternal truth. Christianity is nothing new in its dogmatism; it is but "Platonism for the people," a vulgar eternal truth. With this famous phrase, Nietzsche will lead a campaign against the priests but mainly against Plato. Does this sound familiar? Perhaps another old Nick we have encountered? From beginning to end, it appears, modern political philosophy joins combat against Christianity and its source in the rationalism of the ancients. In place of Machiavelli's effectual truth, Nietzsche posits the notion of "perspective," similar to horizon, as "the basic condition of all life." Both notions rebel against the Platonic conception of philosophy as an end in itself. They instead substitute an unspecified goal for philosophy in politics—Machiavelli for virtue in Italy and Nietzsche for "free spirits" in Europe.

The first "part" of *Beyond Good and Evil* is titled "On the Prejudices of Philosophers." It flings an insult at philosophers by calling into question the virtue of lacking prejudice by which they would distinguish themselves from nonphilosophers. It begins with the distinctive "will to truth" of philosophy:

> The will to truth which will still tempt us to many a venture, that famous truthfulness of which all philosophers so far have spoken with respect—what questions has this will to truth not laid before us! What strange wicked questionable questions! . . . *Who* is it really that puts questions to us here? *What* in us really wants 'truth'? (BGE 1.1)

"Why not untruth," Nietzsche continues. He has adjusted philosophy's quest for truth to "truthfulness" (*die Wahrhaftigkeit*), a moral quality of truth telling rather than truth seeking. As opposed to the intellectual virtue of philosophy, truth telling is one of Aristotle's eleven moral virtues; Nietzsche questions the distinction. He will subject this moral phenomenon, as indicated by the title of the book, to a causal analysis. This makes philosophy into psychology, a physiological psychology, but first he wants to question whether truthfulness is a noble quality, as previous philosophers had assumed.

What is the value of truth, meaning the value for *life*? Does life need truth? Or does life in fact need deception, self-deception? Is the will to truth, then, perhaps akin to the will to deception, or perhaps even identical with it? New philosophers are becoming concerned with these dangerous perhapses. This suggests that conscious thought is not the contrary of instinct but has its root there. To live, man needs regularity; so his instinct produces that regularity in thought. Logic has nothing to do with truth but is indispensable for man's being. To understand thought one must go deeper than thought—yet this is itself a thought. Here is the paradox of the subsequent "depth psychology" that Nietzsche founded. In this context he asserts, as quoted above, that every philosophy is a "personal confession," a morality equivalent to an instinct (BGE 1.6). Every thinker has his specific urge, Nietzsche included, but he is superior to previous philosophers because he is aware of it—and so makes it a thought. Every thinker unmasks other thinkers to discover the urge underneath, but every thinker has a mask himself both concealing and expressing his own urge. Nietzsche generalizes paradoxically about all philosophers by insisting that each of them is intensely personal behind his mask.

One such mask is the idea of living according to nature, for which the Stoic philosophers are best known, though they did not invent it. This is a wrong idea, says Nietzsche—who thereby implies he knows what nature is. He asserts that life means going beyond one's nature by opposing its limitations. The Stoic idea of following nature is a mask for the desire to command nature, a thought whereby Nietzsche shows himself in accord with early modern philosophers such as Machiavelli and Bacon. This commanding he calls the "will to power" (BGE 1.9). Another related mask is the notion of "self-preservation" in Hobbes and Locke. For Nietzsche, self-preservation means that humans are completed and satisfactory as they are; they only need to preserve themselves. For him, this is a delusion. True self-preservation is self-overcoming or creativity toward a goal never reached, an act never completed. To be alive, man must create something new—but how new can new be, especially if the greatest creation is knowledge, as Nietzsche says? Of this urge, the *id* that Freud borrowed from him, he says: "A thought comes when 'it' wishes, not when 'I' wish." In fact, even the "it" contains an interpretation of the process of thinking, as it seems supplied by Nietzsche (BGE 1.17). He denies the usual notion that the will can be separated from a thought and delivers this powerful statement of his thought to illustrate the point:

> In all willing it is absolutely a question of commanding and obeying on the basis . . . of a social structure composed of many "souls." Hence a philosopher should claim the right to include willing as such within the sphere of morals—morals being understood as the doctrine of the relations of supremacy under which the phenomenon of "life" comes to be. (BGE 1.19)

He had said that "our body is but a social structure composed of many souls," referring to the wills of those who obey and the delight of commanding. The will seems determined by the id behind or beneath it but adopts as its own the force that seems to determine it. The body that commands has a social structure consisting of the obstacles it overcomes and wills it forces to obey. In his psychology Nietzsche offers a sociology not of the democratic determination of the will by factors more powerful than itself, but, on the contrary, an aristocratic or tyrannical commanding of factors in its way to make them instruments of itself. The successful will says to itself *l'effet, c'est moi*—not the state is me, as Louis XIV declared, but the effect. Even though the id or urge seems to be in charge, the will commands as the id's executive. The will commands as master but to do so obeys as servant.

One is reminded of Machiavelli's effectual truth, which is the truth that comes about, that one did not intend—but if understood, the truth one desires. Nietzsche is perhaps not so creative as he is given credit for. Or is it the meaning of creativity that one takes over as one's own what was said or done before and gives it a twist? Nietzsche's creativity is a tyranny in the soul taken from Machiavelli's prince, a psychology that takes over from political science. But by not mentioning the soul in his two major works, Machiavelli showed that he very well knew that his politics of *uno solo* was destructive of the soul. To be alone one must use others and be aware of their wills, so that being alone has a "social structure," as Nietzsche says. If the reader permits, let me say here that liberal use of quotation marks in this book is intended to serve accuracy in interpretation. Nietzsche, however, makes the ample use common today of ironic quotation marks, as, for example, when he says both "souls" and souls in this passage. The quotation marks indicate that the soul is a dubious mask over an underlying reality, and without quotation marks, he summons the will to say it anyway. Or is that will a need to surrender to the truth of the soul?

Nietzsche's substitute for traditional philosophy is psychology. But it is not psychology in the sense of classical political philosophy with reason in charge. His psychology is physiological; its source is in the urges of the body. It is, moreover, historical, rather than based on ahistorical nature and ethical rather metaphysical. The latter, for Nietzsche, is the prejudice of philosophers, the mask that conceals the psychological truth. That truth is always a moral interpretation, for one cannot discuss human beings without making value judgments. Every fact is based on an interpretation of value, or a "value" as a verbal noun in the language of today. There cannot be a fact-value distinction in which facts are science and values are emotions, because science is based on a value. Science is interpretation, which is always through language, which is always historical; it is no less interpretive than common sense, religion, or prejudice. Without interpretation science is lifeless and life destroying.

Free Spirits

The second part, titled "The Free Spirit," is also devoted to the subject of philosophy. In this the first two parts differ from the others, which are each devoted to a separate topic. This second part considers the relation of philosophers, known as "free spirits" in the nineteenth century, to nonphilosophers. *O sancta simplicitas*, it begins, describing the world of simplification—that is, falsification—in which we live. The "we" Nietzsche speaks for is not the "we philosophers" he elsewhere stands with but all of us (*Gay Science*, preface, §2); philosophers are not set apart. We live in a thoroughly falsified world with "a passport to everything superficial, our thoughts a divine desire for wanton leaps and wrong inferences!" (BGE 2.24). We live this way because we use language, which is characterized by false opposites where "there are only degrees and many subtleties of gradation." The truth of nature is that it supplies nothing but a disordered chaos of sense data—for example, this, that, or the other human, all of them different. We impose the false universal of "human being," assuming we know what that is. Our science depends unthinkingly on these unexamined assumptions. Our social science today takes for granted that man is "social," meaning that, contrary to Aristotle, man is naturally social rather than political. This issue is never raised by "social scientists" any more than by ordinary people, as both types are united in a quasi-religious—*sancta*!—reliance on falsely distinct definitions.

In general, science depends on a prescientific ordering, a foundation that is not scientific and does not arise from science. This is all very well since it shows that science is fundamentally in harmony with life. For ordinary purposes, for nonphilosophers, we can gaily accept life based on a fundamental falsehood, but philosophers cannot do this. They are the most serious of men and they accept the martyrdom of suffering for the truth in their quest for truth. They live solitary lives without hatred and especially without the moral indignation that causes us to lie to ourselves, pretending to be perfect and demanding that others share our perfection (BGE 2.25). In this Nietzsche parts company with Kant (his pure morality of the categorical imperative) and Marx (the opponent of pure oppression), philosophers for whom he had little sympathy. Yet if philosophy not only has but also *is* a morality, as he says, how can philosophers fail to feel moral indignation (BGE 1.6)? He speaks of a "philosophical sense of humor," but when did common morality ever have a sense of humor (BGE 2.25)? The answer is that Nietzsche had to be a teacher of morality to correct the habitual frustration of moral people, at least in the highest case of a philosopher.

Living a solitary life away from the many may be dangerous to a philosopher, particularly one who identifies philosophy as psychology. This philosopher needs to understand human souls, and to do this he cannot stoop and crawl into their baser aspects himself, but he needs the help of those who bring out what is normally concealed. Nietzsche calls them cynics, who teach the philosopher, who is not himself a cynic (BGE 2.26). He thinks he will probably be misunderstood in this way. Moral men are not good teachers of morality because they do not see its grounds and limits. Indeed, to the extent that moral men are Kantians, they are willfully ignorant of human nature. For Kant, psychology is the enemy of morality. In accordance with your own psychology, you cannot be moral if you know why you are moral, apart from desiring morality itself as a rational being above resort to any psychology. To learn the foundation of morality, you need to learn from teachers who are less admirable than those they expose: Just think of almost any book about a statesman by a suspicious historian.

Philosophy has a tempo, Nietzsche says, a different tempo of thinking in different languages. He cites among others our favorite, Machiavelli, for breathing the dry, refined air of Florence, discussing "the most serious matters in a boisterous *allegrissimo*" and contrasting "long, difficult, hard, dangerous thoughts" with a gallop tempo and "with the very best most capricious humor" (BGE 2.28, p. 41). Here is philosophic humor using cynicism but going beyond it. These tempos are created by the "very few" independent men, the philosophers who look down from above (BGE 2.29). Youth is another cause of difference in tempo: The young cannot understand, because they are always saying yes and no. They are either too reverent or too angry (BGE 2.31). This introduces a discussion of the stages of morality, as if the growth of a human being were comparable to the moral history of the human species (BGE 2.32). Is Nietzsche engaged in overcoming morality as part of its history, or is he creating a new morality regardless of its history? Both ideas are suggested by the title *Beyond Good and Evil.* Then we come to a very important section on the philosopher's morality of truthfulness (*die Wahrhaftigkeit*) and the will to truth that is not easy to understand:

> There would be no life at all if not on the basis of perspective estimates and appearances; and if, with the virtuous enthusiasm and clumsiness of some philosophers, one wanted to abolish the "apparent world" altogether—well, supposing you could do that,

> at least nothing would be left of your "truth" either. . . . Is it not sufficient to assume different degrees of apparentness (*Scheinbarkeit*) and as it were lighter and darker shades of appearances—different values, to use the language of painters? Why couldn't the world *that concerns us*—be a fiction? (BGE 2.34)

Philosophy was originally a search for truth, for the world as it really is, in itself, and apart from human convention. What belongs to a thing itself—its nature or *physis*—is distinct from what is added by human convention or *nomos* (in Greek, because philosophy began in Greece). Thus, for a sacred white cow, the "white" is part of its nature, as a color of some cows, but the "sacred" has been added by humans. This was modified in John Locke's epistemology to distinguish primary qualities, like size and weight, from secondary qualities added by the human perceiver. For this viewpoint, also that of modern physics, the "white" might be part of convention, as well as the "sacred." Nietzsche rebels against the distinction that seems to disparage the human in favor of the nonhuman, and he attacks this attitude of dehumanization by philosophy and especially modern science: The cow that concerns us is the one apparent to us humans, the one we have before us and want to know. He replaces the distinction between nature and convention with a distinction between surface and depth. Science devalues and discards the surface of things as superficial, the mere apparent world. Nietzsche finds a shading of degree from the surface to the depth; the surface is not the dead thing of science to be disregarded but open to interpretation that shades into the thing in its depth, like a darker or lighter shade of the same color. The cow as seen by man is not only white (the surface attribute) but also sacred (the interpretation), so that the thing seen through art and religion means more, and is more profound, than either what every ordinary person can see or the universal dehumanized thing that the scientist can see. Do "sacred" and "white" go together? Is white, the noncolor, really the color of sacred?

The original distinction of philosophy favoring nature over convention is overturned by Nietzsche's analysis: now the *nomos* of the thing is more philosophical than the mere *physis*. The philosopher has a different, broader perspective than the scientist, and his perception is closer to the ordinary person's perspective than the scientist's. One can see this fundamental change by Nietzsche in two contemporary schools of philosophy: phenomenology and ordinary language. Most philosophy since Nietzsche is preoccupied with interpretation, nonscientific or prescientific. For Nietzsche, however, the philosopher is separate from both science and the ordinary person; the philosopher gives things their conventional value, which means their human value. Since different philosophers give different interpretations at different times, convention must be understood historically. Convention has become part nature and part history, with emphasis on history; and philosophy has become interpretation, or hermeneutics. These followers of Nietzsche have in general perhaps lost full sight of his critique of modern science and its truth as "intelligible character" separate from human will. The notion that "every profound spirit needs a mask" yields to the openness and the lack of shame that goes with openness and is characteristic of scientific method (BGE 2.36, 2.40). Nietzsche's "philosophers of the future" are "friends of solitude," something more than the "free spirits" of the nineteenth century whom he analyzes in this second part of his book (BGE 2.44).

The Religious Essence

Following the first two parts on philosophy, and especially the second one on free spirits, is a discussion of the religious essence (*Wesen*). The religious essence is not religion itself but rather the cause of religion, which is not religious. A nonreligious cause of religion is consistent with the rampant atheism of the free spirits he has just discussed. Yet it reveals a much more serious, if not respectful, treatment of religion by Nietzsche. In contrast to Marx, for whom religion is dismissed as a mere interpretive superstructure over the historical developments of economic production, Nietzsche offers the history of religion as the fundamental cause of human history. The free spirits of atheism had eliminated the human soul from history; Nietzsche begins from it:

> The human soul and its limits, the range of inner human experiences reached so far, the heights, depths, and distances of these experiences, the whole history of the soul *so far* and its as yet unexhausted possibilities—that is the predestined hunting ground for a born psychologist and lover of the "great hunt." (BGE 3.45)

The soul is infinite as far as can be known, and its history is best known through the history of religion, not economics as for Marx. Nietzsche turns immediately to the study of original Christianity to understand the religious essence, called a "neurosis"—a sacrifice of the intellect. It was a kind of cruelty to oneself, a revaluation of all the values of antiquity; it came from the spirit of revenge in the Oriental slave, the contrary of confident, assertive aristocracy. Nietzsche develops this thought in his *Genealogy of Morals* (1887), where he presents in his striking graphic exaggeration the rebellion in slave morality and the development of the "ascetic ideal" (see part 3). Here he confines the point to "this whole phenomenon of the saint" that he says is so greatly interesting to so many ages and types of men, including his contemporary, Arthur Schopenhauer (BGE 3.47).

The power of the saint, the strength of his will, attracts notice and wonder. It is not that there is a sudden change from sinner to saint through repentance, for underneath the apparent opposite, sinner and saint are the same. The saint denies life in both its attractions and necessities, so that he denies the will to power, which is the essence of life. But this denial of the will to power is an expression of the will to power—this is the religious essence. The saint is even superior in power to the warrior, and we see that religion must be understood within the universal phenomenon of the will to power. One can wonder whether he succeeded in this: the will to power to do what? Is the sacrifice of the intellect not done for the sake of the intellect, for knowing better rather than for more power?

Next, Nietzsche addresses the religion of the future and asks, "Why atheism today"? In Europe now, theism is disappearing from philosophy, but religion remains. The "whole of modern philosophy" since Descartes is an attempt to "assassinate" the old concept of the soul, attacking its capacity for voluntary action, in order to make an attempt against the basic premise of Christian doctrine that it is possible to know and to love God. Modern philosophy is "covertly or overtly" anti-Christian but by no means anti-religious (BGE 3.54). Just as the saint is a kind of sinner, modern atheism is a kind of religion. It is the cruel sacrifice of the highest, and what is the highest? God. And God is sacrificed for what? For nothing—for a value-free meaningless scientific world. A genuinely religious life is occupied with self-examination and prayer, requiring a certain leisure in which the notion that work disgraces human worth is present if not dominant. Contrast that with "our modern noisy, time-consuming industriousness" stupidly proud of itself, educating people to prepare them for unbelief. Locke praised the "industrious and rational" businessman; Nietzsche extends this description to the scholar and then calls the result "a presumptuous little dwarf and rabble man" (BGE 3.58).

To love man for God's sake has until now been the noblest calling among men, but the love of man without the intent to sanctify that goal, without any higher inclination, is nothing much. It is as if one were to say that some men love cats, others dogs, still others human beings. The philosopher and free spirit, as Nietzsche understands him, will make use of religion just as he makes use of politics and economics for his project of education, which is both destructive and creative and form-giving. The danger of today remains the love of men who are nothing, prepared by Christianity's teaching that all men are equal but kept from being ruinous by the sanctity of the saint, which placed the saint, to men at least, far above the level of ordinary humans. Now, by the sacrifice of God we have lost sight of any elevation in man. Nietzsche ends part 3 with a blast against the calamitous arrogance of Christianity for having created "men not noble enough to see the abysmally different order of rank, chasm of rank, between man and man—such men have so far held sway over the fate of Europe with their 'equal before God' until finally a smaller, almost ridiculous type, a herd animal, something eager to please, sickly and mediocre has been bred, the European of today" (BGE 3.62).

Truthfulness and Shame

Part 4 of Nietzsche's thrilling book contains 122 brief aphorisms (all but §80 and §131 are one sentence long) and is titled "Epigrams and Interludes." This part has puzzles and it is a transition. We readers, challenged and aided by the author's cleverness and brilliance, are to think our way to the reason for the only announced partition in the book's text. It appears that the first three parts on philosophy and religion consider what surpasses or includes man—the whole of things and God—while parts 5 to 9 discuss the morality of man, the specifically human. Part 4 summarizes what precedes and introduces the topic of human morality. In the first aphorism Nietzsche says that a teacher takes things seriously only in regard to students, "even himself" (BGE 4.63). A teacher's thought is not his own except that being a teacher is part of his own. Knowledge is in itself, but it is also *for* someone. Nietzsche always emphasizes his solitude and the individuality of true creativeness, but he also writes books. He is not a mere creative writer who as such has nothing to advise apart from the message to be creative.

What he features in part 4 is shame. Shame is the contrary of pride and vanity but overshadows them in Nietzsche's presentation because it is allied with truthfulness, the virtue of philosophy. Ordinary shame is awareness of one's faults, and philosophic shame is awareness of human boasting, challenging man's prideful assertions. Ordinary shame may be among those assertions as it claims to know what vices deserve shame. In order to gain truth, the philosopher must overcome the ordinary shame that both discloses our faults and evils and protects them with a doubtful awareness. Aristotle said at the opening of his *Metaphysics* that man by nature desires to know, and in his *Nicomachean Ethics* he said that shame is not a virtue because it is better to have nothing to be ashamed of than to be ashamed.[6] For Nietzsche, shame is more positive and more powerful. The shame that suppresses knowledge does not have to contend with Aristotle's affirmation of a natural desire to know, and its greater power that results can be captured by the power of truthfulness and, so to speak, used for good. Truthfulness is the virtue of shame, forging us to lay our souls open and bare. Nietzsche says that knowledge would be much less attractive if one did not have to overcome shame (BGE 4.*65*). Knowledge, it appears, is knowledge of the true self, for which one must overcome the shame of being a man. Man is a "laughable monkey," says Nietzsche in *Thus Spoke Zarathustra*, but he also says there that man is the beast with red cheeks. He is ashamed because of what he finds in himself. What does he find? Evil. "The great epochs of our life come when we gain the courage to rechristen our evil as what is best in us" (BGE 4.118). Shame brings out the value of the evil we are ashamed of and, hence, its virtue.

Here we see Machiavelli's lesson from *Mandragola,* given at the beginning of this book. We are studying the history of modern political philosophy, and for all its diverse turns, Nietzsche at the end is with Machiavelli at the beginning in the modern camp. Nietzsche's twist is to call good evil, as when he describes morality as the revenge of slaves (to be discussed), rather than call evil good, by which he rechristens Machiavelli's plainer advice to do the latter. Machiavelli transforms classical virtue into his own *virtu* with a capacity for dirty tricks, but he did not attempt a rechristening or change in ordinary morality. Nietzsche does that; he brings new virtues of truthfulness and probity (a kind of honesty as shall be seen) for intellectual and moral virtue respectively. The philosopher's truthfulness reveals men to be monkeys, including himself. Shame is the mask of man; truthfulness or probity is the unmasking of man: "One is most disrespectful to one's god; he is *not allowed* to sin" (BGE 4.65a). Here is a failure of shame, said paradoxically to be showing respect. One's "god" is one's ideal. Being true to yourself demands that in your shame you descend to your deepest urges, including the sexual: "The degree and kind of a man's sexuality reach up into the ultimate pinnacle of his spirit" (BGE 4.75). This from Nietzsche has been a clarion call for psychology in our time, more persistent, if not louder, than the honk for socialism from Karl Marx.

Nietzsche includes a dozen aphorisms in part 4 on men and women, never explicitly defining them and, in his own probity, not always complimenting women. His sexism—and racism—one may say, have their origin in the major premise that thought has its origin in bodily urges; the minor premise is that men, women, Aryans, Jews (to whom Nietzsche is favorable) have different bodies that determine their traits; hence, Nietzsche's sexism and racism. One should pay attention to the major premise denying the possibility of pure mind that seems to be found in Plato and Kant. If instead mind is affected by one's body, doctrines of sexism and racism that detail the mind's biases would be open to consideration. To conclude, we humans expose ourselves, but we also conceal ourselves. To deny our shame places us on the level of beasts without red cheeks.

Therefore, Nietzsche says that one must tether one's heart to liberate one's mind (BGE 4.87). A person who fetters neither his heart nor his mind may think himself to be perfectly objective, but without holding a conviction he understands nothing. To have a conviction one must deny something within oneself; one must have shame. The much more liberal self-expression of our time owes its origin to Nietzsche, but it will produce nothing grand because it requires no effort. To exert yourself you must repress yourself and accept the necessity of shame. And in accepting this, you accept the necessity of God (BGE 4.150). The world of convention, created and enriched by the philosopher, the world known to us, requires a fierce conviction from the philosopher, a god or something similar. Machiavelli's world is the world of fact and human necessity;

Hegel's is the world of reason. Both do their best to exclude any world beyond or above this world, which is *the* world. Nietzsche's is the world of convention, anti-Christian to be sure, but requiring a suprahuman source of repression. To summarize: Truthfulness requires overcoming shame, which in turn requires feeling shame, a pleasurable feeling, says Nietzsche. It is shameful that we human beings have to overcome shame, but doing this compels us to create a new conviction and new morality so that we have something new to be shameful about. Part 4 introduces shame to provide a transition from the negative and destructive beginning of *Beyond Good and Evil* to the positive and constructive bulk of the work—the creation of a new morality and a new shame. Nietzsche had said at its beginning that in every philosophy there comes a point where the philosopher's conviction enters the scene: *adventivit asinus, pulcher et fortissimus* (BGE 1.8). The beautiful and very strong donkey hee-haws his conviction, a brute yea-saying. We humans are donkeys but we should be ashamed if we are not beautiful and very strong donkeys. Men create their own shame—which is relativism; yet somehow some men create a beautiful and very strong shame—which is not relativism. Nietzsche makes his way back and forth between these two opposites.

A New Morality

What is the—or rather a—new morality? We learn right away from the title of part 5 that morality has a history, or rather a *natural* history. David Hume had written a *Natural History of Religion* (1757), but Nietzsche's natural history is different. The truth of religion was no longer a question for Nietzsche, and Hume would not have questioned morality by supplying a natural history for it. Nietzsche begins by rejecting a "rational foundation' or "science" of morality, coming to be replaced by a more modest "typology of morality" (BGE 5.186). As is commonplace now, there are only moralities in the plural. But he soon supplies an answer to the question of what a morality is: "Every morality is, as opposed to *laisser-aller*, a bit of tyranny against "nature," also against "reason" (BGE 5.188). Nature and reason have surrounding quotation marks in the text because they are historical and variable, but tyranny does not. Morality is compulsion, as one sees with the Stoics, Port-Royal (Jansenist Catholicism), and the Puritans. The last is common today; one can hardly say "morality" without adding "Puritanical." Nietzsche, however, thinks that this tyranny is a good thing, implying that Puritanism should be welcomed. It gives men discipline and cultivation. Nietzsche promotes creativity, which we like, but he is against the permissiveness often confused today with creativity. One cannot be creative without effort, and effort requires imposing something on oneself. Nietzsche understands this discipline historically, as a stage in the development of man. *Thus Spoke Zarathustra* likewise presents three metamorphoses of man: the camel, the lion, and the child, which signify the carrying of a burden, the assertion of a conviction, and the birth of a new morality.[7]

If the tyranny of morality is good for man, it constitutes the nature of man without quotation marks—which Nietzsche proceeds to do at the end of this same aphorism:

> "You shall obey—someone and for a long time: *else* you shall perish and lose the last respect for yourself"—this appears to me to be the moral imperative of nature . . . which appears not addressed to the individual (what do individuals matter to her?) but to peoples, races, ages, classes—but above all to the whole human animal, to *man*. (BGE 5.188)

The moral imperative of tyrannical nature has no skeptical quotes; Nietzsche looks for history but with a capital H, history with rational meaning, *natural* history. He is led from history to nonhistorical nature. Man has a nature that is improved by the experience of obedience, even of slavery. Usually the experience of tyranny has been held to be living in fear, but Nietzsche rejects "morality as fearfulness" (BGE 5.197–198, 5.201). Fearful morality has its root in the early moderns: Machiavelli shows fear to be more powerful than love, and Hobbes and Locke find their anchor in fear of violent death or fear for one's self-preservation. What they did is to generalize the case of the average person of unremarkable courage. To which Nietzsche replies that one must not generalize the reaction to tyranny in a way that creates average or herd morality. Nietzsche exposes the bad effects of herd or democratic morality. One example of it is the philosophy of empiricism that rests on the reliability of average human senses (BGE 5.192). The power of morality, he says, is such that it governs human senses; even the eye is made to see what morality requires (BGE 5.192).

This is a thrust at Locke's empiricism, in which sense experience determines human actions.

Nietzsche might have joined Aristotle in claiming that moral virtue is both more voluntary and more habitual than tyrannical self-control, and though available to all, achievable only by few. But he does not; he holds to the necessity of tyranny but makes it self-imposed rather than spontaneous like the empiricists, and he keeps it for the few, who excel not in perfect virtue, as for Aristotle, but in the strength of tyranny in enduring and conquering tyranny—in will to power. He describes such a person as having "in addition to his powerful and irreconcilable drives, a real mastery and subtlety in waging war against oneself; in other words self-control, self-outwitting has been inherited and cultivated too—then those magical, incomprehensible and unfathomable ones arise, those enigmatic men predestined for victory or seduction whose most beautiful expression is found in Alcibiades and Caesar" (BGE 5.200). It is hard to see such a villain as Adolf Hitler in these words, but they do remind us again of Machiavelli's *animo* done in the style of Nietzsche's amazing truthfulness.

Nietzsche's description does not include the great deeds of Napoleon and Caesar. Instead, his point is the dominance of mastery against the herd. He is not going to say yet where powerful individuals are to go now, but he does give a sense of the direction toward which they are headed. At the end of part 5 (203), Nietzsche repeats a call for motion "toward" without specifying the end: "Toward new philosophers," in the plural because there can be no science of morality; "toward spirits strong and original enough" to stimulate opposite valuations and invert "eternal values"; "toward forerunners, men of the future" to tie the knot that forces men into new tracks, "to prepare great ventures and overall attempts at discipline and cultivation"; to put an end to "the nonsense of the greatest number"; "to enable a soul to grow to such a height and force that it would feel the compulsion for such tasks."

But it is enough to supply a sample of a sterling passage of Nietzsche's passion that needs to be read in full. It is mostly negative because he thinks things could be no worse even though he despises the certainty of science. Christianity, to be sure, had its virtue, but in the past—no longer now, because Christianity without God is soft and undisciplined. It has produced the degeneration of man under democracy. Nietzsche describes it in a display of unsurpassed philosophic trash talk denouncing "socialist dolts and flatheads" who animalize man, producing "the dwarf animal of equal rights" (BGE 5.203). What has happened to rational control?, one may ask, but note that Nietzsche has not given up on philosophy despite its biases and dangers. He proceeds in part 6 to find a place even for scholars.

The title of part 6 is "We Scholars." Nietzsche was himself a considerable scholar in philology, the field of scholarship arising in the nineteenth century devoted to critical examination of classical texts and the Bible. Its intent was to dissect the author's intention in a whole text to find anterior sources in fragments, thus undoing its integrity and authority. As one of these scholars, Nietzsche defines them by the objectivity they prize that suppresses all values and valuing as personal. The scholar's life is defined by his proud denial of any bias from his life and from life itself. In part 3 of *The Genealogy of Morals,* Nietzsche calls this the "ascetic ideal" and welcomes it as a stage in the formation of a fuller life that would be the opposite of asceticism. Max Weber follows him in his famous essay "Science as a Vocation" (*Wissenschaft als Beruf,* 1917), but Nietzsche is much less admiring. We also note that scholarship as a devotion or calling is the very contrary of Marx's well-rounded human being, who has no special field or specialty and no devotion to anything. The failure to understand devotion is one signal result of Marx's materialism.

Scholarship may be an ingredient in the new philosophy, but Nietzsche begins with an attack on the scholar's declaration of independence from philosophy. His "arrogant contempt" is part of the general democratic degradation of Europe, supported by a degeneration of philosophy itself into a "theory of knowledge" incapable of dominating (BGE 6.204). Early modern philosophers were in the front line of modern science— Bacon, Descartes, Leibniz—but they have been reduced to a lingering remnant of philosophy by the dominance of objective science that despises and fears philosophy. Nietzsche compares the modern scientist or scholar to an old maid: "Like her he is not conversant with the two most valuable functions of man," perhaps commanding mastery and the "giving birth" to genius BGE 6.206). He has the virtue of truthfulness but lacks experience of life, is subject to petty envy, and thinks in measures of mediocrity. The genuine philosopher, Nietzsche says, "lives 'unphilosophically' and 'unwisely' and above all *imprudently*" (BGE 6.205). Not detached from life, meaning common, nonphilosophic life, he cannot afford the irony of Socrates, who in the greatness of his soul looked down from above the common sort (BGE 6.212). Socrates (and his many imitators) distinguished by means of irony between esoteric speech to fellow philosophers and exoteric to the common nonphilosophic multitude. Nietzsche needs the disordered chaos of the philosopher's soul and cannot afford the calm necessary to restrain himself from telling everything to everyone in his truthfulness. To be sure, he wears a mask, but he admits and proclaims that he does (BGE 2.40). For him, it appears, truth seeking has to include truth telling.

The philosopher, as opposed to the scholar, has "ipsissimosity," the superlative of himself (*ipse*) coined by Nietzsche, meaning superlatively personal. This beautiful passage (BGE 6.206; see also 6.212) is another echo of Machiavelli's *uno solo*: it emphasizes the singularity of the phrase yet includes the Machiavellian sense of being on top. However singular and lonely at the pinnacle, however, Nietzsche's philosopher remains a type rather than a mere oneself that commands all others. Nietzsche is not quite the tyrant or proposing tyranny; he and his created similarity deserve their rank, as we learn at the end of part 6. The philosopher is described as a "Caesarean cultivator and violent man of culture" (*Gewaltmenschen der Kultur*, unfortunately translated by Walter Kaufmann as "cultural dynamo"), compared to the objective scholar, who is a mere instrument (BGE 6.207). But what is not merely objective has that objective quality of higher rank, as we learn in the last aphorism:

> Ultimately, there is an order of rank among the states of the soul.... The highest problems repulse everyone mercilessly who dares approach them without being predestined for their solution by the height and power of his spirituality.... For every high world one must be born; or to speak more clearly one must be *cultivated* for it... Many generations must have labored to prepare the origin of the philosopher. Every one of his virtues must have been acquired, nurtured, inherited and digested singly... above all the readiness for great responsibilities, the loftiness of glances that dominate and look down, feeling separated from the crowd and its duties and virtues, the affable protection and defense of whatever is misunderstood and slandered, whether it be god or devil, the pleasure and exercise of the great justice, the art of command. (BGE 6.213)

It is painful to pick apart such gorgeous language but it's essential to see what it means. Nietzsche speaks of a breeder who is bred. Like Plato, he deals with justice, but he cannot say as Plato says that some men have philosophic natures while others do not. He needs a theory of breeding because human nature changes in history, yet the result is the same: The most creative persons have the best or highest natures. He is driven back to the notion of natures in order to escape the nihilism of modern history and the mediocrity of modern science. Somehow he must reconcile the "ipsissimosity" of the philosopher with the objective, natural ranking of men that puts philosophy at the top. In a letter of December 10, 1513, Machiavelli had spoken of his reading of ancient authors as sitting down to "the food that is mine alone."[8] Nietzsche is the latest modern philosopher in the vein of Machiavelli, the earliest and the original: He remains respectful of the philosophic tradition while insisting on, and struggling with, a departure from it.

Nietzsche's Honesty

Part 7 is on "our virtues"—that is, the virtues of us scholars in part 6. The chief such virtue is honesty (or probity, *die Redlichkeit*), which is the will to truth that Nietzsche questions but nonetheless accepts. Honesty turns scholars into skeptics and specialists. They are skeptics because they cannot affirm anything in science without being scientifically dishonest; they are specialists because they cannot know everything. As scholars they are confined to the little footnotes of life. The will to truth, then, is essentially contrary to life: Life requires an affirmation, indeed an affirmation about the whole. Man must affirm himself to be alive; he cannot merely affirm "I am man because I am the world's greatest expert on the brain of a leech" (*Thus Spoke Zarathustra*, pt. 4, §4: "The Leech").[9] Yet Nietzsche accepts the will to truth. How is he going to make it compatible with the will to life—that is, the will to power?

"We modern men," he says, claim to be doubtful of virtue, using a psychological or scientific dissection to take it apart, but we should be ready to psychologize our psychology (BGE 7.215, 7.218). Our "modern ideas," he says pejoratively, focus on a "historical sense" that makes us skeptics. Nietzsche finds that with this sense we deny the "order of rank" that history reveals and take refuge in equality that denies the justice in "high spirituality." Instead of justice to the best, modern men preach pity to the weak. Addressing them, Nietzsche says, "You want if possible—and there is no more insane *if possible*—to *abolish suffering*" (BGE 7.225). "We immoralists" have a duty of our own—honesty, in which we work to perfect "our adventurous courage, our seasoned and choosy curiosity, our subtlest, most disguised, most spiritual will to power and overcoming of the world that flies and flutters covetously around all the realms of the future" (BGE 7.227). Nietzsche brings in the boredom discussed above as a typical complaint of Sherlock Holmes and the nineteenth century: "Let us see to it that out of honesty we do not become saints and bores" and "all moral philosophy so far has been boring" (BGE 7.228). To explain, he cites the British utilitarians, particularly Jeremy Bentham, but we can refer to Bentham's distinguished grandfather, Thomas Hobbes. Skeptical of the power of morality, Hobbes begins from egoism. But then he discovers that man's private good is identical with the common good; the desire for self-preservation induces men to seek peace by consenting to a common sovereign. Hobbes's immoralism is half-hearted and inconsistent; it is egoism set up from the beginning with an eye to its moral overcoming.

Moreover, seeking peace may be exciting, but once attained, peace brings the boring activities of commerce and industriousness that Nietzsche has denounced. He now launches an attack on humanitarianism, which is the pity that Rousseau endorsed as a means to escape the harshness of bourgeois virtue. Against pity, in perhaps the most disliked feature of his thought, he offers cruelty. Man does not have a fundamental pity to accompany his fundamental egoism, as with Rousseau; there is rather a fundamental cruelty. The only self-preservation is a form of self-enhancement or self-heightening in which cruelty replaces pity: "We should reconsider cruelty and open our eyes" (BGE 7.229). We have met cruelty before in this book in the thought of Machiavelli, whom Nietzsche does not mention. Machiavelli had seen cruelty as a necessary opposite to mercy, the contrast between the two making each appreciable and effectual. But in Machiavelli's thinking, cruelty is under the discipline of prudence, which would not recommend cruelty to oneself or unnecessary cruelty to others.

Nietzsche does not suffer these limitations; he wants open cruelty and self-cruelty promoted as honesty. Montesquieu had said in his *Spirit of the Laws* (1748) that "we begin to be cured of Machiavellianism"—of which a major ingredient is cruelty (*Spirit of the Laws*, 21.20). Commerce and industry, the very things that Nietzsche despises, will bring world peace by peaceful means, according to Montesquieu, the canny defender of liberalism. Nietzsche confines his remarks to British utilitarians, lesser figures than Machiavelli, Hobbes, and Montesquieu, but these greater ones are also included in the implication of his argument. His promise for the application of cruelty extends well beyond Machiavelli's and rejects Montesquieu's unfortunate assurance that Machiavellianism is obsolete. In *Ecce Homo* (1888), he says this:

> Let us look ahead a century. Let us suppose that my attempt to assassinate two millennia of antinature and desecration of man were to succeed. That new party of life, which would tackle the greatest of all tasks, the attempt to raise humanity higher, including the merciless extinction of everything that was degenerating and parasitical would again make possible the excess of life on earth. (*Ecce Homo*, Birth of Tragedy, §4)[10]

The party of life will keep us from being bored! This fearsome and sobering assertion shows that Nietzsche knew very well what he was proposing, if for a century in the future. Still, it remains the case that the most interesting feature of cruelty is cruelty not to others but to oneself—the tyrannical cruelty to oneself found in Puritanical morality. Puritanism of this kind is found in the scholar's will to truth. The scholar "forces his spirit to recognize things against the inclinations of the spirit . . . and the wishes of his heart." "In all desire to know there is a drop of cruelty" (BGE 7.229). The will to truth is the most sublime form of self-cruelty because it most fully denies the will to power. It denies the will of man to humanize everything, to conquer all dehumanized nature and to make it the servant of man. Men have always humanized nature in the teleology they attribute to it, giving it human purposes. Flowers are for smelling nice. This commonsense anthropomorphism Nietzsche wants to pick up and use consciously: The essence of man is to impose values with the will to power.

Yet if the will to power is the essence of man, how can Nietzsche accept the will to truth in the intellectual honesty of the scientist? To restate the argument: The will to truth is to see what is, the way it is, whether you like it or not—indeed, especially if you don't like it. We often see the perverse delight that scholars take in telling us unwelcome truths. They love to be messengers of bad news. You can't win in the Middle East, or anywhere. Racial integration is impossible. Human freedom is a delusion. Full employment would be a disaster. Affluence is worse than poverty. The family is a good idea but it won't work. Going to college only makes you forget high school. This cruelty of the scholar is caused by his objectivity; he is after *the* truth, not just *his* truth. Or is he? Nietzsche says that *his* truth is what seems to him *the* truth, and the will to truth is a form of the will to power—the most spiritual form. The will to power turns against itself to become the will to truth. My truth turns against me and becomes *the* truth cancelling *my* truth. Yet Nietzsche says that my truth is not really cancelled; it is expressed in a new way. It is sublimated. Nietzsche invented the notion of sublimation, and as opposed to many who use the term today, he is aware of the connection between sublimation and the sublime. Sublimation by self-cruelty makes men sublime.

Still, he has to face the problem in his brilliant formulations. The will to truth is the will to power turned against itself; it is my truth in the guise of the truth. Now isn't this insight into sublimation by self-cruelty *the* truth? If so, doesn't the will to truth win out, after all? And isn't the will to power, *my* truth, a version of the will to truth, which is *the* truth? We recall Kant's point that the psychologist cannot psychologize himself; he cannot overcome the difference between psychology and philosophy. Here lies the fundamental difficulty, both theoretical and practical, in the modern idea of rational control. Reason as reason does not have control sufficient to establish what it considers reasonable; the will to be reasonable may not have enough power. So, reason needs a formulation that is not fully reasonable to make it powerful. The obvious example we have seen in Machiavelli is necessity, or in Hobbes, Locke, and Rousseau, self-preservation. These are not always reasonable nor always powerful, but they give a certain commonsense support to reason—of course, one does what is necessary for self-preservation. But to make this formula certain, exact, and universal comes at the price of a simplified, even falsified definition of what is reasonable and good.

In their desire for certainty, modern theories abandon whatever advantage they have when taken as shrewd common sense. They try to even out the ups and downs of human fortune so that there is always a ready answer for a problem and prudence in the circumstances is not required. The primary virtues of courage and moderation are not required; in fact, they get in the way of prompt and relentless obedience to necessity. Men are not free of necessity or self-preservation, but they cannot be accurately defined so narrowly as to leave nothing valuable but survival. Survival is not a definite end with a full stop. One must go on to consider survival as what? As cowardly and greedy? Necessity, it appears, needs reference to what is good: There is necessity for mere survival when that is good, and necessary for life with virtue when that is possible. We judge by the primacy of the good even when we want, like Machiavelli, to make things simple by dismissing imagined goods and judging by necessity. Machiavelli's concept leaves us unaware of what is sacrificed when one accepts it. Life beyond acquisition fades from view and one forgets that one acquires in order to spend—and to spend well.

Nietzsche admits this Machiavellian simplification in his analysis of the will to power but claims to overcome its falsity by taking necessity as a stage of self-cruelty to one's spirit. He tries to remake the love of truth into the will to truth, the difference being in the cruelty required by the will. But the cruelty deprives the will to truth of its full rationality; it is a stage of truth seeking that taints the product. It brings a truth that requires "merciless extinction" of humans to establish and thereby to define its control. Reason gives way to control. Philosophy must be compelled to bow to power, and power must do with a sublimated but still simplified philosophy.

Nietzsche attempts "to translate man back into nature," which is to understand the will to power as natural growth as well as the desire to conquer and overcome nature. This is to say Yes to ignorance as well as science, and thus to validate ungrounded conviction, to say yes to what makes us unteachable deep down (BGE 7.230–231). He then returns to the difference between men and women, a topic in several works besides this one. We cannot expect him to give a warm welcome to feminism, since he so forcibly asserts the difference between the sexes, but he blows a kiss in that direction with an attack on the eternal feminine of Goethe or "woman as such." This he renames "the eternally boring in woman" and claims that woman's "great art is the lie, her highest concern is mere appearance and beauty" (BGE 7.232). Equality for the "weaker sex" belongs to the democratic inclination, like disrespect for the old, advocated by "scholarly asses of the male sex." Women have a nature more natural than a man's nature, more instinctual, more vulnerable and in need of love, more condemned to disappointment, more subject to tragic fear and pity. Their concern for indefinable beauty and appearance, as opposed to the male scholarly essence, seems to be a salutary influence in Nietzsche's view, of which the wary reluctance of some feminists today to define women is an odd reminder. But when women want to abandon their vulnerability, as they were doing already in his time, they can only replicate the male will to power and lose their "magic spell," their own will to appearance. Already Europe begins to suffer from this "modern idea," which he names "the borification of woman"—*die Verlangweiligung des Weibes* (BGE 7.239). This mouthful is the exclamation closing part 7.

Part 8 is on peoples and fatherlands, especially the former. Nietzsche prefers peoples (*Völker*) because he dislikes nationalities and wants to present an argument for a united Europe in the present and near future. Patriotism for a nation cramps the style of creative individuals, and he is looking for a World-Historical individual of dubious morality similar to Hegel's but unlike his, identified before the fact. Bismarck is rejected as a petty nationalist who diminished the intellectual force and high culture of Germany in the first half of the nineteenth century. A new Napoleon, Caesar, or Alcibiades, with great strength of will and comprehensive vision, might fill the bill. The emphasis is on language and music, not politics, and the peoples discussed are the Germans, the British, and the French: "The German himself is not, he becomes, he 'develops.'" He "knows no more dangerous and successful disguise than this confiding, accommodating, cards-on-the-table manner of German honesty" (BGE 8.244). The English, however, are "no philosophical race," says Nietzsche, invoking Hobbes, Hume, and Locke as witnesses. But Hobbes, we know, brought "power" to the fore in modern political science and deserves better mention than he gets (*Leviathan*, ch. 10). Nor is this gaily impudent boyish philosopher guilty of the "profound normality" Nietzsche despises in the English (cf. BGE 9.294). The French hold the "foremost school of taste" in Europe, but they have the "good will to resist any spiritual Germanization—and a still better incapacity to succeed." To this sudden knockout punch declaring them to be second-rate, he adds condemnation of the French socialists for their opposition to nationality (BGE 8.254, 8.256). Too bad, one may insert, that Nietzsche did not become acquainted with

Alexis de Tocqueville: Tocqueville had suspicions that Nietzsche might have liked about German pantheism and its excessive democracy. Jews receive more favorable treatment for their "grand style in morality"—a reference to his notable discussion in the *Genealogy of Morals*, where Jews are given credit for the invention of slave morality that so deepened the possibilities of man and extended man's will to power. He remarks ominously, "I have not met a German yet who was well disposed toward the Jews" (BGE 8.250–251).

It appears from part 8 that there is no Hegelian World History of nations representing stages of the development of reason. Nietzsche confines himself to the nineteenth century, particularly the latter half—his own time. Peoples have a bad tendency to degenerate into nations of prejudiced nationalism. Their culture stubbornly becomes political in a manner that questions whether culture or society can be thought and spoken of as apolitical. Perhaps Aristotle was right that politics decides culture rather than the reverse. One may suppose that Nietzsche derived the power of culture and of peoples from his assurance of the power of the outstanding individual, who makes himself *die Meistersinger*, praised by Nietzsche at the opening of part 8 (BGE 8.240).

Nietzsche's Nobility

The chapter title "What Is Noble?" uses the word for *noble* (*vornehm* as opposed to *edel*) that implies high birth, not merely moral elevation; the theme of part 9 is aristocratic nobility:

> Every enhancement of the type "man" has so far been the work of an aristocratic society. Without that pathos of distance which grows out of the ingrained difference between strata—when the ruling caste constantly looks far and looks down on subjects . . . that other more mysterious pathos could not have grown up either—the craving for an ever-new widening of distances within the soul itself. (BGE 9.257)

This will always be true, and the problem of part 9 is to show how the nobility of the barbarous blond beast is connected to the philosopher of Nietzsche's new philosophy. This sort of noble does not regard himself as the servant of the commonwealth but as its purpose. The ruled being for the sake of the rulers must be slaves, though Nietzsche does not concern himself with Aristotle's attempt to define the natural slave. Aristocratic society arises as a condition of the development of a higher type of man.

These "men of prey" belong to a barbarian caste that "accepts with a good conscience the sacrifice of untold human beings" and their "exploitation," which is not a sign of corrupt or imperfect or primitive society but "belongs to the essence of what lives" (BGE 9.257–259). Such exploitation is the "*primordial fact* of all history." But in the following section (BGE 9.260), Nietzsche says that in wandering through the various moralities that have prevailed on earth, he discovered the two basic types that have become known as features of his thought and were explained in his *Genealogy of Morals*, published a year after this work. These are master morality and slave morality, a fundamental distinction that occurs in the higher cultures and in individual higher souls. Higher cultures hold either the slave or master morality, but in higher individuals, master and slave are mixed together rather than completely separate. Master and slave complicate and moderate the primordial fact of exploitation, because it turns out that the slaves are not ground down to lasting, simple inferiority but are able to exploit their masters. In his explanation, we learn the meaning of the "good and evil" in the title of this book and develop the distinctions announced earlier.

"Good and evil" is a change from "good and bad," which precedes it and is characteristic of aristocratic morality. In aristocratic morality "good" is paired with "bad" (*schlecht*); the good are contemptuous of the bad, who are always slaves. Aristocratic goodness is an affirmation by proud aristocrats who frankly proclaim their superiority, and the bad are leftovers who have nothing to be proud of, hence nothing to affirm. They are defined by what they lack. With slave morality, however, the slaves cannot hold the good in contempt, so instead they live and thrive on indignation against "evil" (*böse*) in the aristocrats, who think themselves good. Slave morality is essentially a denial of evil rather than an affirmation of a new conception of "good" that would rival that of the aristocrats. "Good" for the slaves is whatever is not evil, so that good rather than bad is the leftover from what is mainly affirmed; the slave leftover is mostly utility, or justice defined as the useful rather than the noble. The proud aristocrat cannot be vain, because vanity presupposes concern with the opinions of others, while the noble man holds those opinions in contempt. The noble seeks danger, whereas the slave is motivated by fear. From this contrast it might seem that the noble aristocrat is simply superior to the slave, but such is not the case. Nietzsche makes a sudden, striking turn in his argument, giving it a splendid, lasting force.

Slave morality leads to the creation of the soul, when the soul is discovered to be the cause of evil that the slave blames in the master. For the aristocrat, what is real is the superiority that is apparent in his open pride; for the slave, however, the aristocrat's superiority is not obviously apparent but hidden in his soul. Slave morality invents the soul and with it deepens man by creating depth of soul under the prideful—or boastful—surface. In the relationship of master to slave, there is no longer a simple distinction between high and low, as aristocrats presume: There is low in the high and high in the low. To show this Nietzsche exposes the psychology of Jesus, which is

> the story of a poor fellow, unsated and insatiable in love, who had to invent hell in order to send to it those who did not *want* to love him—and who finally, having gained knowledge about human love, had to invent a god who is all love, all *ability* to love—who has mercy on human love because it is so utterly wretched and unknowing. Anyone who feels that way, who *knows* this about love, *seeks* death. (BGE 9.269)

Most men merely admire aristocratic souls, but if one looks keenly, one discovers the defects and feels pity for the torture of great men. Jesus loved men and pitied them for their self-torture, which was *his* self-torture.

Jesus made something noble and divine out of the low in man; indeed, he made God out of man's defects. God is love, which means that God is the ability to love men despite their defects, their dirt. Jesus took the low in man and made it part of the high; he made slave morality out of noble or aristocratic morality. This section on Jesus marks the transition between the old barbarous morality to the new morality of Nietzsche's new philosophers. He begins to speak of saints rather than virile types like Achilles. Saints are preoccupied with cleanliness—that is, with dirt, human dirt. They sanctify human dirtiness by torturing themselves because of it. Nietzsche's new nobility is a nobility of the spirit, in the highest case of the philosopher, who is necessarily a new philosopher. The philosopher is a natural ruler, "by nature a master." He is superior to those who merely suffer, or worse, preach pity (BGE 9.293). "The noble soul has reverence for itself," but this is not shown openly, for the philosopher writes books that conceal what he harbors. He may run away from himself as if afraid, yet he always returns to himself because knowledge comes to its culmination in self-knowledge. This is the glorious passage on the "genius of the heart" with which Nietzsche ends this part and his book (BGE 9.295–296).

The philosopher hates to be understood; he is essentially solitary and cannot stand the smell of other men. He has the will to power that is radically individual. And yet he has a nature that makes him master of other men. How can the solitariness be reconciled with the relationship he bears? In *Beyond Good and Evil* we get the sense that it is through some combination of philosophy and religion. Nietzsche speaks of Dionysius (a god) as a philosopher and then says that all gods philosophize. This contradicts the claim in Plato's *Symposium* that gods do not philosophize (204a). Gods, it is claimed, do not philosophize because they are wise; if you are wise, you do not have to seek wisdom. Nietzsche instead brings gods closer to men so that it is hard to see the difference between the gods who philosophize and the supermen who overcome what men have been. Nietzsche's part 9 culminates in the suggestion that there is no upper limit to human creativity or to man's capacity to overcome himself. To compare Nietzsche in this regard with Marx, one could say that Marx wanted to remove the *barriers* between men with his communism, and Nietzsche wanted to remove the *limits* on humans and therefore reinstate the barriers with hierarchy and exploitation. Neither barriers nor limits are imposed by nature, but Nietzsche, as opposed to Marx, comes to terms with nature.

We have primarily examined this one book of Nietzsche's, but this study leads us to another one of his, *Thus Spoke Zarathustra,* and its doctrine of eternal return. Nietzsche tries to show there that man can conquer everything, literally everything, by willing the past to come again. In this way he redeems himself from bondage to the past and to every other limitation: In the words of an American politician of the 2020s, he is "unburdened by what has been." Without going further, one can note the religious symbolism in *Zarathustra*; its key chapter is titled "Redemption," and the name Zarathustra is borrowed from Persian religion. Nietzsche's "philosophy-religion," if that description is correct, is certainly not Christianity. It is an idea of nature, of the whole and of man's place in the whole. Man's highest creativity is to will nature to return eternally.

MODERN CREATIVITY BEGAN with Machiavelli in the notion that man is free—and then was immediately subjected to human necessities by Machiavelli in the necessity to acquire, and by Hobbes and Locke in the necessity of self-preservation. Every attempt to free man from these necessities has failed. Rousseau tried to show that human necessities, so called, were actually made by men; we ourselves have created our nasty competitiveness and our poverty for ourselves. Yet we cannot escape these necessities—not fully. We can only make them legitimate through political science, which attempts to manage the problems we have made for ourselves. Only the solitary philosopher-artist can go back to nature to find some recourse against human necessities. Nietzsche, like Rousseau, thinks it possible to go back to nature to escape from necessities and thus to attain creativity as freedom. What Nietzsche found is that the end of creativity is to reaffirm nature as the non-created, sometimes with, sometimes without quotation marks. Quotation marks for certain words are the sign of a scholar's urgent need and bad conscience. The great moral difference between Nietzsche and Rousseau is that Rousseau believed in compassion and Nietzsche in cruelty. Consequently, there is a great political difference: In one aspect of his thought, Rousseau proposed a political science to legitimize our bondage; while Nietzsche, in his radical individualism rejected any common good within political communities (BGE 3.43). With no common good, justice is exploitation of the ruled by rulers, exploitation of the worse by their betters. But why? For the good of humans. Nietzsche himself is, after all, a half-hearted immoralist. But what is the cost of his morality? A sacrifice of the freedom of all noncreative humans for the sake of the tortured nobility of the few philosophic souls.

This book on the history of modern political philosophy can be summarized as follows. Throughout the history recorded here from Machiavelli to Nietzsche, freedom consists in an escape from God and nature, by which we are delivered into the bondage of human necessities—"of human bondage" (as a modern philosopher called it, who shall be nameless because not studied in this book). Then we were obliged to understand freedom as the escape from human necessities, from the history we have made for ourselves, back into the arms of God and nature. Isn't there something dubious about an escape into our original prison? Perhaps the original mistake was to define an opposition between freedom and nature, which tried to compel us to escape what cannot be escaped. Perhaps we ought to suppose that our freedom comes from nature and begin our reasoning accordingly. Most humans can be free only through politics, and our political freedom is part of human nature. To suggest an older definition, perhaps man is a political animal by nature. But these are dangerous perhapses, more difficult today than in Nietzsche's day.

ENVOI

A message or blessing is due to readers of this volume, now untested students of the history of modern political philosophy. To be a student of this important topic is a prize without a credential; you have to award it to yourself. But there is one further step necessary that is implied in the book's title. Some sense of what is *modern,* with its initial thrust, its turns, and its developments, has been shown, but the original promise to define *political philosophy* is yet to be fulfilled. What is political philosophy, and what use is it?

Political philosophy is found in the great books, such as those studied in this volume. A long tradition of political philosophy exists, dating from Socrates (who surprisingly never wrote a book himself) and consisting of a series of great books, each written to discuss with favor or disfavor another philosophy, either contemporary or earlier. This history is less accidental than other history because, to a greater degree than citizens or statesmen, philosophers are reacting to thinkers that came before them. This history is also both more and less of a tradition in the usual sense—more, because it is a gift you have to think over rather than merely inherit; and less, because it is a gift open to argument and divided against itself. There are "schools" of thought, each composed of a philosopher surrounded by followers and defenders, normally on terms of war with one another. There is Machiavelli's revolution of modern political philosophy against the ancients, repeated and extended by rather frequent revision we have studied throughout this book, that seems to be in its progressive character. When is progress satisfied with itself? The modernity that by its name is advertised for its novelty is hard to bring to a finish.

"Modern" seems to want a definite stopping point, an "end of history" when it is complete, but not yet to have found one. From Machiavelli to Nietzsche, each philosopher offers a new formula yet admits the need or the possibility of further progress beyond his own. Machiavelli explicitly claims merely "to show the path" to someone else, yet he lays down the notion of "effectual truth" that characterizes modern rational control as a whole. Hegel, on the other hand, did in fact present the end of history, but was overcome and surpassed by his immediate followers. With its idea of progress, modernity is itself a work in progress. Its tradition is to pass along an impulse to question tradition. The philosophic tradition, ancient and modern, is not a sequence of customs, nor is it a "canon" imposed by some political power. Political philosophy and political power coexist in an uneasy relationship; the philosopher in the role of critic is aware and wary of the power he examines and must live under, the politician normally suspicious of an outside overseer with his own particular pride of place.

Beneath the great books are the scholars, the professors like me, who write books somewhat like this one. We are subordinates to the great thinkers we study, or in many cases, out of ignorance or recalcitrance, refuse to study. This book is different in directing readers to the great books rather than distracting readers or disrespecting the books. The great books present themselves as the true guide or guides of humanity, united in intent and divided in performance, and mine is a respectful and secondary guide to the higher guides. One can spend one's life in this tradition or a part of it, and if you want to be serious about political philosophy, this is what you will do.

Yet political philosophy can also be found outside the books in actual politics, where it can be seen in its first strivings before it can say its own name. Citizens and politicians do not claim to be philosophers, whom they regard with genial contempt as perhaps ingenious but inept. Those in or concerned with politics have one quality in common with philosophers, however: they both engage in *argument*. Wherever you follow the news you will see and hear your fellow citizens arguing passionately pro and con, attacking and defending, accusing and denying. Politics means taking sides; it is *partisan*. The sides taken are opposed to one another. It is one side *versus* another—in our day, liberals versus conservatives and often within parties, one faction versus another.

Politics is contradicting argument, and political philosophy is elaborating the grounds of a contradiction to find whether it is fundamental and deciding among the claims of politics which ones are true and to what extent. Political philosophy takes shape in the great books, the scholar-professors, and ordinary citizens; that is its form. But the energy of political philosophy is in the partisanship of the human animal, in actual politics. Not all politics emerges in the conscious form of political philosophy. It was only among the Greeks that it was first discovered and put in books so that it would last. With books, philosophy could become a tradition, and philosophers could talk to one another. Yet if ever there was a calamity in which all great books were lost, the activity of political philosophy could be resurrected directly out of political life. While it may seem to have emerged by accident, political philosophy is potential in the partisan nature of the human animal. In reading this book, you will have seen where your opinions come from and where they lead.

Political life contains parties that defend their particular interests, such as autoworkers or professional women, but in gathering their interests for defense, they also make an appeal to the community and the common good. The appeal is to a kind of judge who would decide issues between the parties. This judge can be a person or a group one is trying to convince or a more official or intelligent judge who is competent. Whether arguments are good or bad, and whether they are complete or incomplete, they are made with reasons intended to convince a judge, actual or implicit. Even in stating a personal interest, one is obliged to generalize one's grievance to appeal to the judgment of another, which one does by giving a reason for it. Reason socializes as it appeals from one individual to others, and beyond that it politicizes as it appeals to the government of a community. With a persuasive reason you can turn a stranger into a fellow partisan, or with an unpersuasive one tune him out. Not all reasons are correct or, if correct, convincing, and so political life is not surely and completely rational. The clear and exact standard of modern political philosophy, trying to produce an "undoubted right" (recall John Locke), does more to silence doubt than to diminish it. Who can oppose the rights to life, liberty, and the pursuit of happiness? But who can define them in practice to avoid partisan confusion?

Political arguments are aimed at a reasonable judge even if they often do not find one or aim well. They will often use reason badly and partially—being partisan in the bad sense—but they do use reason. This is the fact allowing political philosophy, if it is known and available, to enter. With political philosophy one can judge between liberals today, who believe in empathy because all humans are equal; and conservatives, who believe in admiration of those humans who are unequal in some impressive or useful way. An argument like this one is not a clash of conflicting values that cannot be decided by reason. Because both sides look to human nature for support, the difference over policies is also over the facts of human nature, which are more puzzling than they seem at first. Do we admire Franklin D. Roosevelt for his accomplishments or feel sorry for him as a victim of polio? For some reason FDR did not want to be the object of the compassion he showed for others in his politics. Making America more equal was his accomplishment; avoiding victimhood by hiding his wheelchair was his choice. The great Democrat refused America's democratic compassion for a vulnerable human being. As we see in this interesting case, reasoning to a proper judgment is not easy, but what makes it impossible? A better judge might find a better judgment.

A good judgment requires an overall basis for judgment. In this book we have seen two general foundations for political judgment: the ancient and the modern. The ancient principle began with Socrates, the modern with Machiavelli—and they are connected by argument. The ancient principle is that the best regime is the standard by which all regimes are judged; the modern principle is based on Machiavelli's sardonic statement that aspiring to the imaginary best regime, republic, or principality will bring a state to ruin. Aspiring to do good must be replaced by the necessity to do evil that awaits everyone, private or public. The virtue both shining and hiding in the best regime of the ancients must give way to the dirty tricks, both impressive and hidden, taught by Machiavelli.

The ancients defend imaginary virtue on the ground that it is not an arbitrary wish but a fundamental feature of human nature, for philosophy begins from the discovery of nature as opposed to arbitrary convention. But as we have seen, "nature" to Machiavelli is but long-standing custom, and human nature is at its best when it is flexible and ready to create "new modes and orders." The moderns have an uneasy relationship with nature, speaking sometimes of the conquest of nature as if it could be subjugated, more often of how nature can be used against itself, as when what is necessary is arranged to prevail over what is best. Hobbes and Locke try to show, following Machiavelli, that the necessity of self-preservation, when made the basis of rights and duties, will make for greater liberty and strength and even virtue, than chasing the virtues they call utopian.

This is a sketch of the origin and nature of political philosophy. With a variety of hints and statements in the course of the book, it should not come as a surprise when summed up at the end. But what of the *use* of political philosophy? First and most important, political philosophy will allow you to understand further than you knew you could and give enjoyment you did not expect from study you could not complete. The pleasure of trying to understand along the way as you read and reason through readings does not expire but blends with the pleasure of understanding at the end.

It is true that most people do not see these pleasures, stop too soon, and do not reach political philosophy. I once came across a book marker given out by a "think tank," the Cato Institute, quoting the words of a famous economist, Milton Friedman, "One of the great mistakes is to judge policies and programs by their intentions rather than their results." This is almost a direct quotation of Machiavelli's *The Prince* (ch. 15), but Friedman did not say "follow Machiavelli." If he had, he might have had to address the question of whether his advice is what we call Machiavellian. By ignoring intentions, he follows his profession of economist, which holds to analysis of behavior rather than intentions. Intentions of consumers and producers do not matter for economists, but what of the intentions of economists—do they not matter? And those of professors and think tanks? It seems that one might like to know whether the results one judges are got by dirty tricks or virtues. One would like to elaborate the quotation and take a look at Machiavelli himself, his followers, and his opponents. One would need to engage in political philosophy.

That study engages one's self or one's soul. The use of an occupation is not merely the comfort it brings to one's body. Political philosophy combines what is best with what is less than best but real; it covers the meeting of reason with unreason, or of the soul and the body. It deals with satisfactions and with yearnings and dissatisfactions—that is, with the results of economics and with resistance to those results. Together with economics, let us not forget among good results the wonders of modern medicine. In this book these sciences appear, in a general sense, as rational control, the main claim of modern political philosophy. In the rise and fall of rational control, one can see, much better than in the confused terms of our controversies today, great ambition combined with the weaknesses of our thinking. The focus of the moderns is on the body, and it makes the soul serve the body. The ancients aimed at the reverse.

My envoi returns to the distinction of ancients and moderns and to the question of which use comes first: the soul's or the body's. The use of political philosophy is above all to consider that question. The ancients liked to say that philosophy will make you rich in the wealth of learning among the few. The moderns aim for liberty of the self, together with palpable wealth and comfort produced by their sciences, which tend to the body. The purpose of this book and my course at Harvard is to help readers think further with the aid of the best books ever written. It is not to supply a reason to stop thinking! For the way we think is the way we live.

How, then, do we live after the fall of rational control? The fall came with Marx and Nietzsche, especially the latter. Marx found his solution in the inevitable revolution of communism against capitalism—a revolution said to be radical because it did away with the division of labor that he thought irrational because it destroyed the wholeness of human life. The arguments Marx gave did not prove that the proletariat was the universal class whose triumph would make us all whole human beings. But communism has proved to be more lasting than the arguments supporting it, and it survives in powerful regimes as a hope that contrasts with the irrational desire of their rulers but serves to maintain it. Communism should not be dismissed by intelligent readers, however, despite its failures and its contribution to tyranny. It stands for what is common in our lives, a reasonable element in our nature when not used to destroy everything individual. Marx is worth reading to understand his appeal to the spirited and the young, precisely those who are least well explained by his iron laws of history.

What, then, is left over from Nietzsche, who subjugates rational control to the will to power? In Nietzsche's thought (or will), we recall, nature returns from its exile in modernity to distinguish genuine creativity from the cheap, artificial, herd morality of democracy. This is nature without quotation marks. It would be good for all readers to take note of this return and to see how often they, too, need and want a distinction between the imitation, the ephemeral, the stylized, the superficial, the presumptuous—and the real thing. Yet the most obvious leftover from Nietzsche is not his return to nature, which we need, but the present-day concept of the postmodern, a burden to all. "Postmodern" is a notion that treats "modern" as a point of view, not as rational control. It draws from Nietzsche's argument—or is it assertion?—that philosophy, like all other thought, has a certain perspective. Is postmodern, claiming to know this alleged fact, above other points of view by virtue of its awareness? No, there is no support for this claim. Postmodern is the point of view of a point of view! It is unable to escape modernity even in its own name: Postmodern is still present as left behind. The past is still with us in the form of what is passé, as one sees that the novelty that distinguishes modernity since Machiavelli is reduced to "social change," a slogan used without enthusiasm. This is Nietzsche's perspectivism rendered routine and democratic, a weak substitute, a "simulacrum," for what once was declared *progress*. It has nothing of the return to nature that would give it vigor.

Then might there be a "postmodern" position that rescues rational control from its modern critics? It would be one that retains a healthy respect for human nature, especially in its spirited aspect. In accordance with modernity, liberty could be kept as its goal and individual rights as the means to liberty, but it would be a liberty of standing up for one's rights. To stand up for one's rights is the contrary of gaining them through the desire for self-preservation; it's courage versus a kind of cowardice. Hobbes issued the first statement of the rights of man, and Locke adopted it, giving it a twist in the addition of private property. The concern for property invites the desire for gain, fundamentally a slavish thing, but it also fosters a spirit of defense when one's property is at stake. I suggest—this not being the place for a proposal—a reworked liberalism to serve as a rescue for modern rational control hit by the powerful critiques of Marx and Nietzsche.

The early liberals wanted a human motive that would be universal in order to be effectual. This was the desire for self-preservation enshrined in inalienable rights. Such rights, we have seen, are irrational: If they are held as inalienable, a chaos of a war of all against all is the result; if they are given to a sovereign government, the gift is always subject to recall, and they remain a threat to one's promise to obey. But when the exercise of rights calls upon one's sense of honor rather than gain, and thus for virtue rather than survival, rational control becomes reasonable. Modern rational control, we have seen, does not work through an effort of reason by its citizens; its government is indirect, using irrational motives to gain a rational result. It does not appeal to human pride, as would a liberalism attuned to the virtue of citizens in the exercise of their rights. That liberalism would return from an unnaturally constrained self, interested only in survival, to a reliance on the soul, which contains a concern for nobility and sacrifice as well as survival. To pursue this possibility, readers of this book need to read further, beginning with Alexis de Tocqueville's *Democracy in America* and Aristotle's *Ethics*. Fix your attention as well on the American Constitution, intended to surpass the English Constitution in Locke and Montesquieu as a model for modern liberal government.

A professor will always give you something more to read.

Acknowledgments

THIS BOOK is based on lectures from the Harvard University course History of Modern Political Philosophy (known as Government 1061) that I delivered in alternate years at Harvard from 1968 to 2022 (called Government 106b from 1968 to 1980). It was a "department course," not my private property, taught in alternate years to permit my colleagues to have their say to rebut or elaborate what I said. My first acknowledgment is therefore to the Harvard Department of Government for awarding me the honor of serving for fifty-four years as captain teaching the course—half the time.

When the course first came to me it had the title of History of Modern Political Thought, but under my aegis the word "thought" was soon surreptitiously dropped in favor of "philosophy." I wanted to keep the designation of political philosophy as a reminder of its founder, Socrates, not a modern but indispensable to the founders of modern political philosophy. In testimony to this fact, I also taught History of Ancient and Medieval Political Philosophy (Government 1060) of which History of Modern Political Philosophy was the sequel. Modernity, of course, did not begin philosophy, nor did it render premodern philosophy obsolete. Some of the moderns, especially Machiavelli and Hobbes, did deliberately want to render their predecessors obsolete, and today some experts agree with them. The envoi of this book, where I call for a return to the ancients, makes clear that I do not agree.

Some features of this book call for acknowledgment. On the subject of modern political philosophy, it starts early with Machiavelli in the sixteenth century and ends early with Nietzsche in the nineteenth century. To justify the early start, the book is front-loaded with earnest promotion of the truth—not much accepted—that Machiavelli is the founder of modernity, understood as *rational control*. This term is defined along the way in its various forms when later philosophers take their measure of the goal and how to achieve it. My book treats modern political philosophy as a whole and presents many cross-references within its bounds, especially back to Machiavelli. Old Nick is the ghost haunting this book and the philosophers it treats, a figure always present and rarely seen in the texts of those I consider his successors. The scholarship on the relationship is scarce as well. Rational control—so I argue—begins and continues under Machiavelli's banner of effectual truth through its rise to its fall in the thought of Nietzsche.

I end with Nietzsche as the fundamental philosopher of our time, the author of the "postmodern." *Postmodern* stands for loss of belief without being able to replace belief; hence it cannot dispense with the "modern." The philosophers who come after Nietzsche do not surpass Nietzsche and are more likely to cover up their dependence on him than to begin something new or better.

This book transcribes an introductory course (a fairly hard one) for which it was important to read whole books rather than a collection of fragments. Like all philosophers, the modern ones convey their thought in books with parts, themes, and rhetoric, each one fashioned to make a whole. For a course of lectures, reading a philosophic book is as much a lesson to be learned as grasping its overall conclusion. It follows that my treatment of Hobbes, for example, is more a reading of *Leviathan* than a final statement of my view of him. Many problems are not carried as far as they might be and are left purposely unresolved. The second half of the book fastens on the damage done to reason by the resort to history that first emerges in Rousseau. With the time and space available, I could not treat the most authoritative books of Kant and Marx, and I was forced to choose for study only one of Hegel's and Nietzsche's major works.

Readers will find almost no reference to the ample secondary literature on the philosophers included in the book. My view is that it is best for readers and students to wrestle with the original texts without the aid of interpretation. If this is just another interpretation pretending to be above all interpretation, so be it. This one lets authors speak for themselves.

Further acknowledgment must go to Leo Strauss, the inspiration for my thinking and the source of many particular insights in the transcripts of courses he gave at the University of Chicago. What I offer is a survey of the philosophers of modernity with a focus on Machiavelli. Strauss separated his treatment of modern political philosophy in *Natural Right and History* from his *Thoughts on Machiavelli*; in leaving their relation unexplained, he generously left room for his followers—or as Montesquieu would have it, his vassals who defend him. I mention Montesquieu with due respect to say further that there are modern political philosophers besides the eight I have chosen. One could indeed make a team of another eight that would not be a junior varsity to mine.

I wish to thank Sophie Pangle, my research assistant on three books, who, with presence of mind and conscientious intelligence, was my critic and friend as well. With me lecturing in Government 1061 on several occasions were Mark Blitz, Nancy Rosenblum, Michael Sandel, and Peter Berkowitz—thanks to them. I would also like to thank the many teaching fellows (as Harvard calls them) who over the years assisted in Government 1061 in all its recurrences. They are too many to name, but let it be known that I recall the help of every one of them. My wife, Anna, I thank for her patience, love, and ferocious criticism.

Notes

Niccolò Machiavelli

Machiavelli's *Discourses on Livy* (D) is cited by book and chapter or by book, chapter, and paragraph number; "pr." refers to the proemium to book 1. *The Prince* (P) is cited by chapter number of the Chicago (Mansfield) edition.

Thomas Hobbes

The *Leviathan* (L) is cited by chapter and page number of the Cambridge (Tuck) edition.

1. Aristotle, *Nichomachean Ethics*, 1109b30–1115a.
2. Compare with the beginning of Aristotle, *Metaphysics*: "All men by nature desire to know."
3. See the same thought in René Descartes, *Discourse on Method*, part 1.
4. Aristotle, *Nichomachean Ethics*, 1094b.
5. Aristotle, *Politics*, 1252a.
6. Robert Dahl, *After the Revolution* (New Haven, CT: Yale University Press, 1968), 95, on the side of Hobbes.
7. Hobbes comments, opposing Machiavelli, that money is as vital to the militia as militia to money; see D 2.10.1.
8. The same example used by Aristotle and answered by Hobbes to the contrary. Aristotle, *Nichomachean Ethics*, 1110a10; L 21, p. 146.
9. Aristotle, *Politics*, 1257a–58b.
10. Plato, *Republic*, 504a–505a.
11. John Aubrey's *Life of Hobbes* in Thomas Hobbes, *Leviathan: With Selected Variants from the Latin Edition of 1668*, ed. Edwin Curley (Indianapolis: Hackett, 1994), xlviii.

John Locke

John Locke's *First Treatise* (FT) and *Second Treatise of Government* (ST) are cited by section number.

1. Richard Kennington, "Nature and Natural Right in Locke," in *On Modern Origins: Essays in Early Modern Philosophy*, ed. Pamela Kraus and Frank Hunt (Lanham, MD: Lexington Books, 2004), 266–267.
2. See Richard Hooker, *Of the Laws of Ecclesiastical Polity*, ed. Arthur Stephen McGrade (Cambridge: Cambridge University Press, 1989), xiii–xxx, 239.
3. Maurice Cranston, *John Locke: A Biography* (New York: MacMillan, 1957), xi, 80, 323, 434. On Locke's secretive character, see also Roger Woolhouse, *Locke: A Biography* (Cambridge: Cambridge University Press, 2007), 3, 57, 207–223, 393.

4. Cranston, *John Locke*, 246.

5. Felix Waldmann, "John Locke as a Reader of Thomas Hobbes's *Leviathan*: A New Manuscript," *Journal of Modern History* 93, no. 2 (2021): 245–82; Nasser Behnegar, Devin Stauffer, Rafael Major, and Christopher Nadon, "From Laslett to Waldmann: The Case for Reconsidering Strauss on Locke," *Review of Politics* 84, no. 4 (2022): 570–591; Leo Strauss, *Natural Right and History* (Chicago: University of Chicago Press, 1953), 208–209.

6. Aristotle, *Politics*, 1280a7–b10.

7. On the connection of Locke's executive to Machiavelli's *esecuzione* see Harvey C. Mansfield, *Taming the Prince: The Ambivalence of Modern Executive Power* (New York: Free Press, 1989), ch. 8.

8. It would also imply a direct contradiction of what Locke says about the lack of a natural inclination to virtue in his *Essay Concerning Human Understanding* (bk. 1, ch. 2) and his *Essays on the Law of Nature* (essay 6).

9. Plato, *Apology of Socrates*, 23c, 31c.

10. Anatole France, *Le Lys Rouge* (Paris: Calmann-Lévy, 1894), ch. 7.

11. Max Weber, *The Protestant Ethic and the Spirit of Capitalism* (New York: Routledge, 2001 [1905]); see also R. H. Tawney, *Religion and the Rise of Capitalism: A Historical Study* (New York: Harcourt, 1926).

12. *Heidelberg Catechism: Text of Tercentenary Edition* (Cleveland, OH: Publishing House of the Reformed Church, 1877), 3.

13. Is the body of the mother her own? And if so, is the child's fetus the property of the mother to dispose of? The abortion controversy today shows the relevance of the workmanship thesis in Locke.

14. God left men in "penury," forcing them to "subdue the earth," but a prince who is "wise and godlike," Locke says, "by the by," would "by established laws of liberty secure protection and encouragement to the honest industry of mankind" (ST §§32, 42).

15. For references in chapter 5 to what cannot be doubted, denied, complained of, quarreled over, or questioned, see ST §§27, 28, 29, 30, 34, 36, 39, 51. Instead of compromising diverse claims, Locke wants to silence doubt.

16. "Fortify" is the term used in James Madison, *The Federalist* 20, to describe the same operation in the American Constitution.

17. For an attempt to render justice, see Harvey C. Mansfield, *Machiavelli's Effectual Truth* (Cambridge: Cambridge University Press, 2023), ch. 6.

Jean-Jacques Rousseau

References to the *First Discourse* (FD), *Second Discourse* (SD), and *Social Contract* (SC) are to pages of the Chicago (Scott) edition. The *Social Contract* is cited by book and chapter number.

1. See Alexis de Tocqueville, *The Revolution and the Old Regime.*

2. Montesquieu, *Spirit of the Laws*, 10.3.

3. On Bacon's term, see Francis Bacon, *The Works of Francis Bacon*, vol. 4, ed. James Spedding, Robert Leslie Ellis, and Douglas Devon Heath (Texas: Houghton, Mifflin, 1991), 298.

4. Letter from Thomas Jefferson to John Adams, October 28, 1813.

5. On this thesis, see Leo Strauss, *Natural Right and History*, ch. 6.

6. Hobbes L 13, p. 87; Montesquieu, *Spirit of the Laws* 1.2.

7. Edmund Burke, *Thoughts on French Affairs*, in *Reflections on the French Revolution and Other Essays* (London: J. M. Dent & Sons, 1910), 305.

8. Ernst Cassirer, *The Question of Jean-Jacques Rousseau*, trans. Peter Gay (New York: Columbia University Press, 1954).

9. Jean-Jacques Rousseau, "Four Letters to M. the President de Malesherbes," in *The Confessions and Correspondence, Including the Letters to Malesherbes*, trans. and ed. Christopher Kelly, Roger D. Masters, and Peter G. Stillman (Hanover, NH: University Press of New England, 1995), 575.

10. Jean-Jacques Rousseau, *Emile, or On Education*, trans. Allan Bloom (New York: Basic Books, 1979), 193; *Reveries of the Solitary Walker*, Walk 6.

Immanuel Kant

Immanuel Kant's "Idea for a Universal History with a Cosmopolitan Intent" (UH), is cited by page number of the Hackett (Humphrey) edition. *Toward Perpetual Peace, A Philosophical Project* (PP), and "Theory and Practice" (TP) are cited by page number of Kant, *Practical Philosophy*, trans. Mary J. Gregor (Cambridge: Cambridge University Press, 1996). Other works of Kant are cited in *Practical Philosophy* or by the standard Akademie (Ak.) page number.

1. Kant, *Remarks on the Observations on the Feeling of the Beautiful and Sublime*, Ak. 20:44.

2. David Hume, *Treatise on Human Nature*, II 3.

3. Kant, *Prolegomena* (1783), Ak. 4:260.

4. Kant, *Critique of Pure Reason*, preface to 2nd ed., B xxv.

5. Kant, *Groundwork of the Metaphysics of Morals*, Ak. 4:411.

6. Kant, *Lectures on Ethics*, Ak. 27:303.

7. Lincoln regularly quoted the line. See Abraham Lincoln and Stephen A. Douglas, *Debates of Lincoln and Douglas: Carefully Prepared by the Reporters of Each Party at the Times of Their Delivery* (Columbus, OH: Follett, Foster and Company, 1860), 259.

G. W. F. Hegel

G. W. F. Hegel's *Lectures on the Philosophy of History* (PH) is cited by page number of the Oxford (Brown and Hodgson) edition, based primarily on the lectures of 1822–1823. Certain marked passages are taken from the translation of John Sibree (Dover, 1956), which is based primarily on Hegel's lectures in 1830–1831.

1. Hegel, *Elements of the Philosophy of Right*, ed. Allen W. Wood and H. B. Nisbet (Cambridge: Cambridge University Press, 1991), 23.

2. Plato, *The Apology of Socrates*, 20e–23b.

3. Kant, *Conflict of the Faculties*, 7:85.

4. Quotations from the translation of Hegel's *Philosophy of History* by John Sibree are marked accordingly.

5. See Leo Strauss, *Leo Strauss on Hegel*, ed. Paul Franco (Chicago: University of Chicago Press, 2019).

6. Thucydides, *History of the Peloponnesian War*, 1.22.

7. Kant, *Religion Within the Limits of Reason Alone*, trans. Werner S. Pluhar (Indianapolis: Hackett, 2009), p. 179.

8. G. W. F. Hegel, *Werke* (Frankfurt: Suhrkamp, 1970), 2:547.

Karl Marx

References to "On the Jewish Question" (JQ), the *1844 Manuscripts* (MS), the *German Ideology* (GI), *Communist Manifesto* (CM), and *Critique of the Gotha Program* (GP) are from the *The Marx-Engels Reader*, ed. Robert C. Tucker (Norton edition).

1. Aristotle, *Politics*, 1337b–1338a.

Friedrich Nietzsche

Beyond Good and Evil (BGE) is referenced by book and section of the Vintage (Kaufmann) edition.

1. Friedrich Nietzsche, "Zarathustra's Prologue," in *The Portable Nietzsche*, ed. and trans. Walter Kaufmann (New York: Penguin, 1954).
2. Nietzsche, *On the Advantage and Disadvantage of History for Life*, trans. Peter Preuss (Indianapolis: Hackett, 1980), 12.
3. Nietzsche, *On the Genealogy of Morals*, trans. Walter Kaufmann and R. J. Hollingdale (New York: Vintage, 1967).
4. Nietzsche, *Twilight of the Idols*, in *The Portable Nietzsche*, ed. and trans. Walter Kaufmann (New York: Penguin, 1954), 546–547.
5. Nietzsche, *Human, All Too Human*, trans. R. J. Hollingdale (Cambridge: Cambridge University Press, 1996).
6. Aristotle, *Nichomachean Ethics*, 1128b10–33; see also 1108a32–36.
7. Nietzsche, "On the Three Metamorphoses," in *The Portable Nietzsche*, ed. and trans. Walter Kaufmann (New York: Penguin, 1954), 137–139.
8. "Machiavelli's Letter of December 10, 1513," in Niccolò Machiavelli, *The Prince*, ed. and trans. Harvey Mansfield (Chicago: University of Chicago Press, 1985), 109.
9. "That of which I am the master and expert is the brain of the leech: that is my world. And it really is a world too. Forgive me that here my pride speaks up, for I have no equal here." Nietzsche, *Thus Spoke Zarathustra*, in *The Portable Nietzsche*, ed. and trans. Walter Kaufmann (New York: Penguin, 1954), 362.
10. Nietzsche, *Ecce Homo*, trans. Walter Kaufmann (New York: Vintage, 1967).

Envoi

This envoi is drawn in part from a pamphlet of mine, *A Student's Guide to Political Philosophy* (Wilmington, DE: ISI, 2001).

Books To Be Read, Texts To Be Used

THE FOLLOWING ARE THE TRANSLATIONS used in the Harvard University course History of Modern Political Philosophy (Government 1061), chosen to comply with a controversial principle: Translation of great authors should bring the reader to the author rather than the author to the reader. Such translations should be as literal and consistent as can be made readable, to the end that the author's intent, and not the translator's, is always the best guide to what the author thinks. Included are two translations of Machiavelli that I (and my co-translator) made by applying this principle. Translation is a difficult job because it is imperfect at best. It is always better to know the author's language. This means that the best translations should be sought skeptically and, when found, used gratefully—but still skeptically.

Page numbers in the citations to the text in this book are to the editions recommended here.

Chapter 1

Niccolò Machiavelli. *Mandragola*. Edited by M. Flaumenhaft. Long Grove, IL: Waveland Press, 1981.

Niccolò Machiavelli. *Discourses on Livy*. Translated by Harvey C. Mansfield and Nathan Tarcov. Chicago: University of Chicago Press, 1996.

Niccolò Machiavelli. *The Prince*. Translated by Harvey C. Mansfield. 2nd ed. Chicago: University of Chicago Press, 1998.

Chapter 2

Thomas Hobbes. *Leviathan*. Edited by Richard Tuck. Cambridge: Cambridge University Press, 1996.

Chapter 3

John Locke. *Two Treatises of Government.* Edited by Peter Laslett. Cambridge: Cambridge University Press, 1988.

John Locke. *A Letter Concerning Toleration and Other Writings.* Edited by Mark Goldie. Indianapolis: Liberty Fund Press, 2010.

Chapter 4

Jean-Jacques Rousseau. *The Major Political Writings of Jean-Jacques Rousseau: The Two "Discourses" and the "Social Contract."* Translated by John T. Scott. Chicago: University of Chicago Press, 2012.

Chapter 5

Immanuel Kant. *Perpetual Peace and Other Essays on Politics, History, and Morals.* Translated by Ted Humphrey. Indianapolis: Hackett, 1983.

Immanuel Kant. *Practical Philosophy.* Translated by Mary J. Gregor. Cambridge: Cambridge University Press, 1999.

Chapter 6

G. W. F. Hegel. *Lectures on the Philosophy of World History.* Vol. 1. Edited by Robert G. Brown and Peter C. Hodgson. Oxford: Oxford University Press, 2019.

G. W. F. Hegel. *Lectures on The Philosophy of History.* Translated by John Sibree. New York: Colonial Press, 1900; reprint Mineola, NY: Dover, 2004.

Chapter 7

Karl Marx. *The Marx-Engels Reader.* Edited by Robert C. Tucker. 2nd ed. New York: W. W. Norton, 1978.

Chapter 8

Friedrich Nietzsche. *On the Advantage and Disadvantage of History for Life.* Translated by Peter Preuss. Indianapolis: Hackett, 1980.

Friedrich Nietzsche. *Beyond Good and Evil.* Translated by Walter Kaufmann. New York: Vintage, 1966.

Index

Index

Index

Index